AN INTRODUCTION TO
IRISH CRIMINAL LAW

Conor Hanly

Gill & Macmillan

Gill & Macmillan Ltd
Hume Avenue
Park West
Dublin 12
with associated companies throughout the world
www.gillmacmillan.ie

© *Conor Hanly 2006*

ISBN-13: 978 07171 3493 9

Index compiled by Julitta Clancy
Print origination by Carole Lynch

A catalogue record is available for this book
from the British Library.

CONTENTS

Table of Contents

Part III – Inchoate Offences

Part IV – Offences Against the Person

Part V – Offences Against Property

Part VI – Public Order Offences

PREFACE TO THE FIRST EDITION

The study of criminal law in Ireland is at once enjoyable and frustrating. It is enjoyable in that there is interest and excitement inherent in crime and law enforcement, feelings that are no doubt fostered by the prevalence of crime-related issues in popular entertainment and in the media. Yet it is also frustrating in terms of both its sheer volume and complexity. Criminal law is a vast subject drawn from countless judgments and enactments, each of which adds to the law. Many principles of criminal law, especially those developed from the common law, seem contradictory and are difficult to grasp, leaving the student to wonder in exasperation at how such a seemingly muddled collection of legal principles could be allowed to exist. To add to the student's misery is the relative dearth of written commentaries. There are now a number of excellent works dealing with specialised areas of criminal law – Charleton's *Offences Against the Person* and O'Malley's *Sexual Offences: Law, Policy and Punishment* are just two examples. For the student seeking a text that offers an up-to-date overview of Irish criminal law, however, there is little on offer in this jurisdiction. It is with this student in mind, rather than practitioners or academics, that this book has been written, and is based on the syllabus that is likely to be followed at undergraduate level in any Irish third-level institution.

The book is not intended to be an exhaustive commentary on criminal law in Ireland; rather, it is written in the hope of assisting undergraduate students to get to grips with the basic principles, case law and legislation involved in the subject. To that end, this book departs from established practice in three key areas. First, the language used has been simplified as much as possible and analysis has been avoided unless necessary. In many areas of the law, for example, there are few Irish decisions, and recourse has been had to decisions from other jurisdictions, especially Britain. In these circumstances, some minimal analysis has been required in order to assess whether the foreign decisions can be taken as representing Irish law. Second, there is a definite and deliberate bias in favour of Irish materials. In particular, the names of Irish cases have been highlighted in bold italics in order to distinguish them from decisions from other jurisdictions. Furthermore, at the end of every chapter there is a list of modern materials, used in the preparation of this book, that students can refer to in order to develop their knowledge of the matters dealt with in that chapter. Again, there is a heavy bias in favour of Irish materials. Finally, the practice of including the citations of cases in footnotes has not been followed in the hope of simplifying the page layout. Citations for all cases mentioned in the text can be found in the Table of Cases.

Preparing any kind of book is a large undertaking, and I was fortunate to have the assistance of a number of people at Waterford Institute of Technology and elsewhere. My friend and colleague, Grainne Callanan, has consistently been a source of encouragement and advice from the beginning of this project to its completion. Dr Shane Kilcommins, also a friend and colleague, reviewed a number of chapters and freely gave much useful advice. Dr John Ennis, Head of the School of Humanities, Dr Michael Howlett, Head of the Department of Applied Arts, and Neil O'Flaherty, Head of the Department of Languages, Tourism and Sports Studies, were unfailing in their support. All of my other colleagues at W.I.T. were equally generous with their support, with Kathy and Margaret in particular allowing me unrestricted use of the office facilities I needed to complete the book. I also received assistance from others – Claire, Kerry, Mossie and Zeta kindly gave their comments on earlier drafts. At Gill & Macmillan, the experience and considerable patience of Ailbhe O'Reilly and Deirdre Greenan were invaluable. In addition, the encouragement of my parents, brother and sister ensured the book was brought to a conclusion. To all of these people go my sincere thanks. It goes without saying that they bear no responsibility for any errors or deficiencies that exist in the text; such responsibility is mine alone.

I have attempted to state the law as it stood from materials available to me at October 1998.

Conor Hanly
Waterford Institute of Technology
January 1999

PREFACE TO THE SECOND EDITION

When the first edition of this book appeared in 1999, there was no general textbook offering students an overview of the criminal law in Ireland. Anyone seeking such a text was forced to rely on one of several English works, even though such works were not always applicable to this jurisdiction. Since 1999, the landscape has changed. Charleton, Bolger and McDermott published their excellent work, *Criminal Law*, in 1999, and McAuley and McCutcheon published their superb study, *Criminal Liability*, the following year. These are both excellent works that offer detailed and comparative discussions of the criminal law. However, there is still a need for an affordable textbook written for students facing university or professional entry examinations in Criminal Law and such students remain the focus of the second edition of this book. The preface to the first edition stated that the book was written 'in the hope of assisting undergraduate students to get to grips with the basic principles, case law and legislation involved in the subject.' This is equally my hope for the second edition. To that end, I have retained the basic style of the first edition: the language used has been simplified as much as possible, footnotes generally have been avoided so as not to clutter the pages, there is still a bias towards Irish materials, both primary and secondary, and the names of Irish cases are written in bold in order to distinguish them from foreign decisions.

However, I have also taken the opportunity to make some changes. The chapters have been revised and reorganised, and more detail has been added. To avoid increasing the length and therefore the price of the book, I have dropped two chapters (on road traffic offences and drugs offences) that rarely appear on a standard university syllabus. I have also updated the text to take account of the changes that have occurred in the law since 1999. In particular, the chapters on the property offences have been completely revised to take account of the changes brought by the enactment of the Criminal Justice (Theft and Fraud Offences) Act 2001. Developments in the common law have also been noted: the courts are still grappling with the law of provocation and the legacy of *MacEoin*, there have been several new decisions in the area of joint participation in an offence, and with the decision of the Court of Appeal in *Re A (Conjoined Twins)*, the basis of a true necessity defence is finally emerging. Finally, the Law Reform Commission has been very active in the field of criminal law since 1999, with new papers on corporate killing, the *mens rea* of murder and the plea of provocation. Their recommendations in these areas have been fully noted in the text.

I have again been fortunate to have the support of a number of people in the preparation of this new edition. Donncha O'Connell, Dean of the Faculty, and Marie McGonagle, Head of Department, and all my friends and colleagues at the Law Faculty at NUI, Galway gave unstinting support and encouragement. The librarians at NUI, Galway were equally helpful in locating materials. The support of my family was also necessary in finally completing the book. At Gill & Macmillan, Marion O'Brien has shown great patience and understanding at several delays that occurred during the writing process. To all of these people go my sincere thanks. Obviously, responsibility for faults and errors in the text are mine to bear alone. Finally, I must also acknowledge the financial assistance I received from the Millennium Fund at NUI, Galway.

I have tried to state the law as it stood at November 2005.

Conor Hanly
NUI, Galway
January 2006

Table of Cases

Note: Irish cases are indicated in **bold**

Table of Statutes

Table of Articles of the Constitution of Ireland

European Legislation

European Conventions

Table of UK and NI Legislation

United States

ADDENDUM

Since this edition went into production, the Supreme Court handed down a landmark judgment in *CC v. Ireland* **(2006)**. The appellant was a nineteen-year old youth who had engaged in sexual relations with a fourteen-year old girl who had lied about her age. The appellant was convicted of statutory rape under section 1(2) of the Criminal Law Amendment Act 1935 which made it an offence for a male to have sexual intercourse with a female under the age of fifteen. That provision made no allowance for a mistake, even a reasonable mistake, about the girl's age. The Supreme Court ruled unanimously that this aspect of the provision represented an unconstitutional failure by the State to vindicate the appellant's personal rights protected by Article 40 of the Constitution. Hence, section 1(2) of the 1935 Act was struck down and the appellant's conviction was quashed. The Oireachtas responded by enacting the Criminal Law (Sexual Offences) Act 2006 which took account of the Court's objections to the 1935 Act. The following comments, made in the light of these developments should be borne in mind when considering the following sections of the book:

3.3 Voluntary Conduct

In section 3.3 of the book, the requirement that conduct be voluntary before criminal liability can be imposed is noted. However, there is English authority – *R v. Larsonneur* (1933) and *Winzar v. Chief Constable of Kent* (1983) – which suggests that criminal liability can be imposed upon a defendant even where his conduct was physically brought about by someone else. Such defendants are entirely blameless, and in the light of the Supreme Court's decision in *CC*, these authorities can have no application to Irish law.

4.1 Introduction to Mens Rea

In section 4.1, the importance of proving *mens rea* is emphasized. *Mens rea* is the device that the criminal law uses to distinguish between culpable conduct on the one hand and mistaken or accidental conduct on the other. In its judgment in *CC*, the Supreme Court essentially ruled that proof of *mens rea* is now a constitutional requirement necessary to protect the personal rights of citizens, at least as far as serious criminal offences are concerned. The Court noted that section 1(2) of the 1935 Act afforded the appellant 'absolutely no defence once the *actus reus* is established, no matter how extreme the circumstances', and that the appellant would be guilty as charged even though he was unaware that anything unlawful had occurred. The Court ruled that 'to criminalize in a serious way a person who is mentally innocent is indeed to "inflict a grave injury on that person's dignity and sense of worth" and to treat him as "little more than a means to an end", in the words of Wilson J. [in the Canadian case of *Hess and Nguyen v. R* (1990)]'. This approach to the attribution of criminal liability was found to breach the State's guarantee to vindicate the personal rights of the citizen contained in Article 40 of the Constitution.

4.2 Subjective or Objective Fault

In section 4.2 of the book, the common law preference for subjective, as opposed to objective, constructions of criminal guilt is noted. This issue was not expressly dealt with by the Supreme Court in *CC*. The appellant contended that it was not open to the Oireachtas 'to deprive a defendant of a defence of honest mistake, or mistake on reasonable grounds'. In its judgment, however, the Court focused on the appellant's lack of awareness that he was engaging in the activity prohibited by section 1(2) of the 1935 Act. In other words, the Court's focus was on the appellant's lack of subjective fault. However, this does not necessarily mean that objective formulations of criminal guilt, such as those underpinning gross negligence manslaughter, are inconsistent with the Constitution. The Court in *CC* was ruling on a statutory provision that would allow the condemnation of a person who was morally innocent from either a subjective or an objective perspective. It is not clear what the Court would have done had section 1(2) of the 1935 Act allowed the conviction of a person who had failed to take reasonable steps to ascertain the girl's age before engaging in sexual intercourse with her; indeed, the Court expressly left open the question of whether a due diligence defence (i.e., the defendant took reasonable care to avoid the prohibited conduct) would be enough to constitutionally save a serious criminal offence.

4.9 Strict Liability

The common law aversion to strict liability is highlighted in the book at section 4.9. Following the Supreme Court's decision in *CC*, it seems unlikely that the use by the Oireachtas of strict liability to impose criminal liability for a serious criminal offence will survive a constitutional challenge. However, the Supreme Court did not explicitly remove the possibility of using strict liability in connection with minor regulatory offences. The Court was particularly concerned with the imposition of criminal liability on a person who was morally blameless of the charge against him, especially bearing in mind the penalties in mind (a maximum sentence of life imprisonment and enrolment on the Sex Offender's Register) and the social stigma attached to a conviction for statutory rape. Charges of a more minor nature which carry relatively minor sanctions are clearly in a different league to sexual offences that carry lengthy prison sentences. However, the Court suggested, without deciding, that the presence of a due diligence defence might constitutionally justify a regulatory offence of strict liability. This statement could be taken to indicate that even in the case of a minor regulatory offence, the Oireachtas cannot sanction the conviction of a defendant without requiring proof of some degree of fault. On the other hand, this statement was based upon the decision of the majority of the Canadian Supreme Court in *R v. City of Sault Sainte Marie* (1978) and the dissenting judgment of Keane J. in **Shannon Regional Fisheries Board v. Cavan County Council (1996)**. In this latter case, however, the majority of the Supreme Court expressly adopted the suggestion of Lord Wilberforce in *Alphacell v. Woodward* (1927) that the concept of *mens rea* should not be brought into the construction of regulatory offences. This decision was not overruled by the Supreme Court in *CC*, and thus authority continues to exist on which the Oireachtas can construct strict liability for regulatory offences.

13.2 Mistake of Fact

The common law rule that mistakes as to facts should generally result in an acquittal is noted in section 13.2 of the book. The appellant in *CC* honestly believed that the young woman with whom he was having a sexual relationship was aged 16, and he was thus unaware that his conduct breached section 1(2) of the 1935 Act. It was the failure of this provision to offer any defence in these circumstances that lead the Supreme Court to conclude that the provision was unconstitutional. Thus, at least in cases involving charges of serious criminal conduct, it seems that the common law approach to mistakes of fact now appears to have achieved constitutional status. However, it is unclear whether the Oireachtas may demand that a mistake must be reasonable as well as honest before it can negate criminal liability. The Court expressly left open the issue of whether a due diligence defence would be sufficient to constitutionally save a provision.

20.15 Unlawful Carnal Knowledge

Section 20.15 of the book notes that statutory rape was an offence under sections 1(2) and 2 of the Criminal Law Amendment Act 1935, and that under either section mistake as to the girl's age was irrelevant as to the defendant's guilt. Following the Supreme Court's decision in *CC*, which essentially removed the offence of statutory rape, the Oireachtas enacted the Criminal Law (Sexual Offences) Act 2006 which took account of the Court's objections and also updated the law in this area. Under section 2, it is an offence to engage in a sexual act with a child under the age of 15, while under section 3, it is an offence to engage in such an act with a child under the age of 17. In either case, the consent of the child is irrelevant as to guilt. Unlike the 1935 Act, which offered protection only to girls from men, the 2006 Act also protects young boys. Thus, if an older woman now has sexual intercourse with a 16 year old boy, she commits statutory rape. Prior to 2006, such a woman could be charged with sexual assault at most.

The maximum penalty for an offence under section 2 is life imprisonment. The maximum penalty for an offence under section 3 is generally 5 years imprisonment for a first offence and 10 years imprisonment for a subsequent offence. However, if the person convicted under section 3 is a person in authority over the child, the maximum penalties available are 10 years imprisonment for a first offence and 15 years imprisonment for any subsequent offence. A person in authority is defined in section 1 as a parent, step-parent, guardian, grandparent, aunt or uncle, anyone acting in *loco parentis* in respect of the child, or anyone else who is for the time being responsible for the education, supervision or welfare of the child.

Sexual acts are defined in section 1 as including sexual intercourse or buggery between persons who are not married to each other or acts that constitute aggravated sexual assault (see section 20.13 of the book) or rape under section 4 (see section 20.7 of the book). Thus, the offences in the 2006 Act are broader than those under the 1935 Act. The offence of buggery with children under 17, an offence under section 3 of the Criminal Law (Sexual Offences) Act 1993, has clearly been subsumed into the offences under the 2006 Act and is thus unnecessary. Accordingly, section 3 of the 1993 Act has been repealed. However, the 2006 Act also repeals section 4 of the 1993 Act which made it an offence to engage in acts of gross indecency with males under 17. This conduct is not covered by the 2006 Act, and it is unclear why the Oireachtas felt it necessary to abolish the section 4 offence. Grossly indecent acts constitute sexual assault, and up to the age of 15, boys are protected against sexual assault. However, a boy aged 15 can give operational consent to sexual assault, so there is now no legal protection for boys of 15 and 16 against gross indecency.

A defendant charged under either sections 1 or 2 of the 2006 Act will have a defence if he can prove that he honestly believed that the child was over the relevant age. The defendant bears the legal burden of establishing this defence on a balance of probabilities. In assessing the defendant's claim, the jury must have regard to the presence or absence of reasonable grounds for such a belief, but the defence is entirely subjective. Thus, in a case brought under section 2, if the jury concludes that the defendant honestly thought that the girl in question was aged 15 or over, they must acquit even if they also conclude that the defendant's belief was entirely irrational and unreasonable.

Finally, even though the 2006 Act is written in ostensibly gender-neutral language, it is clear that young girls continue to receive greater protection than young boys. Section 5 of the Act provides that a girl under the age of 17 will not be guilty of an offence merely because she engaged in an act of sexual intercourse. Thus, the situation that arose under the 1935 Act also arises under the 2006 Act: if a 16 year old boy has sexual intercourse with his 16 year old girlfriend at her instigation, he commits an offence but she does not. However, section 3(10) provides that if a person is convicted of engaging in a sexual act with a child under 17 and if that person is no more than 2 years older than the victim, the convicted person will not be subject to the registration provisions of the Sex Offenders Act 2001. Thus, in the example just given, the 16 year old boy may be convicted under section 3 but he will not be deemed a sex offender for the purposes of the 2001 Act. However, if a 15 year old boy has sexual intercourse with his 14 year old girlfriend at her instigation, no such allowance will be made. The Oireachtas has clearly determined that sexual intercourse with a girl under the age of 15 is to be treated as a full-scale sexual offence regardless of the age of the offender.

PART I

PRELIMINARY ISSUES

CHAPTER ONE

Introductory Matters

1.1 Introduction

Criminal law is a complex yet fascinating subject, and is in a real sense a reflection of the values held by a society. Its prime purpose is the identification and suppression of criminal activity. It is also the area of law that is most popularly associated with the term 'law', and regularly attracts the attention of the media and politicians. The media, in all its guises, devotes an enormous amount of time and space to crime issues. Some studies, for example, have found that as much as 25 per cent of all newspaper news space is devoted to crime and crime-related issues.[1] Politicians, for their part, are all anxious to address the activities of criminals, and proposals for dealing with criminals form a prominent part of the election manifestos of all political parties, regardless of ideology. Perhaps due to this official attention, criminal law has also entered mainstream consciousness in a way unthinkable for other areas of law. One has only to glance at the television listings to see the sheer number of popular programmes that revolve around crime and the attempts by law enforcement officials to control it. By contrast, there are few television programmes dealing with the law of real property – it would seem that the rule against perpetuities does not hold the same public fascination as the law of murder!

The main purpose of this book is to explain in an accessible manner the substantive criminal law of Ireland found in a typical university syllabus. Part I of the book deals with preliminary issues such as the development and structure of the criminal law; and with the basic rules for the attribution of criminal liability. Part II concerns the general defences to criminal liability; and these two parts make up the so-called general part of the criminal law. The remainder of the book then discusses the main offences, and is broken down by the principal subject area of the offences in question.

The Sources of Irish Criminal Law

1.2 Introduction

As with all branches of Irish law, criminal law is an amalgamation of principles derived from a variety of sources. The principal sources of criminal law are

---

1 See, for example, Surette, *Media, Crime, and Criminal Justice*, California: Brooks/Cole, Pacific Grove, 1992, pp. 62–4. For comments on the media and crime in Irish society, see O'Mahony, *Crime and Punishment in Ireland*, Dublin: Round Hall Sweet & Maxwell, 1995, pp. 2–5.

common law and statute, with international institutions also beginning to have some impact; each of these sources will be considered in turn. However, the reader should also bear in mind the overriding importance of the Constitution, to which all criminal rules and principles must conform. As a result, legislation may not unjustifiably impinge upon the personal rights of citizens that are guaranteed by Articles 40–44 of the Constitution. In particular, criminal legislation must respect the right of personal liberty protected by Article 40.4. By virtue of Article 15.5, the legislators must also avoid enacting retrospective legislation (which is considered later in section 2.2). Additionally, certain provisions of the Constitution have particular importance for criminal law and the trial of criminal offences. For example, Article 34.1 requires justice to be administered in public except in special and limited circumstances. Consequently, any member of the public is generally entitled to attend any criminal trial. However, there are exceptions to this, particularly trials involving incest, rape offences and aggravated sexual assault, in which the evidence is likely to be of a unique and personal nature. Article 38.1 requires all criminal trials to be conducted in due course of law. The essence of this requirement is that all criminal trials must be conducted fairly, with due regard to the personal rights of the defendant. Finally, Article 38.5 requires that all criminal trials be conducted before a jury, with the exception of trials heard in military or special courts, or those involving minor offences. The Constitution, therefore, has helped to shape the course of criminal trials, and creates the framework within which substantive criminal rules are made. The vast majority of those substantive rules, however, come from common law and statute, and it is these sources that are considered next.

1.3 Common Law

Common law is important as a source of criminal law in several respects. First, for centuries the common law courts have exercised the power to declare certain actions illegal without having any statutory basis for doing so. Manslaughter is a good example of a common law offence that has no statutory basis. The decisions of the courts when dealing with such common law offences are obviously of crucial importance, as it is these decisions alone that define and develop the offence. The formal power of the courts to extend the common law no longer exists by virtue of Article 15.2.1, which vests exclusive law-making power in the Oireachtas. It is therefore no longer possible for the courts to prohibit actions even where there is a clear need for it to be done; this is the responsibility of the Oireachtas. This has the advantage that for the creation of new offences and defences, the proper democratic and accountable process must be followed. The disadvantage is that if the Oireachtas is unwilling for political reasons to address an issue (such as abortion, for example), a gap in the law will remain unfilled. The power of the courts to declare and to expand upon existing common law rules, however, remains unaffected by Article 15.2.1 because Article 50 provides that any laws in force in Saorstát Éireann (the Irish Free State) are to continue in force under the present Constitution to the extent that they are compatible therewith. Any pre-existing common law rule (or statutory rule, for that matter) that does not conflict with the Constitution therefore remains in force.

Second, where statutes are enacted by the Oireachtas, many of them merely codify earlier common law rules. A good example of this is provided by sections 18, 19 and 20 of the Non-Fatal Offences Against the Person Act 1997, which set out the statutory basis for the defence of the lawful use of force. For the most part, these provisions simply re-enact the principles developed at common law, and therefore the earlier common law decisions are still relevant as they assist in the interpretation of the statutory provisions. Finally, even when dealing with offences that have no basis in common law, such as the offence of unauthorised interference with computer data under section 5 of the Criminal Damage Act 1991, judicial decisions are important as they interpret the meaning of the words used in the statute. These decisions are authoritative and binding in the same way as common law rules.

In trying to interpret a particular legal rule, Irish courts may also look at the earlier decisions of courts in the other common law countries, especially England. References to precedents, both Irish and foreign, are therefore an essential part of any common law trial; it is necessary to demonstrate that one has legal authority for one's case. Unlike earlier Irish decisions, however, foreign decisions are not binding upon Irish courts; they are of persuasive value only and may be departed from. It is important to remember that while extensive reference will be made to foreign decisions, they do not necessarily represent Irish law unless they have been accepted by the Irish courts or have been incorporated by the Oireachtas into an Irish statute. In order to highlight this point, the names of Irish cases in this book are in bold italics, while foreign cases are in ordinary italics. Unless indicated otherwise, these foreign decisions are from the English courts.

One last point should be made concerning the common law criminal rules. Sometimes the courts will try to trace the development of these rules to discover their full extent. In doing so, they will often have regard to commentaries on the early common law. The most notable of these commentaries are Coke's *Third Institute* (1642), Hale's *History of the Pleas of the Crown* (1736) and Blackstone's *Commentaries on the Laws of England* (1765, Book IV of which deals with criminal law). These classic works are accorded persuasive authority.

1.4 Statute

As the Constitution has removed the power of the courts to create new laws, the source of all innovation and reform is now the Oireachtas. This innovation and reform has not, however, proceeded with any degree of regularity or consistency, and has led to some judicial complaints. It must be recognised that the Oireachtas is a political institution, and its members are influenced by the vagaries of the political process. This can be beneficial in that popular pressure for reform can result in updated legislation. However, it can also result in hasty legislation that is merely responding to a particular incident that may not justify such a response. The creation of a new species of assault involving a syringe is a case in point. Throughout the mid-1990s, the media highlighted a number of robberies carried out with blood-filled syringes. As a result of this exposure, politicians became concerned with this particular form of robbery, and promised speedy measures to deal with it. The Opposition drafted a Bill specifically aimed at syringe attacks, while the government created new syringe offences in their reform of non-fatal offences against the person, which became law in 1997 (these offences are discussed in Chapter 19). It is debateable that such attacks required such a response, for two reasons. First, they could have been dealt with under the existing robbery laws which carry a maximum sentence of life imprisonment, and indeed this exceeds the maximum punishment for most of the new offences. Consequently, it is reasonable to wonder if the public has received any more protection than it had prior to 1997. Second, it is not clear whether syringe attacks were the beginning of a new trend in criminal activity in Ireland, or were merely a passing phase that had been seized upon by the media. If the former, then the new legislation was perhaps justified. If the latter, it is unlikely that any real benefits will accrue to Irish society in the long term. It is difficult to avoid the conclusion that the new offences were created in an attempt to be seen to be 'doing something' about a problem that the media had 'exposed', which is hardly a sound basis for penal reform. In *Gilligan v. Criminal Assets Bureau* (1998), McGuinness J. noted that 'certain elements of the media, both written and broadcast, tend to . . . create in regard to crime an undesirable form of hysteria which has its own dangers.' Principal among these dangers is the possibility of an overreaction to the perception of crime, and the syringe offences in the 1997 Act are arguably such an overreaction. In any case, the process by which these new syringe offences entered the statute books is illustrative of the essentially political character of some legislation. Students should bear in mind the unfortunate fact that legislation is not always the result of sustained reasoning and research.

Criminal statutes tend to take one of three forms. First, they can create entirely new offences that were unknown to the common law. The new syringe offences under the Non-Fatal Offences Against the Person Act 1997 are a good example of this. Second, they can codify existing common law principles, as the Non-Fatal Offences Against the Person Act 1997 did with the defence of the lawful use of force. Third, they can add to existing common law offences and regularise them without affecting the substance of the offence. For example, manslaughter is entirely a common law offence, but is punishable by up to life imprisonment by section 5 of the Offences Against the Person Act 1861, a provision that does not alter the elements of the offence.

Special mention should also be made of the work done by the Law Reform Commission to update the law. The Commission was established by the Law Reform Commission Act 1975 as a body independent of the government to review different areas of the law and to suggest improvements. Since 1975, the Commission has reviewed a number of areas of criminal law: vagrancy, rape, child sexual abuse, handling stolen property, malicious damage, non-fatal offences, sentencing and intoxication. Most recently, the Commission has issued studies of corporate killing, provocation and the mental element of murder. Many of its recommendations have now been incorporated by the Oireachtas into law. Reference will be made throughout this book, where appropriate, to the Commission's recommendations.

1.5 International Sources

Criminal law has traditionally been seen as the preserve of sovereign authorities, and until recently there has been little external influence on the development of Ireland's domestic criminal jurisprudence. However, modern criminal activity such as terrorism, drug trafficking and the trafficking of people are transnational enterprises that cannot be dealt with adequately by individual jurisdictions, but instead require concerted action. Ireland is a member of several international organisations that have drafted legislative responses to these and other criminal activities, responses that are increasingly being incorporated into domestic law. These international organisations consequently form a new source of Ireland's criminal law, albeit still a relatively small one. The two most influential of these organisations are the European Union and the Council of Europe. By virtue of Article 29.4.10º of the Constitution, nothing in the Constitution can be used to invalidate any measure necessitated by Ireland's membership of the EU; in effect, such measures supersede any domestic instrument, including the Constitution itself. Further, in matters covered by the Treaties, the institutions of the EU are entitled to legislate directly for Member States, and such legislation takes direct effect in the same way as legislation enacted by national legislatures. Accordingly, the EU is potentially a powerful influence on criminal law in this country. Some of this potential has been realised.

First, much European law has a distinctly penal character in terms of the sanctions that can be imposed for breaches of that law. European competition law, for example, allows for the imposition of very large fines for anti-competitive behaviour. As will be seen later (see section 1.12), the presence of penal, as opposed to compensatory, sanctions is one of the prime indicia used by the Irish courts to determine whether a legislative measure has a penal character. Second, European law can act as a restraint on domestic legislatures in crafting national criminal laws. For example, in *Conegate Ltd v. H.M. Customs and Excise* (1986), a British legislative prohibition on the import of German-made erotic inflatable dolls was invalidated by European law. Restrictions on the grounds of public morality could be placed legitimately on imports from other Member States, but the measure in question only applied to foreign-made dolls, not to those manufactured in the UK. The restriction therefore could not be justified on the grounds of public morality, and it was declared invalid. Third, while the foregoing examples of European influence on criminal law have arisen primarily as a result of European efforts to enforce European policies on agriculture and economics, the EU is becoming increasingly interested in what might be termed real criminal matters, especially under the so-called Third Pillar of the Union. The Third Pillar, established in 1992 by the Maastricht Treaty, is concerned with justice and home affairs, and establishes a framework within which the governments of EU Member States can co-operate on justice-related issues on a Union-wide basis. For the most part, measures taken within this framework must be incorporated into domestic law. Notable examples of such measures include the Child Trafficking and Pornography Act 1999, the European Arrest Warrant Act 2003 and the Criminal Justice (Terrorist Offences) Act 2005.

Ireland is also a member of other international organisations that have had some influence on criminal law in this jurisdiction. The Council of Europe was formed in the aftermath of World War II to establish some degree of unity among European countries and to allow a forum in which members could discuss matters of common concern. Perhaps its most important instrument is the European Convention on Human Rights, which Ireland signed in 1953. Signatory States are required to ensure that their domestic laws are compatible with the Convention, and a European Court of Human Rights was established under the Convention with the power to declare the incompatibility of national laws and to award damages. The court does not, however, have the power to strike down the domestic law in question. Thus, in *Norris v. Ireland* (1991), the Court declared Irish statutory provisions that punished consensual anal sexual intercourse incompatible with the Convention and awarded damages against Ireland. The provisions in question, however, remained in force until 1993, when they were repealed by the Criminal Justice (Sexual Offences) Act of that year. In an attempt to increase the influence of the Convention, the Oireachtas enacted the European Convention on Human Rights Act 2003, which places a general obligation on the Irish courts to interpret Irish laws in a manner compatible with the Convention, in so far as it is possible, and in so doing to take account of decisions of the European Court of Human Rights. Where such interpretations are not possible, the Irish courts have the power to declare provisions of Irish law to be incompatible with the Convention. Such declarations will not affect the validity of the provisions in question, nor will any right to compensation exist. However, a person in whose favour such a declaration has been made may petition the government for an *ex gratia* payment, and may also seek redress before the European Court of Human Rights. It seems likely that the areas of substantive Irish criminal law most likely to be open to challenge under the Convention are the imprecise definitions of offences like manslaughter under Article 7, the lawful use of lethal force under Article 2 and the insanity defence under Article 6. These issues will be discussed at the appropriate points in the book.

CRIMINALISATION

1.6   Introduction

The criminalisation process is concerned with deciding which actions should be deemed to be crimes and hence subject to criminal sanction. The process is heavily influenced by several competing philosophies, each of which has a different view of what the criminal law should be trying to achieve. However, as noted earlier (see section 1.4), the lawmaking process, and hence the criminalisation process, is now inherently political, and politics is an intensely practical arena. The importance of this aspect cannot be overestimated: legislators are apt to ignore fine philosophical approaches to criminalisation in order to satisfy the perceived concerns of the electorate and their own views of the public interest. Nevertheless, an introduction to the main intellectual currents that underpin the criminalisation process is useful as an aid to understanding the criminal law.

1.7   Moralism

Using morality as a basis for the criminal law involves a consideration of the inherent qualities of actions: immoral actions are prohibited because they are immoral, not because they are harmful to others. Traditionally, there has been a close connection between the criminal law and the morality taught by Christianity, and much of the early common law development of criminal law derived from Christian doctrines. Indeed, as recently as 1984, the majority of the Supreme Court in *Norris v. Attorney General* **(1984)** drew heavily upon Christian moral teachings and the Christian nature of the State, as exemplified by the Preamble to the Constitution, to deny the plaintiff's claim that the criminalisation of homosexual relations was unconstitutional. Thus, the consent of individuals engaged in such relations was overridden at least partly on the basis of a moral teaching (although it is interesting that the majority also felt the need to refer to evidence that homosexual relations could have damaging effects on the community). Few legal moralists would today attempt to use specifically Christian doctrines as a basis for the criminal law, and doing so would almost certainly contravene the European Convention on Human Rights. However, in a famous argument, Lord Devlin argued strongly in favour of a more general sense of morality as a basis for criminal prohibition.[2] Devlin asserted that societies require common moral bonds in order to survive and that society therefore had a legitimate interest in overriding private decisions in order to secure its moral code: 'The suppression of vice is as much the law's business as the suppression of subversive activities; it is no more possible to define a sphere of private morality than it is to define one of private subversive activity.' Thus, society has a right to use the law to prohibit immoral behaviour, even that which is committed in private. However, there are two major difficulties in using morality as a basis for criminal law. First, morality is such a wide concept that using it as a basis for criminalisation could remove any practical limits on the criminal law. Moralists generally recognise the force of this point and do not suggest that morality and the criminal law should be synonymous. Lord Devlin himself accepted that even though the State may be justified in criminalising immoral acts, in many cases the State should not do so. There are other values of concern to society besides its own continuation, such as privacy and tolerance. To effectively prevent immoral conduct committed in private would require police powers so intrusive that the loss in terms of privacy and tolerance, and other values, would negate any advantage gained from the suppression of the activity in question.

Second, there is no single definition of morality, and there are obvious difficulties with adopting a definition derived from one theological source, especially in a multicultural society. As Lord Devlin explained, the 'law can no longer rely on [Christian] doctrines in which citizens are entitled to disbelieve.' Devlin used the word 'morality' in a more general, populist sense: that which 'every right-minded person is presumed to consider to be immoral'. Feelings of disgust that are deeply felt and not manufactured could be taken as an indication that the limits of tolerance were being reached. If an activity is generally regarded as being 'so abominable that its mere presence is an offense', society should not be denied the right to try to eradicate it. Undoubtedly, there are benefits to ensuring that the criminal law is broadly in line with popular sentiment. As Herbert Packer has argued, a prohibitive law that is in line with popular sentiment is likely to be widely obeyed, and if it is broken, the efforts of law enforcement agencies will be all the more zealous.[3] However, there are obvious difficulties in determining whether an activity does in fact create a sufficiently deep sense of disgust, and the danger is that legislators would be able to substitute their own private view of the act in question for that of 'right-minded' people. More fundamentally, basing morality on popular notions of what is acceptable carries a significant risk of incorporating into the criminal law attitudes of blatant prejudice, a risk that seems out of place in a modern society that prides itself on its pluralism and tolerance.

---

2 Patrick Devlin, *The Enforcement of Morals*, Oxford: Oxford University Press, 1965.
3 Herbet Packer, *The Limits of the Criminal Sanction*, San Francisco: Stanford University Press, 1969.

1.8   Liberalism

Liberal legal theory came of age during the nineteenth century and overtook morality as the dominant basis of law. The core liberal value is the autonomy of the individual, and liberalism is primarily concerned with restraining the legal process as far as possible so as to maximise that autonomy. For liberals, the proper extent of the criminal law is defined by the so-called 'harm principle', which is traditionally associated with the work of John Stuart Mill.[4] Mill asserted that 'the sole end for which mankind are warranted, individually or collectively, in interfering with the liberty of action of any of their number, is … to prevent harm to others.' Thus, the consequence of an action rather than its inherent moral quality is the crucial factor in determining whether an act should be criminalised. Acts that cause harm only to the actor himself should not be criminalised; the concept of autonomy that underpins the harm principle requires the State to respect an individual's decisions about how he lives his own life because he knows his own circumstances better than anyone else. This is the general approach of the criminal law in Ireland today. Many of the most important offences require the prosecution to prove absence of consent as a constituent element of the charge – rape, assault, assault causing harm, theft, robbery, burglary. Note that in these offences, consent is not a defence; rather, the absence of consent is an element of the offence. This approach is more consistent with liberal theory than consent being a defence. If consent was a defence to charges of rape, assault, etc., the defendant would have an evidential burden to raise the issue and a failure to do so would result in a conviction despite the defendant's consent. By requiring the prosecution to prove absence of consent, no burden at all is placed on the defendant and this reflects modern society's view that the criminal law should not extend to sexual intercourse, the infliction of physical injury and the transfer of property, where these activities are done consensually. However, on some occasions, the law does treat consent as a defence: a defendant charged with the infliction of serious harm under section 4 of the Non-Fatal Offences Against the Person Act 1997, for example, can raise a defence of consent if the injuries were inflicted in the course of certain activities (see section 19.10). The difference in this approach reflects society's concern with the infliction of serious injury, and grants a defence only where that serious injury arose from conduct deemed socially acceptable.

The harm principle is immediately attractive primarily because of its apparent simplicity. However, the principle is not as simple as it appears, not least because of the difficulty in defining 'harm'. Conceptually, 'harm' could encompass anything from a direct physical assault to moral offense. A Jewish person could plausibly argue that his outrage at the flying of a Nazi swastika constituted harm, as could a Christian moralist at the idea of pre-marital sexual intercourse.

---

4   John S. Mill, *On Liberty* (1859), Everyman ed., London, 1993.

Similarly, it is plausible that harm can be caused indirectly by private actions; for example, the private viewing of pornography is arguably harmful in that it contributes to a demeaning societal view of women. However, basing criminalisation decisions on such a wide view of harm would essentially remove any limitation on the proper extent of the criminal law, thereby undermining the whole point of the harm principle. Mill himself offered only a vague definition of harm; he explicitly denounced any attempt to criminalise actions that either caused no direct harm to anyone or harmed only the actor himself. Later theorists have similarly struggled with a definition of harm; the best known is that offered by Joel Feinberg.[5] Feinberg argued that in addition to harm as defined by Mill, offensive conduct could be criminalised, but Feinberg included many caveats, i.e. the offence caused must be serious, there must be no reasonable alternative means of countering the conduct and the risk of offence was not assumed by the victim. Thus, even Feinberg's expansion of the basis of criminalisation remains tightly restricted. Other liberal theorists have argued that if respect for autonomy is truly the basis for the law, the law must consider what true autonomy entails. Autonomy involves individuals making choices for themselves, but some individuals have few choices to make in how they live due to their social circumstances. Accordingly, Joseph Raz[6] argued that the State has an obligation to assist in the creation of the conditions necessary for true autonomy, and this obligation forms another legitimate basis for interfering with private decisions.

1.9 Paternalism

Paternalistic legislation is that which imposes an obligation upon an individual for his own good, regardless of his wishes. The best example of such a legislation is the requirement that seatbelts be worn in cars; this is done primarily for the benefit of the individuals themselves. The fact that an individual does not want to wear a seatbelt is irrelevant. On its face, paternalistic legislation seems to contravene the harm principle, and indeed, Mill specifically argued against paternalism except in the case of children and the mentally ill. Mill assumed that individuals are better placed to know their own circumstances and needs than anyone else. However, some modern liberal theorists, who are generally within the Millian tradition, have argued that the harm principle can accommodate paternalism. H.L.A. Hart[7] pointed out that Mill's rejection of paternalistic legislation was based on 'a conception of what a normal human being is like which now seems not to correspond to the facts.' Individuals may not, in fact, know what is best for them due to a lack of knowledge. Government has the resources to call on experts in a wide variety of fields, resources that are beyond

---

5 Joel Feinberg, *Offense to Others*, Oxford: Oxford University Press, 1985.
6 Joseph Raz, *The Morality of Freedom*, Oxford: Oxford University Press, 1986.
7 H.L.A. Hart, *Law, Liberty and Morality*, Oxford: Oxford University Press, 1963.

those of most individuals. The decisions made by governments on foot of such expertise are therefore likely to be qualitatively better than any decisions made in relative ignorance by an individual. Further, some people may be incapable of rational decision-making due to factors such as mental disability or addiction. We might, for example, wonder about the ability of a heroin addict to make decisions in his own interests. Clearly there are situations in which the government might know better than the individual, and imposing a good decision might well result in the creation of more good than harm. Further, Gerald Dworkin[8] explicitly located his defence of paternalism within Mill's work. Mill had suggested that an autonomous individual could not be permitted to voluntarily sell himself into slavery because slavery is the antithesis of autonomy; therefore, if voluntary slavery was permitted and enforced, the law would be assisting in a diminution of the core liberal value of autonomy. Dworkin suggests that this argument allows for a limited degree of paternalism, and that the State may restrict the short-term choices available to individuals in order to ensure their ability to exercise autonomy in the future. However, the problem with this argument is that even this 'limited' paternalism is in fact potentially unlimited. Most self-harming actions carry at least some risk of future limitations on the exercise of autonomy, either through death, permanent injury or addiction. As the UK Law Commission put it in its *Consultation Paper* on *Consent in the Criminal Law* (1995), paternalism could be used to turn 'us all into super-fit, clean-living "Spartans" whether we like it or not.'

1.10 Feminism

Feminism is a comparative newcomer to legal theory and holds that the law is inherently male biased, both in terms of its substantive content and in the operation of the machinery of the criminal law. Female perspectives have been excluded because those who hold power within the criminal law – lawmakers, policymakers, judges, prosecutors, lawyers – are, and have always been, predominantly male. As a result, even principles that seem ostensibly gender neutral, such as *mens rea*, are in fact built on male standards, an argument neatly summed up in the use of the phrase 'men's rea' in place of *mens rea*.[9] This kind of argument has been made frequently in murder cases in which abused women killed their husbands in circumstances that seem to indicate cold-blooded decision-making which precludes a plea of provocation (see section 18.15). It is argued that the instant 'heat of the moment' retaliation required by the law is

---

8 Gerald Dworkin, 'Paternalism', (1972) 56 *The Monist* 64.
9 Mark Cousins, 'Men's rea: a note on sexual difference, criminology and the law', in P. Carlen and M. Collison (eds.), *Radical Issues in Criminology*, Oxford: Martin Robertson, 1980; Nicola Lacey, 'General Principles of Criminal Law? A Feminist View', in D. Nicolson and L. Bibbings, *Feminist Perspectives on Criminal Law*, London: Cavendish, 2000.

based on male types of behaviour; that women are more likely to have a 'slow-burn' reaction that will erupt in violence some time later. Thus, women's interests are directly harmed by ostensibly gender-neutral legal principles. However, on many occasions women benefit from the male-driven assumptions that underlie the criminal law. A good example is the old defence of marital coercion; the law presumed that if a married woman committed an offence in the presence of her husband, she did so under his duress. Similarly, Hilary Allen has argued that convicted female offenders are dealt with differently, and generally more leniently, than male offenders.[10] Feminists argue that even in situations such as these, in which women receive an apparent concession from the criminal law, women's interests are harmed because these concessions assume a lack of rational ability on the part of women. Consequently, the 'concession' is in reality an example of the subordination of women and a disregard for female autonomy. However, in countering such discrimination, a sharp divergence has emerged between so-called liberal and radical feminists. Liberal feminists, such as Jennifer Temkin,[11] seek to establish the autonomy of women through legislative and policy changes to the existing law, and they have achieved some notable successes, especially in the area of sexual offences. For example, the abolition of the so-called marital rape exemption by the Criminal Law (Rape) (Amendment) Act 1990 ended the immunity from rape prosecution enjoyed by a husband who had sexual intercourse with his wife without her consent. In so doing, the law explicitly recognised the sexual autonomy of married women. The 1990 Act also made clear that absence of consent is all that is required for a rape charge, and that the absence of resistance by a woman does not equate with consent. Radical feminists such as Catherine MacKinnon,[12] however, assert that the existing law and legal system are inherently patriarchal and cannot be reformed through mere tinkering. They assert that the liberal approach represents at best a mere accommodation of female interests. Consequently, traditional notions of law must be abandoned and a new system of law must be developed that respects the differences between the genders. Merely using apparently gender-neutral words such as 'person' in place of 'men' accomplishes nothing because, as MacKinnon famously commented, the law must accept that there are 'women and men because you don't see many persons around'. Demands for such a widespread reconstruction of the law have met with little success.

---

10 Hilary Allen, *Justice Unbalanced*, Milton Keynes: Open University Press, 1987.
11 Jennifer Temkin, *Rape and the Legal Process*, 2nd ed., Oxford: Oxford University Press, 2002; 'Rape and Criminal Justice at the Millennium', in D. Nicolson and L. Bibbings, *Feminist Perspectives on Criminal Law*, London: Cavendish, 2000.
12 Catherine MacKinnon, *Feminism Unmodified*, Cambridge, MA: Harvard University Press, 1987; *Toward a Feminist Theory of the State*, Cambridge, MA: Harvard University Press, 1991.

CRIME

1.11 Introduction

It goes without saying that the criminal justice system exists to deal with crime. The number of crimes known to the criminal law is enormous: Ashworth estimates that there are about 8,000 offences known to English law,[13] and it is likely that the number in Irish law is at a similar level. Arguably, there has been an overreliance on the machinery of the criminal justice system to deal with social problems, some of which had previously been left to more informal mechanisms. As a result, the reach of the criminal law has grown considerably, perhaps beyond our ability to effectively enforce it. But what is a crime? How do we tell criminal conduct and criminal legislation apart from mere anti-social conduct and regulatory legislation? These questions are not merely of academic interest: if conduct has been rendered criminal, then it must be dealt with within a strict constitutional framework.

1.12 Definition of Crime

Modern Irish cases in which definitions of crime have been attempted have tended to avoid references to the immorality and harmful consequences of the prohibited actions. Instead, the courts have focused on the characteristics of crime and the nature of the proceedings in issue. The leading authority is the Supreme Court decision in ***Melling v. O'Mathghamhna* (1962)**. The defendant had been charged in the District Court with fifteen counts of smuggling butter, the importation of which could be done only under licence. The charges were brought under section 186 of the Customs Consolidation Act 1876, which provided as follows:

> Every person who shall . . . be in any way knowingly concerned in carrying, removing . . . concealing, or in any manner dealing with goods with intent . . . to evade any prohibition or restriction of or applicable to such goods . . . shall for each offence forfeit either treble the value of the goods, including the duty payable thereon, or one hundred pounds, at the election of the [Revenue Commissioners]; and the offender may either be detained or proceeded against by summons.

Additionally, section 232 provided that in default of paying the fine, the defendant must be sentenced to prison for up to twelve months, depending on the amount involved. The defendant argued that the charges related to criminal offences that were not minor and therefore could not be tried in the District Court. The first issue to be decided was the nature of the charges. Were they criminal? Kingsmill Moore J. noted the problem:

---

13 Andrew Ashworth, 'Is the Criminal Law a Lost Cause?', (2000) 116 *Law Quarterly Review* 225.

What is a crime? The anomalies which still exist in the criminal law and the diversity of expression in statutes make a comprehensive definition all but impossible to frame. The criminal quality of an act cannot be discerned by intuition; nor can it be discovered by reference to any standard but one: 'Is the act prohibited with penal consequences?' said Lord Atkin in *Proprietary Articles Trade Association v. Attorney General for Canada* [(1931)].

He then identified several factors which, if present, would indicate the existence of a criminal offence:

(a) it should be an offence against society at large;
(b) the sanction should be of a punitive nature rather than restitutionary;
(c) the action should generally require proof of *mens rea*.

These factors are the principal ones to be used in identifying a criminal charge. However, there are others. In the same case, Lavery J. noted that the procedure to be followed bore all the hallmarks of a criminal prosecution – detention in a garda station, the proferring of a charge, searching the defendant, examination before a District judge, admission to bail and the imposition of a financial penalty backed by the threat of imprisonment in the event of default. Additionally, O Dálaigh C.J. also took note of the language of the provision, which he described as being the 'vocabulary of the criminal law'.

These factors have formed the basis in the Irish courts of the definition of a crime ever since, as the following examples demonstrate. In *DPP v. Boyle* **(1993)**, for example, the High Court considered section 24 of the Finance Act 1926, as amended by section 69(1) of the Finance Act 1982. Section 24(1) required all bookmakers to pay a duty on every bet entered into. Failure to do so would result, on summary conviction under section 24(5), in an excise penalty of up to £500. The court held, following *Melling*, that the provision was a criminal offence. Of particular importance was the language used, especially the words 'offence' and 'summary conviction'. Indeed, the court noted that it was the absence of similar words in *Melling* that resulted in the discussion in that case on the constitution of a crime. In *McLoughlin v. Tuite* **(1986)**, the High Court considered section 500 of the Income Tax Act 1967, which provided a penalty of £500 for failing to produce certain documents. Holding that this provision was civil in character, Carroll J. specifically noted that the penalty was non-criminal and recoverable in civil proceedings, and remarked on the absence of criminal vocabulary. It would seem, therefore, that the language used in a provision is accorded considerable authority. Finally, in *Gilligan v. Criminal Assets Bureau* **(2001)**, the issue arose as to the nature of the forfeiture proceedings allowed by the Proceeds of Crime Act 1996. The Act allows for the forfeiture of property that the High Court believes on a balance of probabilities to be derived directly or indirectly from criminal activity. This power can be exercised even where the property owner has not been charged with, much less convicted of, any criminal offence. The plaintiff argued that this power was criminal in nature, and that as the High Court proceedings were civil in nature, he would suffer a criminal sanction without the protection of due process of law required by the Constitution in all criminal trials. The Supreme Court held that an action under the Proceeds of Crime Act was of a civil character, principally as there was no provision in the Act for the indicia of criminal proceedings. In the High Court (***Gilligan v. Criminal Assets Bureau* (1998)**), McGuinness J. had made a similar finding, noting also that proceedings under the 1996 Act were *in rem* (against property) rather than *in personam* (against a person), as would be usual in a criminal trial.

1.13 Classification of Crimes

Common Law

The law recognises that some crimes are more serious than others, and has accordingly adopted a number of classification systems. At common law, there were three types of offences: treasons, felonies and misdemeanours. Originally, all crimes were classified as felonies, with treason being a specific type of felony. They all attracted the death penalty and forfeiture of all property. However, the judges recognised that there was a need for a lesser category of offences, and created misdemeanours, which attracted only terms of imprisonment or fines. The title of felony was kept for the more serious offences, such as murder, rape and kidnapping, with misdemeanours being less serious offences, such as perjury.

The old common law distinction carried some important consequences. First, a person suspected of committing a felony could be arrested without a warrant,[14] a power that did not exist in relation to misdemeanours. Second, felonies attracted two related offences that did not apply to misdemeanours. It was a misdemeanour not to report a felony. This offence, called misprision of felony, was defined by the Supreme Court in ***Heaney and McGuinness v. Ireland* (1997)** as 'conceal[ing] or procur[ing] the concealment of a felony known to have been committed. It is the duty of all citizens to disclose to the proper authorities all material facts as to the commission of a felony of which the citizen has definite knowledge.' It was also a misdemeanour, called compounding a felony, for a person to agree not to prosecute a felony in return for a reward of any kind.

Statute

The distinction between felonies and misdemeanours has been abolished by section 3 of the Criminal Law Act 1997. However, as many statutes still refer to offences in these terms, section 3(2) provides that for the purposes of these

---

14 An arrest warrant is a written authority allowing the apprehension of a specified person for a specified offence. It is usually given by a District Court judge on the application of the gardaí.

statutes, all offences will be treated as misdemeanours, thus effectively abolishing the consequences of the distinction noted above. The Act goes on to create a new category of offences to replace felonies, called arrestable offences. Arrestable offences, or attempts to commit any such offences, are those that carry a penalty of at least five years' imprisonment. Where a person has committed or is in the process of committing an arrestable offence, that person may be arrested without a warrant by either a garda or a private citizen (sections 4(1) and (2)). A 'citizen's arrest' may, however, only be made to prevent the offender avoiding arrest by the gardaí. It is an offence to impede the arrest of anyone who has committed an arrestable offence (section 7(2)). Finally, it is also an offence to accept a reward (other than fair compensation for any harm done) in return for concealing the commission of an arrestable offence (section 8(1)).

It is the practice in modern statutes to distinguish between offences on the basis of the manner in which they will be tried: summary offences and indictable offences. Summary offences are of a minor nature and are tried in the District Court, without a jury. They are usually prosecuted by the gardaí or some other State agency, such as the Environental Protection Agency in the case of some environmental offences. Indictable offences are more serious, and are usually tried in the Circuit or Central Criminal Courts before a jury. Indictable offences of a subversive nature may be tried without a jury in the Special Criminal Court, as may any other offence that the DPP decides is unsuitable to be tried in the ordinary criminal courts. Additionally, many indictable offences may be tried in the District Court if it is just to do so and the defendant agrees.

Constitution

The Constitution also contains a classification system, namely minor and non-minor offences. The importance of this distinction can be seen from Article 38.5, which requires that anyone charged with a criminal offence, other than a minor offence or one to be tried before a special or military court, is entitled to a trial before a jury. As the Constitution contains no definition of a minor offence, this task has fallen to the courts. In *Melling v. O'Mathghamhna* **(1962)**, the Supreme Court laid down the following criteria by which an offence could be classified as minor or non-minor:

(a) how the law stood when the statute was passed;
(b) the severity of the penalty;
(c) the moral quality of the alleged offence; and
(d) the relationship between the alleged offence and common law offences.

However, it is clear from the judgment that the severity of the punishment is the single most important consideration. Later cases suggest that offences which might attract punishments of a fine or imprisonment of up to six months are minor, but sentences of two years or more render the offence non-minor. Furthermore, following the acceptance of the Sixteenth Amendment to the Constitution (the Bail Referendum), Article 40.7 refers to a further category of offences, namely serious offences. The Bail Act 1997 defines a serious offence as one that might attract a term of imprisonment of five years or more, and includes in the Schedule to the Act murder, manslaughter, assault and aggravated assault, rape, incest and drugs offences. Whether or not the courts will accept this definition remains to be seen. It may well turn out that the courts will substitute 'serious' offences for 'non-minor' offences.

PUNISHMENT

1.14 Introduction

The real function of the criminal law is a matter of some debate. Its formal function is to establish a code of acceptable behaviour, and by so doing to allow a peaceful and ordered society to exist. As Lord Hailsham said in *R v. Howe* (1987), the 'overriding objects of the criminal law must be to protect innocent lives and to set a standard of conduct which ordinary men and women are expected to observe if they are to avoid criminal responsibility.' As such, criminal law is a means of social control. However, whether its control is benign or something more sinister depends on one's perspective. Some commentators, especially those writing from a Marxist perspective, see criminal law as a reflection of the interests of the ruling class, and as a means of ensuring the continuation of that class's power. Others see it simply as a reflection of the will of society; it lays down the standards of behaviour expected of members of that society and outlaws anti-social behaviour. There are probably elements of truth in both views: legislation does reflect the view and ideology of the group that holds power, but the prohibition of seriously anti-social behaviour, such as killing and rape, also represents the will and needs of society. This is an ongoing debate that will not be resolved any time soon, if ever. For the purposes of this book, however, it is sufficient to note that the criminal law is an agent of social control and is designed to curb people's behaviour.

Criminal law is far from being the only agent of social control. Most branches of law fulfil a similar role. Contract law, for example, requires those who make contracts to honour them, while tort tries to ensure that people do not injure others through negligent behaviour. There are also other means of controlling behaviour that fall outside the law altogether. Religion and social norms are obvious examples of such non-legal methods of control: religion holds it to be a sin to tell a lie, while skipping a queue is a breach of social convention. Neither action, however, is illegal and neither will ordinarily attract any legal sanction. Thus, criminal law is but one of the methods used by society to order itself. It differs from the others by the sanctions attaching to it; only a breach of the criminal law will attract a State-imposed punishment. Society has deemed such breaches to be sufficiently serious to the common good as to warrant direct intervention by the State. A breach of contract can be left to the injured party to pursue, but a killing requires some formal punishment to be imposed by the State. There can be little objection to this when the matter is as serious as killing. However, not all criminal actions are as serious, or affect the common good as much as killing; some offences are very minor, such as dropping litter. It might be felt that such minor actions could be prevented by some other means, such as a civil action. Nevertheless, society has decided that they too should be policed by the State, and result in a punishment directed by the State. It is to this punishment that the discussion now turns.

1.15 Objectives of Punishment

Traditionally, four objectives of punishment have been put forward: incapacitation, retribution, deterrence and rehabilitation. Which of the four is the most important is a matter of opinion, and those opinions tend to vary over time. In the 1950s and 1960s, the major concern seemed to be rehabilitation. However, since the 1970s, there has been a trend towards retribution, particularly in political circles. As will be seen later, this trend has apparently been resisted by the Irish courts.

Incapacitation

Where a criminal offence has been committed, especially a serious offence, it is obviously important that its perpetrator is not free to commit a similar offence, at least for the duration of the punishment. The law therefore seeks to incapacitate the offender, and thereby to prevent him from causing any more harm. This objective is particularly important when dealing with persistent offenders – in the English case of *R v. Sargent* (1975), it was noted that when dealing with such offenders, 'the only protection which the public has is that such persons should be locked up for a long period.' However, such an approach to punishment can be unjustifiably harsh. In the first place, it would require that the only punishments on offer should be those that prevent the offender from committing other offences, which in practice would mean either imprisonment or execution. Yet the imposition of either penalty may not be appropriate for the actual offence committed. Most people would consider a long jail sentence to be somewhat harsh for the offence of dropping litter, even where it is done repeatedly. Second, even where a custodial sentence is warranted, the incapacitation approach would require that sentences be considerably longer than the actual offence committed deserves. It may, of course, be argued that persistent offenders deserve longer sentences because, having been in trouble before, they know full well what they are doing and risking. Be that as it may, the incapacitation approach can be used as a form of preventative justice which, as will be seen later (see section 1.17), is not tolerated by the Irish Constitution.

Retribution

The retributive theory of punishment has had a long history and various revisions. For a time it lost ground to rehabilitation, but it seems that it is again the dominant theory, at least in the political arena. In earlier times, the theory of retribution meant what its name suggests: vengeance. It operated almost according to the biblical 'eye for an eye' standard. Through the public process of the trial and the imposition of a punishment in the name of society, the law was said to demonstrate the revulsion felt by society for the offender's actions. The offender had attacked society, so society felt justified in attacking the offender. By doing so through the medium of the law, moreover, the chances of a private citizen seeking personal retribution were minimised. The law was thus seen as a social safety valve. This view of retribution now has little academic or judicial support, although one feels that it might have greater following in the general populace.

In its next guise, retribution was seen to be a form of expiation of guilt – the offender had committed an offence against society which had to be made good by serving a punishment. In so doing, the offender accepted his guilt, paid for it and then re-entered society with a clean slate. The language of expiation is still prevalent today – it is common to speak of a criminal 'paying his debt to society'. However, true expiation works in much the same way as the Roman Catholic rite of Confession – the penitent confesses his sins and receives absolution. Likewise, a criminal may accept his guilt and seek redemption. Unfortunately, society cannot force this on the offender, and can do no more than to provide, through punishment, an opportunity for expiation. Society can accept the punishment as payment for the crime, even though the offender accepts no remorse for his actions.

The modern theory of retribution is better known as the 'just dessert' theory. According to this theory, offenders receive punishment simply because they deserve it. Central to the theory is the belief that human beings are free, autonomous beings who act as they choose to act. Those who choose to break the law do so out of free will, and therefore morally deserve to be punished. The focus of this approach is exclusively on the past criminal conduct of the offender. It follows that the future misconduct of the offender, or indeed his rehabilitation, is irrelevant. Furthermore, as dessert theorists believe that the offender's conduct alone is justification for the punishment, the possibility of deterrence is also irrelevant, although such theorists are quite willing to accept deterrence as a useful by-product of retribution. All that is of concern to the dessert theorist is the moral blame attaching to the offender due to his criminal action. He must 'get what he deserves'. This in turn places a limit on the punishment that can be imposed. Unlike the theory of incapacitation, which might attract a heavier punishment than the actual offence deserves, the dessert judge will try to measure the harm done and the guilt of the offender, and impose a sentence that visits a proportionate amount of harm on the offender. In other words, dessert theory holds that the punishment must be proportionate to the crime. This is the proportionality principle. It is this principle that distinguishes a just desserts approach from that of pure vengeance, which held that the punishment should equal the crime.

Deterrence

Theories of deterrence operate on the basis of 'prevention is better than cure'. The hope is that by imposing a punishment, there will be less crime in the future. Hence, the deterrent effect of a criminal punishment assumes great importance, and works in two ways. First, it is hoped that the individual offender will be taught that 'crime does not pay' and that he will not reoffend. This is known as individual deterrence. The court must look at the individual offender and impose a sentence that is likely to make a lasting impression on him. This necessarily involves the court in making a prediction as to the offender's likelihood of committing further offences. If the court feels that there is little such likelihood, then a lenient sentence such as probation might be justified. If, however, the likelihood is high, then a lengthy prison sentence may be required. The necessity for such predictions, however, is also the greatest weakness of the individual deterrent approach. Predicting the future behaviour of a person can never be an exact science, and the high rate of repeat offending is a testament to this difficulty. Additionally, this approach could lead to sentences that bear little or no relation to the severity of the crime. If X, a young man with an unblemished record, kills his wealthy father in order to receive his inheritance, the court may have no reason to believe that X will commit another offence in the future. On a strict individual deterrent basis, the court should therefore impose a lenient sentence. Indeed, if there is no chance of X committing other offences, theories of deterrence would suggest that there is no point in imposing any punishment at all. The opposite is also true: if Y is a persistent litterbug, individual deterrent theory would suggest a severe sentence in order to deter his littering habits. It is likely that the disparity in the treatment of X and Y would result in considerable public concern.

The second form of deterrence hopes that criminal punishments will encourage others to avoid becoming involved in criminal activity, thus reducing the overall level of crime in the community. This is known as general deterrence. Under this form of deterrence, the offender's guilt is not the central issue; rather, it is the public perception of his conduct that will decide his sentence. So, if the offender commits a crime that is on the increase, he might receive a punishment that would ordinarily be considered excessive. If, for example, the courts believe that there are too many burglaries, and X is convicted of burglary, the courts may decide to make an example of him by imposing a sentence of life imprisonment. Alternatively, if X commits a rare offence, the courts might be justified in imposing a very light sentence as to do otherwise would be superfluous because no one else is committing that kind of offence anyway. Such an approach attracts the same criticism as individual deterrence: there is no necessary connection between the offence and the punishment imposed. Furthermore, there is little real evidence that other criminals will be deterred from their intended conduct. General deterrence is dependent in part on the perceived ability of the gardaí to catch criminals. If the gardaí are perceived to have a low rate of success against criminals, potential criminals may be more willing to take the chance of committing a crime. The greater confidence the criminal has in his own law-breaking skill, the less thought he will give to being caught, and therefore to the possibility of severe punishment.

Rehabilitation

The law is also concerned that an offender be given a chance to rehabilitate himself to become a useful member of society. In this respect, crime can be seen as a form of illness, and punishment as a form of therapy or cure. It should be stressed that this is not entirely for the benefit of the offender alone, but also for that of society as well. It is obviously in society's best interests that offenders turn away from crime, thereby contributing to the overall well-being of society. However, while rehabilitation is a noble and ambitious goal, it does have certain difficulties. First, it requires a high level of State intervention, which in turn requires a high level of resources. Second, in common with deterrence, rehabilitative measures have no necessary connection with the crime committed. From a rehabilitation perspective, the sentence imposed should be the one most likely to rehabilitate the offender, not the one that his crime actually deserves. Indeed, the more serious the offence, the more 'ill' the offender, and therefore the greater the necessity for him to be rehabilitated instead of punished. Finally, there is little evidence that rehabilitative schemes actually work. The usual method of assessment is to look at the rate of repeat offending, or recidivism: if it decreases, then rehabilitation is working; if it increases or remains the same, then rehabilitation has failed. There seems to be general agreement that rehabilitative schemes in this country and in others have had little effect on recidivism.

1.16 Modes of Punishment

Until recently, the most severe punishment that could be imposed was the death penalty, given in cases of capital murder, treason or some offences against military law. However, the Criminal Justice Act 1990 formally abolished the death penalty (sentences for which were, as a matter of policy, commuted anyway since the 1950s). The imposition of the death penalty is now unconstitutional by virtue of the 21st Amendment of the Constitution 2001; further, the constitutional prohibition on the death penalty has been removed from the ambit of the emergency powers provisions of Article 28. Consequently, the death penalty cannot be lawfully reinstated in Ireland even if the Constitution is suspended due to an emergency. Additionally, the use of corporal punishment is expressly prohibited by section 12 of the Criminal Law Act 1997. It might also be noted that, in line with the recommendations of the Law Reform Commission (*Report on Non-Fatal Offences Against the Person* (1994)), the immunity from prosecution that a teacher once had in respect of corporal punishment imposed upon a student has been abolished by section 24 of the Non-Fatal Offences Against the Person Act 1997.

The sanctions available today are imprisonment, fines, forfeiture, community service orders, probation and compensation orders.

Imprisonment

The most severe punishment available is imprisonment. Until recently, there were technically three types of imprisonment: imprisonment, imprisonment with hard labour, and penal servitude. There was, however, little practical difference between them. In any case, section 11 of the Criminal Law Act 1997 has now formally abolished penal servitude and hard labour. Sentences of imprisonment may be suspended if the court feels it is appropriate in the circumstances to do so. Where a person is convicted of a number of offences, he may receive a number of sentences which will usually run concurrently. However, sentences passed by the District Court may run consecutively, as shall sentences imposed for offences committed while on bail (Criminal Justice Act 1951 and Criminal Justice Act 1984, respectively). The Law Reform Commission, in its *Report on Sentencing* (1996), recommended that imprisonment be viewed as the sanction of last resort.

Fines

Financial penalties account for the bulk of criminal sanctions imposed by the courts. They may be imposed either as a penalty in themselves or in addition to another penalty and represent a source of revenue that helps to defray some of the cost of the criminal justice system. The amount of the fine will depend on the relevant statute, which will usually specify the maximum amount that can be imposed. However, inflationary pressures can reduce the effectiveness of statutory fines, and to combat such pressures, the Law Reform Commission, in its *Report on the Indexation of Fines* (1991), recommended that the values of fines be linked to a price index. This recommendation has not been enacted. If a fine is imposed and is not paid, the defaulter can be imprisoned; such imprisonment is not in lieu of the fine, but rather in addition to the fine.

Forfeiture

In modern Irish law, the most important forfeiture provisions are found in the Proceeds of Crime Act 1996 as amended by the Proceeds of Crime (Amendment) Act 2005, both of which are enforced by the Criminal Assets Bureau (CAB). These Acts permit the courts to order the forfeiture of property in Ireland and, under certain conditions, property outside Ireland with a value in excess of €13,000 where such property directly or indirectly represents the proceeds of criminal conduct. The CAB was established under the Criminal Assets Bureau Act 1996 for the purpose of identifying assets that have been gained directly or indirectly from criminal activity and to initiate any necessary legal steps required to seize such property. The staff of the CAB is drawn mainly from the gardaí, but it also contains personnel from the Revenue Commissioners and the Department of Social Welfare. Orders under the 1996 Act can be granted even where the respondent has not been convicted of any criminal offence. In *Gilligan v. Criminal Assets Bureau* **(2001)**, the appellants argued that the absence of the protections granted by Article 38 of the Constitution to criminal defendants rendered the 1996 Act unconstitutional. The Supreme Court, confirming the earlier decision of the High Court, ruled that proceedings under the 1996 Act were civil in nature: the 1996 Act does not contain the typical indicia of criminal proceedings, such as powers of arrest and detention, the provision of bail, the power to order imprisonment for default or the initiation of proceedings by summons or indictment. Further, the court ruled that there is no constitutional right to the use of the proceeds of crime and therefore no interference with constitutionally protected property rights.

The Criminal Justice Act 1994 also contains some forfeiture provisions that are aimed specifically at drug traffickers. Where a person has been convicted of drug trafficking offences (supplying, transporting, storing, importing or exporting drugs), the DPP can apply to the High Court to determine whether that person has received and benefited from any payments or property in connection with those offences. The court is entitled to assume that any property gained by the offender during the period of six years prior to the conviction was gained in connection with such offences. This assumption may, however, be rebutted. If not, the court may then order the offender to pay the full value of the property to the State.

Community Service Orders

Community Service Orders were introduced into Irish law by the Criminal Justice (Community Service) Act 1983. Any court other than the Special Criminal Court may impose a community service order against any offender over the age of sixteen. It can only be imposed in lieu of imprisonment, although the Law Reform Commission, in its *Report on Sentencing* (1996), recommended that this restriction should be removed. The order can be for between forty and 240 hours of unpaid work that will be completed under the supervision of a probation officer. The offender must, however, consent to the order and the court must be satisfied that the order is appropriate in the circumstances of the case. Failure to perform the service is itself an offence under the 1983 Act.

Probation

Probation is an option that has a long history in Ireland, and is now governed by the Probation of Offenders Act 1907. It may be applied to any offender who has been convicted of an offence punishable by imprisonment. There are two forms of probation: one that operates only in the District Court and one that operates in all courts. The former, sometimes called an absolute discharge, allows the District Court, despite having concluded that the offence has been proven, to order the release of the defendant without formally proceeding to a conviction. The other form of probation, sometimes called a conditional discharge, allows any court to release the defendant following conviction, subject to the defendant entering into a recognisance to be of good behaviour for a period of up to three years.[15] If during the probation period the defendant breaches his recognisance, he must appear in court to be sentenced for the original offence. During probation, the defendant will be under the supervision of a probation officer. Finally, the District Court has the power to bind a defendant over to keep the peace under the Courts (Supplemental Provisions) Act 1961. Such an order operates in much the same way as a conditional discharge.

Compensation

Compensation Orders may also be imposed, either as an alternative to some other sanction or in addition thereto. There are three principal means by which the victim of criminal actions may receive compensation. First, in 1974, the Criminal Injuries Compensation Tribunal was established to provide compensation to those who suffered personal injury as a result of criminal activity occurring since 1972. Since 1986, however, the Tribunal has been precluded from awarding compensation for general damages such as pain and suffering. Compensation is now limited to special damages only, such as medical bills and any other quantifiable losses.

Second, under the Malicious Injuries Act 1981, the Circuit Court could order compensation for malicious damage to property to be paid by local authorities. The cost of this scheme was enormous, and led to the passing of the Malicious Injuries (Amendment) Act 1986, which limited claims to malicious damage arising out of riots or actions connected to the conflict in Northern Ireland. In *Cleary & Co. (1941) Plc v. Dublin Corporation* (**1997**), the plaintiff claimed interest on an award for damage arising from incendiary devices in its Dublin

---

15 A recognisance is a formal agreement entered into by a defendant to keep the peace.

store. It was held that such interest is excluded by the terms of the 1981 Act because it is not compensation for damage done.

Finally, under the Criminal Justice Act 1993, the courts have the power to order an offender to pay compensation to the victim, and this should be exercised unless the court has good reason not to do so. However, the Court of Criminal Appeal has recently confirmed that the payment of compensation should not of itself preclude the imposition of a sentence of imprisonment. In *The People (DPP) v. McLaughlin* **(2005)**, the defendant pleaded guilty to a charge of rape and offered the sum of €10,000 in compensation, and the complainant had indicated that she was willing to accept the offer. Carney J. imposed a sentence of five years' imprisonment, but felt compelled to suspend the sentence on foot of this compensation. The Court of Criminal Appeal ruled, however, that 'there is no jurisprudence, principle or practice which renders the payment of compensation to a rape victim inconsistent with the imposition of a custodial sentence.' The court confirmed that the selection of the appropriate sentence was a matter for the trial judge's discretion and the payment of compensation was only a factor to be considered.

1.17 Sentencing in Ireland

The imposition of sentences, and in particular the perceived disparity in sentencing, is an area of criminal justice that has caused considerable public concern, with regular calls for the introduction of sentencing guidelines. The policies followed by the courts in choosing an appropriate sentence can be difficult to discern, as sentencing policy does not always figure prominently in judicial decisions. Additionally, there is a virtual absence of guidance on sentencing from either the Constitution or from statutes. Any such attempt must extract policies piecemeal from various judgments, leading to at least the appearance of incoherence. Nevertheless, there are some general points that may be made.

Constitutional Guidance

The Constitution does establish some general principles upon which sentencing should be based. In *Deaton v. Attorney General* **(1963)**, the Supreme Court held that sentencing forms an integral part of the administration of justice. As a result, sentencing must follow the constitutional requirements of justice, fairness and independence that apply to all other aspects of a criminal trial. In *The State (Healy) v. Donoghue* **(1976)**, Henchy J. held that these constitutional requirements created

> [A] guarantee that a citizen shall not be deprived of his liberty as a result of a criminal trial conducted in a manner or in circumstances calculated to shut him out from a reasonable opportunity of establishing his innocence, or where his guilt has

been established or admitted, of receiving a sentence appropriate to his degree of guilt and his relevant personal circumstances.

This statement suggests that the Irish courts are constitutionally prohibited from imposing sentences that are excessive in relation to the crime and the degree of blameworthiness of the offender. In effect, the Irish courts are constitutionally required to exercise proportionality in their sentencing practices. This was the attitude of Flood J. in *The People (DPP) v. WC* (**1994**), when he stated that:

> The selection of the particular punishment to be imposed on an individual offender is subject to the constitutional principle of proportionality. By this I mean that the imposition of a particular sentence must strike a balance between the particular circumstances of the commission of the relevant offence and the relevant personal circumstances of the person sentenced.

Similarly, in *The People (DPP) v. Connolly* (**1996**), the defendant had been sentenced to three years' imprisonment for causing the deaths of two people by dangerous driving. The sentence was reviewed after five months, and the balance was suspended. The DPP appealed on the basis that this was unduly lenient. The Court of Criminal Appeal held that while it certainly was lenient, providing the trial judge maintained a balance between the particular circumstances of the offence and the relevant personal circumstances of the defendant, the sentence should not be disturbed.

Second, in *The People (Attorney General) v. O'Callaghan* (**1966**), Walsh J. held that the concept of personal liberty protected by the Constitution prevents the punishment of any person in respect of any matter of which he has not been convicted. The only exceptions to this general rule would have to be carefully spelled out by the Oireachtas, and would in any event have to be limited to the 'most extraordinary circumstances' where the preservation of public peace, order or safety, or the safety of the State was at stake.

Third, in *O'Callaghan*, the Supreme Court made it clear that the Constitution will not allow any form of preventative justice. Therefore, an offender cannot receive a sentence that is excessive in relation to the crime he committed and to his degree of guilt. Consequently, the incapacitation approach to punishment could run into serious constitutional problems. This is well demonstrated in *The People (DPP) v. G* (**1994**). The defendant, a thirty-year-old man, had pleaded guilty to twelve counts of rape involving three girls aged between six and twelve over a period of six years. The Central Criminal Court had sentenced him to twelve concurrent sentences of life imprisonment, and it was this sentence the defendant appealed against. He had acknowledged his guilt from the very first interview with the gardaí, and he argued that he deserved a discount as a result. The trial judge had recognised that he had a duty to take account of all mitigating factors, which included the guilty plea. However, the judge also stated that he had a duty towards society. His conclusion was to give:

> ... total priority to the protection of the community and [to impose] a sentence [of life imprisonment] which is designed to ensure that the defendant will not be released until the Minister [of Justice]'s advisers are fully satisfied that there is no danger of the defendant re-offending ...

The Supreme Court disagreed, substituting a sentence of fifteen years for each count instead. The court held that a sentencing court must take into account all mitigating factors, including an early guilty plea, in arriving at an appropriate sentence. The protection of the community, by implication, cannot override this principle. Similarly, in *The People (DPP) v. FB* (**1997**), the defendant had committed numerous acts of rape and incest on his three daughters, and pleaded guilty to a token number of charges. The trial judge stated that he believed that a life sentence was the appropriate sentence for a number of reasons, one of which was that the defendant could only be released from such a sentence when he was no longer a danger to society. This, however, was a form of preventative justice and was unconstitutional. For this and other reasons, a sentence of fifteen years was imposed. Since these cases were decided, section 29(2) of the Criminal Justice Act 1999 has granted to the courts the power to impose the maximum sentence even where a guilty plea has been received. However, the essential point made in these cases remains valid: a sentence calculated to prevent the commission of possible future crimes is likely to be unconstitutional.

Statutory Guidance

Statutory influence on sentencing is comparatively light. In *The People (DPP) v. WC* (**1994**), Flood J. made the following observation:

> The role of legislation, subject to some exceptions, has been to provide a power to sentence an accused person, and to set the outer limit of its use. The sentence to be imposed on an accused person in a particular case is solely a matter for a trial judge in the independent and impartial exercise of judicial discretion.

The central role in sentencing is therefore occupied by the courts. Nevertheless, there is some general guidance given in legislation. First, as noted by Flood J. in *WC*, the primary role of the legislature in sentencing is to decide on the maximum sentence that can be imposed. This legislative decision is inevitably based on the Oireachtas' view of the seriousness of the offence and is generally unreviewable by the courts. In some cases, the Oireachtas has imposed mandatory and minimum sentences. The best example of a mandatory sentence is that for murder: under the Criminal Justice Act 1964, the penalty to be imposed upon conviction for murder is life imprisonment. Minimum sentences have been imposed in respect of drug trafficking offences under section 15A of the Misuse of Drugs Act 1977, as amended by the Criminal Justice Act 1999. Anyone convicted under this provision is to receive a sentence of at least ten years' imprisonment, unless there are specific and exceptional circumstances in the case relating to either the offence or the offender that would make such a sentence unjust. A study commissioned by the Department of Justice in 2005 shows that this caveat has allowed the judiciary to avoid imposing the minimum sentence in most cases: out of fifty-five cases studied, the minimum sentence was imposed only three times.[16]

Second, section 8 of the Criminal Justice Act 1951 allows courts to take into account offences admitted to by a defendant who has been convicted of another offence. The advantage to the defendant of doing this is set out in section 8(2), which prohibits any subsequent prosecution for the offences so taken into account. However, in *DPP v. Gray* (1987), Henchy J. stated that section 8 only applied to offences that were within the jurisdiction of the court that convicted the defendant. Therefore, the District Court cannot take an admission of murder into account. If the court agrees to take these other offences into account, a higher sentence may be imposed, but it may not exceed the maximum sentence allowed for the offence for which the defendant has been convicted.

Third, the Criminal Justice Act 1993 contains two provisions that can have an effect on sentencing. First, section 2 allows the DPP to appeal to the Court of Criminal Appeal any sentence that he feels is unduly lenient. The Court of Criminal Appeal has the power to substitute a new sentence or to refuse the appeal. A further right of appeal to the Supreme Court on a point of law in respect of the sentence exists for both the prosecution and the defence. The Law Reform Commission, in its *Consultation Paper on Prosecution Appeals from Unduly Lenient Sentences in the District Court* (2004), has provisionally recommended that this power of appeal be extended to sentences in summary cases heard in the District Court. Second, section 5 provides that when sentencing a defendant for a sexual or violent offence, the court must take into account the effect of the offence on the victim. Further, the provision gives to the victim a statutory right to give evidence as to that effect, and as such acts as a balance to the defendant's right to present mitigating evidence on his behalf.

Finally, some attempt at encouraging consistency in sentencing was made by the Criminal Law Act 1997. Section 10(1) provides that if a person is convicted on indictment of a statutory offence, the penalty for which is imprisonment, but the term is neither specified nor expressed to be up to life imprisonment, then that person should be sentenced to no more than two years. In the case of an attempt to commit an indictable offence for which a maximum penalty is specified, section 10(2) provides that the sentence should not be greater than that which would be imposed for the commission of the complete offence. For example, if the penalty for the full offence is ten years' imprisonment, the penalty

---

16 Patrick McEvoy, B.L., *Research for the Department of Justice on the Criteria Applied by the Courts in Sentencing under s.15A of the Misuse of Drugs Act 1977 (as amended)*, 2005, available at www.justice.ie.

for an attempt should be less than ten years. The courts are also given the general power, in section 10(3), to impose a fine either in addition to some other punishment or in lieu thereof. This power is, however, subject to any other statute under which the offence must be dealt with.

Aside from these statutory measures and the constitutional framework mentioned above, a judge has almost absolute discretion in imposing sentences. This independence is perceived to lead to wide disparity in sentencing and has provoked calls for the introduction in Ireland of sentencing guidelines. In England, for many years the Court of Appeal issued binding guidelines on sentencing, such as those for the crime of rape in *R v. Billam* (1986). In issuing such guidelines, the Court of Appeal was required to consider the advice of an independent Sentencing Advisory Panel consisting of members drawn from the judiciary, academia and criminal justice practice. The Criminal Justice Act 2003 transferred the Court of Appeal's function to a newly created Sentencing Guidelines Council consisting of eight judicial members and four non-judicial members. The Council published its first set of *Final Guidelines* in 2004, which are available at www.sentencing-guidelines.gov.uk.

The Irish courts take a different approach, however, endorsing the principle of judicial independence in sentencing. The justification for this principle was given by the Supreme Court in **Deaton v. Attorney General (1963)**, *per* O Dálaigh C.J.:

> Where the legislature has prescribed a range of penalties the individual citizen who has committed an offence is safeguarded from the executive's displeasure by the choice of penalty being in the determination of an independent judge. The individual citizen needs the safeguard of the courts in the assessment of punishment as well as on his trial for the offence. The degree of punishment which a particular citizen is to undergo for an offence is a matter vitally affecting his liberty; and it is inconceivable to my mind that a constitution which is broadly based on the doctrine of separation of powers . . . could have intended to place in the hands of the executive the power to select the punishment to be undergone by citizens.

However, the English Sentencing Guidelines Council, chaired by the Lord Chief Justice and comprising mainly members of the judiciary, is arguably properly located within the judicial branch of government. Hence, any guidelines it issues would come from the judicial branch and therefore would not contradict the separation of powers. This was the conclusion of the United States Supreme Court in *Mistretta v. US* (1989) in respect of the creation of the United States Sentencing Commission, which was charged with the creation of sentencing guidelines for federal courts in the US. Consequently, an arrangement in Ireland similar to that established under the Criminal Justice Act 2003 in England might well overcome the objections set out in *Deaton*. However, the Irish courts have also indicated their hostility to judicially created sentencing guidelines. In *The People (DPP) v. Tiernan* (1988), the Supreme Court was specifically asked by the Attorney General for guidelines in rape cases. This request was beyond the scope of the appeal, but the court dealt with it indirectly. In particular, the court endorsed the 'fundamental necessity for judges in sentencing in any form of criminal case to impose a sentence which in their discretion appropriately meets all the particular circumstances of the case.' Because of this, the court felt it inappropriate to 'appear to be laying down any standardisation or tariff of penalty for cases.' The most that the court would do was to state that rape should be punished with an immediate and substantial custodial sentence unless there were some exceptional reasons for not doing so. Beyond that, the courts continue to enjoy the freedom to impose whatever sentence they deem fit.

Objectives

The basic objectives of criminal punishments in Irish law were set out by Walsh J. in *The People (Attorney General) v. O'Driscoll* (1972):

> The objects in passing sentence are not merely to deter the particular criminal from committing a crime again but to induce him in so far as possible to turn from a criminal to an honest life and indeed the public interest would best be served if the criminal could be induced to take the latter course. It is therefore the duty of the courts to pass what are the appropriate sentences in each case having regard to the particular circumstances of that case – not only in regard to the particular crime but in regard to the particular criminal.

In a similar vein, in *The State (Stanbridge) v. Mahon* (1979), Gannon J. had this to say:

> The first consideration in determining sentence is the public interest, which is served not merely by punishing the offender and showing a deterrent to others but also by affording a compelling inducement and an opportunity to the offender to reform. The punishment should be appropriate not only to the offence committed but also to the particular offender.

These passages indicate that the Irish courts follow an amalgamation of three punishment theories: retribution (of the desserts kind), deterrence and rehabilitation. The sentence passed must take account of the particular crime and the degree of guilt of the defendant. In *The People (DPP) v. M* (1994), the Supreme Court indicated that once the trial judge has decided the seriousness of the crime, 'it is the duty of the court to consider ... the particular circumstances of the convicted person. It is within this ambit that mitigating factors fall to be considered' (*per* Denham J.). However, in passing sentence, the courts must also bear in mind the possibility of rehabilitation. Accordingly, even where the circumstances warrant it, a sentence should not be so harsh as to prevent the possibility of reform by the offender. Finally, the importance of deterrence, both individual and general, to the public interest is recognised. As noted above, deterrence of either kind could in theory result in excessive or lenient sentences being imposed, but the possibility of this is minimised by the requirement that the sentence reflect the crime committed and take account of the possiblity of reform. Thus, each of these principles acts as a check to the others.

Guilty Pleas

In *The People (DPP) v. Tiernan* (1988), the Supreme Court specifically recognised that an early guilty plea was a relevant factor to be taken into account when sentencing an offender. The facts of that case were as follows: the complainant had been sitting with her boyfriend in her boyfriend's car when the defendant and two others forced their way into the car and drove it some distance away. The boyfriend was assaulted and locked in the boot of the car. The complainant was then raped on more than one occasion by two of the men, suffered violence and was forced to engage in acts of sexual perversion. The complainant suffered severe psychiatric trauma resulting in a serious nervous disorder which rendered her unfit for work for six months. The defendant himself had a number of prior convictions for violent offences. He had, however, pleaded guilty from the outset, and argued that the trial court's sentence of twenty-one years' imprisonment was excessive and did not reflect the guilty plea. The Supreme Court accepted that an early guilty plea was an important and relevant factor in determining a proper sentence for any offence. How relevant it is would depend on the circumstances of the case in question. In this case, the Supreme Court accepted that it was important because it had spared the complainant from giving evidence – Finlay C.J. specifically stated that had the defendant forced the complainant to testify, he would have had little hesitation in affirming a sentence of twenty-one years' imprisonment. As it was, however, the complainant had been spared and, bearing in mind the 'desirability of contemplating that the accused should some day be rehabilitated into society', the sentence was reduced to seventeen years' imprisonment.

Three justifications are usually put forward for allowing a discount for an early guilty plea. First, a guilty plea may be an expression of genuine remorse. In *The People (DPP) v. WC* (1994), one of the factors that influenced Flood J. in deciding to impose a nine-year suspended sentence on the defendant for rape was the fact that the defendant had 'shown real and convincing remorse virtually from the moment of commission of the crime'. Second, by admitting the charge, the defendant spares the victim the ordeal of testifying in court and having to suffer cross-examination. This is particularly important in sexual offences, where the victim's evidence would be especially distressing. The Supreme Court placed special emphasis on this justification in *Tiernan*, where the plea was made at an early stage of the investigation and was followed by a subsequent guilty plea in court. Third, if the defendant pleads guilty at an early stage, the trial will be considerably shorter, and the criminal justice system will be able to proceed more efficiently. In *WC*, Flood J. acknowledged that the defendant's guilty plea had 'saved the State the expense of what could have been a lengthy trial'. However, this is one of the few instances where efficiency has been accepted by the Irish courts as a justificiation for allowing a reduced sentence for a guilty plea. The principal justifications therefore are remorse and sparing the victim.

It must be stressed that a guilty plea is not automatically followed by a discount in the sentence. Section 29 of the Criminal Justice Act 1999 requires the courts, if appropriate, to take into account both the stage at which the guilty plea is entered and the circumstances in which it was entered. Further, section 29(2) specifically permits the imposition of the maximum sentence available for the offence in question despite a guilty plea if there are exceptional circumstances which warrant the maximum. This provision essentially deals with situations such as that which arose in *FB*, in which the trial judge indicated that he was obliged by precedent not to impose the maximum sentence because a guilty plea had been entered. Finally, where a defendant does not plead guilty, he may not be punished for not doing so through the imposition of a heavier sentence.

Other Factors

Given the Irish courts' commitment to handing down individualised sentences, it is difficult to summarise the kind of factors that they will take into account in determining a sentence. Typically, the courts are quite lenient to young offenders, on the basis that such offenders should be given a chance to mend their ways. The courts may also occasionally exercise leniency in respect of defendants who might find prison life exceptionally difficult. In *DPP v. Clarke* (1997), the defendant was a Jamaican national who had been sentenced to seven years' imprisonment for possession of crack cocaine with intent to supply. The Court of Criminal Appeal accepted that his nationality made prison life more difficult in that he was a target for other prisoners. On this basis, coupled with the fact that he was young and of previously good character, the court reduced the sentence to five years' imprisonment. Similarly, particular hardship to a defendant's family may also result in leniency. A good support network is another factor that will be taken into account, on the understanding that such support will increase the chances of successful rehabilitation. Thus, in *The People (DPP) v. M* (1994), the Court of Criminal Appeal reduced a sentence passed on a member of a religious order for sexual offences against children on the basis that on his release, he would return to his order where he would receive treatment and would never again have access to children. Similarly, in *The People (DPP) v. G* (1994), the religious defendant's seven-and-a-half-year sentence for buggery was reduced to eighteen months in prison with the balance suspended provided that he spent the rest of the sentence at a secure religious institution. Finally, co-operation with the gardaí in an investigation will usually also warrant a discount. The defendant's complete co-operation with the gardaí in *The People (DPP) v. G* (1994) was one of the factors, in tandem with his early guilty plea, that influenced the Supreme Court to reduce twelve concurrent life sentences to fifteen years' imprisonment on each count.

It should also be stressed that the courts are not limited to looking at mitigating factors. As was made clear in *O'Driscoll* and *Stanbridge*, the courts must pass a sentence that is appropriate to the crime and to the criminal. Accordingly, they must also consider any aggravating factors. What precisely constitutes an aggravating factor will depend on the facts of the case and the nature of the offence committed. In *Tiernan*, the Supreme Court described the following factors as aggravating the rape: the fact that it was a gang rape; it was accompanied by violence and abduction; the rape was repeated; there were accompanying acts of perversion; the effect of the experience on the victim was severe; and the defendant had prior convictions for violent offences. The English Court of Appeal in *R v. Billam* (1986) also accepted each of these factors as aggravating a rape, but added a further factor: where the victim is either very young or very old. Had such a fact been relevant in *Tiernan*, there is no doubt that the Supreme Court would have agreed.

Consecutive and Concurrent Sentences

If a defendant is charged with committing multiple offences or multiple counts of the same offence and is convicted, he will be sentenced for each offence or count of offence for which he has been convicted. The question then arises as to whether those sentences should run concurrently or consecutively. The main statutory authority that exists applies to offences committed while on bail, and in such a case, the sentences are to run consecutively (Criminal Justice Act 1984, section 11). In other cases, the courts have discretion although there is a clear preference for concurrency. The leading authority on this point of sentencing principle is *The People (DPP) v. McC* (2003). The Court of Criminal Appeal was dealing with a serial child abuser who had pleaded guilty to a variety of sexual offences including rape, sexual assault and possession of child pornography. There were six young victims and the acts in question occurred on different occasions. The trial Court imposed concurrent sentences in order to take account of the defendant's guilty plea and absence of previous convictions. The Court of Criminal Appeal accepted that if there are several unconnected offences involving different victims, the trial judge has discretion to impose consecutive sentences. However, the court went on to point out that 'it has long been the sentencing practice in this jurisdiction that a discretion in favour of consecutive sentences is exercised sparingly.' Further, the court indicated that one of the factors that should influence a trial judge in his discretion is the maximum sentences available for the offences in question. If they are quite short, then the totality of the sentence might be inadequate and consecutive sentences might be required. If, as in this case, the maximum sentences are long (rape, for example, carries a maximum sentence of life imprisonment), then the need for consecutive sentences should recede.

Law Reform Commission Recommendations

The Law Reform Commission has reviewed the whole area of sentencing (*Consultation Paper 12* (1993) and *Report on Sentencing* (1996)). However, the discussion on the objectives of sentencing caused a division in the Commission. The majority set out five statements of principle in relation to sentencing:

(1) society requires a system that will demonstrate a rejection of anti-social behaviour, and by so doing, will create and reinforce a sense of social values;

(2) punishment must be proportionate to the harm done or risked, and to that end, the law must publicly create a hierarchy of wrongs that roughly accords to the damage or potential damage involved;

(3) the criminal justice system exists to provide protection to the community, and the imposition of punishments is one of the main methods of securing this objective;

(4) punishment must not be inflicted for its own sake, but should have a purpose such as to demonstrate society's rejection of criminal behaviour; and

(5) punishment must bear some relationship to the offender's capacity to control his behaviour, and therefore to his degree of guilt.

The majority recommended that, on the basis of these statements of principle, when imposing a sentence, the judge should completely disregard deterrence, and should also disregard rehabilitation if the sentence is to be imprisonment. Instead, the judge should be guided solely by the 'just desserts principle'. In other words, the offender should receive the sentence that his crime and his culpability deserves. The majority felt that this was the best way to introduce some degree of uniformity and consistency into sentencing policy.

The Commission felt that the best way to implement its proposals would be to introduce non-statutory guidelines which would provide that:

(a) the severity of the sentence should be measured solely by the seriousness of the offence;

(b) the seriousness of the offence should be measured by the harm caused or risked by the defendant, and his degree of guilt;

(c) deterrence and rehabilitation (when the sentence was for imprisonment) should be irrelevant in determining the severity of the sentence; and

(d) possible mitigating and aggravating factors should be specified.

Aggravating factors include the use or threat of violence or a weapon, the fact that the victim was a law enforcement officer, the use or threat of excessive cruelty, or the abuse of a position of confidence or trust. Mitigating factors included provocation, the absence of serious injury, the fact that the offence was committed through strong temptation or was motivated out of compassion or sympathy, or that the defendant was suffering from reduced mental capacity at the time of the commission of the offence.

1.18 Further Reading

Carey, 'The Rule of Law, Public Order Targeting, and the Construction of Crime', (1998) 8 *ICLJ* 26.

De Londras, 'Kow-Towing to the Twin Gods of Time and Money: The Guilty Plea Discount in Sentencing', (2004) 14(1) *ICLJ* 14.

Law Reform Commission, *Consultation Paper on Sentencing,* 1993.

————, *Report on Sentencing*, LRC 53–1996.

————, *Consultation Paper on Prosecution Appeals from Unduly Lenient Sentences in the District Court,* LRC CP33 2004.

————, *Report on the Indexation of Fines*, LRC 37–1991.

O'Donnell, 'Challenging the Punitive Obsession', (1998) 8 *ICLJ* 51.

O'Malley, 'Community-Based Sentences and Social Control', (1993) 11 *ILT* 201.

————, 'Principles of Sentencing', (1991) 1 *ICLJ* 138.

————, 'Punishment and Moral Luck', (1993) 3 *ICLJ* 40.

————, 'Resisting the Temptation of Elegance: Sentencing Discretion Reaffirmed', (1994) 4 *ICLJ* 1.

————, *Sentencing: Law and Practice*, Dublin: Round Hall, 2000.

————, 'Sentencing Murderers: the Case for Relocating Discretion', (1995) 5 *ICLJ* 31.

————, 'The First Prosecution Appeal Against Sentence', (1994) 4 *ICLJ* 192.

Osborough, 'A Damocles' Sword Guaranteed Irish: The Suspended Sentence in the Republic of Ireland', (1982) 17 *Ir Jur (ns)* 221.

————, 'Deferment of Imposing Sentence', (1981) 16 *Ir Jur (ns)* 262.

————, 'Dismissal and Discharge under the Probation of Offenders Act, 1907', (1981) 16 *Ir Jur (ns)* 1.

CHAPTER TWO

OVERVIEW OF CRIMINAL LIABILITY

2.1 Introduction

The principal issues to be decided by criminal law are how to attach criminal liability and to whom. Superficially, this would be easy to answer by saying that anyone whose actions make him culpable of a crime should suffer a criminal sanction. So, if X kills Y, X should be punished for murder. However, attributing criminal blame is not that easy, for there are many other factors that must be considered before deciding if X's actions deserve a conviction for murder. Perhaps he did not intend to kill anyone and Y's death was an accident. Perhaps Y attacked X, and X was only acting in self-defence. Perhaps X was insane at the time and was unaware of what he was doing. These possibilities, if true, all affect the degree of X's culpability and may reduce it partially or completely. Accordingly, criminal liability cannot be imposed on X simply by reference to his actions alone; the law must consider whether his actions were, in the circumstances, blameworthy, and if so, to what extent. Only if his blameworthiness reaches a certain level will liability be imposed. The foregoing issues deal with the substantive rules of criminal liability. However, decisions on these issues must take place within the principles established by the Constitution, and a brief consideration of these principles is required.

2.2 Constitutional Principles

The Constitution establishes the State, the organs of the State and regulates the interaction between the State and private individuals. For the most part, the Constitution is silent as to the substantive content of the criminal law, but the principles embodied in the Constitution act as a guide to, and a limitation on, both the Oireachtas and the courts in their respective efforts to progress the criminal law. A full exposition of constitutional principles is beyond the scope of this work, but four principles deserve particular mention.

Nullum crimen sine lege, nulla poena sine lege

It is a fundamental principle that a person's conduct cannot be the basis of criminal liability unless the law recognises such conduct as an offence. This principle is expressed in the Latin maxim *nullum crimen sine lege, nulla poena sine lege* – no crime without law, no punishment without law. Thus, lawmakers are prohibited from making up the law as they go along: proscribed conduct must be known in advance, thereby giving people a chance to alter their behaviour so as to avoid criminality. Any person who engages in proscribed conduct after the proscription has been made known can fairly be said to have chosen to engage in criminality and is thus deserving of punishment by the State. This principle is so well entrenched that it is difficult to find many modern examples of it. However, the point arose in *The People (DPP) v. Kavanagh* **(1997)** as a result of an unfortunate error in the drafting of the Non-Fatal Offences Against the Person Act 1997. There, the defendant had been charged with a series of offences including three counts of false imprisonment contrary to common law. These charges were laid prior to the enactment of the 1997 Act, but the trial occurred after the 1997 Act came into force. Section 28 of the Act abolished the common law offence of false imprisonment and replaced it with a new statutory offence in section 5. The defendant argued that as a result of the 1997 Act, the offence of common law false imprisonment was no longer known to the law and trial on those counts could not proceed. The Special Criminal Court noted that the draftsmen had neglected to include in the 1997 Act any provision saving the prosecution of proceedings initiated prior to the Act which were affected by the enactment of the Act. The court rejected the prosecution's argument that there was a pre-existing statutory offence of false imprisonment created by section 11 of the Criminal Law Act 1976, which would be unaffected by section 28 of the 1997 Act. This provision classified the offences of kidnapping and false improvement as felonies with a maximum punishment of life imprisonment. The court ruled that this provision was concerned with the classification and punishment of the common law offences. Thus, the court concluded that there was no statutory or common law basis for the three counts of false imprisonment, all of which had to be dismissed.

In *Quinlivan v. Governor of Mountjoy Prison* **(1998)**, an almost exact replica of *Kavanagh*, the High Court disapproved of the reasoning in the earlier case. McGuinness J. ruled that the effect of section 28 should be interpreted according to the presumption of constitutionality: it should be presumed that the repeals in section 28 were intended to apply prospectively only, as to hold otherwise would constitute an unconstitutional interference with the judicial function. However, the matter came before the Supreme Court in *Grealis and Corbett v. DPP* **(2001)**. There, Keane C.J. ruled that the wording in section 28 of the 1997 Act was clear and unambiguous, as was its effect:

> Common sense, as well as authority, leads one inexorably to the conclusion that, where a common law offence is repealed by statute, in the absence of any saving provision it ceases to exist for all purposes and no prosecution can be maintained in respect of it after the repealing statute has taken effect.

Orders of prohibition were therefore granted to the applicants to restrain prosecutions being brought against them for the common law offence of assault. This issue is unlikely to arise again because in the aftermath of the decision in *Kavanagh*, the Oireachtas enacted the Interpretation (Amendment) Act 1997, which provides that if an enactment abolishes a common law offence, that abolition will not prejudice any proceedings already instituted under the previously existing law.

Prohibition of Retrospective Legislation

Related to the requirement that the offence charged be known to the law is the prohibition of retrospective legislation. Even where certain conduct has been formally proscribed, the defendant's behaviour must have been illegal at the time it was committed. It is considered fundamentally unjust to impose criminal liability on a person for an action that was not a criminal offence when that action was committed. For that reason, Article 15.5 of the Constitution provides: 'The Oireachtas shall not declare acts to be infringements of the law which were not so at the date of their commission.' Article 7 of the European Convention on Human Rights contains a similar proscription. In other words, if X tells a lie today, and the Oireachtas passes a statute tomorrow making lying a crime, X cannot be prosecuted. However, Article 15.5 only applies in situations in which the Oireachtas seeks to retrospectively criminalise what had been lawful behaviour; the provision has no application when the behaviour has always been unlawful. In *Gilligan v. Criminal Assets Bureau* (**1998**), a constitutional challenge was brought against the Proceeds of Crime Act 1996 which allows for the forfeiture of assets that directly or indirectly represent the proceeds of crime. Section 1 of the Act defines proceeds of crime as 'any property obtained or received (whether before or after the passing of the Act) by or as a result of or in connection with the commission of an offence.' The applicant argued that the portion of this definition in brackets gave the Act a retrospective effect and therefore was in breach of Article 15.5. The High Court rejected this argument on the basis that the acquisition of ill-gotten wealth was not legal prior to the passing of the Act, and therefore the Act did not declare any activity to be illegal prior to its enactment that was not so at the date of its commission. The Act therefore was not retrospective within the meaning of Article 15.5. The Supreme Court later confirmed that the 1996 Act was not in breach of Article 15.5 but did not elaborate on its reasoning.

Void for Vagueness

In keeping with the general requirement that proscriptions of conduct be known in advance, there is a general requirement in the Constitution, and one which has been included in Article 7 of the European Convention on Human Rights, that the proscription be defined with some degree of certainty. Without such certainty, it would be difficult for people to know what conduct has been proscribed and hence difficult for them to take steps to avoid engaging in criminality. An excellent example of this point is provided by *King v. Attorney General* (**1981**). The applicant challenged the constitutionality of section 4 of the Vagrancy Act 1824, as amended, under which he had been convicted of the offence of 'loitering with intent'. The effect of the impugned provision was that to secure a conviction, the prosecution merely had to prove that the person charged was a 'suspected person or reputed thief' loitering in virtually any public place with intent to commit a felony. Further, no overt proof of intent was required in that the required intent could be inferred from the circumstances or even from the person's known character. Not surprisingly, the Supreme Court struck down this provision; Henchy J., who delivered the leading opinion, was especially harsh in his language:

> the ingredients of the offence and the mode by which its commission may be proved are so arbitrary, so vague, so difficult to rebut, so related to rumour or ill-repute or past conduct, so ambiguous in failing to distinguish between apparent and real behaviour of a criminal nature, so prone to make a man's lawful occasions become unlawful and criminal by the breadth and arbitrariness of the discretion that is vested in both the prosecutor and the judge, so indiscriminately contrived to mark as criminal conduct committed by one person in certain circumstances when the same conduct, when engaged in by another person in similar circumstances, would be free of the taint of criminality, so out of keeping with the basic concept inherent in our legal system that a man may walk abroad in the secure knowledge that he will not be singled out from his fellow-citizens and branded and punished as a criminal unless it has been established beyond reasonable doubt that he has deviated from a clearly prescribed standard of conduct, [that the provision breaches several constitutional provisions].

Despite Henchy J.'s strong language, it is clear that some uncertainty is tolerated in Ireland's criminal law on at least two levels. First, unlike most common law jurisdictions, the criminal law in this country remains largely uncodified; many of the general principles are still based on common law decisions, and it is not unusual to find conflicts in those decisions: for example, see the discussion in Chapter 18 on the modern Irish authorities on the defence of provocation. Further, many of the criminal statutes that are in force are well over 100 years old and have been the subject of multiple amendments: the law on rape, for example, is contained primarily in five statutes stretching back to 1861. Thus it can be difficult for people without legal training to determine what conduct exactly is proscribed, a situation made worse by the general unwillingness of the law to allow for ignorance of the law (see Chapter 13). Admittedly, some improvements have been made: for example, the property offences have been largely codified in the Criminal Law (Theft and Fraud Offences) Act 2001, as have non-fatal offences in the Non-Fatal Offences Against the Person Act 1997. However, many areas of the law, including most of the general principles of criminal liability, have not received this level of attention. Consequently, there is a need for a systematic codification of the law, not only to improve certainty, but also to ensure that the law reflects the need of modern Irish society.

Second, even where the scope of an offence can be determined with some certainty, the law in its definitions makes extensive use of various concepts that are

41

inherently vague. For example, in many areas of the criminal law, a reasonable standard of behaviour is expected. Whether the defendant acted reasonably is largely a matter for the court to determine objectively after the fact. Implicit in such a determination is an assumption that there is general agreement as to what constitutes reasonable behaviour, an assumption that probably cannot withstand scrutiny. Ideas of what is reasonable in a particular circumstance are likely to vary: a homeowner who kills a home-invader may honestly believe that he acted reasonably, but a jury might equally honestly disagree. In such a case, the homeowner could be convicted of homicide even though he tried in good faith to stay within the law but failed to do so due to the inherent ambiguity of the standard to which he was held. Similarly, the offence of gross negligence manslaughter contains an inherent ambiguity – the jury is required to determine whether the defendant's behaviour was grossly negligent so as to warrant condemnation. In effect, the jury is allowed to decide after the fact whether the defendant's conduct deserves criminal punishment. Such uncertainties have not yet formed the basis of a constitutional challenge, and it seems unlikely that the courts would accede to such a challenge unless the ambiguity is of a similar degree to that seen in *King*. There have, however, been challenges brought in the English courts alleging that such uncertainties breach Article 7 of the Convention. In *R v. Misra* (2004), for example, the Court of Appeal considered whether the lack of precision in gross negligence manslaughter breached the certainty requirement of Article 7. The court drew a distinction between uncertainties in the ingredients of an offence and uncertainties in the process by which it is decided whether the required ingredients have been established in an individual case. Uncertainties of the former kind breach Article 7 in that individuals would be unable to regulate their conduct so as to avoid contravening the law. Uncertainties as to the process apparently do not breach the requirements of Article 7: the fact that the offence is defined in such a way that different tribunals might come to different conclusions on the basis of the same set of facts does not necessarily make the offence itself too uncertain (*Wingrove v. UK* (1996)). The courts seem likely to maintain the assumption that there are reasonable standards of behaviour in the community, and that both defendants and jurors, as members of the community, can be expected to know them and to apply them.

The Presumption of Innocence

In *Woolmington v. DPP* (1935), Viscount Sankey made the following famous statement:

> Throughout the web of the English criminal law one golden thread is always to be seen, that it is the duty of the prosecution to prove the prisoner's guilt … if at the end of and on the whole of the case, there is reasonable doubt, created by the evidence by either the prosecution or the prisoner, as to [the prisoner's guilt], the prosecution has not made out the case and the prisoner is entitled to an acquittal.

This is the presumption of innocence enjoyed by all criminal defendants: the defendant does not have to prove innocence; rather, the prosecution must prove guilt and must do so beyond a reasonable doubt. However, Viscount Sankey identified two exceptions: the legislature was entitled in its enactments to shift the burden of proof to the defendant, and the defence of insanity must be proven by the defendant. In both cases, the defendant can discharge his burden on a balance of probabilities rather than beyond a reasonable doubt. Thus, the defendant generally bears no legal burden to prove his innocence; that burden rests with the prosecution. However, the defendant may have to meet an evidential burden in order to raise a defence. In *The People (Attorney General) v. Quinn* (**1965**), for example, the Supreme Court explained this point:

> Before [a] possible defence can be left to the jury as an issue there must be some evidence from which the jury would be entitled to find that issue in favour of the appellant. If the evidence for the prosecution does not disclose this possible defence then the necessary evidence will fall to be given by the defence.

In *The People (DPP) v. Davis* (**2001**), the Court of Criminal Appeal noted that the evidential burden was not especially heavy, but it does involve tendering evidence that suggests that the elements of the defence might be present. If the defendant fails to meet this evidential burden, the defence is not a live issue and cannot be considered by the jury. This evidential burden must not be confused with the legal burden of proof, which remains with the prosecution. A failure by the defendant to meet an evidential burden in respect of an issue means that that issue cannot be considered by the jury, but the jury can still acquit him based on the totality of the evidence in the case. A failure by the prosecution to meet the legal burden, on the other hand, means that the defendant must be acquitted.

That the presumption forms part of Irish law is beyond doubt; indeed, in *O'Leary v. Attorney General* (**1995**) the Supreme Court accepted that the presumption has constitutional status, holding that it forms part of the requirement in Article 38.1 of the Constitution that criminal trials be conducted in due course of law. As a result, the defendant is entitled to benefit from any reasonable doubt as to his guilt. Thus, if two or more reasonable interpretations of the evidence are possible, the jury must adopt the explanation that favours the defendant: *DPP v. Byrne* (**1974**). In *DPP v. Wallace* (**2001**), Keane C.J. held that the rule in *Byrne* requires only that the alternative interpretations are reasonable. It is a misdirection to instruct the jury that *Byrne* applies only when the interpretations are equally reasonable. Regarding the exceptions identified by Viscount Sankey, the burden placed on the defendant to establish an insanity defence has been accepted by the Irish courts without comment on numerous occasions. Indeed, in *Hardy v. Ireland* (**1994**), Egan J. specifically noted that insanity is 'something which must be established by an accused person in a criminal prosecution if he wishes to rely on it.'

There are several instances in Irish criminal legislation in which the legal burden of proof is placed on the defendant to disprove an element of the charge. For example, section 15 of the Misuse of Drugs Act 1977 requires a person charged with possession of controlled drugs with intent to supply to prove that he did not intend to supply others if, bearing in mind the quantity of the drugs found and any other matter the court thinks relevant, the court feels it is reasonable to assume that the drugs were not for the defendant's own immediate use. In other words, the court in these circumstances can presume a key element of the charge, thus shifting the legal burden onto the defendant to disprove that element of the charge. In *The People (DPP) v. Lawless* (**1985**), the gardaí raided a flat under a search warrant and recovered seventeen paper packages, each containing between 5 and 10 mg of heroin. Despite evidence that the total quantity was probably less than the daily intake for a heroin addict, the Court of Criminal Appeal accepted that there was sufficient evidence to raise the presumption. There was no evidence that the defendant was actually a heroin addict, and therefore no evidence that he would need the heroin for his own use. Further, the fact that the heroin had been divided into seventeen separate packages indicated an intention to supply others. Accordingly, the court was entitled to presume an intention on the part of the defendant to supply others, and the burden was on him to prove that this was not his intention.

The constitutional status of provisions like section 15 that shift the legal burden of proof is unclear. The Supreme Court has accepted, in *O'Leary*, the constitutionality of legislative provisions that shift an evidential burden. In other words, it is acceptable for a statute to place a burden on the defendant merely to introduce sufficient evidence to raise an issue on a point that he wishes to contest while at all times leaving with the prosecution the legal burden of proof. Further, in *Hardy*, two judges (Egan and Murphy JJ.) of the Supreme Court accepted that the provision under challenge had shifted the legal burden of proof and still upheld its constitutionality. However, both judges attached importance to the fact that the shift occurred in the context of exculpation: the provision allowed the defendant to avail of a defence if he was able to prove the necessary facts on a balance of probabilities. It is unclear whether they would have been so willing to uphold a shift in the legal burden relating to an element of the charge. However in *DPP v. Byrne* (**2001**), the Supreme Court considered the effect of section 50(8) of the Road Traffic Act 1961, as amended. The defendant was charged with being in charge of a vehicle in a public place with intent to drive while having excessive alcohol in his body. Section 50(8) provides that once it is shown that the defendant was in charge of the vehicle, there is a presumption that he had an intention to drive. The Supreme Court ruled that once this presumption was raised, the defendant would have to show 'the contrary so as to raise a reasonable doubt'. In other words, the Supreme Court accepted that the provision shifted the legal burden of proof as to an element of the charge. Finally, it is worth noting that the European Court of Human Rights has accepted the compatibility with

Article 6.2 of the Convention (which mandates a presumption of innocence in criminal trials) of presumptions that reverse the burden of proof. However, in *Salabiaku v. France* (1988), the court stressed that any such presumption must be confined 'within reasonable limits which take into account the importance of what is at stake and maintain the rights of the defence.'

2.3 Overview of the Elements of Criminal Liability

It is for the prosecution to establish beyond a reasonable doubt the criminal liability of the defendant. In most cases, criminal liability is attached to an individual person. However, in some circumstances, liability can also attach to incorporated and unincorporated bodies. Additionally, the net of criminal liability will be extended to include anyone who assists in the commission of an offence. This extended liability may attach either on the basis that the defendant was fully a part of a criminal enterprise, in which case he will be liable for all the acts of the other members of the enterprise carried out in furtherance of the plan. This is known as the doctrine of common design or joint enterprise. Alternatively, liability may attach on the basis that the defendant was a secondary participant in the crime. In other words, he helped to commit or plan the commission of the offence. This is known as secondary liability.

The prosecution's duty contains both positive and negative elements.

The Positive Duty

The fundamental basis of criminal liability is expressed in the Latin maxim *actus non facit reum nisi mens sit rea* – an act does not make a man guilty unless his mind is also guilty. Criminal liability thus involves two distinct elements: a physical element, or *actus reus*, and a mental element, or *mens rea*. Some doubt has been expressed about the utility of maintaining the phrases *actus reus* and *mens rea*. For example, in *R v. Tolson* (1889), Stephen J. wrote that the term *mens rea* is misleading in that it has multiple meanings that can be ascertained only through an examination of individual offences, and that it implies that immorality is an element of criminal liability. Similarly, in *R v. Miller* (1983), Lord Diplock suggested that the term *actus reus* is equally misleading since it suggests that a positive action is required for the attachment of criminal liability. There is truth in these comments, but the concepts of *actus reus* and *mens rea* provide a time-honoured shorthand for proscribed conduct and fault, respectively; as Lord Simon of Glaisdale pointed out in *Lynch v. D.P.P. for Northern Ireland* (1975), the terms have 'justified themselves by their usefulness'. Further, within each concept there are general principles that apply broadly across the criminal law to the extent that a generic shorthand is justified. These principles will be considered in the following two chapters.

Both *actus reus* and *mens rea* must be established by the prosecution beyond a reasonable doubt before the defendant can be convicted, and must also be shown to have been present contemporaneously. The *actus reus* comprises the activity that has been proscribed by the law, activity that may consist of actions, words, possession or inaction, depending on the offence in question. Additionally, the *actus reus* may require proof that a particular result followed from the defendant's activity: for example, the offence of murder requires proof not only of activity on the defendant's part, but also that this activity resulted in the death of the deceased. Whatever the requirements of the *actus reus* of the particular offence charged, all of its elements must be proven by the prosecution; there can be no criminal liability without proof of the *actus reus*. However, while proof of the *actus reus* is a necessary prerequisite of criminal liability, such proof is generally not sufficient for a conviction. The prosecution must also prove that the defendant's actions were directed by a culpable state of mind. This is the *mens rea* of the offence charged. Further, when there is more than one element of the *actus reus*, each must be accompanied by a corresponding element of *mens rea*. However, as with all general legal rules, there are exceptions. The *actus reus* must always be proven, but there are some offences the definition of which dispenses with at least one element of the *mens rea*. Such offences are known as strict liability offences. Thus, in a prosecution for statutory rape, i.e. sexual intercourse between a male and a girl under the age of seventeen, it is not necessary for the prosecution to prove that the male knew the girl was aged under seventeen.

The Negative Duty

In addition to positively establishing the *actus reus* and the *mens rea* of the offence, the prosecution also bears the duty of negating any defence put forward by the defendant (except for insanity, the burden of proving which rests on the defence – see section 2.2). These defences may be exculpatory, in the sense that they go to the defendant's innocence or guilt, or non-exculpatory, in the sense that they do not affect the defendant's innocence or guilt but are more technical in nature, such as the rule against double jeopardy. The discussion in this book focuses on the exculpatory defences. The criminal law recognises many different exculpatory defences, some specific to particular offences and others more general in nature. Broadly, these defences fall into one of two categories: those that involve a denial of an element of liability and those that assert a special circumstance. The former category includes most of the general defences known to the law. If these defences are raised, the defendant is pleading that the prosecution has failed to establish a required element of liability. Suppose X is charged with the murder of Y. The prosecution must prove the *actus reus* of murder, which is the unlawful killing of a human being. During X's trial it emerges that X killed Y legitimately in self-defence. X's actions were thus justified and were not unlawful. In other words, an essential element of the *actus reus* has been negated and the prosecution must fail. Alternatively, suppose X kills Y, but due to insanity X thought that he was killing a snake. Here, a human being has been unlawfully killed, thus establishing the *actus reus* of murder: X's insanity does not in any sense justify killing another person. However, the *mens rea* of murder is an intention to kill or to cause serious injury to another person, an intention that X could not have formed due to his insanity. Therefore, the *mens rea* of the offence has been negated, and again the prosecution must fail. In effect, X is excused from responsibility for his actions. In either case, whether X's actions were justified or excused, a required element of criminal liability has not been established. It is accordingly something of a misnomer to label these pleas as *defences*: they are more correctly labeled as negations of criminal liability. Nevertheless, attaching this label to these pleas is a time-honoured tradition, and this tradition is followed in this book.

Defences involving the assertion of special circumstances are defences in the true sense of the word, and a good example is the plea of provocation. This plea involves an acceptance that the *actus reus* and *mens rea* were present, but that special circumstances existed whereby only reduced liability should be attributed to the defendant. Thus, if X kills Y having been provoked, there is no question that the *actus reus* and *mens rea* of murder are present. However, X may argue that full responsibility should not rest with him as the incident was caused by Y's provocative conduct. The prosecution again bears the burden of negating these true defences beyond a reasonable doubt.

2.4 Further Reading

Ni Raifeartaigh, 'Reversing the Burden of Proof in a Criminal Trial: Canadian and Irish Perspectives on the Presumption of Innocence', (1995) 5 *ICLJ* 135.

Robinson, 'Criminal Law Defences – A Systematic Analysis', (1982) 82 *Col. LR* 1.

Robinson, 'Should the Criminal Law Abandon the *Actus Reus – Mens Rea* Distinction?', in Shute, Gardner and Horder (eds.), *Action and Value in Criminal Law*, Oxford: Clarendon Press, 1993, p. 187.

CHAPTER THREE

THE *ACTUS REUS*

3.1 Introduction

The *actus reus* is the action necessary for the crime to have been committed. It is often described as the physical element of the crime. While this definition is useful and is basically accurate, it can be misleading in that the *actus reus* is not limited to the physical action itself, but can include the result of the act and the surrounding circumstances. As Lord Hope of Craighead stated in *Attorney General's Reference No.3 of 1994* (1996):

> The *actus reus* of a crime is not confined to the initial deliberate and unlawful act which is done by the perpetrator. It includes all the consequences of that act, which may not emerge until many hours, days or even months afterwards.

Most offences require proof of the result of the accused's action. Murder, for example, requires proof of death. Such offences are called 'result' offences. In other cases, mere proof of the accused's action will suffice. These offences are called 'conduct' offences. Perjury is a good example: the offence is committed as soon as a person makes a false statement under oath, irrespective of the result.

The precise requirements for the *actus reus* will vary according to the offence. For example, the Criminal Justice Act 1990 makes it a special and distinct offence to murder a member of the gardaí in the execution of his duty. To convict a person charged with this offence, the prosecution must prove that the defendant engaged in proscribed conduct towards the officer who was acting in the course of his duty and that the defendant's conduct caused the officer's death. The *actus reus* of the offence thus has three elements:

(a) the proscribed conduct by the defendant;
(b) towards a member of the gardaí acting in the course of his duty; and
(c) which caused the officer's death.

It would not be sufficient to show that the defendant disliked and killed a fellow member of the local golf club who just happened to be a member of the gardaí.

The action must be carried out by a person. At common law, 'person' referred only to a natural or corporate person; an unincorporated body could not commit a criminal offence. However, criminal liability can be imposed on such a body by the terms of a statute. In *DPP v. Wexford Farmers' Club* (**1994**), the defendant club advertised a function on the club's premises in contravention of the Intoxicating Liquor Act 1988, which prohibited such publications by any person. The District Court stated a case to the High Court as to whether or not an unincorporated body could be considered a 'person'. It was held by the High Court that, under the terms of the statute, the club could be prosecuted as a person.

Generally, if there is no evidence of an *actus reus*, then a conviction is impossible. This applies even where the accused believes himself to have committed a crime, and fully intended to do so. So, in *R v. Deller* (1952), X believed that a certain car was mortgaged to a finance company. Knowing this, he fraudulently induced Y to buy the car with assurances that it was free from any charges. Unknown to X, however, the mortgage document on the car was invalid in law. He was charged with, and convicted of, obtaining by false pretences under the Larceny Act 1916. His conviction, however, was overturned on appeal; while he certainly had the necessary *mens rea*, he had been, accidentally, telling the truth. Therefore, there was no *actus reus*, and consequently no crime.

3.2 Types of Conduct

Broadly speaking, four forms of conduct can constitute the *actus reus*: acts, words, possession and omissions. Of the first two – acts and words – little needs to be said. In most cases, the prosecution must prove that the defendant committed some act that has been proscribed by law. The precise action will obviously vary according to the offence – the act of killing in a murder charge or the act of stealing in a theft charge – but the defendant must be shown to have *done* something illegal. Alternatively, words might constitute the criminal conduct. A charge of incitement, for example, might involve an allegation that the defendant induced another person to commit a crime simply through verbal persuasion (note that incitement might also be committed through coercive acts – see Chapter 17). Similarly with perjury: the offence is committed as soon as the defendant tells a lie while under oath.

Possession and omissions require a more detailed explanation.

Possession

Possession essentially means having control of certain proscribed things such as controlled drugs, firearms or explosives. The criminal conduct involved in possession consists of no more than having the proscribed articles under one's control; it is not necessary to show that the things were used in any particular way or even that they were used at all. In *Minister for Posts and Telegraphs v. Campbell* (**1966**), Davitt P. described the essence of possession in the following terms:

> In my opinion a person cannot, in the context of a criminal case, be properly said to keep or have possession of an article unless he has control of it either personally or by someone else. He cannot be said to have actual possession of it unless he personally can exercise physical control over it; and he cannot be said to have constructive possession of it unless it is in the actual possession of some other person over whom he has control so that it would be available to him if and when he wants it.

Thus, there are two forms of possession: actual or constructive. So, if X has stolen jewellery on his person or under his direct control, he has actual possession. If, however, X has the jewellery on his person, but he is acting under the direction of Y, then Y has constructive possession of the jewellery.

Possession may be inferred even when the article in question was not actually found on anyone's person. Thus, in *Campbell*, the defendant had been charged with possessing a television without a licence. The television had been found in a cottage, the occupier of which was the defendant. The High Court accepted that possession could be inferred from the presence of an unlicenced television in a person's dwelling, but found on the facts insufficient evidence that the cottage was the defendant's dwelling. Similarly, in *People (Attorney General) v. Nugent and Byrne* (1964), the Court of Criminal Appeal accepted that the owner of a car could normally be inferred to be in possession of the contents of his own car. A passenger in the car, however, could not be the subject of such an inference, and proof would have to be offered that the passenger was in control of the article. Proximity may also lead to an inference of control. In *The People (DPP) v. Foley* (1995), the gardaí searched an apartment and found the defendant sitting on a bed beside a shotgun, a handgun was on a nearby table and there was a bag in which the butt of another firearm was clearly visible. The Court of Criminal Appeal held that while mere proximity to an article does not automatically indicate control over that article, the circumstances of this case, i.e. the proximity of the defendant to the weapons and the fact that the weapons were on open display, were such that there was ample evidence to support an inference of possession of the firearms in question. This case also illustrates the fact that an article can be jointly possessed by two or more people simultaneously – the circumstances of the case allowed an inference of possession not only against Foley but also against another man who was also present in the apartment.

An important factor in all possession cases is knowledge of the existence of the article in question. In *Campbell*, Davitt P. held that a defendant cannot 'properly be said to be in control or possession of something of whose existence and presence he has no knowledge.' This kind of knowledge, despite clearly relating to the defendant's mind, is considered to be part of the *actus reus* of possession: as McCauley and McCutcheon point out, this is an important point in relation to the imposition of strict liability in some jurisdictions for certain drugs offences.[1] In such cases, even though the controlling legislation has dispensed with proof of *mens rea*, the prosecution must still prove that the defendant knew of the existence of the article. Once this has been done, there is no need for the prosecution to prove that the defendant was aware of the nature of the articles. So, in *Warner v. Metropolitan Police Commissioner* (1969), the defendant's claim that he was unaware that the bottles in his possession

---

1   F. McCauley, and P. McCutcheon, *Criminal Liability,* Dublin: Round Hall Sweet & Maxwell, 2000, p. 215.

contained controlled drugs was held by a majority of the House of Lords to be irrelevant to the charge. As Lord Pearce put it, '[t]hough I reasonably believe the tablets that I possess to be aspirin, yet if they turn out to be heroin, I am in possession of heroin tablets. This would be so I think even if I believed them to be sweets.' Further, in *R v. McNamara* (1988), the Court of Appeal ruled that knowledge of the presence of the container was sufficient; in that case, the defendant knew that he had in his custody a box of what he believed to be videos. The box turned out to contain cannabis. The court reasoned that the defendant knew that he was in possession of a box and that the box contained something. There was no requirement on the prosecution to prove that the defendant had knowledge of the nature of the contents.

The courts on this island appear to be more reluctant to impose strict liability in these kinds of cases. In *The People (DPP) v. O'Shea* **(1983)**, the defendant was involved in transferring boxes of drugs, but was unaware of their contents. He was aware that something was wrong and that one of his fellow workers was carrying a gun. He thought the boxes contained explosives. The defendant's conviction for possession was quashed, and although not explicitly stated, it seems clear that the defendant's lack of knowledge of the contents of the box was crucial. In *The People (DPP) v. Kelly* **(1996)**, the Court of Criminal Appeal decided that if the jury accepted that the defendant had been given a plastic bag, that he had opened the bag and looked inside and then placed the bag under the front seat of the car in which he was travelling, then the jury would be entitled to find that the defendant had possession of the bag and its contents. The clear implication is that evidence that the defendant was aware of the contents of the bag was required in order to prove possession of those contents. More explicitly, in *R v. Murphy* (1971), when dealing with a charge of possession of firearms, Lord MacDermott C.J. held that possession involved 'knowledge of the nature of what is kept or controlled', not merely knowledge of the existence of a container.

In all cases, while reasonable inferences may be drawn, they do not have to be drawn. In *R v. Whelan* (1972), the police had raided an apartment occupied by the three defendants and found a firearm hidden in a drawer. The Northern Ireland Court of Appeal accepted that the evidence was sufficient to raise an inference that at least one of the three men was in possession of the firearm, but that the evidence could not indicate which of the three was guilty. Thus, the court declined to draw the inference of possession sought by the prosecution against all three defendants. This decision was distinguished in *Foley* on the basis that the gun was hidden and was therefore under the control only of the person or persons who knew it was there, while in *Foley* the weapons were in the open and could have been grabbed by either man. Thus, both men had control over the weapons and therefore joint possession could be inferred. A third co-defendant in *Foley* was acquitted, however, on the basis that he had only called to the apartment on a social visit and claimed not to have seen the guns. He was thus able to offer an innocent explanation for his presence, an explanation that, if accepted, undermined any suggestion that he controlled the weapons. The Court of Criminal Appeal accepted that the third man's claims could reasonably have been true, although it does seem to be a stretch that he had not noticed a shotgun and a handgun that were in plain view. His claim that he had only made a social call is more compelling: a social guest in an apartment has as little control over the contents of that apartment as the passenger in *Nugent and Byrne* had over the contents of the car in which he was traveling.

Omissions

In most cases, the prosecution must prove that the defendant committed some act, said something or took possession of a proscribed article. In all such cases, the defendant's actions indicate that he has chosen to do something that the law regards as unlawful. What about a situation in which the defendant did not do anything but merely allowed an evil to occur? Suppose X is walking by a river and he sees a young child drowning in the river. Suppose also that X could save the child with ease and with little risk to himself, but does not do so and the child drowns. Morally, X's failure to act is reprehensible, but is X legally responsible for the child's death? Traditionally, the common law generally has answered this question in the negative, and has distinguished between people who cause harm and those who merely allow harm to occur. Thus, in *R v. Lowe* (1973), the Court of Appeal ruled that there is a 'clear distinction between an act of omission and an act of commission likely to cause harm.' This attitude to omissions flows logically from the liberal ideology underpinning modern criminal law which emphasises the importance of individual autonomy. Within this ideology, individuals should be free to live their lives in as unvirtuous a manner as they please, and the law should intervene only when an individual chooses to act in a manner that is harmful to others. Individuals should not be compelled to choose a virtuous path; therefore there should be no legal compulsion upon them to come to the assistance of others. In short, the criminal law exists to suppress the doing of evil, not to promote the doing of good. Further, not penalising omissions allows the law to avoid practical difficulties in defining the limits of criminal liability for failures to act.

A minority of common law jurisdictions have enacted legislative provisions providing for general criminal liability for a failure to come to another person's assistance (known colloquially as 'Good Samaritan' laws). Section 519 of the Vermont Statutes, for example, creates a general duty to provide reasonable assistance to anyone exposed to grave physical harm subject to three conditions: the assistance can be given without danger to the person giving it, rendering assistance will not interfere with important duties owed by the person to others and assistance is not already being rendered by someone else. This legislation is aimed at those who are in a position to help others but who fail to do so, and as such constitutes a new departure for a common law jurisdiction. However, the maximum penalty for breach of this provision is a mere $100; clearly, the Vermont legislators intended this provision to allow the Vermont courts to express a moral condemnation of the defendant's selfishness rather than to impose true criminal liability. No common law jurisdiction has yet enacted a general duty to act backed by full-scale criminal sanctions.

The distinction between a failure to act and a positive action will often be quite clear. However, on some occasions the courts have blurred the distinction. In *Fagan v. Metropolitan Police Commissioner* (1968), the defendant parked his car on a police officer's foot. He claimed this was accidental. However, when the officer instructed him to move the car, the defendant refused. He was charged with assaulting a police officer. In his defence, the defendant argued that the original action was not an assault due to a lack of *mens rea*, while his refusal to move the car could not amount to assault as it was a failure to act. The court agreed that assault cannot be committed by omission. However, the defendant's actions should be taken as one continuing action. It began with driving over the police officer's foot, and only ended when the car was removed. His refusal to remove the car therefore constituted part of a continuing action. In a similar vein, in *Kaitamaki v. R* (1985), the defendant was convicted of rape. He appealed on the grounds that he had genuinely believed the victim to be consenting, and had only realised after penetration that this was not the case. Notwithstanding this realisation, he had failed to withdraw, but argued that, under the relevant New Zealand legislation, rape was completed at penetration. As he had no *mens rea* at penetration, he had not committed rape, while his subsequent failure to withdraw could not be considered to be an action. The court noted that the legislation in fact provided that rape was complete (not *completed*) upon penetration. It could only be completed upon withdrawal. Therefore, the defendant's failure to withdraw constituted part of a continuing action, and his conviction was upheld. In both cases, the crucial element of the defendant's conduct was clearly an omission, yet the courts construed it as merely part of a continuing positive action.

Fagan and *Kaitamaki* involved omissions being deemed to be part of continuing acts. On other occasions, the courts have taken the opposite view and deemed positive acts to be omissions. The best example is the decision of the House of Lords in *Airedale NHS Trust v. Bland* (1993). Here, a patient was in a persistent vegetative state and the House of Lords authorised the discontinuance of life support. Doing so necessarily involved a series of actions, but Lord Goff, giving the leading judgment, ruled that doing so was no different than failing to initiate life support in the first place: in each case, 'the doctor is simply allowing his patient to die in the sense that he is desisting from taking a step which might, in certain circumstances, prevent his patient from dying as a result of his pre-existing condition.' Thus, a positive act was deemed to be an omission and not punishable unless the failure to act constituted a breach of a legal duty. It is only when a defendant is legally required to act that an omission *per se* is punishable under criminal law, and such a duty to act arises in one of three ways: under contract, under statute and under common law.

Under Contract

In *R v. Pittwood* (1902), the defendant was employed as a gatekeeper at a railway crossing. Part of his duties consisted of ensuring the gate was closed when a train was approaching. On one occasion, however, he forgot to close the gate and a train collided with a hay cart that was crossing the line. One man was killed and another was seriously injured. The defendant was convicted of manslaughter on the basis of his contractual obligations. The fact that the victim was not a party to the contract was found to be irrelevant – the defendant was employed specifically to protect the public. However, the defendant's contract was of a private nature, and the fact that the public derived some benefit from his work did not alter the nature of that contract: the defendant worked for his employer's benefit, not that of the public. Accordingly, it is difficult to see how a public duty could truly arise, especially as the doctrine of privity of contract usually prevents any rights or duties accruing to persons other than the parties to the contract. Interestingly, in *R v. Dytham* (1979), the Court of Appeal cited with apparent approval the comments of the trial judge in *R v. Llewellyn-Jones and Lougher* (1967) to the effect that a breach of a private contract leaves the defaulter open only to civil liability. This approach is more consistent with the fundamental principles of contract law and consequently seems preferable to that in *Pittwood*.

Under Statute

There are numerous instances where a statute imposes a duty upon people to act. Failure to act in such circumstances will result in the imposition of criminal liability. For example, the Road Traffic Act 1961, section 56, as amended, imposes a duty upon all car users to obtain third party liability insurance. Failing to do so is a criminal offence.

Under Common Law

Common law recognises that a duty to act arises in one of four broad situations: where the defendant is employed in a public capacity, where the defendant created the danger to others, where the defendant has voluntarily assumed a duty towards another person and where there is a familial relationship between the parties.

Public Officials

In *R v. Dytham* (1979), the defendant was a police officer. While on duty in the early hours of the morning, he witnessed the deceased being ejected from a nightclub. A fight developed in which the deceased was kicked and beaten to death. At no time did the defendant make any attempt to assist the deceased, whose plight was clearly visible to him, but merely stood by and watched. He was charged with misconduct of an officer of justice. He argued that this was an offence unknown to the law. It was held, however, that where the holder of a public office wilfully fails to perform any duty that common law or statute requires him to perform, he is guilty of a common law offence called misconduct in a public office. However, his conduct must be shown to have been calculated to injure the public interest and to require condemnation. Providing the action was so calculated, liability would not be restricted to fraud or dishonesty, but could be imposed for any action or omission. The same applies in Ireland. In ***DPP v. Bartley* (1997)**, the High Court dealt with a case involving the sexual abuse of a woman by her stepbrother which had continued for a long time. Very early on, she made a complaint to the gardaí, one of whom apparently responded by asking, 'Well, did you not enjoy that? Did you not feel good about all the fondling and what your brother was doing?' Because of this rejection, and that of her parents, she was incestuously abused for a quarter of a century longer than was necessary, she bore a child by her stepbrother, she was incestuously abused while married, and she developed suicidal tendencies and was seriously intimidated and beaten. While not necessary to decide the matter in issue, as a result of the actions of the gardaí, Carney J. took the opportunity to specifically endorse the decision in the *Dytham* case. If a member of the gardaí receives a credible complaint of a serious crime, that member is under a common law duty to investigate it. Failure to do so is illegal and will render that member liable to prosecution.

Creation of Danger

If a person creates a dangerous situation, the law may impose a duty to at least minimise the dangers. In *R v. Miller* (1983), the defendant, a squatter, fell asleep while smoking a cigarette. He awoke to find the mattress on fire, but failed to take any steps to extinguish the fire. On the contrary, he merely went to another room where he fell asleep again. He was charged with, and convicted of, arson, and appealed on the grounds that a failure to put out a fire started accidentally cannot establish the *actus reus* of arson. The House of Lords accepted that the defendant may have started the fire accidentally, but noted that when he awoke, he could have put out the fire with little difficulty or danger to himself. From that moment, he had sufficient *mens rea*. The remaining issue was whether he had *actus reus*. It was held that arson can be committed by omission in circumstances where the defendant created the fire. In effect, the House established that where a defendant has created a dangerous situation, he is under a legal duty to mitigate its effect (although Lord Diplock, who delivered the leading judgment, suggested that the word 'responsibility' be used instead of 'duty'). The House also considered whether or not the defendant's actions should be viewed as one continuing action, which was the basis of the Court of Appeal decision. However, their Lordships decided that the duty approach was preferable in that it would be easier to explain to a jury. The conviction was upheld.

Similarly, in *DPP v. Bermudez* (2004), the defendant was brought to a police station for questioning. Before being searched, the defendant was asked to empty his pockets. He placed some items on a table and assured the police officer that he had nothing else in his pockets. The police officer then searched the defendant and pierced her finger on a syringe in the defendant's pocket. The defendant was charged with an aggravated assault offence. He argued that there was no evidence from which the *actus reus* of assault could be shown. However, the Divisional Court of the Queen's Bench accepted that if a person creates a danger which exposes another person to a reasonably foreseeable risk of injury, then the *actus reus* of assault could be established. In this case, the defendant's dishonest assurance that he had nothing in his pockets had exposed the police officer to a reasonably foreseeable risk of injury. In effect, the defendant had been under a duty to warn the police officer of the danger posed by the syringe in his pocket, and his failure to do so was sufficient evidence to establish the *actus reus* of assault.

Voluntary Assumption

The courts have regularly noted a duty to assist relatives or others for whom the defendant had voluntarily accepted responsibility. In *R v. Gibbins and Proctor* (1918), the wife of the first defendant had left him, and he had begun living with the second defendant. They both had children, and all of them lived in the same house. There was no shortage of money, which was given by the first defendant to the second for housekeeping expenses, but one of the first defendant's children, a daughter of seven years, was allowed to starve to death while all of the others were well cared for. There was evidence that the second defendant hated and cursed the deceased child. Both defendants were convicted of murder. On appeal, both convictions were upheld. Regarding the first defendant, it was argued on his behalf that he was not guilty of murder because he had given sufficient money to provide for the upkeep of all the children. The Court of Appeal held, however, that he lived in the same house and must therefore have known that his daughter was in a serious condition merely from her appearance, and that no doctor had been called. He must also have known that the second defendant hated the child. The jury could well have inferred that he preferred his own daughter's death than to risk a break-up with the second defendant, and this was sufficient for a murder conviction. Implicit in this judgment is a condemnation of the first defendant's failure to come to his daughter's aid. It was not acceptable for him to turn a blind eye to her sufferings, and it was no defence for him to say that he had provided sufficient money for her upkeep. The appeal of the second defendant was more straightforward. She had taken charge of the child while under no obligation to do so. She was to all intents and purposes the child's mother, and had excluded the child's real mother from caring for the child. The child's welfare was therefore the second defendant's responsibility. Despite this, the child had been physically abused and had deliberately been denied food by the second defendant, which caused her death. Her murder conviction was therefore also upheld.

In *R v. Stone and Dobinson* (1977), the deceased was an elderly woman who lived with her brother and his housekeeper and mistress, who were the defendants. The brother was a man of low intelligence, with failing senses of hearing, sight and smell. The deceased paid for her lodgings, which consisted of a small room. She had a morbid fear of putting on weight, and refused to eat proper meals. She apparently lived in squalid conditions, mainly of her own making. The deceased became bedridden, and the second defendant tried, with the help of a neighbour, to wash her. An attempt was made by neighbours to summon a doctor, but this was unsuccessful. Some weeks later, she was found dead in her room, and her body was in a dreadful condition. In particular, she was soaked in urine and excreta, and had deep ulcerations all over her body, many of which contained maggots. These ulcerations would have taken at least two to three weeks to develop to that extent. A doctor gave evidence to the effect that if the deceased had received assistance at any time up to two weeks before she was found dead, there was a real prospect that she could have been saved. The defence argued that at no time had either or both of the defendants agreed to accept responsibility for the deceased. She was a lodger who died through her own eccentricity, and the situation was the same as if a person failed to help a stranger who was drowning. The Court of Appeal rejected the argument for a number of reasons: the deceased was a blood relative of the first defendant's; she lived in the same house as the defendants, both of whom knew of her condition; the second defendant had taken on the responsibility of washing the deceased; they tried to summon a doctor three weeks before the deceased died; and the defendants provided food. On these facts, a jury would be entitled to conclude that the defendants had accepted responsibility for the deceased, and were therefore under a duty to act to prevent harm coming to her. Their convictions for manslaughter were upheld.

In *Airedale NHS Trust v. Bland* (1993), Lord Mustill described *Stone and Dobinson* as 'troubling', and indeed, the case illustrates some of the difficulties involved in criminalising failures to act. The deceased was an adult woman and was therefore ostensibly responsible for herself. She was paying for her room in the defendants' house and was therefore essentially a tenant notwithstanding her relationship to the first defendant. It is difficult in principle to see why a landlord should be criminally responsible for the welfare of his tenants. Further, the actions that the defendants undertook with respect to the deceased, from which the court inferred an assumption of responsibility, were minimal. The decision suggests that responsibility for another person can be assumed on foot of only one or two kindly acts. Thus, if X goes shopping for his elderly neighbour on one or two occasions, and the neighbour dies some time later of starvation, it would seem that X could be deemed to have accepted the responsibility of providing food for the neighbour and is therefore implicated in her death. Nor is there any indication in the judgment as to how a responsibility that has been assumed in this way can be renounced. The decisions in *Stone and Dobinson* could be used to greatly extend the net of criminal liability, and the courts have not yet indicated the full extent of this liability or how it is to be limited.

Most of the cases on this point concern the death of close relatives. However, it seems clear that this duty is not necessarily confined to dependent relatives. In *R v. Nicholls* (1875), it was held that a 'grown up person who chooses to undertake the charge of a human creature helpless either from infancy, simplicity, lunacy, or other infirmity, he is bound to execute that charge without (at all events) wicked negligence.' There is no suggestion that the dependent person must be a relative (although in this case, the child was the defendant's grandson). This is also suggested in *Gibbins and Proctor*, where the second defendant had taken responsibility for the first defendant's child. In the American case of *Jones v. United States* (1962), the federal Circuit Court ruled that a legal duty to act could arise where the defendant had 'voluntarily assumed the care of another and so secluded the helpless person as to prevent others from rendering aid', and did not limit this assumption by reference to any relationship between the parties. In *R v. Taktak* (1988), the defendant, a heroin addict, had procured a young prostitute for his heroin dealer, who wanted to take the prostitute with him to a party. Some time later, the defendant collected the woman, who was almost unconscious, outside a building. He brought her back to the dealer's premises where they were alone, and he tried for some time to assist her but did not call a doctor. Some hours later, the dealer arrived, and following unsuccessful attempts to revive the woman, he (not the defendant) called a doctor, who pronounced her dead. All three New South Wales appellate judges accepted in principle that the defendant had assumed a responsibility for the woman by taking her into his exclusive care, thereby removing any possibility of her receiving aid from anyone else. The fact that the defendant was unrelated to the deceased was irrelevant; Carruthers J. pointed out that in modern society, the assumption of a legal duty of care, a breach of which can be grounds for criminal liability, cannot be confined to specific legal relationships such as husband and wife or parent and child. On the facts of the case, however, the defendant's manslaughter conviction was unanimously overturned as there was insufficient evidence to establish the degree of negligence required for a conviction.

Familial Relationship

There is ample authority for the proposition that a legal duty is owed to close relatives that is independent of any assumption of responsibility, being derived from the relationship itself. A well-known example is *R v. Senior* (1899). The defendant was a member of a religious group that believed that medication was immoral in that it constituted a lack of faith in God. The defendant's infant son contracted pneumonia but, in line with his religious beliefs, the defendant did not provide medication but in all other respects did his best for his son. The child died and the defendant was convicted of manslaughter. In more recent times, the Court of Appeal (in *R v. Lowe* (1973)) has questioned the decision in *Senior*. In *Lowe*, the court was concerned to distinguish between positive acts that cause death and omissions that lead to death. In the former case, a prosecution for homicide would be appropriate, but in the latter case, a similar prosecution might not be appropriate in the absence of a high degree of neglect. The court did not question, however, the earlier assumption that a father owes a duty of care to his infant son.

In *Senior*, the child was clearly unable to protect himself or to make his own decisions. Whether a duty would arise in respect of non-dependent children is unclear. In *R v. Chattaway* (1922), the deceased was twenty-five years old when she moved back to her parents' house, where she later fell into ill health and died. There was evidence that the deceased was completely under the control of her parents to the extent that she was effectively helpless to control her own affairs, despite her age. The Court of Criminal Appeal ruled that in these circumstances, the parents owed a legal duty to take proper care of the child despite her age, and that their failure to do so in this case justified the manslaughter conviction. By contrast, in *R v. Shepherd* (1862), an eighteen-year-old pregnant daughter was purposefully denied any midwifery support during labour by her mother. A complication arose and the daughter died. Erle C.J., giving the leading opinion, ruled that the mother owed no duty to her daughter, who was entirely emancipated. The distinguishing feature between these cases seems to be the degree of emancipation enjoyed by the child. In *Chattaway*, the child was under the parents' control; in *Shepherd*, the child seems to have been more independent. Nevertheless, it seems unlikely that a modern Irish court would easily forgive a parent who refused to assist his or her independent child with at least the basics necessary for life when the child was clearly in need of that assistance.

3.3 Voluntary Conduct

As a general rule, the defendant's conduct must be voluntary before criminal liability will be attached to him: Lord Denning said in *Bratty v. Attorney General for Northern Ireland* (1963) that the 'requirement that there should be a voluntary act is essential … in every criminal case. No act is punishable if it is done involuntarily.' The courts have not adopted a formal definition of 'voluntary conduct', preferring instead to allow juries to use their own common sense in defining the term. The great American judge Oliver Wendell Holmes suggested that a voluntary act is one involving a willed contraction of the muscles,[2] but this definition is perhaps a little artificial: if X wishes to pick something up from the floor, can it truly be said that he wills the muscles in his back to extend to allow him to bend over, then wills the muscles in his arm to extend and contract to allow him to pick up the object, and then wills the muscles in his back to contract in order to stand upright again? To remove this artificiality, H.L.A. Hart suggested that a voluntary act is one in which movements are 'subordinated to conscious plans of action'.[3] Under this definition, all of the individual muscular movements referred to in the example above are subordinated to the conscious plan of picking up the object from the floor and can thus be labeled voluntary.

The requirement of voluntariness is grounded in the liberal assumptions that underlie the criminal law. The criminal law should be drafted in such a way as to protect to the greatest extent possible the autonomy of individuals, who are assumed to be rational actors capable of directing their own lives. The core of autonomy is individual choice, and criminal liability should attach only to those who have chosen to engage in behaviour that is harmful or potentially harmful to others. A person whose actions are not chosen, and therefore are involuntary, consequently should not suffer criminal penalty. In *R v. Boshears* (1961), the defendant killed a woman while he was asleep. As he had no control over his actions, he was acquitted on a charge of murder. This case illustrates the issue of automatism, although the circumstances in which a plea of automatism will be successful are limited (see below).

One could be forgiven for thinking that consideration of the requirement of voluntariness would fit more naturally within a discussion of *mens rea* than *actus reus*. After all, conscious plans of action, to which voluntary movements are subordinated, occur in an individual's mind. However, it is clear that voluntariness is an element of the *actus reus*: in *R v. Theroux* (1993), MacLachlin J. confirmed that the '*actus reus* has its own mental element; the act must be the voluntary act of the accused for the *actus reus* to exist.' The reasoning behind the inclusion of a mental element in the physical element of the crime is that acting in the true sense of the word requires some control by the actor. The defendant in *Boshears*, for example, was not truly acting when he killed the deceased; instead, he effectively *suffered* an act to be done by his body. Thus, the concept of acting which lies at the heart of the *actus reus* inherently contains a mental element. A useful by-product of this approach is that the plea of automatism, as a negation of *actus reus* rather than *mens rea*, should generally be available even in cases of strict liability in which it is unnecessary to prove elements of the *mens rea*.

---

2 Oliver W. Holmes, *The Common Law*, New York: Dover, 1881.
3 H.L.A. Hart, *Punishment and Responsibility*, Oxford: Oxford University Press, 1968.

Automatism

Automatism was defined by Lord Denning in *Bratty v. Attorney General for Northern Ireland* (1961) as '[A]n act done by the muscles without any control by the mind such as a spasm, a reflex action or a convulsion, or an act done whilst suffering from concussion or whilst sleep-walking.' Broadly, automatism can arise in one of two ways: from internal factors or from external factors. Internal factors are physical or mental conditions that cause the defendant to lose control over his actions. In effect, they constitute a disease of the mind, and accordingly, this form of automatism is known as insane automatism and if successful will result in a finding of 'guilty but insane' under the M'Naghten Rules (see Chapter 8) and indefinite detention in the Central Mental Hospital. The reasoning here was again provided by Lord Denning in *Bratty*:

> Suppose a crime is committed by a man in a state of automatism or clouded consciousness due to a recurrent disease of the mind. Such an act is no doubt involuntary, but it does not give rise to an unqualified acquittal, for that would mean that he would be let at large to do it again. The only proper verdict is one which ensures that the person who suffers from the disease is kept secure in a hospital so as not to be a danger to himself or others.

External factors are conditions that arise outside of the body and give rise to non-insane automatism. However, to constitute an external factor for the purposes of non-insane automatism, the event must be something unusual. In *R v. Rabey* (1980), Ritchie J., for the majority, agreed with the Court of Appeal in the same case that 'the ordinary stresses and disappointments of life which are the common lot of mankind do not constitute an external cause.' In that case, the defendant alleged that he entered a dissociative state following a rejection by a young woman with whom he was infatuated, and assaulted her violently. The majority ruled that the true cause of the incident was an abnormality in the defendant's mind caused by his infatuation, and that consequently, the defendant's defence was more properly characterised as insanity. Classic examples of external factors were given in *Hill v. Baxter* (1958) in the context of a road traffic offence: the driver being hit on the head by a stone thrown up by a passing motorist or attacked by a swarm of bees while driving. In such circumstances, the driver might react instinctively rather than consciously, resulting in an accident. So, if X is charged with dangerous driving for having suddenly swerved up onto the pavement and struck a pedestrian, and X can show that he lost control of the vehicle due to being concussed by a flying stone that struck him on the head, he should have a full answer to the charge. Unlike automatism caused by internal factors, non-insane automatism arises from factors that are unlikely to recur; thus, in the example just given, X is unlikely to be struck again on the head by a flying stone and there is consequently no reason to detain him. A further distinction lies in the operation of these two forms of automatism. Insane automatism provides an answer to a criminal charge in that proof of insanity negates proof of *mens rea*. However, non-insane automatism provides an answer to a criminal charge due to a negation of the voluntary element of the *actus reus*.

The situation is somewhat different if the automatism derived from self-induced external factors such as the ingestion of alcohol or drugs. Suffering an automatic episode due to a flying stone or a swarm of bees is not the fault of the defendant and it would be unreasonable to hold him to account in any way for such an episode. Intoxication, however, will usually be at the choice of the defendant and it seems wrong in principle to allow an intoxicated defendant to benefit from such a choice. Accordingly, the English courts have developed some complex rules to deal with intoxication, rules that have recently been adopted into Irish law by the Court of Criminal Appeal in *The People (DPP) v. Reilly* **(2004)**. These rules will be dealt with in detail later (see Chapter 9), but in essence they allow an intoxicated defendant an answer to a charge involving a crime of specific intent but not to a charge involving a crime of basic intent. A crime of specific intent is an offence that requires proof of intention, and intoxication negates the ability of a person to form an intention. However, a crime of basic intent is one that requires proof of recklessness only. As the effect of intoxication (at least from the ingestion of alcohol and dangerous drugs) upon the mind is well known, a person who ingests intoxicants can be taken to have known the risk that he was running, and this constitutes the legal definition of recklessness. Thus, becoming intoxicated is a reckless thing to do, and as recklessness is sufficient for a charge of basic intent, intoxication can offer no answer to such a charge.

Finally, it is important that the true cause of the automatic episode be ascertained. Thus, in *R v. T* (1990), the defendant was involved in a robbery. The defence argued that the defendant was suffering from post-traumatic stress disorder at the time of the robbery, which would be an internal factor. However, the disorder arose as a result of a rape that the defendant had suffered, which would constitute an external factor. Thus, the true explanation for the defendant's involvement in the robbery was an external factor and the Crown Court accepted that the issue of non-insane automatism should be considered by the jury (which still convicted her).

Non-Insane Automatism

The courts seem to be somewhat suspicious of automatism, and so limit its exercise. In particular, the courts have noted – as the House of Lords did in *Bratty* – that claiming not to remember an action may simply be a ruse to avoid liability. For that reason, Lord Denning stated in *Bratty* that automatism was more than simply not being able to remember an action, or being unable to control an impulse to commit an action. The requirements for a successful plea were discussed in the High Court in the civil case of *O'Brien v. Parker* **(1997)**. The defendant had been involved in a road traffic accident. His actions were the cause of the accident, but he argued that at the time of the accident, he had suffered an epileptic attack, which had come on with no warning. However, he conceded that at the time, he had some degree of awareness and could still make decisions. He argued that he should not be held accountable on the grounds of automatism. The High Court noted the existence of automatism as a defence in criminal cases, and saw no reason why it should not also apply in civil cases, subject to the same limits. In particular, it must be shown that the defendant had no control at all over his actions. Where he retained any degree of control, the defence would fail. In this case, as the defendant had admitted to having had some control, his defence failed, and he was found fully liable for the accident. (It must be remembered that this was a civil case, and that had it arisen before a criminal court, the issue would have been somewhat different. In particular, in *R v. Sullivan* (1983), it was decided by the House of Lords that epilepsy is a disease of the mind, and would therefore give rise to insane automatism. Issues of insanity were, of course, irrelevant in *O'Brien*.) The High Court's decision fully accords with the approach taken in England. In *Attorney General's Reference No.2 of 1992* (1993), the defendant was a lorry driver who had crashed into a broken-down vehicle parked on the hard shoulder, resulting in the deaths of two people. He was acquitted on the grounds of automatism. The Attorney General sought the opinion of the Court of Appeal on the limits of automatism (although the court's decision would not affect the acquittal). The evidence suggested that the defendant had been lulled into a trance-like state by the monotonous nature of the journey, and was therefore suffering from reduced awareness. Because his awareness was only reduced, the Court of Appeal held that automatism was inappropriate; a defendant must have no awareness at all for such a defence to succeed.

Penalising Involuntary Conduct

Despite the general requirement that the defendant's conduct be voluntary before criminal liability can be attached to him, there are some occasions in which involuntary conduct can attract criminal sanctions. First, as already noted, an intoxicated offender can be convicted of an offence of basic intent despite his lack of awareness of his actions. This issue is more fully dealt with in Chapter 9.

Second, an offence may be defined in such a way that a 'state of affairs', or a specific situation, constitutes the *actus reus*. This state of affairs exception has led to some particularly harsh decisions. In *R v. Larsonneur* (1933), the defendant was required to leave the UK. She went to Ireland, from where she was deported back to the UK, and was handed over to the police. She was charged with, and convicted of, being an alien found in the UK without permission under the Aliens Order 1920. A more extreme example is found in *Winzar v. Chief Constable of Kent* (1983). The Licensing Act 1872 made it an offence to be found drunk on a highway or in a public place. The police were called to remove the drunken defendant, who had refused to leave a hospital. They took him out of the hospital, formed the opinion that he was drunk and placed him in their squad car, which was parked on the highway. The defendant was subsequently convicted of being found drunk on the highway. The fact that the offence was effectively committed by the police, and that no fault could attach to the defendant, was irrelevant. The court justified this decision by comparing the defendant to a drunk man who was asked to leave a restaurant, and did so. Such a man would clearly be capable of being found drunk in a public place because he had entered that place voluntarily. If the defendant in *Winzar* should be acquitted in similar circumstances, he would effectively be receiving a reward for non-cooperation, while the other man would effectively be receiving a punishment for his co-operation, and this would be unjust.

Whether or not these cases would be followed in Ireland is unclear. Charleton notes a New Zealand decision, *Finau v. Department of Labour* (1984), which is similar to *Larsonneur*. The accused had been ordered to leave New Zealand, but argued that her pregnancy had prevented her from doing so. The argument was accepted, and she was acquitted. Charleton argues that this decision is to be preferred as it is more just, and therefore more in line with Irish constitutional requirements of justice.[4]

Third, there are situations in which a person accepts a duty to act responsibly towards others and a failure to do so can result in criminal liability even if the person was in an unconscious state at the time the offence was committed. This is the so-called doctrine of prior fault. In *Kay v. Butterworth* (1945), the defendant fell asleep while driving and collided with a group of soldiers who were marching along the side of a road. Humphreys J. ruled that a driver is under a legal duty to remain awake at the wheel of his vehicle. If 'drowsiness overtakes a driver while he is at the wheel, he should stop and wait until he shakes it off and is wide awake again.' The prior failure of the defendant in this case to stop as soon as he felt drowsy meant that he had failed in his duty to other road users and criminal liability could be attached to him on that basis.

3.4 Causation

It is obviously not necessary to establish causation in conduct offences: no result is required to establish the offence, thereby removing causation from the equation. Causation is, however, essential in result offences. The prosecution must, therefore, prove that it was the conduct of the defendant that brought about the particular result. This issue does not arise very often and when it does it is invariably in homicide cases. The classic example is *R v. White* (1910). The defendant put potassium cyanide into his mother's drink, intending to kill her.

---

4 Charleton, *et. al., Criminal Law,* Dublin: Butterworths, 1999, para. 1.31.

She was later found dead, but the evidence disclosed that she had died from heart failure rather than from the poison. The defendant was consequently convicted of attempted murder only.

There is a distinction between factual causation and legal causation. Factual causation refers to the objective connection that exists between two events, and is often couched in terms of the well-known 'but for' test: would the subsequent event have occurred but for the preceding event? Suppose X's car skids off the road at night and strikes a tree, killing a passenger. Subsequent investigation shows that X was traveling at 150 kph. X is charged with causing death by dangerous driving and the prosecution wants to show that the speed at which X was driving was the cause of the accident. The jury will be asked, would the crash not have occurred but for the speed at which X was driving? If the answer is negative, then a factual causal link between the defendant's conduct and the death has been shown. The difficulty with the 'but for' test is that it is inherently simplistic. There may be many causes of a particular consequence: in the example just given, the road might have been wet from rain, there might have been reduced visibility due to poor street lighting, X might have been trying to avoid an animal that was in the middle of the road, etc. Each of these factors can be implicated equally in the crash through the use of the 'but for' test, and the test is unable to distinguish between them as principal or lesser causes of the accident. Further, the 'but for' test is also quite blunt and can spread the net of criminal liability very far. So, in the example just given, the accident could not have happened but for X having a car to drive: should the automobile industry be implicated in the death of the passenger simply because it produced a car that was later driven by X? The stretch of factual causation therefore needs to be limited by legal causation, which is essentially a set of guidelines designed to determine which factually causative conduct carries sufficient moral responsibility for the consequence as to warrant criminal condemnation. Actions that are too remote from the consequence (such as those of the car industry in the example above) are unlikely to attract such condemnation. However, causation is ultimately a matter of fact for the jury to decide, applying its common sense and knowledge of the world: *R v. Finlay* (2003). Nevertheless, the law has developed rules to assist the jury and it is to these rules that the discussion now turns.

Proving Causation

The required causal link between the defendant's conduct and the result can be inferred from the circumstances even where the precise cause of the result cannot be shown. This point is well illustrated in ***The People (DPP) v. Murphy* (2005)**. The defendant was appealing against his conviction for the murder of a young German woman whose body was found over a month after she had disappeared. Her body had been damaged by wild animals and a pathological examination was unable to determine the exact cause of death. Semen was recovered from the body, which was shown through DNA analysis to have come from the defendant. However, the defendant argued that this evidence showed only that sexual intercourse had occurred between the defendant and the deceased and did not establish any causal link between the defendant and the death of the deceased. Perhaps she died from natural causes, or from an accident or had been killed by another person. In the absence of any evidence as to cause of death, the defendant argued, his conviction could not be maintained. However, the Court of Criminal Appeal ruled that there was 'abundant evidence from which a virtually irresistible inference [of causation] could be drawn.' In particular, the deceased had been young and in good health; the state of undress in which the deceased's body had been found indicated that her death occurred during or just after recent sexual activity; and, not least, the defendant had made a statement to the gardaí in which he had apologised for taking the deceased's life. Thus, the court held that there was sufficient evidence from which the jury could conclude that the defendant had murdered the deceased, even if the precise mechanism whereby she died remained uncertain.

It is clear that the defendant's actions do not have to be the sole cause of the result. Providing his actions were an 'operating and substantial cause' of the result, he can be convicted. In *R v. Hennigan* (1971), the defendant was driving a car, at night and in a restricted area, at approximately 80 mph along a main road that divided two minor roads. As he drove through the intersection, he crashed into another car emerging from one of the minor roads, killing two of its three occupants. The issue before the Court of Appeal was whether the defendant was responsible for the collision, and therefore for the two deaths. The court noted that in a civil case, the other driver might be held to be substantially at fault as she had been crossing a main road. However, the evidence also indicated blame on the defendant's part, especially with regard to his speed. The trial judge had directed the jury at trial that the defendant's action did not have to be the sole cause of the collision providing it was a substantial one. He explained that 'substantial' meant that the actions must have been more than a remote cause of the deaths; they must have been an appreciable cause. The Court of Appeal endorsed this explanation, and found ample evidence to suggest that the defendant had substantially caused the accident. However, in *R v. Cato* (1976), the Court of Appeal held that it was not necessary to actually use the word 'substantial' as long as the jury was aware from the direction that something more than a minor contribution was required. The court quoted Smith and Hogan's assertion that anything more than a trivial contribution would be sufficient, but expressly stopped short of endorsing it. In the circumstances of the case, the jury clearly knew what the judge had been talking about, so the lack of reference to a 'substantial' cause was irrelevant.

Irish law adopts a similar attitude. In **The People (DPP) v. Davis (2001)**, the defendant was charged with murder. The deceased's body showed evidence of considerable injuries, some of which the defendant suggested had been caused either in an earlier altercation with other people, falling down the stairs, or had been inflicted during attempts to revive the deceased. The Court of Criminal Appeal found these explanations to be scarcely credible, and concluded that the defendant's own admitted attack was probably the sole cause of the deceased's death. The court pointed out, however, that it is 'unnecessary to go so far: it is sufficient if the injuries caused by the applicant were related to the death in more than a minimal way.'

Novus Actus Interveniens

It is possible for the actions of a third party to intervene between the defendant's actions and the result. To take an extreme example, suppose X stabs Y in the arm during a robbery, and Y is brought to hospital. The wound is nasty but not life-threatening. However, the hospital doctor is utterly incompetent and allows the wound to develop a gangrenous infection which spreads throughout Y's body, killing him. In these circumstances, there is authority to suggest that X is not liable for murder (although, as will be seen later, the scope of this authority has been narrowed in recent years). The actual cause of Y's death was the doctor's incompetence rather than the stab wound. As such, the doctor's incompetence breaks the chain of causation that must be shown if X is to be convicted of murder. Circumstances such as these are known by the Latin phrase *novus actus interveniens*. A *novus actus* typically arises through the conduct of a third party, but in some circumstances, the conduct of the victim can also break the chain of causation. More rarely, a so-called 'act of God' can also constitute a *novus actus*, provided the act in question is the 'operation of natural forces so unpredictable as to excuse a defendant all liability for its consequences' (*Southern Water Authority v. Pegrum* (1989)).

There are a number of conditions to be satisfied before the action of a third party can break the causal link. Where it is alleged that a third party's actions are a *novus actus*, the jury must be satisfied that the actions were voluntary. In *R v. Pagett* (1983), a sixteen-year-old girl, pregnant by the first defendant, was used by him as an unwilling shield during a stand-off with the police who were trying to arrest him for serious offences, and was killed by police bullets in the cross-fire. He was convicted of murder and appealed. It was held by the Court of Appeal that the issue was whether the actions of the police, which were the immediate cause of the girl's death, could constitute a *novus actus* to the extent that the defendant could be relieved of responsibility for her death. The court rejected this contention on a number of grounds, one of which was the involuntary nature of the police officers' actions. When the police officers returned fire, they were acting in self-defence and so were not acting voluntarily: in essence, they had been compelled to return fire in order to protect themselves. Further, the court stated that where police officers act in the course of their duty in response to the actions of a defendant, the officers' actions cannot be regarded as voluntary, and hence cannot constitute a *novus actus*. By using the deceased as a shield in circumstances where he knew that the police might return his fire, the defendant had committed an unlawful and dangerous act that had resulted in death. Accordingly, a manslaughter conviction at least was warranted, and where there was sufficient *mens rea*, a murder conviction might be appropriate.

In *Pagett*, the defendant himself had clearly brought about the actions of the police. A series of cases concerning medical intervention to deal with injuries inflicted by defendants present a different problem. Suppose X breaks Y's leg, and Y is brought to hospital where he is forced to remain in traction. While in the hospital, Y contracts a serious infection from bacteria that flourish due to the unhygienic condition of the hospital, and later dies from that infection. Is X responsible for Y's death? It can be argued that X initiated a sequence of events that led directly to Y's demise, and that X should be held responsible for Y's death. On the other hand, it can be argued with equal force that a broken leg is not usually a life-threatening injury and that the real cause of Y's death was the negligent maintenance of the hospital. On this view, X would not be held responsible for Y's death. The courts have generally adopted the former view unless the original wound was no longer a 'substantial and operating cause' of the deceased's death. Thus, the actions of doctors who try to deal with an injury inflicted by the defendant will not generally constitute a *novus actus* because their efforts are a normal part of the sequence of events brought about by the defendant. The first case in the series in which these issues were considered was *R v. Jordan* (1956), in which the defendant was convicted of murder. He had stabbed the deceased, resulting in hospitalisation. In hospital, the deceased's wound was stitched and he was treated with an antibiotic to prevent infection. However, he was allergic to the particular antibiotic used, and this became clear after the first doses when he developed diarrhoea. This treatment was stopped, but was then recommenced the following day by a different doctor. Furthermore, abnormally large quantities of liquid were given to the deceased intravenenously, which waterlogged his lungs, which in turn caused a form of pneumonia, and it was this condition that resulted in his death. The Court of Appeal accepted that death following normal medical treatment required after an unlawful injury could be said to have been caused by the injury. In such a case, the treatment would be dependent upon the injury which was caused by the defendant, and he would therefore be responsible for the consequences of the treatment. In this case, however, the medical treatment was not only not normal, it was 'palpably wrong'. The wound could not be said to have contributed to the deceased's death; the cause was the medical treatment received in hospital, treatment that was independent of the defendant's actions. The defendant's conviction was therefore quashed, the medical treatment constituting a *novus actus*.

In ***People (Attorney General) v. McGrath* (1960)**, the deceased had been assaulted by the defendant and lay unconscious in the road. He was examined at the scene by a passing doctor (who later departed to call an ambulance) who saw no evidence of internal bleeding. Twenty minutes later, and before an ambulance arrived, the deceased was put into a private car by a number of passers-by and brought to hospital where internal bleeding was discovered, which allowed blood to enter the deceased's lungs and which caused his death. The defendant argued on appeal that the deceased's death was caused by the inexpert actions of the passers-by who brought the deceased to hospital instead of waiting for the ambulance. The Court of Criminal Appeal distinguished *Jordan* on the basis that the deceased in that case had died from the medical treatment rather than from the wound inflicted by the defendant. In **McGrath**, however, the medical evidence showed that the cause of death was inhalation of blood into the lungs consequent upon the wound caused during the assault. The court concluded that the actions of the passers-by had not introduced any new cause of death:

> Any such interference was admittedly a humane and well-intentioned act, brought about by the wrongful act of the applicant; far from being a new act that negatives causation by cutting the chain of causation between the blow struck and the death, it formed a normal link in the chain.

Similarly, in *R v. Smith* (1959), inappropriate medical treatment was given to a soldier who had been stabbed with a bayonet during a fight with other soldiers. The treating doctor had not appreciated the seriousness of the wound and his treatment probably impeded the soldier's chances of recovery, and the soldier died from haemorrhaging in the lung. The Court of Appeal noted that the original wound was still an operating and substantial cause of the death; of particular note was the fact that the soldier died within two hours of the original wound, and within that period, there had been insufficient time for a proper medical examination. The court concluded that *Jordan* was an unusual case that depended on its own facts and should be distinguished. The defendant's appeal was dismissed.

The influence of *Jordan* was further restricted in *R v. Cheshire* (1991). The deceased developed breathing difficulties requiring a tracheotomy, having been shot in the abdomen and thigh. His wounds healed, but he died two months later from complications arising from the tracheotomy. It was accepted by the Court of Appeal that these complications should have been diagnosed by the attending doctors, and that had they done so, the deceased would not have died. However, specifically upholding the judgment in *Smith*, the court held that these complications were a direct result of the gunshot wounds and the attempts by the doctors to deal with the damage done by them. Therefore, the defendant's actions were a significant cause of the death. The court went on to indicate that only extraordinary and unusual treatment could constitute a *novus actus*, and even then only if the jury was satisfied that this treatment was so significant a cause of death that it completely overshadowed the original injury. In a similar vein, in *R v.*

Mellor (1996), the deceased, aged seventy-one, suffered injuries in an assault, and died two days after being admitted to hospital. The defence argued that death was a result of medical negligence rather than the assault. The court held that the jury had to decide if the prosecution had established if the defendant's actions were a substantial cause of death. Medical negligence could be an issue for a jury to consider in this respect, and the onus was on the prosecution to negative it as the cause of death. However, the court went on to say that provided the jury was sure that the defendant's actions contributed significantly to the deceased's death, it was irrelevant that incompetence or mistakes on the part of doctors were also a significant cause of death.

Acts of the Victim

Typically, a *novus actus* will arise due to the actions of a third party, but there are occasions when the actions of the victim might also break the chain of causation. Suppose X assaults Y, breaking Y's ribs. Y does not call an ambulance but instead drives to the local hospital for medical attention. However, Y drives recklessly, loses control of the car and is involved in a crash in which Y is killed. It is difficult to see why X should be held responsible for Y's death in these circumstances in that Y was killed by his own act, i.e. driving recklessly. In principle, a defendant should not be held responsible for the voluntary acts of his victim.

However, the courts are wary of laying blame on the shoulders of the victim, especially as the defendant initiated the events that led to the death. A good example of these issues is the so-called escape cases, in which the deceased is killed trying to escape from violent conduct on the part of the defendant. In *R v. Williams and Davis* (1992), the deceased, a hitch-hiker, was given a lift by the defendants, who intended to rob him. In trying to escape, the deceased jumped from the car and was killed. The defendants argued that the deceased's own action had brought about his death and that they should not be held responsible for it. The Court of Appeal held, however, that a victim's response will not excuse a defendant if that response was one of the range of responses that could reasonably be foreseen as a consequence of the defendant's actions. Only where the victim's action was 'so daft as to make it his one voluntary act' could the chain of causation be broken, and even then the jury should bear in mind that in the heat of the moment, the deceased would not have been thinking entirely rationally. To put the court's reasoning another way, the defendant is responsible for all the normal links in the sequence of events that he himself initiated, and if the deceased's response formed part of that sequence, the chain of causation is not broken. What constitutes a normal link is defined and limited by reasonable foreseeability: if the deceased's response could not have been foreseen by reasonable people, the response will be connected to the defendant's actions only remotely and cannot be considered to be a normal link in the chain of causation.

Reasonable people can reasonably foresee all but the most 'daft' responses; thus only responses that are 'daft' can break the chain of causation, thereby releasing the defendant from responsibility for the response.

This reasoning does not extend to situations in which the defendant's actions form part of those of the victim. In such situations, the actions of the deceased are also the actions of the defendant and the defendant bears full responsibility for them. Thus, in *R v. Rogers* (2003), the defendant tied a tourniquet around the deceased's arm to raise a vein into which the deceased injected a heroin mixture, which caused the deceased's death. The Court of Appeal ruled that both the deceased and the defendant had been 'playing a part in the mechanics of the injection which caused death', and this act constituted an offence under the Offences Against the Person Act, section 23 (administering a noxious substance). Thus, the unlawful act of the deceased was also the unlawful act of the defendant, and as that act caused the deceased's death, the defendant was rightly convicted of manslaughter. This principle of joint action has recently been extended by the Court of Appeal in *R v. Kennedy (No.2)* (2005). The defendant had prepared a heroin mixture in a syringe and given it to the deceased, who injected it into his own arm and then returned the syringe. The court ruled that the original conviction was correct on the basis that as the mixture prepared by the defendant was for immediate injection, it was open to the jury to find that the defendant and the deceased were both equally engaged in the one activity of administering the heroin to the deceased, an activity that caused the deceased's death.

The preceding paragraphs concern the defendant's responsibility for the actions of the victim; what responsibility does the defendant have for the omissions of the victim? Suppose X causes a treatable injury to Y, but Y fails to seek medical attention and as a result the wound becomes infected and Y dies. Is X responsible for Y's death? As noted earlier (see section 3.2), the common law has traditionally tended to view failures to act as being beyond its purview, and this attitude extends to not allowing defendants to escape criminal liability for a deceased's failure to deal with his injury. Thus, in the old Irish case of **R v. Flynn (1867)**, the deceased had suffered a head injury from a stone thrown by the defendant during a fight. For two days, the deceased did nothing about the injury but instead followed his usual regimen. By the time a doctor was called, it was too late. It was held that the deceased had done nothing to make his wound worse; had he done so, his actions might have constituted a *novus actus*. The cause of death was the original head wound that had been caused by the defendant. A more recent analysis of a similar issue was provided by the Court of Appeal in *R v. Dear* (1996). In this case, the defendant had slashed the victim with a knife, causing the latter's death two days later. It was argued on appeal that the victim had either left his wound untreated or had actually reopened his wound as a means of committing suicide. However, the court ruled that the defendant's actions were irrelevant: if the wound caused by the defendant was an operating and substantial cause of the deceased's death, then causation was established on ordinary principles regardless of the deceased's contribution to his own demise.

Eggshell Skull Rule

Lastly, the tortious principle of the 'Eggshell Skull Rule' also applies in criminal law. In other words, it is no defence that the victim suffers from some abnormality that accentuates the injury. For example, suppose X strikes Y over the head with a club, intending merely to knock him out. However, Y has an unusually weak skull ('as thin as an eggshell'), and he dies as a result. It is no defence on a charge of manslaughter or murder for X to say that he only wanted to knock Y out. In *R v. Blaue* (1975), the deceased was an eighteen-year-old Jehovah's Witness who had been seriously attacked by a man with a knife after she had refused to have sexual intercourse with him. Because of her serious loss of blood, she was advised that she would need a blood transfusion. She refused in writing to consent to the procedure, despite being told that she would die without it, and she died the following day. It was argued that the deceased's refusal was unreasonable and therefore constituted a *novus actus* that broke the chain of causation. The Court of Appeal noted that the policy of the law has always been that those who inflict violence upon others must take their victims as they find them, and this includes the religious and spiritual values held by those victims. It should not be open to the defendant to escape liability for the consequences of his actions on the basis that he thinks his victim was being unreasonable. Her death was brought about by the stab wound that he inflicted upon her, and he was therefore responsible for her death.

3.5 Further Reading

Charleton, 'Causation in the Law of Homicide', (1991) 1 *ICLJ* 68.

Hart and Honore, *Causation in the Law*, 2nd ed., Oxford: Oxford University Press, 1985.

Heaton, 'Dealing in Death', [2003] *Crim LR* 497.

Lanham, '*Larsonneur* Revisited', [1976] *Crim LR* 276

Mackay, 'The Automatism Defence – What Price Rejection?', (1983) 34 *NILQ* 314.

McAuley, 'The Action Component of *Actus Reus*', (1988) 23 *Ir Jur (ns)* 218.

McCutcheon, 'Omissions and Criminal Liability', (1993–1995) 28–30 *Ir Jur (ns)* 56.

Williams, 'Criminal Omissions: The Conventional View', (1991) 107 *LQR* 432.

CHAPTER FOUR

THE *MENS REA*

4.1 Introduction

Mens rea is the mental element of the offence. It is a comparative newcomer in that early conceptions of guilt focused exclusively on the proscribed conduct. However, under the influence of canon law and conceptions of sin, regard began to be had to the defendant's mental state at the time he committed the offence. *Mens rea* has now become so entrenched that, with some specific exceptions, proving it is an essential part of the prosecution's duty. Modern society considers it to be fundamentally unjust to punish those who do not understand the consequences of their conduct or those who bring about harm accidentally or under a mistaken impression of the circumstances. *Mens rea* provides the mechanism by which we can make these distinctions. It is best understood as shorthand for the requirement of culpability or fault on the part of the defendant. *Mens rea* today encompasses a wide range of fault situations that may be mental states – intention, knowledge, 'subjective' recklessness, belief – and some that are not really mental states at all, but rather failures to consider consequences – 'objective' recklessness and negligence. Each of these forms of culpability may result in criminal liability being attached to the defendant, depending on the offence charged. The consequences that flow from a finding of fault will depend on the degree of fault found. Thus, if X shoots and kills Y, X's punishment will depend on whether he fired the gun intentionally or recklessly; if the former, X will be convicted of murder and will be sentenced to life imprisonment, but if the latter, X will be convicted of manslaughter and may be sentenced to anything up to life imprisonment.

Further, there must be an element of *mens rea* for every element of the *actus reus*. Take the offence of capital murder, for example (note that capital murder, while still an offence distinct from murder, is no longer punished by the death penalty, but the phrase 'capital murder' is a useful shorthand). The *actus reus* of capital murder broadly has two elements:

(a) murder,
(b) of a garda acting in the course of his duty.

The *mens rea* of the offence similarly has two elements:

(a) an intention to kill or to cause serious injury, and
(b) knowledge that, or recklessness as to whether or not, the person killed was a garda acting in the course of his duty.

There is therefore an element of *mens rea* for each element of the *actus reus*.

Before considering what *mens rea* is, it is essential to consider what it is *not*. In particular, motive should never be confused with *mens rea*. Evidence of motive is useful to the prosecution to show that the defendant had a reason to commit the offence with which he has been charged, and it may also be relevant in sentencing. However, the fact that the defendant had a motive to commit the offence does not prove that he in fact committed the offence, or if he did commit the offence, that he intended to do so. Suppose X is the sole beneficiary of his rich grandmother's estate and he accidentally hits and kills her with his car. The fact that X had a good motive for killing his grandmother does not change the fact that the killing was accidental. If X is charged with his grandmother's murder, he should be acquitted due to a lack of *mens rea*. Similarly, the fact that a person intentionally commits an offence out of laudable motives does not change the fact that he acted with *mens rea*. In *The People (DPP) v. Kelly* (2004), the defendant was charged with causing criminal damage to a warplane belonging to the United States Navy that had stopped at Shannon Airport on its way to participate in the United States' war in Iraq. The defendant admitted causing the damage but claimed that she did so for a laudable motive: to protect the lives of Iraqi people. The Circuit Court judge ruled that while the applicable legislation allowed a defence of lawful excuse, this defence was not open on the facts of the case. The defendant's motive in attacking the aircraft may have been prompted by her conscience and concern for the Iraqi people, but if the law had been broken she would have to accept the legal consequences of her actions.

4.2   Subjective Fault or Objective Fault

It has been noted earlier that modern liberal conceptions of guilt are built on an assumption that people are autonomous individuals who are capable of making their own choices about their own lives (see section 1.8). The key to autonomy is choice, and the law should preserve to the greatest degree possible the ability of individuals to choose between different courses of conduct. The law should also hold individuals responsible for their actions and for the consequences of those actions, to the extent that those consequences were foreseen and therefore chosen. Those individuals who choose to engage in conduct that is harmful to others are morally deserving of punishment. Those whose actions, while harmful, were not chosen should escape criminal punishment (although they may well be open to civil liability). Thus, under traditional liberal conceptions of guilt, the proper extent of *mens rea* is defined by the defendant's own intention and foresight. The focus of the trial should be on what the defendant intended or foresaw rather than on what a reasonable person might have intended or foreseen in similar circumstances. Delivering the leading judgment in *R v. G* (2003), Lord Bingham stated:

> It is a salutary principle that conviction of serious crime should depend on proof not
> simply that the defendant caused (by act or omission) an injurious result to another

but that his state of mind when so acting was culpable ... It is neither moral nor just to convict a defendant ... on the strength of what someone else would have apprehended if the defendant himself had no such apprehension.

This conception of guilt is referred to as subjective *mens rea*. Thus, in *DPP v. Morgan* (1975), Lord Hailsham held that a man charged with rape should not be convicted if he honestly believed that the sexual intercourse was consensual, even if that belief was unreasonable.

The principal difficulty with the subjective approach is that it makes criminal liability depend on an individual's perceptions, which will vary according to the characteristics of the individual in question. Thus, great harm could be caused by a person's inadvertence to an obvious risk, leaving the victim without any redress from the criminal justice system. As Lord Simon of Glaisdale pointed out in his dissenting opinion in *Morgan*, in the context of rape, a 'woman who has been ravished would hardly feel that she was vindicated by being told that her assailant must go unpunished because he believed, quite unreasonably, that she was consenting to sexual intercourse with him.' If the law wishes to prevent individuals from injuring others, it must, in Lord Simon's words, 'hold a fair balance between victim and accused' by requiring of people a minimum standard of conduct which will not vary according to the characteristics and perceptions of individuals. That minimum standard of conduct would be set by reference to what reasonable people would deem appropriate in a given situation. A failure to reach this standard should constitute sufficient fault to justify attaching criminal liability in at least some circumstances. This is what is known as objective *mens rea*. The major difficulty with objective fault is that all people must be held to this minimum standard of behaviour even if they are incapable of reaching that standard, perhaps due to a disability (*Elliot v. C* (1983)). It seems harsh in the extreme to punish such a person; doing so comes close to punishing that person for his disability.

These two standards of fault permeate the criminal justice system. In a recent House of Lords decision (*B v. DPP* (2000)), Lord Nicholls indicated his view that subjective *mens rea* is the default position of the common law. A statute may depart from this position in a particular instance, but such a departure is limited to the application of that statute and has no general application. Even more recently, the House of Lords in *R v. G* (2003) overturned twenty-five years of precedent when it overruled the decision in *MPC v. Caldwell* (1981), holding that recklessness in the context of causing criminal damage could no longer be defined objectively. In that case, Lord Steyn indicated his view that in modern times, there has been a shift in favour of subjectivism. However, Lord Bingham and Lord Rodger in that case also made it clear that objective recklessness might be retained for some offences. Further, there are numerous instances throughout the criminal law of an objective standard being applied through the use of strict liability and negligence. Also, many of the general defences require reasonable standards before they can succeed – for example, in using force in self-defence, a person is permitted only to use the degree of force that is reasonably necessary in the circumstances. Further, it is worth noting that in the United Kingdom, the effect of the *Morgan* decision in rape cases has been reversed by the Sexual Offences Act 2003, which now requires a belief in consent to be reasonably held before the defendant can escape liability. There are also occasions in which the two standards are mixed. Taking self-defence again as an example, a defendant may plead self-defence even where he was mistaken as to the circumstances: it was held in *R v. Williams (Gladstone)* (1987) that in such circumstances, the defendant will be judged according to his view of the circumstances (a subjective standard), but within that view, his actions must have been reasonable (an objective standard). This approach to the use of force has been enacted in Ireland in the Non-Fatal Offences Against the Person Act 1997 (see Chapter 7).

4.3 Intention

The courts have generally tried to avoid defining intention, preferring instead to rely on the jury's own sense of the common meaning of the word. However, it is clear from the case law that the courts have recognised two forms of intention: direct and oblique.

Direct Intention

A person directly intends a result when he desires to bring about that result and deliberately sets out to do so. In ***The People (DPP) v. Murray* (1977)**, Walsh J. defined intention in the following terms:

> To intend to murder, or to cause serious injury ... is to have in mind a fixed purpose to reach that desired objective. Therefore, the state of mind of the accused person must have been not only that he foresaw but also willed the possible consequences of his conduct.

Similarly, the Court of Criminal Appeal approved the following definition in ***The People (DPP) v. Douglas & Hayes* (1985)**:

> An 'intention' to my mind connotes a state of affairs which the party 'intending' ... does more than merely contemplate: it connotes a state of affairs which, on the contrary, he decides, so far as in him lies, to bring about, and which, in point of probability he has a reasonable prospect of being able to bring about, by his own fruition.

A direct intention therefore involves a focus by the defendant on a particular object and a desire to achieve that object. In cases such as this – and they constitute the majority of cases – the courts have found little need to provide any further explanation to the jury. Thus, in *R v. Christofides* (2001), the Court of Appeal ruled that there was no need for a special direction in a case where the defendant repeatedly hit the victim on the head with a stick; the defendant's intention was clear from his actions and any attempt to provide a formal definition could only have the effect of confusing the jury.

Oblique Intention

The definitions of intention in ***Murray*** and ***Douglas & Hayes*** might be sufficient for the majority of cases, but there is a small class of cases where those definitions might prove to be too narrow. Suppose X is an animal rights activist and plants a bomb at the local abattoir because he believes that the butchery of animals is immoral and wants to stop it. The bomb explodes and kills an employee of the abattoir. Can X be convicted of murder, bearing in mind that an intention to kill or to cause serious injury is an essential element of that offence (Criminal Justice Act 1964, section 4)? The focus of the definitions in ***Murray*** and ***Douglas & Hayes*** is on the defendant's objective, but in this example, X's objective was not to kill or to cause serious injury but merely to stop what he believed to be the immoral practice of killing animals for food. Under these definitions, assuming the jury accepted X's explanation, he would have to be acquitted of murder. But suppose X knew that there would be employees in the abattoir when the bomb exploded and knew that almost certainly some might be killed in the explosion. An acquittal of murder in these circumstances seems wrong in principle: the defendant has acted deliberately knowing that someone would die as a result of his actions. His moral culpability is virtually identical to that of a person who intends directly to kill or cause serious harm. Thus, the definition given by Walsh J. in ***Murray*** needs to be expanded to include a deliberate act done with at least some degree of appreciation of the unintended consequences of the act. This is what is known as oblique intent, and the crucial issue for the courts has been the degree of foresight of the unintended consequence required to support a finding of intention.

In *Hyam v. DPP* (1974), the defendant set fire to a house, did nothing to warn the occupants of the house, and two people were killed. The defendant admitted that she knew that what she had done was dangerous both for the occupants of the house and for the neighbours, but claimed that her intention was to scare the owner of the house into leaving the neighbourhood. The defendant was convicted of murder and appealed on the basis that she lacked the necessary *mens rea* (which was an action carried out with malice aforethought). The House of Lords held that a deliberate act carried out with the knowledge that death or grievous bodily harm was a highly probable result of the act amounted to malice aforethought. The majority of the Lords also indicated that this level of foresight would constitute an intentional act, although two of the majority did not formally decide the issue. Lord Hailsham, however, argued – surely correctly – that while foresight of likely consequences was an element of intention, foresight and intention were distinct concepts.

Ten years after *Hyam*, the Court of Criminal Appeal in ***Douglas & Hayes*** handed down the only reported Irish decision on oblique intent. The defendants were charged with shooting with intent to commit murder under section 14 of the Offences Against the Person Act 1861. The court held:

> In the circumstances of any particular case, evidence that a reasonable man would have foreseen that the natural and probable consequences of the acts of the accused was to cause death and evidence of the fact that the accused was reckless as to whether his acts would cause death or not is evidence from which an inference of intent to cause death may or should be drawn, but the court must consider whether either or both of these facts do establish beyond a reasonable doubt an actual intention to cause death.

This holding was heavily influenced by the decision in *Hyam*, and indicates that recklessness as to whether or not death is caused is sufficient to infer an intention. In so holding, the Court of Criminal Appeal effectively blurred the distinction between the *mens rea* of murder and that of manslaughter. This precise blurring effect led the English courts to reconsider the level of foresight of consequences necessary to support an inference of intention.

Following two House of Lords decisions in *R v. Moloney* (1985) and *R v. Hancock and Shankland* (1986), the Court of Appeal in *R v. Nedrick* (1986) attempted to crystallise their Lordships' opinions into a model direction. The court held that the jury should be asked to decide whether death or serious harm was a virtually certain result of the defendant's acts, and if so, whether the defendant knew this. If the answer to both questions was affirmative, the jury would be justified in inferring that the defendant intended to kill or to cause serious harm. Thus, the Court of Appeal ruled that foresight of consequences as a high probability was insufficient to infer intention; the level of foresight necessary to support a finding of intention could not be less than virtual certainty. In *R v. Woollin* (1998), the House of Lords endorsed the *Nedrick* ruling (with one modification), and rejected any attempt to dilute it. In particular, Lord Slynn expressed concern that allowing a lower level of foresight to suffice for intention would '[blur] the line between intention and recklessness, and hence between murder and manslaughter', thereby effectively increasing the scope of the offence of murder. The *Nedrick* test was altered in one way, however: the Lords felt that finding intention based on foresight of consequences as a virtual certainty, rather than merely inferring it, would be less confusing for a jury. Thus, in England, the test for oblique intention sufficient to support a charge of murder is as follows:

> Where the charge is murder and in the rare cases where the simple direction is not enough, the jury should be directed that they are not entitled to find the necessary intention, unless they are sure that death or serious injury was a virtual certainty (barring some unforeseen intervention) as a result of the defendant's actions and that the defendant appreciated that such was the case.

The state of the law in Ireland is unclear, as the only reported decision on oblique intent is that in ***Douglas & Hayes***. In particular, it is not clear whether the Irish courts have moved from the high probability test set out in *Hyam,* and adopted here in **Douglas & Hayes,** to the virtual certainty test elaborated in *Nedrick* and *Woollin.* It is submitted that the *Woollin* test should be adopted in Ireland. The Criminal Justice Act 1964 mandates an intention to kill or to cause serious injury as the *mens rea* of murder, and this level of *mens rea* is the only distinction between murder and manslaughter. If 'evidence of the fact that the accused was reckless as to whether his acts would cause death' is sufficient to constitute an intention to kill, where then lies the distinction between murder and manslaughter? Acceptance of such evidence to fulfil the *mens rea* of murder sets the bar too low and, as Lord Slynn feared in *Woollin,* essentially pushes the boundary of murder into what should be regarded as manslaughter. It is noteworthy that the Law Reform Commission, in its recent *Consultation Paper on the Mental Element of Murder* (LRC CP17-2001) has provisionally recommended that the *Woollin* formulation be adopted into Irish law for this very reason.

Double Effect

Another issue concerning oblique intent requires mention. Suppose X is a hospital patient dying from terminal cancer and is suffering from intense pain. Y is a doctor who wishes to end X's pain by administering a morphine injection. However, Y knows that only a lethal dose of morphine would be sufficient to deal with X's pain. If Y administers the injection, he has acted deliberately not to cause death but knowing that death was virtually certain to occur as a result. As such, Y would have sufficient *mens rea* for murder under the *Woollin* formulation, and certainly under the **Douglas & Hayes** formulation. However, there is substantial English authority to the effect that doctors in such a situation can benefit from the so-called doctrine of double effect: the *mens rea* of murder will not be satisfied when a doctor acts deliberately to deal with a patient's pain knowing that a side effect of his actions will be the death of the patient. In *Airedale NHS Trust v. Bland* (1993), Lord Goff described this doctrine as 'an established rule'. He said:

> [The doctor's] decision may properly be made as part of the care of the living patient, in his best interests; and, on this basis, the treatment will be lawful. Moreover, where the doctor's treatment of his patient is lawful, the patient's death will be regarded in law as exclusively caused by the injury or disease to which his condition is attributable.

Lord Steyn in *R (Pretty) v. DPP* (2002) adopted these comments, saying that 'medical treatment may be administered to a terminally ill person to alleviate pain although it may hasten death.' How this doctrine is to be reconciled with *Woollin* is not clear, but it may be that in these precise circumstances, there is an exception to the normal rules relating to oblique intent.

Transferred Intent

In some instances, it is possible for a person to be convicted of committing an offence against a person for whom he bore no ill feeling. For example, suppose X tries to shoot Y, but misses and kills Z. It would clearly be unjust to allow X to defend his actions on the grounds that he had in fact intended to kill Y rather than Z. The law therefore allows the intent that X had in respect of Y to be transferred to Z. This is the doctrine of transferred intent. The classic example of the doctrine is *R v. Latimer* (1886), an assault case. The defendant was involved in a pub brawl with another man. He swung his belt at the other man, but the belt bounced off the other man's arm and struck the owner of the pub in the face, causing injury. The defendant appealed against his conviction on the grounds that he had struck the owner by accident and therefore had insufficient *mens rea*. Lord Coleridge C.J. stated that 'if a person has a malicious intent towards one person, and in carrying into effect that malicious intent he injures another … he is guilty of what the law considers malice against the person so injured.' This doctrine applies to all offences, but has been given statutory effect in the case of murder (see section 18.7).

There are, however, limits to the application of the doctrine. In particular, the *mens rea* for the offence intended can only be transferred to an offence that has a similar *mens rea* requirement. Again, the classic example is an old case, *R v. Pembliton* (1874). The defendant threw a stone at another person, but missed and broke a window instead. The jury concluded that he had intended to hit a person, but convicted him of causing criminal damage anyway. On appeal, the conviction was quashed due to a lack of *mens rea*; his intention to hit a person with the stone, i.e. an intention to commit an assault, could not be transferred to the offence of criminal damage, whose *mens rea* requirement was of a different nature. The same principle was applied to a more complex problem in *Attorney General's Reference No.3 of 1994* (1996). The defendant had stabbed a pregnant woman, knowing that she was pregnant. He admitted an intention to cause the woman a serious injury but denied any similar intent with respect to the unborn child. As a result of the stabbing, the child was born prematurely and lived for 121 days before dying. It was undisputed that the child died as a result of being born prematurely, which was in turn caused by the stabbing. The question for the House of Lords was whether the defendant could be properly convicted of homicide even though at the time of the stabbing, the unborn child was not regarded by the law as being alive (see section 18.5). It was suggested by the Attorney General that the defendant's admitted malice towards the mother could be transferred to the unborn child and then transferred again to the child once born. The Lords refused to accept such a double transfer, saying that:

> To make any sense of [transferred intent] there must … be some compatibility between the original intention and the actual occurrence, and this is, indeed, what one finds in the cases. There is no such compatibility here. The defendant intended

to commit and did commit an immediate crime of violence to the mother. He committed no relevant violence to the foetus, which was not a person, either at the time or in the future, and intended no harm to the foetus or to the human person which it would become.

4.4 Knowledge and Belief

To act knowingly is the moral equivalent of acting intentionally in different kinds of circumstances: knowledge is the required *mens rea* for a large number of offences, especially those involving possession, and it is the most serious form of *mens rea* required to support the offence of rape. To act knowingly requires an appreciation by the defendant of certain facts: if X is unaware of the presence of a quantity of drugs in his suitcase, he cannot be said to have knowingly imported drugs. Further, as noted in the previous chapter, X cannot be said to have been in possession of the drugs either (lacking the knowledge element of the *actus reus* of possession). However, it is not clear what level of appreciation is required: must X appreciate the relevant facts as a matter of absolute certainty and beyond any doubt before it can be said that he is acting knowingly? It seems unlikely that such a high standard would be required because to do so would effectively prevent convictions from ever being obtained. As a practical matter, therefore, the fact that the defendant entertained some level of doubt should not be fatal to the prosecution's claim that he knew of the facts alleged. At the same time, knowledge as to the facts alleged is not the same as mere belief as to those facts. In ***Hanlon v. Fleming* (1981)**, Henchy J., speaking for the Supreme Court, explained the difference in the following terms:

> I may believe that there is life in outer space, that evolution is the origin of species, that a particular person did a particular act, but I may have to admit that I do not know, or do not know with any substantial degree of certainty, that such beliefs are well founded. Without entering into the intricate logical, metaphysical and philosophical problems involved in a comparison of knowledge with belief, and keeping the matter on the plane of ordinary usage (which is, presumably, how it would be dealt with by both judge and jury), I would point to the commonly used expression 'I believe it to be so, but I do not really know.'

Henchy J. accepted that a requirement of knowledge is very strong and the courts should not dilute it by equating knowledge with belief. Thus, a statute that penalises a defendant for acting while knowing that a fact is true carries a higher standard of culpability than a statute penalising a defendant for acting while knowing *or believing* a fact to be true.

While knowledge and belief may be distinct, evidence of belief may negate a finding of knowledge on the defendant's part. In *R v. Dunne* (1998), the defendant had been charged with knowingly evading a prohibition on the import of obscene videos. The defendant appealed on the grounds that he did not know that the videos were obscene, he was merely of that opinion. The Court of Appeal accepted that a defendant 'who believes that the heroin he is carrying is glucose is entitled to be acquitted, just as is the defendant who believes that the obscene videos he is carrying comprise recordings of sporting events.' In other words, if the defendant believed that the videos he was carrying were innocent, such belief would necessarily preclude a finding that he was knowingly importing obscene videos. However, as indicated by Henchy J.'s comments, the courts tend to regard the term 'knowledge' as an ordinary term within the understanding of the jury and therefore rarely feel the need to provide a definition.

4.5 Recklessness

Recklessness is usually defined as engaging in conduct that involves taking an unjustifiable risk of causing harm to others. There is no question in cases involving reckless criminal conduct that the defendant wanted to cause harm – if this was the case, then the defendant could be found to have intended the harm. The point, rather, is that the defendant engaged in conduct that risked harming others. The principal issue that has exercised the courts, especially in England, is whether the law should require the prosecution to prove that the defendant consciously considered the risk before imposing criminal punishment. Take the following example: X is living in an apartment in a residential area. He is sitting in his bedroom holding his hunting rifle. Out of sheer boredom, he starts shooting at birds sitting on a telephone wire across the road from his house. One of his shots hits Y, who was walking along the street, and Y later dies as a result of his injuries. At trial it emerges that X only wanted to hit the birds and gave no thought at all to the possibility of hitting a person. Was X reckless in his actions? Traditionally, the common law required evidence that the defendant perceived the risk that he was running in order to find that the defendant had acted recklessly. In *R v. Cunningham* (1957), the defendant broke open a gas meter, without turning off the gas, in order to steal the money therein. Gas escaped into a neighbour's house, which partially asphyxiated the neighbour. The defendant was charged with unlawfully and maliciously administering a noxious thing so as to endanger life contrary to section 23 of the Offences Against the Person Act 1861. The issue was whether the defendant had acted with malice. The Court of Appeal ruled that malice required proof of intention or recklessness, and that for recklessness to exist it must be shown that the defendant had known of the risk he was running and had consciously decided to take that risk. Proof of actual ill will towards the person injured, however, was not required.

Two decisions of the House of Lords handed down on the same day in 1981 changed the legal conception of recklessness. In *Metropolitan Police Commissioner v. Caldwell*, the defendant had set a fire in a hotel while drunk. He claimed that the risk of endangering others had not crossed his mind. Lord Diplock, who delivered the leading judgment, considered the moral distinction between a defendant who stopped to consider the risks that he was taking and the defendant who failed to do so and concluded that any such distinction was impracticable. He held that the word 'reckless' in a statute does not have a special meaning, but should be given its ordinary meaning. Such a meaning would include a situation in which a person failed to consider the existence of a risk that would have been obvious if he had stopped to think about it. Therefore, Lord Diplock ruled that recklessness exists if the defendant created an obvious risk, and either failed to consider the possibility that such a risk existed or consciously decided to run that risk. In this case, the fact that the defendant had been drunk was irrelevant to the issue of recklessness if the risk would have been obvious had he been sober. In *R v. Lawrence* (1981), a case involving a charge of reckless driving, the House issued a slight modification to the test proposed in *Caldwell*: the jury should be satisfied that the defendant acted in such a manner that he created a serious and obvious risk of causing harm to others, and that the defendant either had appreciated the risk he was running and decided to accept it or had failed to consider the possibility of there being such a risk. Whether or not such a risk had been created was a matter for the jury to determine according to the standards of an ordinary and prudent driver.

The decisions in *Caldwell* and *Lawrence* thus created two conceptions of recklessness in English law, one purely subjective and the other objective. Three issues arose in the aftermath of these decisions. First, it was not clear in 1981 which test should be used in a particular case. However, in *R v. Morrison* (1989), the Court of Appeal held that where malice was the required *mens rea*, the *Cunningham* test should be used. Where recklessness was the standard of culpability, the *Caldwell* test should be used.

Second, the two forms of recklessness articulated in *Caldwell* left a gap between them, the so-called *Caldwell* lacuna. Take the facts in *Caldwell* as an example. If the defendant had stopped to think about the risk of endangering lives associated with setting a fire in a hotel, but had concluded that no such risk existed, his actions could not be considered to be reckless. *Caldwell* required proof that the defendant either consciously ran a risk or that he had failed to consider the possibility that such a risk existed. Clearly, a defendant who mistakenly concluded that there was no risk fulfils neither test. He might have been negligent, but negligence is not recklessness. Thus, such a defendant would fall into a lacuna between the two strands of recklessness identified in *Caldwell* and *Lawrence*. The House of Lords acknowledged the existence of this lacuna in *R v. Reid* (1992), but suggested that cases that fell within the lacuna would be rare. However, the lacuna arose squarely before the Divisional Court in *Chief Constable of Avon v. Shimmen* (1986). There, the defendant was a martial arts expert who launched a kick at a plate-glass window believing that his skill was such that he could stop the kick just short of the window. In fact, he broke the window and was charged with causing criminal damage. The court accepted that the lacuna existed but found that it did not arise in this case. The defendant had not mistakenly concluded that there was no risk; rather, he believed that his martial arts skills were such that any risk had been minimised. Therefore, he had obviously adverted to the possibility that the window might be damaged and had decided to run that risk. Consequently, he had acted recklessly and could be convicted of causing criminal damage.

Third, the test elaborated in *Caldwell* and *Lawrence* was clearly objective in its formulation and did not depend on any appreciation of risk by the particular defendant. In *Elliot v. C* (1983), the defendant, a young girl with some learning difficulties, set a fire in a shed, but the fire spread and the shed was destroyed. On a charge of arson, the Court of Appeal held that it was irrelevant that the defendant did not think about the risks in her actions or that she would have been unable to appreciate those risks if she had stopped to think about them. If the risk would have been obvious to a 'reasonably prudent person' and the defendant had not thought about the risks involved in her action, the jury could find that she had acted recklessly. Thus, the objective formulation of recklessness made no allowance for immaturity or disability, but instead held everyone to the standard of an ordinary reasonable adult. This ruling was the subject of considerable academic and judicial criticism, and indeed, in *Elliot* itself, Robert Goff L.J. expressed his dismay at the result, which he clearly felt was unjust.

Despite criticism such as this, *Caldwell* remained in currency until the issue of recklessness was revisited by the House of Lords in *R v. G* (2003), a case that bears a striking resemblance to *Elliot*. The two defendants, aged ten and eleven, had set a fire under a plastic wheelie bin which was adjacent to a shop and then left. The fire spread to the shop and some neighbouring buildings, causing about £1 million worth of damage. The defendants were convicted of arson under the Criminal Damage Act 1971 (the same provision under consideration in *Caldwell*). The House of Lords unanimously held that *Caldwell* had been wrongly decided. Lord Bingham, who delivered the leading judgment, ruled that prior to the enactment of the 1971 Act, the word 'reckless' had always required advertence by the defendant to the risk that he was running. Parliament had not intended to alter the contemporary meaning of the word, and thus Lord Diplock's construction of the 1971 Act in *Caldwell* was incorrect (perhaps in an attempt to ensure that the drunken defendant would not be able to avoid criminal liability). Lord Bingham was also swayed by broader policy considerations, and he delivered a powerful endorsement of the subjective approach to constructions of criminal culpability. He ruled that a defendant who engaged in risky conduct while genuinely failing to perceive the risks he was running 'may fairly be accused of stupidity or lack of imagination, but neither of those failings should expose him to conviction of serious crime or the risk of punishment.' Further, the objective formulation set down in *Caldwell* could lead to injustice, as illustrated by the facts in *G* itself and the unease at the verdict expressed by the trial judge. The trial jury had also plainly been offended at the standard they were being asked to impose; following the judge's explanation of the *Caldwell* standard, the jury had asked the trial judge why they had to consider the risk from the perspective of the reasonable person rather than that of the defendant. Lord Bingham argued that the 'sense of fairness of 12 representative citizens sitting as a jury ... is the bedrock on which the administration of criminal justice in this country is built', and laws offensive to that sense of fairness must be a matter of concern. Accordingly, he held that to be found reckless for the purposes of the Criminal Damage Act 1971, a defendant must have perceived the risk that he was running, thereby returning the construction of liability under that Act to its pre-*Caldwell* condition.

The precise application of the decision in *G* is not clear. Lord Bingham himself explicitly noted that his comments were confined to a construction of the Criminal Damage Act 1971, and that he did not want to throw any doubt on the decision in *Lawrence*. Similarly, Lord Rodgers, in his concurring comments in *G*, argued that an objective formulation of recklessness might be better suited to some offences. However, it seems highly unlikely that this decision will be confined to criminal damage cases; the decision in *Caldwell* was made in a similar context but was quickly given an extended application, and it seems certain that *G* will be treated similarly. Further, there is an obvious attraction in having one meaning only attached to a concept that pervades the criminal law.

G does not affect the liability of a person who considers the risk of causing harm but mistakenly concludes that there is no risk; such a person continues to be outside the definition of recklessness. What about a person who deliberately closes his mind to the existence of the possibility of a risk of causing harm? This issue was considered by the Court of Appeal in *R v. Parker* (1977), which concluded that such a person could be considered to have acted recklessly within the *Cunningham* formulation of that word. The court reasoned that deliberately closing one's mind to an obvious risk equates to knowledge of the risk: as Glanville Williams later explained, a person cannot realistically close his mind to the possibility of a risk unless he has realised, at least fleetingly, that a risk exists. Therefore, such a defendant will have appreciated that a risk existed and by definition he will have acted recklessly.[1] The decision in *Parker* was effectively subsumed into *Caldwell*, but in light of the decision in *G*, it is submitted that the decision in *Parker* can and should now stand on its own again.

Recklessness in Ireland

The meaning of recklessness in Ireland is not clear. The Irish courts have traditionally tended towards a more subjective view of the law, which would suggest that Irish law will follow *Cunningham*. The leading Irish case is ***The People (DPP) v. Noel and Marie Murray* (1977)**. It should be noted that this

---

1 Glanville Williams, *Textbook of Criminal Law*, 1st ed., 1978, p. 79.

case was decided several years before *Caldwell*; what the Supreme Court might have done if the *Caldwell* decision had been before them is impossible to guess. *Murray* was a capital murder case in which the second defendant had killed an off-duty garda who was about to apprehend the first defendant following a bank robbery. The Court held that a conviction for capital murder required evidence that the defendants either knew that their victim was a garda acting in the course of his duty or were reckless as to that fact. This conclusion led to consideration of the meaning of recklessness. All of the judges accepted that a conscious disregard of a risk would constitute recklessness. Henchy J. is representative of this view; he endorsed the definition of recklessness set out in the American Law Institute's Model Penal Code at section 2.02(2)(c): 'A person acts recklessly with respect to a material element of an offence when he consciously disregards a substantial and unjustifiable risk that the material element exists or will result from his conduct.' However, in a passage that almost exactly foreshadowed the House of Lords' decision in *Caldwell*, Walsh J. stated that:

> Recklessness may be found either by applying a subjective test as where there has been a conscious taking of an unjustified risk of which the accused actually knew, or by applying an objective test as where there has been a conscious taking of an unjustified risk of which the accused did not actually know but of which he ought to have been aware.

Thus, there is authority from the Supreme Court for both definitions of recklessness, and it is not clear the extent to which either definition should apply. Henchy J. indicated that his definition applied 'in this context', i.e. in the context of a capital murder case, while Walsh J.'s comments seem more general in their application. The extent of application of the other judges' comments is equally open to question.

Case law since *Murray* is inconclusive. In *Re Hefferon Kearns Ltd.* (1993), Lynch J. quoted a definition of recklessness for the purposes of reckless trading under section 33 of the Companies Act 1990 that was explicitly based on *Caldwell*. Similarly, in *PSS v. JAS & Others* (1995), Budd J. ruled, in the context of the offence of scandalising the court, that a person was reckless if he 'recognised that [interference with the due process of justice] was a possibility and deliberately took the risk that it might occur [or] if he was heedless of what was a perfectly obvious risk.' Given that the first branch of the test requires appreciation of the test, the meaning of 'heedless' in the alternative branch suggests a failure to consider the possibility of an obvious risk. Most recently, in the joined cases *The People (DPP) v. McGrath* and *The People (DPP) v. Cagney* (2004), the Court of Criminal Appeal considered the statutory offence of endangerment. This offence, created by section 13 of the Non-Fatal Offences Against the Person Act 1997, required proof that the defendants' actions were either intentional or reckless. In determining the definition of recklessness, Denham J. adopted the subjective definition provided by Henchy J. in *Murray*.

Thus, there is at present conflicting Irish authority on the meaning of recklessness, and it will be interesting to see the effect, if any, that the House of Lords' decision in *G* will have in this jurisdiction.

4.6 Negligence

Negligence is defined as falling below the standard of behaviour to be expected of reasonably prudent people. It is a completely objective form of *mens rea* and requires no advertence to risk at all on the part of the defendant. So, in *R v. Lamb* (1967), the defendant pointed a loaded gun at his friend in jest and pulled the trigger. He did not understand the firing mechanism and thought it was safe, and expert evidence demonstrated that this was a reasonable error. The defendant's state of mind was therefore innocent, but the Court of Appeal ruled that there was ample evidence on which the jury could find that the defendant had been negligent (the defendant's manslaughter conviction was overturned on other grounds). Thus, negligence does not constitute a state of mind as such; rather, negligence is more properly described as a standard of behaviour. Traditional liberal conceptions of criminality would exclude such a standard as a basis for attaching criminal liability because there is no reference required to the defendant's own state of mind. Nevertheless, there are many offences that take negligence as their fault standard. However, for the most part, these negligence-based offences are of a lesser nature; the only serious offence that can be established by negligence is manslaughter, and even then the degree of negligence must be very high. Thus, as far as the serious offences are concerned, the traditional view of *mens rea* remains largely preserved.

The structure of negligence in criminal law is identical to that in the law of tort: the prosecution must prove that the defendant owed the victim a duty of care and breached it, and that the breach of duty caused the harm in question. To obtain a conviction for manslaughter, however, there is a further step required of the prosecution: the jury must be satisfied that the degree of negligence was sufficiently high to warrant a criminal sanction. The phrase used is 'gross negligence', and the courts have struggled to provide some guidance to juries on what constitutes gross negligence as opposed to ordinary negligence. However, in *R v. Adomako* (1994), the House of Lords indicated that the matter must be decided by the jury in each case according to the circumstances, and accepted that 'an attempt to specify [the degree of negligence required] more closely is ... likely to achieve only a spurious precision.' The Irish courts have had similar difficulties. They have stressed that a conviction for manslaughter requires finding fault considerably in excess of ordinary negligence. In *The People (Attorney General) v. Dunleavy* (**1948**), the Court of Criminal Appeal ruled that a jury should not convict a person of manslaughter unless they find that his negligence involved a high degree of risk of substantial personal injury to others. More recently, in *The People (DPP) v. Cullagh* (**1999**), the deceased had been killed at a fairground while riding a machine called a 'chairoplane'. Due to the negligence of the defendant, the chair on which the deceased was sitting became detached from the machine, causing the deceased to fall to her death. The equipment was old and clearly rusted. The Court of Criminal Appeal confirmed that the 'negligence required [for a manslaughter conviction] is a matter of degree.' The jury had to consider whether the defendant had 'so failed in the duty which he owed [the deceased] as to be liable criminally for her death.' No further specification was given and the court upheld the defendant's manslaughter conviction, finding sufficient evidence to support the jury's decision.

In deciding whether the defendant's negligence was sufficient to warrant a manslaughter conviction, the jury must be careful to base its decision on the degree to which the defendant breached his duty of care alone and not be swayed by the consequences of that breach. In *R v. Akerele* (1943), the defendant was a doctor who had given inoculation injections to a number of children. He had negligently prepared an excessively strong solution for injection and ten children died. The Privy Council concluded that the defendant's negligence related to one act of preparing a solution which was then dispensed to a number of children, rather than the repeated injections, and that this one act could not be considered sufficiently grave as to constitute gross negligence. In particular, the Council ruled that it would be improper to judge the defendant's negligence by reference to the number of people affected by his one negligent action.

4.7 Accident

If a person causes harm accidentally, he will not usually be found liable in criminal law. Such accidental harm rises where the defendant reasonably fails to foresee the consequences of his actions. The facts in *R v. Lamb* (1967) provide a good example. The defendant argued that killing his best friend had been an accident in that when he pointed a loaded gun he did not understand the firing mechanism and thought it was safe. Three witnesses testified that this mistake was entirely understandable given the defendant's lack of experience with firearms. The Court of Appeal felt that there was evidence on which a jury could have found that the defendant acted negligently, but quashed the conviction for manslaughter on the grounds that the defendant's defence of accident should have been put to the jury. Thus, if the jury concludes that what happened was due to a reasonable accident, the defendant must be acquitted.

4.8 Proving *Mens Rea*

To prove the *actus reus*, the prosecution will typically call witnesses who can testify to what the defendant did or said, forensic experts, garda officers, etc. This evidence is usually relatively straightforward in that it relates to the external and observable elements of the defendant's alleged crime. Proving *mens rea*, however, requires a different kind of proof. Objective forms of *mens rea*, such as negligence, require the jury to consider the defendant's conduct in relation to a supposedly common standard of behaviour. In its deliberations, the knowledge and understanding of the jurors themselves constitute the best source of information as to that common standard. The twelve jurors are selected at random and, collectively, are taken as being broadly representative of the population, and consequently, their collective view of what is a reasonable standard of behaviour is largely determinative. Thus, it will not usually be necessary to introduce evidence as to this standard. This holds true in Ireland, even though questions about the true representativeness of Irish juries can be raised given the extensive list in the Juries Act 1976 of those who are, or can be, excused from jury service. Evidence as to a reasonable standard will be required, however, when the standard in question relates to those who profess special skill, such as doctors. These people are held to the standard to be expected of ordinary and reasonably competent experts in that area, a standard that will generally be beyond the knowledge of jurors. So, in *R v. Adomako* (1994), the defendant was an anaesthetist who failed to notice that a tube had become disconnected during an operation, as a result of which the patient died. Expert evidence was called to show that a reasonable and competent doctor would have noticed the disconnected tube, and that the defendant had failed to reach this standard of expert behaviour and therefore had been negligent.

Proof of subjective *mens rea* is more problematic. Subjective *mens rea* relates to the defendant's own state of mind at the time of the incident and, as has been stated by numerous judges, it is not possible to look into a person's head to see what was going on. Instead, the jury will be invited to draw inferences from the facts that have been objectively proven. Just as it is possible to gauge a person's subjective appreciation of a meal from his physical reactions – for example, the fact that he finished the meal and then asked for more – it is equally possible to gain insight into a person's thinking from his actions and words. Certainly, the defendant can be asked what his intention was at the time or what he foresaw happening as a result of his actions. However, the defendant in a criminal case has a clear vested interest in putting the best possible gloss on his actions, and the jury should not take his answers at face value. Instead, they should consider all the evidence – including any testimony from the defendant – and from the totality of that evidence use their collective sense and knowledge of the world to draw inferences as to what was going on inside the defendant's head. Doing so may well lead the jury to conclude that the defendant's testimony should be disregarded. As Lord Bingham said in *R v. G* (2003):

> The defendant rarely admits intending the injurious result in question, but the [jury] will readily infer such an intention, in a proper case, from all the circumstances and probabilities and evidence of what the defendant did and said at the time. Similarly with recklessness: it is not to be supposed that the [jury] will accept the defendant's assertion that he never thought of a certain risk when all the circumstances and probabilities and evidence of what he did and said at the time show that he did or must have done.

It was his faith in the jury's ability to use its common sense to accomplish this task that allowed Lord Bingham to reject the prosecution's argument in *G* that abolishing objective recklessness would allow defendants to escape criminal responsibility, thereby lowering the protection that the law can offer to the public.

The foregoing comments apply equally to cases involving intention or recklessness. However, in the case of intention, the law has developed a presumptive mechanism to assist the jury in its deliberations: the law presumes that people intend the natural and probable consequences of their actions. This presumption has been given statutory effect in relation to murder in section 4(2) of the Criminal Justice Act 1964, and it is with this provision that the case law has been concerned. However, the presumption also exists at common law in connection with all offences that require proof of intention. In *Hosegood v. Hosegood* (1950), Lord Denning explained that this presumption is 'a proposition of ordinary good sense'. As people are generally able to foresee the natural and probable consequences of an action, it is reasonable for the law to presume that if a person takes an action, the person has foreseen, and therefore intended, the natural and probable consequences of that action. Lord Denning further explained that the presumption is not absolute and may be displaced by the evidence in a particular case. But, in *DPP v. Smith* (1960), the House of Lords held that if death or serious harm were natural and probable consequences of the defendant's action, then the defendant must have intended to cause death or serious harm. The decision provoked enormous criticism as it effectively removed any semblance of subjective *mens rea* in murder cases. It is now clear that *Smith* is not good law, having been legislatively reversed by the 1964 Act, which explicitly provides that the presumption may be rebutted.

It is essential that juries understand that the presumption does not alter the burden of proof, which remains at all times with the prosecution. As a result, judicial instructions to juries can become somewhat awkward; in *The People (DPP) v. McBride* (**1997**), the Court of Criminal Appeal held that the jury must consider 'whether the State had satisfied them beyond reasonable doubt that the presumption had not been rebutted.' The correct approach to the presumption was explained in *The People (DPP) v. Hull* (**1996**). The defendant had fired his shotgun through a door of a house that had just been closed by the occupant of the house. The occupant was killed by the shot and the defendant was charged with murder. The trial judge instructed the jury to consider section 4(2) of the Criminal Justice Act 1964 in two steps. The first step was to consider whether death or serious injury was a natural and probable result of the defendant's actions. If the jury answered this question negatively, then the presumption of intention could not arise. If, however, the jury concluded that death or serious injury was a natural and probable result of the defendant firing his shotgun through a door that had just been closed, then the jury could presume that the defendant had intended to cause death or serious injury. The second step would then be to decide whether the presumption had been rebutted. The defendant had argued that the shotgun had gone off accidentally, and the jury had to decide whether the prosecution had been able to counter this argument. If the jury concluded that they had done so, then the presumption would not have been rebutted and the defendant should be found to have intended to cause death or serious harm. The Court of Criminal Appeal rejected the argument that these instructions were defective, ruling that they correctly explained the import of section 4(2).

Lastly, in considering whether the presumption has been rebutted, the jury should have regard to the defendant's explanations of his actions at the time of the incident; actions and words after the incident throw no light on the issue of the defendant's state of mind at the time the crime was committed. Thus, in *The People (DPP) v. McDonagh* (**2001**), the Court of Criminal Appeal ruled that evidence of remorse expressed at the scene of the crime after the killing could not properly be considered rebuttal evidence.

4.9   Strict Liability

In some offences, liability may be imposed despite at least one element of *mens rea* being absent. A good example of such an offence is unlawful carnal knowledge of a young girl, which is also known as statutory rape (see section 20.15). The Criminal Law Amendment Act 1935 makes it an offence for any male to have sexual intercourse with any girl under the age of seventeen. The *actus reus* of the offence has three elements: (a) intercourse, (b) with a girl, and (c) who is under the age of seventeen. There must be *mens rea* with respect to the first two elements. The third element, however, does not require any *mens rea*. It is therefore no defence for the defendant to argue, on a charge of statutory rape, that he genuinely believed the girl to be aged seventeen or over, even where he had good grounds for so believing.

At common law, only two offences are of strict liability: public nuisance and criminal libel. All other strict liability offences are the creatures of statute. Very often, statutes do not indicate whether an offence is one of strict liability and it will be a matter for the courts to determine the intention of the legislature using the canons of statutory interpretation. In *Gammon Ltd v. Attorney General for Hong Kong* (1984), Lord Scarman set out five principles to be followed in making this determination, all of which apply equally in Ireland. First, there is a general presumption that the legislature intended that *mens rea* be required. The leading authority on this point in England is *Sweet v. Parsley* (1969), in which Lord Reid said:

> [T]here has for centuries been a presumption that Parliament did not intend to make criminals of persons who were in no way blameworthy in what they did. That means that whenever a [legislative provision] is silent as to *mens rea* there is a presumption

that, in order to give effect to the will of Parliament, we must read in words appropriate to require *mens rea.*

In Ireland, the Supreme Court accepted this point in *DPP v. Roberts* (**1987**).

Second, this presumption is very strong when dealing with an offence that is 'truly criminal' in character as opposed to being of a regulatory nature. In making this distinction, the consequence of a conviction is an important matter to consider. Thus, in *Director of Corporate Enforcement v. Gannon* (**2002**), the High Court decided that the limited penalties imposed for breaching section 187(6) of the Companies Act 1990 (acting as auditor for a company while disqualified) indicated that the offence created by that provision was not 'truly criminal' in character. Similarly, in *Re Employment Equality Bill 1996* (**1997**), the Supreme Court found that the various offences set out in the Bill for which an employer could be made vicariously liable were not merely regulatory in character, as they would attract a substantial measure of public opprobrium.

Third, the presumption of *mens rea* can only be rebutted where the statute in question clearly so states or does so by necessary implication. This point was accepted by Walsh J. in the Supreme Court in *The People (DPP) v. Murray* (**1977**). In *B v. DPP* (2000), Lord Nicholls stated that a necessary implication 'connotes an implication which is compellingly clear', which can be found in the words of the statute, the nature of the offence, the mischief which the statute was intended to rectify or any other circumstances which might assist in determining the legislature's intentions. However, the courts should not lightly conclude that an offence is one of strict liability; as Lord Goddard pointed out in *Brend v. Wood* (1946):

> It is of the utmost importance for the protection of the liberty of the subject that a court should always bear in mind that, unless a statute either clearly or by necessary implication rules out *mens rea* as a constituent part of the crime, the court should not find a man guilty of an offence against the criminal law unless he has a guilty mind.

Fourth, the presumption can be rebutted only when the statute concerns a matter of social concern involving public safety, and fifth, even in such cases, strict liability should be necessary to the attainment of the goals of the legislation. In *Lim Chin Aik v. The Queen* (1963), the Privy Council suggested that there must be something that the class of persons to whom the legislation is addressed can do through the supervision, inspection or exhortation of those whom he controls, or through the improvement of business practices. Thus, in *R v. Brockley* (1994), the Court of Appeal considered the statutory offence of acting as a company director while being an undischarged bankrupt created by section 11 of the Company Directors Disqualification Act 1986. The court accepted that construing the offence as one of strict liability would ensure that bankrupts would have to take steps to ensure that their bankruptcy had been discharged before acting again as a company director, which clearly assisted in attaining the goals of the legislation. Similarly, in **Gannon**, the High Court accepted that a strict construction of section 187(6) would encourage greater vigilance on the part of auditors to avoid being involved in the auditing of companies in which they had a personal involvement. However, in **Re Employment Equality Bill 1996**, the Supreme Court held that the imposition on employers of vicarious liability for equality offences committed by employees without the knowledge of the employer, (i.e. they had no *mens rea*), was too great an imposition and was disproportionate to the social goal of the legislation.

Certain words, when used in statutes, suggest that *mens rea* is generally required. For example, adverbs such as 'intentionally' or 'recklessly' will always establish a *mens rea* requirement. Others such as 'knowingly', 'wilfully' or 'maliciously' will generally do so. Still others, however, such as 'causing', have sometimes been held not to establish *mens rea*. In **Maguire v. Shannon Regional Fisheries (1994)**, the High Court considered the meaning of this word in the context of section 171(1)(b) of the Fisheries (Consolidation) Act 1959, which makes it an offence to cause any deleterious matter to fall into any waters. It was held that the offence was made out whether or not it was done intentionally, recklessly, negligently or accidentally. Consequently, proof of *mens rea* was unnecessary. Similarly, in **DPP v. Behan (2003)**, the High Court ruled that the offence of failing to provide a breath specimen in section 13(1) of the Road Traffic Act 1994 was one of strict liability, even though section 23 of the same Act provided a defence to the charge that the defendant had a special and substantial reason for so failing. However, the courts have been somewhat inconsistent in their findings, making it difficult to predict in advance whether or not an offence is one of strict liability.

4.10 Vicarious Liability

Vicarious liability refers to the legal liability of one person for the actions of another, and is most commonly associated with tort. It arises most frequently when an employee commits a tort for which the employer is then held liable. The criminal version is much the same; an employer can be prosecuted for the crimes of an employee. This may apply even where the employer has no knowledge of the crime, or even where the employee has acted contrary to the employer's instructions. Where an employer is prosecuted in such circumstances, proof of *mens rea* on the part of the employer is clearly unnecessary.

Criminal vicarious liability is primarily centred on statute law; the general rule at common law was that no one could be held vicariously liable for the crimes of another person. In the old English case *R v. Huggins* (1730), it was held that 'the principal is not answerable for the act of the deputy as he is in civil cases; they must each answer for their own acts, and stand or fall by their own behaviour.' Common law did, however, recognise two exceptions to this general rule: in criminal libel, a publisher could be convicted in respect of an article published without his permission or knowledge; and an employer could be convicted where his employee created a public nuisance by causing substantial annoyance or inconvenience to others, again without his knowledge or permission.

Most offences that give rise to vicarious liability are created by statute and can arise in one of three ways. First, a statute can expressly impose vicarious liability for an offence. Second, a statute can imply vicarious liability. For example, in **M'adam v. Dublin United Tramways Corporation (1929)**, the defendant was charged with overloading a tram contrary to the Dublin Carriage Act 1853. The passengers had been allowed onto the tram by a conductor who had written instructions to obey the law. The District Court stated a case to the High Court which held that the owner of a tram was criminally liable for the overloading of the tram, even if done without the owner's knowledge. The High Court reached this conclusion by considering the purpose of the legislation:

> The object of the regulation is to protect the public against the danger that may result from the over-loading of an omnibus, and that object could be achieved only by absolutely prohibiting the carriage in any omnibus of more than a limited number of passengers, and by penalising the owner for any breach of such prohibition, irrespective of his knowledge of such a breach.

Further, the court noted that the offence in question was of a regulatory nature and not criminal in a real sense.

Third, where an employer is under a statutory duty to do something, and he delegates that duty to an employee, he will be responsible for any crime committed by the employee while carrying out that duty. In *Allen v. Whitehead* (1929), the owner of a public house left his manager with strict instructions that prostitutes were not to be allowed onto the premises, an instruction that was not followed. It was held by a Divisional Court that the legislature may sometimes prohibit an action absolutely, and that in doing so, the guilt of an employee must be imputed to his employer. The owner had delegated his duty and discretion, and was responsible for the manager's action. However, later cases have confirmed that the delegation must be complete; if an employer has retained any authority, then vicarious liability will not be imposed. In *Vane v. Yiannopoullos* (1964), an owner of a public house left a waitress instructions that only customers who were buying a meal could be served a drink, as required by the licence. The owner then retired to a basement in the premises. The waitress sold a drink to two customers who were not eating, and the owner was charged under the Licensing Act 1961. It was held, quashing his conviction, that before guilt on the part of the employee can be imputed to the employer through delegation, the employer must have delegated full managerial power to the employee. In this case, complete control had not been given to the waitress as the employer was still on the premises. A further issue was discussed by the Supreme Court in **DPP v. Roberts (1987)**. Here, the defendant was prosecuted for after-hours sales of alcohol in a hotel premises. The defendant held the licence but the premises was owned by a limited company, and the defendant had played no part in the running of the premises since her marriage several years earlier. A majority of the Supreme Court found that the defendant was the company's nominee for the purposes of renewing the licence in accordance with a long-standing practice. However, the company was deemed by the majority to be the real licensee, and it was the company that was responsible for the offences complained of rather than the defendant. Thus, despite the company having formally delegated the licence to the defendant, the delegation was for a specific purpose only that had nothing to do with the management of the premises, and the majority declined to extend criminal liability to the defendant.

4.11 Further Reading

Law Reform Commission, *Consultation Paper on Homicide: The Mental Element of Murder*, LRC CP17-2004.

Keane, 'Murder: The Mental Element', (2002) 53 *NILQ* 1.

McAleese, 'Just What is Recklessness?', (1981) 4 *DULJ* 29.

McAuley, '*Mens Rea*: A Legal-Philosophical View', (1982) 17 *Ir Jur (ns)* 84.

———, 'Modelling Intentional Action', (1988) 23 *Ir Jur (ns)* 218.

Stannard, 'Murder, Intention and the Inference of Intention', (1999) 34 *Ir Jur (ns)* 202.

Wilson, 'Doctrinal Rationality after *Woollin*', (1999) 62 *MLR* 448.

CHAPTER FIVE

COINCIDENCE OF *ACTUS REUS* AND *MENS REA*

5.1 Introduction

Both *actus reus* and *mens rea* must coincide in terms of time. In other words, when a person commits an unlawful act, he must have the necessary *mens rea* at that time. For example, suppose X is driving over to Y's house with a shotgun, intending to kill Y. On the way, he accidentally hits and kills a pedestrian, who turns out to be Y. X is not guilty of murder because at the time of the killing, he did not have the intention to kill or to cause serious injury. The situation would be different, however, if X saw Y walking along the pavement and deliberately swerved to hit him. In that case, at the time of the killing, X would have the necessary *mens rea*. The reason for this requirement of coincidence was set out in the old case of *Hales v. Pettit* (1563):

> For imagination of the mind to do wrong, without an act done, is not punishable in our law, neither is the resolution to do that wrong, which he does not, punishable, but the doing of the act is the only point which the law regards; for until the act is done it cannot be an offence to the world, and when the act is done it is punishable.

Thus, the law will not punish mere thoughts or intentions, no matter how morally culpable and repugnant they may be.

An overly literal application of this rule could have some very unjust results. For example, suppose that X commits a number of actions over a period of time that ultimately result in Y's death. Strictly speaking, finding a coincidence of *actus reus* and *mens rea* could be difficult, but an acquittal would be unjust. The law has developed a number of responses to such situations: the continuing act approach, the duty approach and the 'supposed corpse rule'. All of these approaches are somewhat artificial, and should be seen for what they are: an attempt by the law to balance principle with reality in order to avoid unjust decisions.

5.2 Continuing Act

Under the continuing act approach, a number of nominally separate acts can be seen as one continuing act. In *Fagan v. Metropolitan Police Commissioner* (1968), the defendant accidentally parked on a policeman's foot and then refused to move. He argued that he was not guilty of assault because his first action was accidental and therefore was not culpable, while his refusal to move the car (the second 'action'), which was culpable, could not constitute an assault. It was held by a Divisional Court that the assault was one continuing action that began with the accidental parking of the car on the policeman's foot, and ended with the removal of the car. The court further ruled that it is not necessary for the *mens rea* to be present at the 'inception of the *actus reus*; it can be superimposed on an existing act.' In other words, the *actus reus* comprised both the initial accident and the subsequent refusal to move the car. Consequently, the *mens rea* which developed with the refusal to move was able to coincide with the continuing *actus reus*. Similarly, in *Kaitamaki v. R* (1985), the defendant was having sexual intercourse with a woman under the mistaken impression that she was consenting. He realised that this was not the case, but did not withdraw. The relevant legislation provided that sexual intercourse for the purposes of a charge of rape was 'complete upon penetration', and the defendant argued that this provision meant that once penetration had occurred the *actus reus* of the offence was committed. As he had no *mens rea* at that time, believing the woman to be consenting to intercourse, he could not be convicted of rape. The Privy Council held, however, that the word 'complete' meant only that the required element of sexual intercourse was fulfilled once the prosecution had proven that penetration had occurred; the word did not mean that the intercourse was completed or finished. The *actus reus* of rape was a continuing action that began at penetration and ended at withdrawal. When the defendant realised that the woman was not consenting, but continued to have intercourse, he formed the *mens rea* necessary for rape. As the *actus reus* was still continuing, it was able to coincide with the *mens rea*.

5.3 Duty

As an alternative to the continuing act approach, the House of Lords has created a duty approach to the problem of coincidence. In *R v. Miller* (1983), the defendant was a squatter who fell asleep on a mattress while smoking a cigarette. He awoke to find the mattress on fire, but simply got up and went into another room and fell asleep again. He was charged with, and convicted of, arson on the grounds that having caused the fire, he was under a duty to try to put it out. The Court of Appeal upheld the conviction, but did so under the continuing action approach. The House of Lords again upheld the conviction, and discussed the two approaches. It was held that the duty approach was preferable as it would cause less confusion to a jury. Thus, when a person accidentally sets a certain event in motion, he has a legal duty to take reasonable measures to counter that event; failure to discharge this legal duty constitutes the *actus reus* and, as the person is at that point aware of the event that he caused, he has *mens rea* and can be convicted. It is worth noting that the courts in both *Fagan* and *Kaitamaki* could easily have reached the same decision under the duty approach. Nevertheless, given that *Kaitamaki* was decided after *Miller*, it would seem that the courts may still use the continuing act approach.

5.4   The 'Supposed Corpse Rule'

Suppose X strikes Y over the head with a club, with the intent to kill. Y falls to the ground unconscious, but X believes him to be dead. An hour later, X decides to make the 'death' look like an accident by placing the 'body' on the rail tracks in front of an oncoming train. Unknown to X, it is only when the train strikes him that Y dies. There are two distinct actions involved: the first was when X struck Y with the club, the second was when X placed Y on the railway tracks. In the first action, X has *mens rea* because he intended to kill Y, but he has no *actus reus* because Y did not die. In the second action, there is an *actus reus* because Y died, but X has no *mens rea* because, believing Y to already be dead, X could hardly have intended to kill or cause serious injury. The continuing act and duty approaches to the problem of coincidence will not work in this situation: as to the first, there is clearly no continuing action, and as to the second, arguing that having knocked Y unconscious, X was under a duty not to put his body in the path of an oncoming train is artificial to the point of absurdity. Strictly speaking, therefore, X is not guilty of murder, and can only be convicted of attempted murder. This would obviously be a very unjust result that would allow X to quite literally get away with murder. The 'supposed corpse rule' has been developed by the English courts to get over this problem.

In *Thabo Meli v. R* (1954), the defendant and others seriously assaulted the deceased and believed that they had killed him. They then threw the body over a cliff, but it was the fall and the resulting exposure that actually killed the deceased. It was held that these actions were part of a preconceived plan and could not therefore be viewed as two separate actions; rather, both actions were part of a continuing transaction. As both the *actus reus* and the *mens rea* were present during the transaction, the defendant's conviction was upheld. The key to the decision in *Thabo Meli* was the existence of a preconceived plan. Where such a plan is shown to exist, there is a certain logic to viewing all the elements of that plan together: as was said in *R v. Ramsay* (1967), the plan suggests 'a dominating intention running throughout a series of acts which can fairly be taken as the intention actuating the fatal act.' However, suppose there was no preconceived plan and the defendant's subsequent action was borne out of panic – can he be convicted? In *Ramsey*, the New Zealand Court of Appeal ruled that *Thabo Meli* had no application to a case in which there was no evidence of an underlying plan. In *R v. Church* (1965), however, the English Court of Appeal appeared to come to a different conclusion. The defendant had assaulted a woman who had been taunting him and knocked her unconscious. He had been unable to revive her and, in a panic, threw her body into a river. A post-mortem later showed that she had died from drowning rather than from the assault, as the defendant had believed. The jury was directed that unless the prosecution had proven that the defendant knew that the woman was still alive when he threw her into the river, a conviction for murder was not permitted. The Court of Criminal Appeal held that this direction was 'unduly benevolent' to the defendant: on the basis of the reasoning in *Thabo Meli*, a murder conviction was possible if the jury concluded that the two actions were part of a series of acts designed to cause death or grievous bodily harm. However, there was no evidence of a preconceived plan, and the court did not explain why two separate actions could be viewed as one transaction where there was no such plan. Some light was thrown on the matter, however, in *R v. Le Brun* (1991). In that case, the defendant and his wife had been to a friend's house, and were on their way home. A heated argument developed, during which the defendant punched his wife, knocking her down. He then tried to move her body in order to prevent detection, but in trying to lift her, he accidentally dropped her, which caused her death. Again there was no evidence of a preconceived plan, and indeed the defendant did not believe that the initial assault had caused the deceased's death. The conviction for manslaughter was upheld on the basis of the two actions being one transaction. The fact that there was an interval between the two actions did not of itself affect this, nor did the lack of a preconceived plan. Where the second event is designed to cover or conceal the first event, a single transaction can easily be established. It is not clear, however, what would have happened if the second action had been designed to assist the victim (such as by trying to take her to a hospital), rather than to avoid detection, but it is suggested that so doing would break the chain of causation, rendering the defendant not guilty of homicide.

5.5   Further Reading

Marston, 'Contemporaneity of Act and Intention', (1970) 86 *LQR* 208.

Stannard, 'Stretching Out the *Actus Reus*', (1993–95) 28–30 *Ir Jur (ns)* 200.

Sullivan, 'Cause and Contemporaneity of *Actus Reus* and *Mens Rea*', [1993] *Cambridge LJ* 487.

CHAPTER SIX

PARTICIPATION IN A CRIME

6.1 Introduction

A person who commits an offence is traditionally known as the principal offender. However, the law has always recognised that principal offenders may have had help, and indeed, very often the offence could not have been committed without such help. Accordingly, criminal liability stretches to cover not only the principal offender but also those who provide the principal with assistance, either before, during or after the commission of a offence. These offenders have traditionally been known as accessories. Thus, common law recognised four degrees of participation in a offence:

(a) principal in the first degree, who was the actual perpetrator of the offence;
(b) principal in the second degree, who aided and abetted the commission of the offence at the time of its commission;
(c) accessory before the fact, who assisted in the commission of the offence before its commission; and
(d) accessory after the fact, who knowingly provided assistance to a felon.

The first three categories applied to felonies and misdemeanors equally, while the fourth applied only to felonies. However, the common law view of secondary participation has been largely overtaken by statute: the Criminal Law Act 1997 provides that anyone who aids, abets, counsels or procures the commission of an indictable offence is liable to be indicted, tried and punished in the same way as a principal offender.

PRINCIPAL LIABILITY

6.2 Introduction

It is a cardinal rule of common law conceptions of criminal liability that such liability is imposed on a personal basis only; the common law has been reluctant to impose liability on one person for the actions of another (see section 4.10). If criminal liability is a personal liability, then it follows that criminal liability can be imposed only on an entity that has a personality recognised by law. In most cases, offences are committed by individuals, acting either on their own or in concert with others. However, the law has also had to confront the possibility of criminal actions being committed by entities other than human individuals: incorporated companies that exist legally independently of their owners and employees, and unincorporated groups that have no legal standing.

6.3 Corporate Criminal Liability

The common law has always had difficulty accommodating the view that a non-human entity can commit an offence. The closest to such an accommodation that the common law got until recently was the concept of the deodand. Anglo-Saxon law recognised that inanimate objects and animals could cause death, and in such cases, the object – the deodand – or its value was forfeit to the Crown to be used for pious purposes. This concept was still in use in the 1840s: in *R v. Semini* (1949), Lord Goddard C.J. noted a case in that period in which the London and Birmingham Railway Company had to pay the sum of £2,000 as the value of a railway engine that ran over and killed a man. The deodand was abolished by statute in 1846.

Aside from the deodand, the common law did not recognise that non-human entities could commit criminal offences and suffer punishment for so doing. However, following the famous decision of the House of Lords in *Salomon v. Salomon & Co.* (1897), incorporated companies were definitively recognised by law as having the same legal existence as human beings. Thus, a company was a 'person' as far as the law was concerned, and could be made criminally liable under the terms of a statute. There are now numerous instances of companies being subject to criminal sanctions for breaches of statutory duties under health and safety legislation, competition laws and the Companies Acts. Further, in 2001, the Company Law Enforcement Act established the Office of Director of Corporate Enforcement with the specific power to enforce the penal elements of the Companies Acts. However, these statutes impose criminal liability only in specific instances; they do not provide a general basis for criminal liability to be attached to companies, especially for common law offences such as manslaughter. One of the principal difficulties in prosecuting companies for such offences is the common law requirement of *mens rea*: how can a company have a culpable state of mind? In *R v. ICR Haulage* (1944), the Court of Criminal Appeal suggested that in some circumstances the knowledge or intention of an agent of a company could be attributed to the company itself. However, it was not until the latter half of the twentieth century that this attribution approach evolved into a definitive test.

In *HL Bolton (Engineering) Co. Ltd v. TJ Graham & Sons* (1957), Denning L.J. set out the controlling mind test for corporate criminal liability:

> A company may in many ways be likened to a human body. They have a brain and nerve centre which controls what they do. They also have hands which hold the tools and act in accordance with directions from the centre. Some of the people in the company are mere servants and agents who are nothing more than hands to do the work and cannot be said to represent the directing mind or will. Others are directors and managers who represent the directing mind and will of the company, and control what they do. The state of mind of these managers is the state of mind of the company and is treated by the law as such.

In *Tesco Supermarkets v. Natrass* (1971), Lord Reid acknowledged the 'personality which by a fiction the law attributes to a corporation'. He upheld Denning L.J.'s comments in *HL Bolton*, but specifically rejected any attempt to include any lower-level managers within the concept of a controlling mind. Instead, Lord Reid limited the test to the board of directors, the managing director and other superior officers who 'carry out the functions of management and speak and act for the company.' It is these people alone whose minds can be identified with the company. Thus, if the controlling mind is culpable, then the company is similarly culpable. By this process of identification, the common law requirement of *mens rea* can be maintained even against a company that in reality has no mind of its own.

It has become clear since these decisions that the controlling mind test, while overcoming the problem of *mens rea*, has created problems of its own. In particular, most prosecutions for corporate manslaughter have failed because the prosecution has been unable to find a person who is sufficiently high in the corporate chain to be considered a controlling mind, but who is also low enough in the chain to have personal responsibility for the procedures and processes that brought about the offence in question. In effect, the prosecution falls between the two stools of controlling mind and personal fault. The real problem is that the controlling mind test is built on a vision of corporate governance that is at once simplistic and outdated. It assumes direct and close connections between the upper levels of management and the actual workings of the company at the shop floor level, such that both control and responsibility will be vested in the same people. In small companies, this assumption is not unwarranted, and it is worth noting that the first successful prosecution for corporate manslaughter in English legal history was brought against a one-man company (*R v. Kite and OLL* (1994)). In larger, more complex companies, however, the controlling minds are likely to be so divorced from the day-to-day operations of the company as to have no direct responsibility for the incidents. Thus, in *R v. P & O Ferries* (1991), a prosecution was brought against P & O Ferries for manslaughter in respect of the deaths caused when the ferry *Herald of Free Enterprise* capsized outside Zeebrugge harbour. The prosecution named several employees as well as the company, and two of these employees had sufficient seniority to satisfy the controlling mind test. The trial court ruled that an indictment for manslaughter could be laid against the company, and rejected the company's contention that homicide could be committed only by a human being. However, the trial judge ended proceedings before the prosecution had even presented its case on the basis that there was no evidence of sufficient responsibility on the part of the controlling minds to allow for attribution of criminal liability to the company.

In recognition of these problems, attempts have been made to expand the test for corporate criminal liability. In *P & O Ferries* itself, an attempt was made by the prosecution to base liability on a principle of aggregation. This principle would allow the court to add together all the individual culpable acts of employees of the company being prosecuted, and if the aggregate of those acts reached the standard of fault required, i.e. negligence or recklessness, then the company could be found liable. However, Turner J. ruled that the proposed principle of aggregation went against rulings from the House of Lords and was not part of the common law. A similar argument in *Attorney General's Reference No.2 of 1999* (2000) failed for the same reason.

A second attempt to expand corporate liability was also rejected by the Court of Appeal in *Attorney General's Reference No.2 of 1999*. This case grew out of a failed prosecution for manslaughter brought against Great Western Railway Co. in respect of a serious collision between two trains that resulted in seven deaths and numerous serious injuries. An enquiry found that the defendant company had rostered only one train driver, and that he had been distracted when the collision occurred. There was also evidence that the train in question was equipped with two anti-collision alarms, neither of which had been switched on. There was further evidence that the company encouraged train drivers to leave on time even if safety equipment was not working. Thus, there was ample evidence of negligence. The Attorney General made two principal arguments. First, since the House of Lords' decision in *R v. Adomako* (1994), the *mens rea* of gross negligence manslaughter was entirely objective. Accordingly, it was now unnecessary to attribute a state of mind to the company. Rather, it was sufficient that the company had failed to discharge its duty of care to its passengers and that the failure had caused death and was of such a degree as to constitute gross negligence. Second, the Attorney General argued that if state of mind was irrelevant in a prosecution for manslaughter against a human, then it should be equally irrelevant in a similar case against a company. The Attorney General further argued that the public interest required the sort of emphatic denunciation of a company that has caused death that is inherent in a manslaughter conviction, and argued that there was authority for either dispensing with the controlling mind test or at least broadening it. In *Meridian Global Funds Management v. Securities Commission* (1995), a successful prosecution had been brought by the Securities Commission in respect of an acquisition of shares that had not been notified to the Commission as required by statute. Lord Hoffman ruled that the purpose of the legislation was to compel immediate disclosure to the regulatory body of the identity of people who became substantial security holders in public issuers. To achieve this purpose, it would be necessary to attribute to the company the mind of the person acquiring the interest in question: the 'company knows that it has become a substantial security holder when that is known to the person authorised to do the deal.' Lord Hoffman did not limit this attribution to company directors. Similarly, in *R v. British Steel* (1995), the Court of Appeal ruled that the proper application of safety at work legislation was not necessarily dependent upon the controlling mind doctrine. Steyn L.J. ruled that 'it would drive a juggernaut through the legislative scheme if corporate employers could avoid criminal liability where the potentially harmful event is committed by someone who is not the directing mind.'

The Court of Appeal accepted that proof as to the defendant's state of mind is not a prerequisite to conviction for gross negligence manslaughter. However, the Court of Appeal held that the decision in *Adomako* was an attempt to clarify the law on gross negligence only, and the decision there did not impact on the existing requirements for corporate manslaughter. *Meridien* and *British Steel* were distinguished on the basis that they concerned prosecutions derived from statutory offences, the proper construction of which excluded the controlling mind doctrine. The Court of Appeal concluded that it had no authority to expand the application of corporate manslaughter beyond the controlling mind test.

6.4 Unincorporated Associations

Unincorporated bodies, such as clubs and associations, are not generally recognised by the law as having an existence independent of their members. Thus, legally, such bodies do not exist, and therefore at common law cannot commit an offence. As a result, a prosecution for a common law offence can be brought only against individual members of the group rather than against the group as a whole: in *Attorney General v. Able* (1984), Woolf J. held that 'there can be no question of [an unincorporated] society committing an offence.' However, it is clear that statute can impose criminal liability on the group itself. This was confirmed by the High Court in *DPP v. Wexford Farmers Club* **(1994)**. There, O'Hanlon J. ruled that section 45 of the Intoxicating Liquor Act 1988 allowed for the imposition of criminal liability on an unincorporated club for advertising a club function in breach of that provision.

SECONDARY PARTICIPATION

6.5 Statutory Forms of Secondary Liability

The Criminal Law Act 1997 provides that a person is a secondary participant in the commission of a crime if he aids, abets, counsels or procures the commission of that offence, and that a secondary participant should be treated by the courts as a principal offender. The initial question is, what do these terms actually mean? This issue occupied the Court of Appeal in *Attorney General's Reference No.1 of 1975* (1975), which considered the meaning of those terms as they appeared in the Accessories and Abettors Act 1861. The court stated:

> We approach s.8 of the Act of 1861 on the basis that the words should be given their ordinary meaning, if possible. We approach the section on the basis that if four words are employed here, 'aid, abet, counsel or procure', the probability is that there is a difference between each of those four words and the other three, because, if

there was no such difference, then Parliament would be wasting time in using four words where two or three would do.

The logic of this approach is impeccable: by using four different words, it is reasonable to assume that the legislature intended the four different words used in the 1997 Act to have distinct meanings and to cover distinct forms of conduct. However, as will be seen in the following paragraphs, the approach of the courts has been largely to treat the words as interchangeable. Indeed, the court in *Attorney General v. Able* (1984) preferred to look at the four words as a single entity meaning 'helping'. Thus, it is far from clear that the courts will apply different meanings to these words.

Aiding and Abetting

Aiding and abetting are almost always taken together. In general, to aid and abet the commission of a crime will require that the secondary participant be present at the scene of the crime. In this respect, one is aiding and abetting where one gives assistance or encouragement to the principal offender while the crime is being committed. However, this is not always the case. In *Gillick v. West Norfolk and Wisbech Area Health Authority* (1985), the House of Lords considered whether or not a doctor could lawfully prescribe contraceptives for an under-age girl without the consent of her parents, which was allowed in exceptional circumstances by UK government guidelines. One particular issue was whether such a doctor could be said to have aided and abetted the commission of unlawful sexual intercourse. The Lords decided that such a crime could be committed depending on the doctor's intention; aiding and abetting would not occur if the doctor honestly acted in the best interests of the girl in prescribing contraceptives. However, it is worthy of note that the Lords felt that aiding and abetting could occur even though the doctor would not be present when the offence of unlawful sexual intercourse was committed. This decision effectively took the concept of aiding and abetting into the realm of counselling and procuring, and is illustrative of the fact that the Court of Appeal's approach in *Attorney General's Reference No.1 of 1975* has not commanded widespread respect.

Counselling

Counselling generally refers to help or advice given prior to the commission of the offence. The precise form of help required to fulfil the definition of counselling is unclear, but, in common with all other forms of secondary participation, it seems to be quite minimal. It does not have to be shown that there is a causal connection between the assistance given and the commission of a crime. So if X advises Y that the best way to kill Z is by poisoning him, but Y decides in the end to shoot Z instead, X has still given counseling towards the commission of an offence. Thus, in *R v. Calhaem* (1985), the defendant had been convicted of murder. The defendant was infatuated with her solicitor, and had instructed a man to kill a woman who was supposedly having an affair with the solicitor. The prosecution case was that the defendant had counselled or procured the murder. She appealed on the grounds that there was no causal connection, on the facts, between anything she might have said to the man and what actually happened, and therefore she could not be said to have counselled the murder. The Court of Appeal gave the word 'counselling' its ordinary meaning, and stated that counselling meant to '"advise", "solicit", or something of that sort'. The court also decided that no causal connection as such was required. All that was required was that the prosecution show a contact of some sort between the defendant and the man, and that the man acted within the scope of that contact. To that extent, there must have been a connection between the counselling and the offence. Beyond that, however, there was no need for the prosecution to prove a causal connection. Incidentally, this case also demonstrates the overlap between counselling and procuring, in that the defendant's actions clearly constitute what would normally be considered procuring.

Procuring

Procuring means to bring about a desired result through one's efforts. Suppose X wishes the death of Z, and to that end, he hires Y to do the killing and supplies Y with Z's address and picture. X's actions clearly come within the ambit of 'procuring', in that he not only desires Z's death, but also takes steps to bring about that result. However, it is clear that no formal agreement is required, and indeed the other party may be entirely unaware of the effort. In *Attorney General's Reference No.1 of 1975* (1975), the defendant had 'spiked' a friend's drinks with significant quantities of spirits. The friend was arrested for being over the limit while driving home. The defendant was charged with being a secondary participant in the offence of driving with an excess quantity of alcohol in the blood. The Court of Appeal held that procuring does not require a conspiracy or agreement between the procurer and the principal offender. In this case, the defendant had spiked his friend's drinks without the knowledge of the friend, thereby ensuring that the friend was not in a position to prevent the commission of the offence. In these circumstances, it was clear that the defendant had procured the commission of the offence. Accordingly, the court had no difficulty in upholding the conviction.

6.6 Basis of Secondary Liability

Before secondary liability can be imposed, there must be proof that an offence has been committed. In this respect, secondary liability differs from the inchoate offences, i.e. attempts, conspiracy and incitement (see Chapters 15, 16 and 17, respectively) in that the latter can be committed irrespective of the commission of

106

the full offence. Thus, if X wishes to kill Z, and hires Y to do the killing, but Y does not in fact do so, X can be charged with incitement or conspiracy, but not as a secondary participant. In *Thornton v. Mitchell* (1940), a bus driver was charged with careless driving and a conductor was charged as a secondary participant. The driver had been reversing his bus, and had been relying on the directions given to him by the conductor. The conductor, however, failed to see two pedestrians standing behind the bus, and both were injured. The driver was acquitted on the basis that he had not been careless, but the conductor had still been convicted as a secondary party. The High Court held that in effect this penalised the conductor for aiding and abetting 'the driver in doing something which had not been done', and quashed the conviction.

Once the commission of a crime can be shown, charges of secondary complicity may be brought, even where the principal offender is either unknown or acquitted. In *R v. Bourne* (1952), the defendant had on two occasions forced his wife to commit buggery with a dog, which was an offence. The wife was not charged, but the defendant was convicted of aiding and abetting the commission of buggery, and appealed. The Court of Criminal Appeal was content to allow the prosecution to argue that not charging the wife as the principal offender was not fatal because had she been charged, she would have been able to secure an acquittal on the basis of duress (see Chapter 10). As duress allows an excuse from criminal liability due to threats, the lack of a conviction against the wife would not have meant that no offence had been committed, only that she was excused from responsibility for it. Thus, the offence of buggery had been committed, and the defendant had clearly been an accessory to it. His appeal was consequently dismissed. Similarly, in *R v. Cogan and Leak* (1975), Leak had compelled his wife to have sexual intercourse with Cogan, who believed that the woman was consenting. Cogan, accordingly, was acquitted of rape, but Leak was convicted of aiding and abetting a rape. He appealed on the basis that he could not suffer secondary liability, as the principal offender had been acquitted. The Court of Appeal noted that the wife had been raped in that she had not consented to the intercourse, and that this had happened as a result of Leak. He had accordingly procured the commission of the offence, and his conviction was upheld (this is another example of the interchangeability of aiding, abetting and procuring). The principal offender in cases such as *Bourne* and *Cogan and Leak* are excused from any criminal liability for their actions, usually on the basis that they lack *mens rea*. In such cases, the person who actually commits the offence is known as an innocent agent. In *R v. Stringer* (1991), Woolf L.J. approved the following definition of an innocent agent:

> A person acts through an innocent agent when he intentionally causes the external elements of the offence to be committed by (or partly by) a person who is himself innocent of the offence charged by reason of lack of a required fault element or a lack of capacity.

Finally, by virtue of section 7(3) of the Criminal Law Act 1997, if a person is charged with an arrestable offence which is shown to have been committed, but there is not enough evidence to convict him as a principal offender, he may, if the evidence warrants it, be convicted under section 7(2) instead (acting with the intent of impeding the arrest of a principal offender).

6.7 *Actus Reus*

Irrespective of the meaning given to the four forms of participation, i.e. whether they have distinct meanings or are interchangeable, there must be proof of actual assistance given to the principal offender.

The kind of act required varies from case to case, and the cases discussed already give a number of different actions that have resulted in the imposition of liability. In *R v. Brown* (1968), an Australian case, the defendant's action was a simple cough which acted as a warning to the killer that the victim was leaving his room and was vulnerable to attack. The cough was therefore intended to assist in the commission of a murder. Similarly, in *R v. Gianetto* (1996), the Court of Appeal held that any involvement in a crime 'from encouragement upwards would suffice' for a conviction. In that case, the trial judge, in his summation to the jury, had stated as an example that if someone had told the defendant that he was going to kill the defendant's wife, and the defendant had patted him on the back, nodded and said 'Oh goody', that would have been sufficient for a conviction. These cases not only demonstrate that minor acts can constitute the *actus reus* of secondary participation, but that the accessory's act must have been of assistance to the principal in committing the offence.

Generally speaking, a failure to act, such as merely being at the scene of a crime or not preventing the commission of a crime, does not give rise to secondary liability. So, if X stands by eating popcorn while watching the murder of a child, he generally commits no crime. However, this is not always the case. In *R v. Clarkson* (1971), a woman, recently out of hospital, went to a party given by members of the British army on duty in Germany. While there, she was raped violently by a number of soldiers. At some point during the rapes, a number of other soldiers, including the appellants, entered the room eagerly, having heard the woman's screams, and remained there for some time. Some even assisted by holding the woman down. The appellants, however, apparently had not committed any such positive act to assist the rapes. The Courts-Martial Appeal Court acknowledged that if their convictions for aiding and abetting were to be upheld, inferences would have to be drawn from their mere presence. It was accepted that their presence was not accidental, they having entered the room because they had heard the woman screaming. However, this was not enough; the fact that the offenders derived encouragement from the presence of the appellants did not make them guilty. It would also have to be shown that the appellants intended their presence to encourage the commission of the crime. If that was so, secondary liability could be imposed on the apellants on the basis of their mere presence.

A failure to act may also constitute secondary participation where the defendant is under a duty to act or is in a position of authority. So, if a garda stood by and watched as a child was murdered, liability could be imposed upon him. In *Tuck v. Robson* (1970), the owner of a pub allowed a customer to continue drinking after closing time, thereby breaching the licensing laws. The publican's failure to act was held to constitute aiding and abetting as he was in control of the premises, knew of the situation and was under a legal duty to act. Similarly, in *R v. Dytham* (1979), the defendant was a police officer who watched as a man was kicked to death and did nothing to intervene. He was convicted of misconduct in a public office, but it is submitted that on the facts, he could have been charged with complicity in the murder.

6.8 *Mens Rea*

As with liability for most offences, secondary liability cannot be imposed in the absence of *mens rea*. Indeed, *mens rea* can turn innocent presence at the scene of the crime into active participation, as noted in *Clarkson*. However, the *mens rea* requirement for secondary participation is the subject of considerable conflict in the authorities. All agree that the defendant must be shown to have offered his participation intentionally; recklessness or negligence will not be sufficient. Additionally, all agree that the secondary party must have some knowledge or foresight of the offence planned. The authorities are in conflict, however, as to the degree of knowledge required by the defendant of the principal's plans. Irish authorities suggest that the defendant must know the nature of the planned offence, although it is not necessary that he know the precise details or means by which the offence is to be carried out. Other authorities suggest that if the defendant knows that the principal *might* commit a particular offence, the defendant can be convicted of complicity in that offence, thereby casting the net more widely.

Intention

In *Clarkson*, the Courts-Martial Appeal Court held that it was not sufficient that the offenders derived encouragement from the presence of the defendant; it would also have to be shown that the defendant intended to give encouragement or wilfully gave encouragement. The position is the same in the Irish authorities. Thus, in **The People (Attorney General) v. Ryan (1966)**, the defendant was convicted of aiding and abetting a murder. The defendant and two others had been involved in an altercation with another group of people who were attending a dance. Some time later, after the dance had ended, the two groups met again, the defendant's group being armed with various car tools. The ringleader of the defendant's group killed one member of the other group and seriously injured another. The evidence indicated that the defendant had been one of the men who had been armed. The Court of Criminal Appeal approved the direction of the trial judge who had said that the jury must be satisfied the defendant had been knowingly giving the ringleader encouragement. If that was the case, then simply standing around with a weapon in his hand could constitute an act sufficient to impose liability. However, it is not necessary for the prosecution to prove that the defendant intended to go through with the planned offence. In *R v. Rook* (1993), the defendant was part of a plan to kill another man, but on the day of the killing he did not turn up. He argued that he had never intended to go through with his part of the killing. This was found by the Court of Appeal to be irrelevant because the defendant had intended to assist or encourage the commission of the crime and had believed that the offence probably would be committed. The court ruled further that to withdraw from participation, the defendant should give timely notice to the other participants that he does not intend to go through with his part of the plan unless it was impracticable for him to do so.

Knowledge

The first element of *mens rea*, therefore, is that the encouragement or assistance is given intentionally. This will, in practical terms, protect the person who innocently stumbles across a crime scene. All the authorities are agreed that this element is essential. However, some disagreement arises as to the second aspect of *mens rea* – the degree of knowledge that the defendant must have as to the intentions of the principal offender. Some degree of knowledge is essential. So, if X helps Y believing that Y only intends to steal from Z, but Y kills Z, liability should not be imposed on X for murder. In *DPP for Northern Ireland v. Maxwell* (1978), the defendant was a member of the UVF. He was told to take his car and guide some other men in a following car to a public house. The men in the following car threw a bomb at the building, but the owner's son was able to foil the attack by picking up the bomb and throwing it away. The defendant was convicted of doing an act with intent to cause an explosion likely to endanger life, and appealed. He argued that he was only involved in the UVF in respect of welfare matters rather than military operations, and that he had had no idea what the purpose of this operation was going to be. The House of Lords held that a defendant cannot be convicted of aiding and abetting unless he knows what is intended. It was unnecessary, however, for the defendant to have knowledge of the intended crime, and he could be convicted for any offence that he had contemplated. The House held that this defendant, being a member of an organisation that continually performs acts of violence, must have known that he was on a military operation, and that the operation would involve the use of bombs, guns or incendiary devices. Because of this knowledge, he assisted in whatever form the attack took, and his conviction was accordingly upheld.

The position in Ireland is more restricted. In ***The People (DPP) v. Madden*** (**1977**), the defendants had been convicted of aiding and abetting the murder of a man in Cork by machine-gun fire. The Court of Criminal Appeal held that it was necessary to establish that the defendants had intentionally given assistance to the commission of a crime of which they had known, or the commission of a crime of a similar nature. This matter was again visited by the Court of Criminal Appeal in *The People (DPP) v. Egan* (**1989**). The defendant was told that 'a small stroke' was planned and was asked to make his garage available, a request to which he agreed to participate in. As it happened, what was planned was an armed robbery. The defendant argued that while he had known that a theft was planned, he had not known that it was going to be an armed robbery, something to which he would never have agreed. It was held, on the basis of *Maxwell* and *Madden*, that it was not necessary to show that he had known the precise means of the theft; all the prosecution had to do was show that he knew the nature of the intended crime. As the defendant had known that some form of theft would occur, the conviction should stand. Despite the apparent endorsement of *Maxwell* in *Egan*, it would seem that the English position is capable of being interpreted more widely. For example, the guns, bombs or incendiary devices referred to in *Maxwell* might have been used for a robbery, an offence that is entirely different in nature to that of causing an explosion. A robbery might, however, conceivably have been contemplated by the defendant. It would seem that given the defendant's knowledge of the UVF's operations, and the inferences that could be drawn from that knowledge, he would be guilty of either offence. Under *Egan*, however, it would be necessary to show that the defendant knew the nature of the offence; knowledge of violent activities alone would not be sufficient.

There is considerable English authority to the effect that a secondary participant can be convicted as a principal offender for the commission of an offence incidental to the one planned. For example, X is assisting Y in a burglary, and Y is carrying a gun intending only to use it as a threat. If X foresees that Y might use it to kill, and Y subsequently does intentionally kill, X can be convicted of murder on the basis of his foresight. This is implicit in the *Maxwell* judgment, and has arisen in other decisions. These decisions, however, have mainly arisen in cases involving the doctrine of common design (discussed below – section 6.10). Under this doctrine, some English decisions have suggested that a secondary party who contemplates the commission of an offence by the principal ancillary to the original offence is guilty of that ancillary offence if it is committed.

However, in *R v. Powell; R v. English* (1997), the House of Lords, in dealing with two cases of common design, confirmed the existence of a principle in secondary participation under which the participant can be convicted of an incidental offence if he foresaw that the principal may commit that other offence. In such cases, it is irrelevant that the secondary party has not agreed to the commission of the further offence. Ni Raifeartaigh suggests that there is also dictum in *The People (Attorney General) v. Ryan* (**1966**) to support this view. The Court of Criminal Appeal in that case said that the defendant must have contemplated the principal using a weapon on any member of the other party that he met, and that such contemplation was sufficient to attach liability to him.[1] However, this dictum is not in line with the English decisions in that using the weapon was not incidental to the original offence; using the weapon was part of the original offence. The English decisions, however, involve liability for offences that are not necessarily connected to the original offence. This approach is difficult to defend, certainly where the ancillary offence requires proof of intention. If the offence requires proof of recklessness only, as in rape, for example, it could be argued that the secondary party acted recklessly where he foresaw that the offence might occur but went along with it anyway. Where the incidental offence requires proof of intention, however, such a justification cannot be maintained, for two reasons. First, as noted in Chapter 4, foresight is not intention, nor is it even evidence from which intention can be inferred unless the defendant foresees the consequence as a virtual certainty. So far, the English courts have not insisted on such a high standard of foresight in secondary participation cases. Indeed, in *Rook*, it was held that the standard was satisfied by showing that the risk of the offence was substantial. Yet, this very same test was rejected by the House of Lords in *R v. Woollin* (1998) as expanding the scope of oblique intention too far (see section 4.3). Second, the effect of these decisions is that liability may be imposed on a participant on a standard that is lower than that required to convict the principal. In *Powell*, Lord Hutton accepted the force of this argument in terms of logic, but argued that logic is not the sole basis for law. There may be times, and this was found to be one of them, when logic must give way to practical concerns such as the need to give effective protection to the public against criminal gangs. However, on the other hand, if one accepts Lord Hutton's point, the virtual certainty test endorsed in *Woollin* makes little sense, as it sets the standard for *mens rea* so high as to make the protection of the public more difficult. Additionally, it is difficult to reconcile the difference in treatment between principals and participants with the clear wording of the Criminal Law Act 1997, that anyone who aids, etc. the commission of indictable offence is liable to be indicted, tried and punished *in the same way as the principal offender* (emphasis added). Consequently, it is submitted that the standard required in *Powell* is too low for the imposition of secondary liability for an offence requiring proof of intention.

6.9   Accessories After the Fact

As far as accessories after the fact are concerned, section 7(2) of the 1997 Act provides that if a person believes another person to have committed an arrestable offence, any action done with the intent of preventing the arrest of that person is an offence. In effect, this provision simply updates the common law definition of an accessory after the fact.

---

1 Ni Raifeartaigh, 'The Mental Element of Accessories to Murder', (1994) 4 *ICLJ* 31.

6.10 The Doctrine of Common Design

The doctrine of common design (or joint enterprise, as it is also known) applies to situations in which a number of individuals act in concert to achieve an unlawful common goal. The doctrine holds that each party to a common unlawful purpose is fully liable for all the acts done by the other parties in furtherance of that purpose. By agreeing to such a purpose, all participants clearly intend to commit whatever actions are required to achieve that purpose, subject to any agreed limitations. Accordingly, each participant has the moral fault necessary to justify a conviction for all offences involved in bringing the agreed enterprise to fruition. Included are any consequences that are related to the enterprise; thus, in a common design to rob a bank, the shooting of a bank security guard would normally be included in the common design, as this action is related to the enterprise, and all participants will be guilty of murder. However, if one of the participants to the robbery takes the opportunity to rape a female bank teller, he must bear responsibility for that action alone as it goes beyond what was agreed and is therefore unrelated to the agreed enterprise.

It is not clear whether common design is distinct from secondary liability or is merely a form of secondary liability. At a conceptual level, the two approaches to the attachment of criminal liability to members of a group seem to be distinct. As the Court of Appeal noted in *R v. Stewart and Schofield* (1995):

> A person who is a mere aider and abetter, etc. is truly a secondary party to the commission of whatever crime it is that the principal has committed although he may be charged as a principal ... In contrast, where the allegation is joint enterprise, the allegation is that one defendant participated in the criminal act of another. This is a different principle.

In other words, with common design, the parties *are* principals, whereas with secondary participation, the parties are *treated* as principals. Thus, if X, Y and Z jointly agree to rob a bank, the doctrine of common design arises, but if X hires Y and Z to help him rob a bank, secondary liability should arise with respect to Y and Z. However, making the distinction can be difficult in practice as common design and secondary liability clearly cover similar ground; in either of the examples just given, an external observer would simply conclude that three men robbed a bank. The case law is mixed. In *R v. Powell; R v. English* (1998), the House of Lords, in its approach and in its language, effectively subsumed common design into secondary liability, thereby removing any real meaning to the phrase 'common design'. But in *R v. Bryce* (2004), the Court of Appeal ruled that a distinction must be made between secondary participants and parties to a joint enterprise, holding that special rules apply to the latter. In *The People (DPP) v. Doohan* (**2002**), the defendant had hired a co-defendant to beat up the deceased, but the co-defendant shot the deceased with a shotgun. The Court of Criminal Appeal upheld the defendant's conviction on the basis of a common

113

design, yet his actions more properly constituted an archetypal example of procuring the commission of an offence under the Criminal Law Act 1997. Thus, the relationship between common design and secondary participation remains unclear.

Limits of a Common Design

The leading formulation of the doctrine of common design was provided by the Court of Criminal Appeal in *R v. Anderson and Morris* (1966):

> Where two persons embark on a joint enterprise, each is liable for the acts done in pursuance of that joint enterprise … that includes unusual consequences if they arise from the execution of the agreed joint enterprise but if … one of the adventurers goes beyond what has been tacitly agreed as part of the common enterprise, his co-adventurer is not liable for the consequences of that unauthorised act.

This statement neatly covers all of the major points in the doctrine, and was specifically endorsed by the Court of Criminal Appeal in *The People (DPP) v. Cumberton* (1994). The starting point for the jury is whether the defendant was involved in a common design. The phrase 'common design' suggests a degree of planning, but it is clear that a common design can arise through spontaneous concerted actions. In *R v. Uddin* (1998), the Court of Appeal accepted that the 'spontaneous behaviour of a group of irrational individuals who jointly attack a common victim' could constitute a joint enterprise, depending on the foresight of the participants. What is important is that the participants act in concert according to a common goal. So, in *R v. Petters and Parfitt* (1995), one man attacked a victim in a car park, and another man joined in. The Court of Appeal ruled that there was no evidence that the two attackers were acting in concert and thus were not parties to a common design. They were, however, liable as principals for their own actions. Further, the defendant must *act* in concert with the other participants; mere presence at the scene is not in itself sufficient to support a finding that the defendant was part of a common design. In *The People (DPP) v. Rose* (2002), the Court of Criminal Appeal explained that the 'applicant could not be convicted of anything for mere callousness. If she was not a participator in the crime as part of a joint enterprise but was merely a spectator she had no criminal liability even if she did not express any words or take any steps to prevent what was happening.'

The jury must then consider the true extent of the common design. The test is what was agreed explicitly or tacitly by the participants, and each participant is fully liable for every action committed to realise the agreed goal. In determining the extent of the common design, it is unnecessary for the prosecution to prove precisely who did what as long as the jury is convinced that the actions fit within the agreement that underpins the common design. The jury should view the plan in its entirety. As most offenders have every wish to get away with their crimes, actions taken to ensure a safe and clean getaway may be considered part of the common design: *The People (DPP) v. Casey* **(2004)**. In making their determination, the jury is not bound by the defendant's explanation of what was agreed, but may draw inferences from all the evidence. This was made clear in *Doohan*; the defendant argued that he had authorised a beating of the deceased, and he explained in his testimony that he had intended that the deceased should be put in hospital with his arms and legs broken. As it turned out, the co-defendant had shot the deceased with a shotgun, and the deceased died from loss of blood. The Court of Criminal Appeal noted that the defendant wanted the deceased to suffer serious injury and had given the co-defendant unfettered discretion as to how the attack would be carried out. The court ruled that there was evidence from which the jury could conclude that the use of a gun did not go beyond what had been tacitly agreed.

As agreement forms the basis of common design liability, it follows that, as the Court of Criminal Appeal noted in *The People (DPP) v. Kenny* **(2003)**, 'a person must have knowledge of what is to occur to be part of a common design'; it can hardly be said that a person has agreed to something of which he is ignorant. To prove such knowledge, it is not necessary for the prosecution to show that every aspect of the plan was explicitly articulated; the jury is entitled to infer that a participant must have realised that certain actions were implicit in achieving the common goal. By continuing to participate in the light of such realisation, the participant has effectively given unspoken assent to the unarticulated aspects of the common plan. In *The People (DPP) v. Pringle* **(1981)**, a member of the Garda Siochana was killed during a raid on a post office van. The court held that once the appellants were aware that resistance from the gardaí would be met with the use of firearms, they became responsible for the actual use of the firearms. In other words, the possibility of killing members of the gardaí was part of the plan and had therefore been tacitly authorised by each participant.

If the jury concludes that the actions of one participant went beyond what had been agreed, then that participant alone bears responsibility for those actions; liability cannot be attributed to the other participants. In *The People (DPP) v. Noel and Marie Murray* **(1977)**, the husband and wife defendants had carried out a bank robbery and in making their escape were chased by an off-duty garda. Marie Murray shot the garda at point blank range to prevent him from catching her husband. Both defendants were convicted of capital murder, Noel Murray on the basis of common design. The trial court clearly regarded Marie Murray's actions as an action in furtherance of the planned crime and therefore part of the common design. The Supreme Court ruled, however, that capital murder and murder were distinct. While there was evidence that murder formed part of the common intention, there was no evidence that the shooting of gardaí was even discussed, much less agreed. Accordingly, the Supreme Court ruled that on the facts of the case, there could be a common design as to murder but not to capital murder. Therefore, the killing of the garda went beyond what had been agreed, and Noel Murray's conviction for capital murder was quashed.

Actions Incidental to the Common Design

Suppose X and Y plan to steal various electronic items from a house. They break into the house and collect the items they have come for. They are challenged by the female owner of the house, Z, and Y struggles with and eventually kills Z. There is no doubt that X is equally guilty of murder, as Y's actions are either part of the burglary plan or are unusual consequences of the plan. However, suppose instead that Y rapes Z. Is X equally liable for rape? In Irish law it seems clear that X should be acquitted; indeed, in **The People (DPP) v. Hourigan and O'Donovan (2004)**, this precise scenario was given to the jury by the trial judge, and later endorsed by the Court of Criminal Appeal, as an example of an action that goes beyond a common design. The British courts, however, have taken a different approach to a situation like this. In *Chan Wing-siu v. R* (1984), three men armed with knives broke into an apartment occupied by the deceased and his wife. The appellant guarded the wife in one part of the apartment while the other two men took the deceased to another part, where they killed him. The appellant argued that his murder conviction could not be sustained as he had played no part in the killing and that killing went beyond what had been agreed. The Privy Council ruled that the appellant had joined in an expedition in which he knew dangerous weapons were to be carried, and that he should not be allowed to 'escape the consequences by reliance on a nuance of prior assessment, only too likely to have been optimistic.' In *R v. Hyde* (1990), the Court of Appeal used the decision in *Chan Wing-siu* to rule that English law recognised two distinct forms of common design, at least where death results to the victim. The first, relatively simple kind arises where the primary object of the design is to cause physical injury to the victim. The principle in *Anderson and Morris* applied here; if a participant joined such an enterprise, then his agreement formed the basis of his liability for all actions done in furtherance of the enterprise. The second, more complex kind of common design arises where causing physical injury is not the object of the common design but arises incidentally to it. The court gave the example of an agreement to commit a burglary, during which a person is killed. This kind of case would be governed by the principle set out by the Privy Council in *Chan Wing-siu*: if the defendant foresaw a risk that someone would be killed and still participated in the enterprise, he could be convicted of homicide. In such a case, the fact that the defendant did not intend, or agree, that lethal force be used was irrelevant.

In *Hui Chi-ming v. R* (1991), the Privy Council took this analysis one step further and ruled that it was unnecessary for the possibility of incidental harm to be in the contemplation of all parties to the enterprise. It was sufficient that the incidental harm was contemplated by the participant on trial, providing such contemplation was coupled with continued participation in the enterprise. Finally, the matter reached the House of Lords in *R v. Powell; R v. English* (1997), which endorsed the analysis of the Privy Council and the Court of Appeal, and explicitly brought that analysis to its logical conclusion. Both appeals related to offences carried out by principals allegedly in excess of what had been agreed. Lord Hutton, who delivered the leading judgment, expressly extended the analysis to include a participant in a common design who did not agree to the use of a weapon but who participated in the design knowing that another participant was carrying a weapon and might use it. Lord Hutton expressed the rule of law in the following terms:

> When two parties embark on a joint criminal enterprise one party will be liable for an act which he contemplates may be carried out by the other party in the course of the enterprise even if he has not tacitly agreed to that act.

English law, therefore, allows a conviction on the basis of common design where there is only foresight, not agreement. However, Lord Hutton also held that criminal liability should only be extended to the non-killing participant if the killing was of a type that he actually contemplated. Thus, in the case of *English*, the appellant had contemplated the use of a wooden club, but the killer had used a knife. Lord Hutton ruled that a knife is fundamentally different to a wooden club; therefore, *English* had not contemplated the kind of attack actually committed, and his conviction was quashed.

The Irish courts have maintained that the basis of common design liability is an agreement, explicit or implicit, and that the defendant must have knowledge of what has been agreed. It is to be hoped that the Irish courts do not adopt the extensions allowed by the British courts. The foreseeing participant in a common design that so exercised Lord Hutton in *Powell* is certainly not morally blameless in that he assisted in bringing about the circumstances in which the incidental offence was committed. To that extent, he consciously accepted the risk that the incidental offence that he foresaw as a possible outcome would be committed, and this is the very definition of recklessness. Thus, no objection can be raised to convicting such a participant of an offence of basic intent, i.e. one supported by recklessness. To convict him of a specific intent offence is another matter, however. We have already seen (section 6.8) in the context of secondary liability that convicting an accessory of murder on foot of mere foresight is untenable, and that argument applies with equal force in the context of common design. The Criminal Justice Act 1964 mandates a finding of intention to kill or to cause serious injury, but a participant who foresees the possibility of death and continues to participate anyway is at most reckless, and recklessness is insufficient for a finding of murder. Further, it is plainly illogical that a participant who has not agreed to the incidental offence should be convicted on foot of a lower fault standard than the person who actually committed the incidental offence.

Furthermore, if the phrase 'common design' is to have any real meaning, it must be underpinned by an agreement. It is difficult to see how foresight by one person of a possible incidental action can truly constitute a common design. To hold otherwise, as the British courts have done, is to make nonsense of the phrase and can only cause confusion for jurors. As Lord Mustill pointed out in his reluctant concurring speech in *Powell*:

> I cannot accommodate [the extended form of] culpability within a concept of joint enterprise. How can a jury be directed at the same time that S is guilty only if he was a party to an express or tacit agreement to do the act in question, and that he is guilty if he not only disagreed with it, but made his disagreement perfectly clear to S? Are not the two assertions incompatible?

This incompatibility, and the confusion that results from it, serves no useful purpose. The justifications given by the British courts for extending common design are all policy based. In *Powell*, Lord Hutton accepted that his ruling involved a degree of illogicality, but argued that the 'rules of the common law are not based solely on logic but relate to practical concerns' and, in relation to crimes committed in the course of joint enterprises, to the need to give effective protection to the public against criminals operating in gangs. However, it has never been suggested that a defendant such as *Powell* should escape liability altogether; if such a participant contemplated that a killing might occur as part of the plan, for example, then by continuing to participate in that plan he has acted recklessly and he can be convicted of manslaughter. No good reason was given in *Powell* as to why the foreseeing participant must be convicted of *murder* in order to protect the public. Further, one would think that the public requires a similar level of effective protection from all killers, including those acting on their own, yet it is clear that a solo killer cannot be convicted of murder on the basis of recklessness. Accordingly, it is submitted that the British courts have extended the doctrine of common design so far that it no longer has any real meaning.

6.11 Further Reading.

Charleton et al., *Criminal Law*, Dublin: Butterworths, 1999, Chapter 3.
———, 'The Scope of the Doctrine of Common Design', (1985) 3 *ILT* 199.
Clarkson, 'Complicity, *Powell* and Manslaughter', [1998] *Crim LR* 556.
Ni Raifeartaigh, 'The Mental Element for Accessories to Murder', (1994) 4 *ICLJ* 31.
Smith, 'Criminal Liability of Accessories', (1997) *LQR* 453.

PART II

GENERAL DEFENCES

CHAPTER SEVEN

LAWFUL USE OF FORCE

7.1 Introduction

From the foundation of the common law, the State has claimed a near-monopoly on the use of force in order to end the cycle of tribal feuding characteristic of early societies. Agencies have been created (the police and the courts) both for protection and as a means of providing redress of grievances, thus removing the need for private action. By relying on the State's promise of protection and redress, a less violent society is possible. However, the State's protection exists only in general terms; as the gardaí cannot be everywhere at once, they cannot guarantee protection to every individual person all of the time or to suppress all crime as it occurs. Thus, the law has always recognised that in certain situations, individuals will have to take private steps to protect themselves and others and to prevent the commission of crimes. However, this recognition is far removed from the right to self-help that existed in early societies. The law will not allow individuals to engage in private retribution; rather, individuals may use only such force as is necessary to provide protection from an immediate threat or to prevent the immediate commission of a crime, but thereafter they must involve the relevant State agencies. Thus, the legitimate use of force represents a balance between the needs of an ordered society and the right of individuals to ensure their own protection.

At common law, the law allowed for the use of private force in three circumstances: defending oneself or others, assisting a police officer in the discharge of his duty or preventing the commission of a crime. Generally, the same rules applied to each scenario, but there were some differences. For example, if X was defending himself, he would be expected to retreat as far as possible before using force; if X was a police officer attempting to arrest a fugitive, however, there would be no duty to retreat. The basis for the use of force today is contained in sections 18, 19 and 20 of the Non-Fatal Offences Against the Person Act 1997. For the most part, these provisions simply put the rules and restrictions developed by the common law on a statutory footing.

7.2 Lawful Basis for Using Force

The Non-Fatal Offences Against the Person Act 1997 sets out the circumstances in which force might be used, and it is clear from the wording used that these circumstances constitute a justification for the use of force. Section 18 allows reasonable force to be used to protect oneself or others, to protect property or to prevent the commission of a crime or a breach of the peace. Not surprisingly, these provisions cannot generally be used to justify the use of force against the gardaí. Section 18(6) prohibits any such defence being used against a person that the defendant knows is a member of the gardaí acting in the course of his duty. However, this provision does permit the use of force against the gardaí if the defendant believed that force was immediately necessary to prevent harm to himself or to another. So, if X sees members of the gardaí beating his son with truncheons, X would be entitled under section 18(6) to use reasonable force to prevent harm coming to his son. He would not, however, be entitled under this provision to use force to secure his son's escape from the gardaí. Section 19 allows for the use of reasonable force to assist in the making of a lawful arrest, and this provision is not limited to members of the gardaí. Under section 4(4) of the Criminal Law Act 1997, a person who is not a member of the Garda Síochána may lawfully effect an arrest without warrant in respect of an arrestable offence if he reasonably believes that the person being arrested would otherwise attempt to escape or evade the gardaí. The arrested person must then be handed over to the gardaí as soon as practicable. Combining section 4(4) with section 19, therefore, an individual may make what is commonly termed a 'citizen's arrest' and may use reasonable force to do so.

7.3 Existence of a Lawful Justification

Whether one of the justifications discussed above exists is ultimately a matter of fact for the jury to consider. Nevertheless, there are some legal principles that the jury must bear in mind in making its determination. The threat against which force is deployed does not have to be blameworthy to justify the use of force: section 18(3) provides that a criminal act, for the purposes of the use of force, may exist even though the threatening person could plead infancy, duress, automatism, intoxication or insanity. Thus, the fact that the person could not be convicted of a crime in respect of his conduct is irrelevant, and this makes eminent sense. The whole point of these provisions is to allow individuals to protect themselves from danger in circumstances where recourse to State agencies is impracticable. The fact that a dangerous person is insane, and therefore not responsible for his actions, does not make him or his actions any less dangerous. This point was made in *Re A (Conjoined Twins)* (2001) in which the Court of Appeal authorised the separation of two Siamese twins knowing that one would die as a result. Medical evidence showed that one of the twins (Mary) was effectively killing the other (Jodie) by using Jodie's heart and lungs, which was putting these organs under too great a strain. Ward L.J. ruled:

> The reality here – harsh as it is to state it, and unnatural as it is that it should be happening – is that Mary is killing Jodie … I have no difficulty in agreeing that this unique happening cannot be said to be unlawful. But it does not have to be unlawful. The six-year-old boy indiscriminately shooting all and sundry in the school playground is not acting unlawfully for he is too young for his acts to be so classified

122

… I can see no difference in essence between that resort to legitimate self-defence [i.e. killing a six-year-old boy who is shooting indiscriminately] and the doctors coming to Jodie's defence and removing the threat of fatal harm to her presented by Mary's draining her life-blood.

Whether a section 18 justification exists must be judged from the perspective of the person using the force: section 18(5). Section 19(3) contains a similar provision in respect of the use of force to assist in the making of an arrest. The defendant who pleads that the use of force was lawful must therefore honestly believe that he is meeting an unjust attack against himself, another person, etc. However, under section 1(2), the jury should consider the presence or absence of reasonable grounds for such a belief in determining whether the belief was honestly held. Thus, in **DPP v. McGinty (2003)**, the Court of Criminal Appeal struck down jury directions which suggested that the defendant should have reasonable grounds for his perspective of the facts. This reflects the position at common law. In *R v. Williams (Gladstone)* (1987), the defendant witnessed another man dragging a youth along the street. The other man explained that he was a police officer and that he had arrested the youth for stealing a lady's handbag, but he was unable to show any identification. The defendant struggled with the other man, causing injury. It turned out that the other man was not a police officer, but that the rest of his story was true and that the arrest had been lawful. The Court of Appeal ruled that the defendant was entitled to be judged in the light of the circumstances as he believed them to be. In other words, in evaluating the defendant's claim of lawful use of force, the jury should assume that the injured man had in fact unlawfully assaulted the youth and that the defendant had gone to the youth's assistance. Further, the fact that the mistake was unreasonable was irrelevant except in so far as it might indicate whether or not the mistake was genuine. The Privy Council came to a similar conclusion in *Beckford v. R* (1988), and that a belief in the existence of a justificatory circumstance will negate guilt is now well established at common law.

What about the reverse situation: the defendant causes injury without being aware that a justification exists for him doing so? In *R v. Dadson* (1850), the defendant was a police officer who shot and wounded a man he had challenged for trying to steal a quantity of wood. English law at the time allowed police officers to shoot at escaping felons, and the wounded man was in fact a felon but this was unknown to the defendant at the time he opened fire. Pollock C.B., for the court, ruled that the defendant was properly convicted because when he fired, he knew of no justification for doing so. This decision suggests that the objective existence of a justification for the use of force will not benefit a defendant unless that justification was in his knowledge at the time the force was used. It seems clear that this principle has been incorporated into section 18; section 18(5) requires the defendant's actions to be judged from the circumstances as the defendant believed them to be. A defendant cannot sensibly be said to have believed that his use of force was justified unless he was aware that the justificatory circumstances exist. Further, section 18(5) exists as a protection for those who, having made a genuine error as to the circumstances, are morally innocent. A person such as Dadson clearly is not innocent; the fact that a justification turned out to exist was a matter of blind luck.

One last point needs to be made clear. The defendant's actions are to be judged from his own perspective, but that does not mean that he has a licence to define for himself what constitutes a crime against which he can deploy force. Section 18 allows people to use force to protect themselves or others when they mistakenly believe that a criminal act is being committed. To take advantage of section 18(5), the defendant's belief must relate to the factual circumstances that prompted his use of force, not to a moral evaluation of those circumstances. In a democracy, individuals are entitled to hold moral opinions on whether a particular action should or should not be lawful and to use the political process to try to have their opinions enacted as law. They are not entitled to disregard that process and to define as criminal that which society accepts as lawful. Neither a system of law nor a society that claims any degree of civilisation could long survive a system in which individuals were permitted to use force whenever they deemed it appropriate according to their private beliefs. Thus, X might genuinely believe that killing animals for food constitutes murder, but he is not entitled to use that belief to justify the shooting of workers in an abattoir in order to defend cattle about to be slaughtered. Similarly, in *The People (DPP) v. Kelly* (2004), the defendant was not permitted to argue that her belief that the US invasion of Iraq constituted a crime against the Iraqi people justified her in causing criminal damage to a US Navy warplane at Shannon Airport.

7.4 Motive for Using Force

The only time that force can be used is to meet one of the situations outlined in sections 18 and 19 of the 1997 Act. Force used out of a desire for revenge, to extract information or to teach a lesson will never be justified. In *The People (Attorney General) v. Coffey* (1966), the defendant armed himself and some friends with car tools and went looking for some other men who had earlier assaulted him. It was held by the Supreme Court that an acquittal on the grounds of self-defence would be unjustifiable on these facts; to hold otherwise would be 'contrary to any system of justice in any civilized country.' Similarly, in *R v. Bond* (1993), the defendants kidnapped and threatened a young man they thought might have information about a series of thefts. The Court of Appeal condemned the defendants' actions in the strongest terms:

> It may seem a trite observation, but it has to be said; that a civilized society cannot tolerate individuals taking the law into their own hands. That applies to exacting revenge for any perceived wrong, even if the perpetrator of the wrong is clearly established ... Such conduct is in itself indefensible, but, if not put down, it would

lead to retaliation, to feuds and fights, to injustice and to a breakdown in public order. We fully understand the frustration felt when a crime is committed and the offender is not traced or brought to justice, but such frustration can never justify this sort of self-help.

Force should only be used as a last resort to meet an imminent threat. Once that threat has ended, the justification for using force similarly ends.

As a general rule, force may not legitimately be used by a defendant if he has provoked the attack in the first place. Section 18(7) provides that 'the defence provided by this section does not apply to a person who causes conduct or a state of affairs with a view to using force to resist or terminate it.' This is in line with common law. In *R v. Browne* (1973), a Northern Ireland decision, it was held that to qualify as a defence, the need for defensive action 'must not have been created by the conduct of the accused in the immediate context of the incident which was likely or intended to give rise to that need.' In other words, where the defendant acts in a way that he knows will result in a violent outburst from another person, he cannot then claim to be using force to defend himself against the violence.

However, several caveats need to be mentioned here. First, the limitation in section 18(7) only arises when the defendant acts in such a way as to bring about a violent attack 'with a view to using force' to resist it. This suggests that the defendant's actions must have been calculated to bring about the violent response. If he acted without realising how the other person would react, section 18(7) will not apply, even if a reasonable person would have appreciated the likely response. Second, the limitation does not apply when the defendant's 'provocation' consisted of lawful conduct. Section 18(7) itself provides that the use of force may be justified if the defendant's actions were lawful even if he knew that they would provoke a violent response. Thus, in *R v. Field* (1972), it was held that a defendant was justified in remaining in a public place even though he knew that someone was coming to attack him. Similarly, if X acts to stop Y from assaulting Z, and Z then attacks X, X can use force to defend himself. Preventing a crime is a lawful act, and X therefore fits within the exception in section 18(7). Finally, it is submitted that a claim of lawful use of force may still succeed where the defendant provoked the incident if the reaction of the other party was excessive. Suppose X lightly slaps Y, and Y responds by beating X with an iron bar. Y's response is excessive and X can surely defend himself even though he initiated the incident. By responding so excessively, Y was no longer a victim of an unjust attack trying to repel that attack; rather, Y became an aggressor against whom X could deploy defensive force. In ***The People (DPP) v. Doran* (1987)**, the defendant broke into the deceased's house but ran when confronted by the deceased, who was wielding a golf club. However, the deceased then chased the defendant and began striking him with the golf club. The defendant drew a knife that he was carrying and stabbed the deceased a number of times, killing him. The fact that the defendant was carrying a knife indicates that he foresaw the possibility of violence, but the Court of Criminal Appeal did not disapprove in principle of his plea of self-defence. Indeed, the court appears to have accepted that the jury could have acquitted the defendant on this ground. The court's rationale was not made explicit, but it seems to be that the deceased's reaction was excessive, not least because the threat had at that point ended.

7.5 Necessity to Use Force

The wording of sections 18 and 19 makes it clear that the defence contained in those provisions is fundamentally purpose driven. Reasonable force may only be used when it is necessary to achieve one of the purposes set out in sections 18 and 19, as judged from the defendant's perspective. Necessity in this sense has a number of aspects to it. In the first place, the type of force permitted will depend on which purpose the individual is trying to achieve, and it is that purpose that provides the backdrop against which the use of force must be judged. If a private individual is trying to protect against an attack, there is generally no necessity for anything other than defensive force to be used. If, however, the individual is trying to prevent the commission of a crime or to make an arrest, a more offensive posture might be necessary. It would be absurd if a police officer, in trying to make an arrest, was required to act only defensively; the officer's duty requires him to be more assertive than a private individual acting in self-defence.

Second, the use of force will be necessary only when it is used against an imminent threat. As noted earlier, the use of force by private individuals is a derogation from the State's general monopoly on force, and that derogation is allowed only in recognition of the impossibility of State agencies being able to guarantee protection to all individuals at all times. It then follows that if the threat is not imminent, the individual has the time to seek the assistance of the appropriate authorities, and hence there is no need for the use of force by that individual. This does not mean, however, that a person is required to wait until the blows are raining down on him before he can respond. If an individual was required to allow the other party to land the first blow, the defence of use of force would be useless in that the victim of the attack could well be incapacitated by the first blow and therefore be unable to defend himself. In *The People (Attorney General) v. Keatley* (1954), the Court of Criminal Appeal quoted with approval the following statement: '[a person] has a right to defend himself, and to strike a blow in his defence without waiting until [his attacker] has struck.' So, if an attack is imminent, the target of the attack may strike first, although doing so may well cause evidential problems in the event of a trial. Simply put, getting in the first blow means striking first, and in the more objective atmosphere of a courtroom, striking first does not always sit well with a claim of defensive force.

The prohibition on pre-emptive strikes does not extend to reasonable acts taken in preparation of an anticipated attack. Section 20(2) extends sections 18 and 19 to 'acts immediately preparatory to the use of force'. It is likely that this provision will be interpreted in the light of the pre-existing common law. In *The People (DPP) v. Kelso* **(1984)**, the defendant RUC officers carried their service revolvers while visiting a pub across the border. It was accepted that their possession of these weapons could be for a lawful purpose if they held an honest and reasonable belief that their lives might be in danger and the weapons were needed to guard against that danger. Interestingly, in the earlier decision of *The People (Attorney General) v. O'Brien* **(1969)**, the Court of Criminal Appeal looked less favourably on possession of a knife, describing it as an offensive weapon. In *R v. Fegan* (1972), a Northern Ireland decision, the defendant married a woman from a different religious denomination, and faced threats from a number of sources. He illegally bought and maintained a handgun and ammunition in anticipation of an attack. The Northern Ireland Court of Appeal ruled that his possession of the weapon could be lawful providing three conditions were met: the threat was honestly and reasonably anticipated, the threat could not be met by other means and the steps taken were proportionate to the threat faced. A more extreme example of preparatory acts occurred in *Attorney General's Reference No.2 of 1983* (1984). The defendant's shop had been looted during riots that the police had been unable to control. The defendant anticipated further attacks and he made up a number of petrol bombs to throw at looters. The Court of Appeal accepted that the possession of these bombs could be lawful to deter unlawful acts that were beyond the ability of the police to control, providing the bombs were destroyed once the threat had passed.

Third, the use of force is not necessary unless it has effectively been forced upon an individual by the actions of another. The easiest way for a defendant to establish this is to show that he physically retreated and only used force when the aggressor came after him. However, there is no duty as such to retreat from a fight; section 20(4) provides that the fact that a defendant had an opportunity to retreat before using force and did not avail of the opportunity is only a fact to be taken into account in determining whether the individual's use of force was reasonable. At common law, it used to be fatal to a claim of self-defence if the defendant had an opportunity to escape and did not avail of it. The reasoning appears to have been that as force can only be used when necessary, if there was an escape route open to the defendant it was unnecessary to use any force. This duty to retreat did not apply, however, where the defendant was trying to prevent the commission of a crime or to make a lawful arrest. Neither did it apply if a person was attacked in his home; a person's home is his ultimate refuge from which retreat cannot be demanded. So, in the eighteenth century, Hale wrote that a person attacked in his home 'need not flee as far as he can as in other cases of *se defendendo*, for he hath the protection of his house to excuse him from flying, as that would be to give up the protection of his house to his adversary by his flight.' By the end of the 1960s, the courts were beginning to reformulate the duty to retreat. In *R v. Julien* (1969), the Court of Appeal held that 'what is necessary is that [the defendant] should demonstrate by his actions that he does not want to fight. He must demonstrate that he is prepared to temporize and disengage and perhaps to make some physical withdrawal.' In *R v. McInnes* (1971), the same court ruled that a failure to retreat was not conclusive evidence that the defendant had not acted in self-defence. In *R v. Bird* (1985), the Court of Appeal ruled that there was no duty to retreat; rather, an unwillingness to retreat was one factor to be considered in deciding the defendant's true motivation for fighting. Nevertheless, the fact that the defendant retreated will obviously be powerful evidence to negate any suggestion that force was used out of revenge or aggression.

7.6 Reasonable Force

Sections 18 and 19 authorise the use of such force as is reasonable in the circumstances as the defendant believed them to be. Section 20(1) includes in the definition of the use of force the causing of an impact on another person's body, threats to use force as defined or threats to detain another person without actually using force. Using force against property includes threats made to a person against his property. The key issue is whether the defendant's use of force was reasonable, and this issue is decided using a test of proportionality. The basic rule is that the victim's response must be proportionate to the threat he faced. If this rule is met, the defendant should be acquitted on any charge; if the force used was excessive in the circumstances, the defence will fail.

What constitutes a proportionate reaction will necessarily depend on the circumstances of the case. However, a number of general points may be made. First, the proportionality test is objective and the defendant's level of force will be judged according to the standard of a reasonable person. This is clear from the requirement in sections 18 and 19 that the force used be reasonable. The English courts toyed with a more subjective standard: in *Palmer v. R* (1971), for example, the Privy Council ruled that evidence that 'in a moment of unexpected anguish a person attacked had only done what he honestly and instinctively thought was necessary that would be most potent evidence that only reasonable defensive action had been taken.' However, in *R v. Owino* (1996), the Court of Appeal forcefully restated the traditional objective standard. This standard prevents the defence of lawful force being claimed by people who have totally overreacted to a threat, and thereby encourages restraint on the part of all individuals. However, the reasonable person will share the defendant's perspective of the circumstances. Thus, the test is an objective standard set within subjective parameters: if a reasonable person might have reacted with the same force as used by the defendant in the circumstances as the defendant believed them to be, the defendant's response was proportionate and he should be acquitted.

Even though the test for proportionality is objective, individuals are not held to an absolute standard of mathematical proportionality. Anyone using force is expected to assess the situation he is in and to weigh an appropriate response, but allowances need to be made for the impact of fear, adrenaline, passion, etc. on an individual's assessment of the situation and of his own response to that situation. Consequently, an individual under attack cannot be expected to precisely weigh his response to that attack, an attitude exemplified by Justice Holmes' famous comment in *Brown v. US* (1921) that 'detached reflection cannot be demanded in the presence of an uplifted knife.' In ***Ross v. Curtis* (1989)**, the defendant fired on some thieves who had broken into his shop and were menacing him in his adjoining home, and hit one of the thieves in the head. The High Court noted that the defendant could have accomplished his purpose of scaring away the thieves by firing into the ceiling, but ruled that in the heat of the moment, he had simply failed to aim the shot properly. In the case of a police officer attempting to prevent the commission of a crime or to effect an arrest, the officer needs to consider the seriousness of the crime involved: a higher level of force may be justified to prevent a murder than to prevent a youngster from writing graffiti on a wall. But here again, it must be conceded that police officers are subject to the same passions as everyone else, although the fact that such professionals have a level of training and experience that ordinary people lack is also of relevance.

Subject to the foregoing, the level of force that can be used must bear some relationship to the threat faced. So, as a general guideline, a gun can be met with a gun, a knife with a knife, a fist with a fist. It would generally not be reasonable for a person to meet a low-level threat with a lethal weapon; so, in *R v. McInnes* (1971), Edmund Davies L.J. said that the use of a knife in a fist fight was 'totally unreasonable'. However, if a person is faced with a deadly threat, he may respond with deadly force. In the case of defending property, generally lethal force can never be justified, as property, regardless of its value, cannot be equated with human life, although there are three caveats to this general proposition. First, it is conceivable that some forms of property are so necessary for the preservation of life – such as medical equipment, for instance – that lethal force might be employed to protect them, but in such cases it is arguably the life that is dependent upon the property that is really being protected. Second, even in defending ordinary property, it is likely that the aggressor will retaliate against the defender, thereby putting the defender in danger. In such a case, the defender will be defending himself as well as his property, and his use of force should be considered against that backdrop. Given that the defender has the right to defend his property, it would be absurd to hold that if he uses such force and the thieves retaliate against him, he may not then defend himself according to the ordinary principles of self-defence.

Third, a person's home has always been treated by the criminal law as a special form of property; hence the non-application of the common law duty to retreat if attacked at home. Similarly, it seems likely that somewhat more force can be tolerated in defence of one's home than in defence of other forms of property even of equal value. This can be justified on two grounds. First, a person's home is supposed to be his sanctuary, and has a different place in a person's life than virtually any other kind of property. Second, a home invasion may not necessarily be an attack on property; rather, it might be the prelude to a far more serious personal attack. Therefore, defending one's home and defending one's person are closely related. For these reasons, some jurisdictions in the US have departed from the reasonable force standard in cases of home protection. These laws, known popularly as 'Make My Day' statutes, are well illustrated by a statute enacted in Colorado that allows home-occupants to use deadly force against a person making an unlawful entry into their home if the occupant reasonably believes that the person intends to commit a further crime against person or property in the dwelling and might use any physical force, no matter how slight. Few other common law jurisdictions have gone so far, although the Crown Prosecution Service in England indicated in 2005 (*Householders and the Use of Force Against Intruders*, 2005) that prosecutions against homeowners will only be brought where there is evidence of gratuitous violence being deployed against a home-intruder. It seems likely that a similar policy would prevail in Ireland.

Ultimately, the decision regarding the reasonableness of the force used is a matter for the assessment of the jury. Thus, in **The People (DPP) v. Clarke (1994)**, the deceased had assaulted the defendant and made threats against his family. The defendant retrieved a gun from his home, went looking for the deceased, and during a confrontation, the defendant shot and killed the deceased. The trial judge commented in summing up that the facts of the case would hardly allow for an acquittal on the grounds of self-defence. This was held by the Court of Criminal Appeal to be a misdirection in that it interfered with the function of the jury. Accordingly, the jury has almost unfettered scope to apply their own standards to the question and may have regard to factors that are not strictly permitted by law, especially in cases in which the defendant has presented himself in a sympathetic light. If the jury concludes, however, that the force used was excessive in the circumstances, the defendant will be convicted as charged, even where the defendant honestly thought he used reasonable force (although there is a middle ground in cases involving murder charges; see section 7.7). Such a belief may, however, be taken into account in sentencing.

7.7 Use of Lethal Force

Providing the force used is reasonable and is directed to one of the purposes set out in sections 18 and 19, there is no limit to the degree of force that can be used. All of the foregoing principles apply equally to charges of homicide as to non-fatal charges. However, pleading the lawful use of force to a murder charge involves some special issues that must now be considered separately. As noted above, if the force used was reasonable, the defendant must be acquitted even if he killed the attacker; if the force used was excessive, the defendant must be convicted even if he honestly believed that he used no more force than was necessary. This remains the case in England; the House of Lords ruled in *R v. Clegg* (1995) that it was irrelevant that the defendant's situation justified the use of some force if the force actually used was excessive. There, the defendant had opened fire on a car that drove through a checkpoint in Northern Ireland, and a passenger in the car was killed. The House of Lords rejected the defendant's attempt to create a middle ground which would result in a manslaughter conviction if the jury was satisfied that the defendant had used excessive force but no more force than he honestly believed to have been necessary. In Ireland, however, the Supreme Court accepted this very argument in *The People (Attorney General) v. Dwyer* **(1972)**. The Supreme Court noted that a murder conviction required a finding of intent, a subjective fault requirement. A person who does not intend to kill or to cause serious injury cannot be convicted of murder: Criminal Justice Act 1964. If the jury accepted that the defendant had killed in self-defence and used no more force than he thought was necessary, he believed himself justified in using the lethal force and therefore did not intend to commit murder. Accordingly, the defendant should be convicted of manslaughter. However, if the defendant knowingly used more force than was reasonably necessary, he must be convicted of murder. So, in *The People (Attorney General) v. Commane* **(1975)**, the defendant was attacked by the deceased but succeeded in knocking him out. The defendant then strangled the deceased and killed him. The Court of Criminal Appeal noted that the deceased had already met the threat posed by the defendant and, having rendered him unconscious, any further violence was clearly excessive. Thus, in Ireland, almost alone in the common law world, a jury in a murder case involving a plea of lawful use of force has three verdicts open to them: guilty of murder (the defendant used excessive force knowing that it was excessive); guilty of manslaughter (the defendant used excessive force but honestly believed that the force he used was reasonable); and not guilty (the defendant used objectively reasonable force in the circumstances as he believed them to be).

The European Convention on Human Rights

The impact of the European Convention on Human Rights on the defence of the lawful use of force in homicide cases is unclear. Article 2 of the Convention provides:

1. Everyone's right to life shall be protected by law.
2. Deprivation of life shall not be regarded as inflicted in contravention of this article when it results from the use of force which is no more than absolutely necessary:
    a. in defence of any person from unlawful violence;
    b. in order to effect a lawful arrest or to prevent the escape of a person lawfully detained;
    c. in action taken for the purpose of quelling a riot or insurrection.

Article 2(1) clearly requires that signatory States ensure that the law of the land provides protection for the right to life, and it is unclear whether the defence of lawful use of force as it stands contravenes this requirement. At first sight, the Convention imposes what amounts to a standard of absolute necessity rather than one of reasonable necessity, as in sections 18 and 19 of the 1997 Act. In *McCann v. United Kingdom* (1996) and again in *Andronicou v. Cyprus* (1998), the European Court of Human Rights indicated that the taking of life must be strictly proportionate to the achievement of one of the objectives in paragraphs a-c in Article 2(2) in order to comply with the Convention. On its face, this standard of proportionality appears to be higher than that employed under sections 18 and 19, which make allowances for human frailties. However, in *McCann*, the Court held that the taking of life might be justified under article 2(2) if based on an honest and reasonable belief that the taking of life was absolutely necessary to protect innocent lives. The fact that the belief turned out to be incorrect would not then create a breach of Article 2. The Court went on: 'To hold otherwise would be to impose an unrealistic burden on the State and its law-enforcement personnel in the execution of their duty, perhaps to the detriment of their lives and those of others.' Further, the Court accepted in the same case that the 'difference between the [absolute necessity and reasonable necessity] standards is not sufficiently great that a violation of Article 2 para. 1 ... could be found on this ground alone.' The clear implication of these statements is that the standards required for compliance with Article 2 of the Convention are not as absolute as it appears. Thus, it seems that a Convention challenge to the standard required in sections 18 and 19 would not succeed.

However, sections 18 and 19 couch the objective test within subjective parameters: the defendant's actions are judged according to his view of the circumstances, and a genuine mistake as to those circumstances will not be fatal. By holding in *McCann*, and later in *Andronicou*, that the mistake must be honest and reasonable, the European Court of Human Rights clearly requires a more objective approach to the assessment of the defendant's actions. Such a holding is fully in keeping with the stricter language employed in Article 2, and it seems that in this respect sections 18 and 19 might require revision to avoid incompatibility with the Convention.

7.8 Further Reading

Doran, 'The Doctrine of Excessive Defence: Developments Past, Present and Future', (1985) 36 *NILQ* 314.

Dwyer, 'Homicide and the Plea of Self-Defence', (1992) 2 *ICLJ* 73.

Stannard, 'Excessive Defence in Northern Ireland', (1992) 43 *NILQ*.

CHAPTER EIGHT

INSANITY

8.1 Introduction

Broadly speaking, insanity is relevant to criminal law in two ways. First, the defendant must be fit to plead to the charge. If it is shown that the defendant, because of insanity, is unable to understand the charge against him or the difference between guilty and not guilty, or is unable to instruct counsel, challenge jurors or follow the evidence, the trial cannot proceed, essentially because its fairness cannot be guaranteed due to the defendant's condition. The test to be followed in such instances was laid down by the Supreme Court in *The State (Coughlan) v. Minister for Justice* (1968):

> ... has the prisoner sufficient intellect to comprehend the course of the proceedings of the trial, so as to make a proper defence, to challenge a juror to whom he may wish to object, and to understand the details of the evidence.

This test is not limited to any particular definition of insanity; it simply assesses the defendant's ability to comprehend what is going on. If he is found to be unfit to plead, section 2 of the Criminal Lunatics Act 1800 provides that he should be detained in strict custody until the pleasure of the government be known. The consequences of such a finding can be severe. The Committee on the Prevention of Torture, formed under the auspices of the European Convention for the Prevention of Torture, referred in its 1999 Report to the Irish Government to a man who had been found unfit to plead and had spent over sixty years in the Central Mental Hospital. The Committee noted other cases in which people had spent periods of up to thirty-eight years in the hospital. No provision has yet been enacted requiring reviews of cases such as these. However, the Criminal Law (Insanity) Bill 2002, which at the time of writing has been passed by the Seanad and is before the Dáil, proposes to establish an independent Mental Health Review Board to ensure reviews of all detentions in the Central Mental Hospital (or other designated centres) at periods of not more than six months. Once a person is found to be no longer unfit to plead, the director of the designated centre is required to notify forthwith the court that ordered the detention.

Second, where the defendant is fit to plead, the trial will proceed, but the defendant may raise the defence of insanity. The law will presume that every defendant is legally sane and, if over the age of fourteen (due to infancy – see Chapter 12), is fully accountable for his actions. However, if the defendant is able to show, on a balance of probabilities as opposed to beyond reasonable doubt, that at the time the offence was committed he was legally insane, he will have a defence. In these circumstances, the defendant will be deemed to have lacked the necessary *mens rea*, and should not therefore be held accountable. It is with this defence of insanity that this chapter is concerned.

8.2 Beginning of the Defence

Common law was slow to recognise any such defence, and what limited mercy it did show tended to be somewhat restricted. Chief Justice Coke wrote that insanity was no defence unless the defendant more resembled a beast rather than a man. Hale, however, would have allowed a defence where a man had the understanding of a child under fourteen.[1] It was not until *R v. Hadfield* (1800) that the modern defence began to take shape. The defendant believed he had to die in order to save the world. Because suicide was a sin, he could not kill himself, so he fired a shot at the king, which was a capital offence. It was held that he was not accountable for his actions because of insanity, and was acquitted.

The watershed as far as modern insanity is concerned was reached in *R v. M'Naghten* (1843). The defendant suffered from an insane delusion that Sir Robert Peel was persecuting him, and believed that Peel had to be killed. However, the defendant killed Peel's secretary instead. At his trial, the defendant was acquitted because of insanity. The decision caused such outrage that the House of Lords asked the Law Lords a series of questions designed to explain the defence of insanity. The judges complied with the request, although they protested the impropriety of having to do so outside a case. The answers to these questions became known as the M'Naghten Rules, and they have formed the basis of the insanity defence ever since.

8.3 The M'Naghten Rules

It should be noted that the questions put to the Law Lords, and consequently their answers, were principally concerned with the issue of insane delusions. The reason for the importance of this point will be seen later.

The principal M'Naghten Rules were set out by Lord Tindal C.J.:

> The jurors ought to be told in all cases that every man is to be presumed to be sane, and to possess a sufficient degree of reason to be responsible for his crimes, until the contrary be proved to their satisfaction; and that to establish a defence on the ground of insanity, it must be clearly proved that, at the time of the committing of the act, the party accused was labouring under such a defect of reason, from disease of the mind, as not to know the nature and quality of the act he was doing; or, if he did know it, that he did not know what he was doing was wrong ... If the accused was conscious that the act was one which he ought not to do, and if the act was at the same time contrary to the law of the land, he is punishable.

Irish and English law on insanity has been built around these rules ever since, although the Irish courts have been considerably more enterprising in their

---

1 Both quoted by O'Hanlon, 'Not Guilty Because of Insanity', (1968) *Ir. Jur.* 61.

willingness to expand the rules than their English counterparts. In **Doyle v. Wicklow County Council (1974)**, a seventeen-year-old youth had burned down an abattoir while suffering from a mental disorder, and the plaintiff, who owned the abattoir, claimed compensation from the defendant. The Supreme Court ruled that the M'Naghten Rules are not the 'sole and exclusive test' for determining insanity. The questions asked of the Law Lords were limited to insane delusions, and the Lords' answers should be similarly limited, and situations that do not fall precisely within the Rules may still amount to legal insanity. It is clear, then, that the Irish courts consider themselves free to depart from the specific Rules if doing so is required in the interests of justice.

8.4 Presumption of Sanity

Everyone is presumed to be sane until the contrary is shown. The burden of proving the defence of insanity therefore rests on the defendant. In this respect, insanity is unique among the general defences, and an exception to the *Woolmington* principle. However, even though the burden of proving insanity is on the defendant, the law does recognise that defendants do not have the power or resources of the State. Consequently, the standard of proof required of the defendant is proof on a balance of probabilities rather than beyond reasonable doubt. Providing X can convince the jury that it is more probable than not that he was insane at the time he committed the act, he will be acquitted.

8.5 Disease of the Mind

Whether or not the defendant was suffering from a disease of the mind is a question of law rather than one of medicine. The purpose of this requirement is to exclude from the ambit of insanity conditions such as drunkenness or anger. The authors of these conditions are people themselves, but the defence of insanity exists only to provide a defence to those who commit actions through no fault of their own. Nor do the Rules apply to forgetfulness or carelessness. In *R v. Clarke* (1972), the defendant had been charged with larceny arising from her failure to pay for certain items in a supermarket. Her defence was that she had taken the goods without paying for them due to absentmindedness brought on by depression. The trial judge held that this raised the issue of insanity, but this was rejected on appeal. There, it was held that insanity only applies to people who have lost their powers of reasoning due to a disease of the mind. It does not apply to those who 'retain the power of reasoning but who in moments of confusion or absentmindedness fail to use their powers to the full.'

A disease of the mind is not limited to psychiatric conditions; even physical conditions can qualify as 'diseases of the mind' if they manifest themselves in such a way as to impair the defendant's ability to reason. In *R v. Kemp* (1956), the defendant had brutally attacked his wife with a hammer. He was a man of excellent character and, until this incident, he and his wife had been regarded as a devoted couple. He argued that he suffered from arteriosclerosis which had, on the occasion in question, caused a lack of blood to the brain, in turn causing a loss of consciousness so that he had had no control over his actions. It was argued by the prosecution that this was not a disease of the mind as there was no evidence of brain damage, and it was in fact a physical condition. It was held by Devlin J., however, that the M'Naghten Rules focus on the condition of the mind:

> The law is not concerned with the brain but with the mind, in the sense that 'mind' is ordinarily used, the mental faculties of reason, memory and understanding … In my judgment the condition of the brain is irrelevant and so is the question of whether the condition of the mind is curable, transitory or permanent.

Thus, any condition, whether physical or mental, that impacted on the working of the defendant's mind at the time the act was committed could be classified as a disease of the mind. This definition clearly included the defendant's condition of arteriosclerosis. Similarly in *R v. Quick* (1973), in which the defendant was a nurse who assaulted a patient. He argued that he was diabetic and had not followed his doctor's instructions in taking his insulin. He had apparently taken the insulin but had eaten very little, and had then gone out drinking. As a result, he claimed that he had suffered a hypoglycaemic shock, and that he had no knowledge of his actions at the time. He argued that he should be acquitted on the grounds of automatism (see section 3.3). However, the trial judge directed that his defence was consistent only with insanity, and he pleaded guilty. On appeal, the Court of Appeal held that the essence of a disease of the mind is a malfunction of the mind caused by a disease, and therefore diabetes could qualify as a disease of the mind. However, a malfunction of the mind caused through the application of an external factor such as drink or drugs cannot fairly be said to have arisen as a result of a disease, and so must be excluded from the ambit of insanity. In this case, the defendant's condition did not emanate from the diabetes but from the defendant's failure to follow his doctor's advice. Therefore, the causative factor was external rather than internal. Consequently, there was no disease of the mind, and therefore no insanity.

In essence, therefore, a 'disease of the mind' may be caused by any internal factor. It will be recalled from Chapter 3 (section 3.3) that an internal factor is a condition that arises within the body. Such factors lead to a defence of insanity rather than non-insane automatism. In *R v. Sullivan* (1983), the House of Lords considered the case of a man who suffered from epileptic fits. During one such fit, he kicked an eighty-year-old man about the head, causing injury. He wished to raise the defence of non-insane automatism rather than insanity. The Lords, while expressing their sympathy for the defendant in his wish to avoid the label of insanity, endorsed the approach taken in *Kemp* and *Quick*. Epilepsy was an internal factor, and must therefore be considered under the heading of insanity.

8.6 Defect of Reason

Merely suffering from a disease of the mind is not sufficient; the defendant must also show that the disease caused a sufficient impairment of his ability to reason (a 'defect of reason'). This is done in one of two ways: by showing that he did not know the nature and quality of his actions, or that he did not know they were wrong. These principles are alternatives: the defendant does not have to show both. Knowledge of the wrongful nature of his actions will be dealt with in the next section; knowledge of the nature and quality of the action is the subject of this section.

The Rules do not define the concept of 'nature and quality', but it seems to refer in effect to situations where the defendant did not know what he was doing. So, if X throws his baby into a washing machine while believing that he is washing a shirt, he does not know the nature and quality of his actions. In other words, he does not comprehend the physical nature of his actions. In *R v. Codere* (1916), the defendant, an officer in the Canadian army, had killed a fellow soldier and was convicted of murder. He argued that 'nature' and 'quality' suggested different aspects of the test for insanity. 'Nature', it was argued, referred to the physical nature of the act, while 'quality' referred to its moral character. It was held by the Court of Appeal that the defendant's ability to discern the moral character of his actions was irrelevant. In other words, if he knew that he was killing but believed that he was justified, he could still be convicted because he knew the nature and quality of his actions. Similarly, in *R v. Dickie* (1984), the defendant had set fire to a wastepaper basket, knowing that he had done so. There was evidence that he was suffering from a manic-depressive episode at the time, but as he had known what he was doing, this was held to be irrelevant. The fact that he was unable to appreciate the consequences and dangers of his actions was also immaterial.

This approach has drawn considerable criticism, and has not been followed in many common law jurisdictions. It is unlikely that the Irish courts will favour it. In *The People (Attorney General) v. Hayes* (**1967**), the defendant killed his wife, but claimed that he had been unable to stop himself. Henchy J. held that it would be unjust not to allow a defence of insanity even where the defendant knew the nature and quality of his actions, and knew that they were wrong, but was unable due to a disease of the mind to prevent himself from committing them. This decision was approved by the Supreme Court in *Doyle v. Wicklow County Council* (**1974**). If Irish law will allow insanity where the defendant knew what he was doing and that it was wrong, there is no reason why a similar defence should be denied to a defendant who knew what he was doing but was unable to appreciate the consequences of his actions. Indeed, a defendant in a case similar to *Dickie* would surely have a greater claim in justice to a defence of insanity than one in a case such as *Hayes*. It seems likely, therefore, that Irish law will adopt a more liberal approach to this requirement, in an appropriate case.

8.7 Wrongful Nature of the Act

The alternative method of showing that the defendant had suffered a defect of reason is by showing that even though he knew what he was doing, he did not know that it was wrong. The Lords in *M'Naghten* further explained that this element of the Rules would be defeated if the defendant was conscious that he ought not to commit the action, and that it was contrary to the law of the land. In *R v. Windle* (1952) the defendant had killed his wife by giving her an overdose of aspirin (100 tablets). His wife had complained many times about her life, and had frequently mentioned committing suicide. At trial, the doctors giving evidence were satisfied that she was insane. They were equally satisfied that the defendant was suffering from a form of communicated insanity that might constitute a disease of the mind. However, there was also evidence that when he surrendered to the police, the defendant had stated, 'I suppose they will hang me for this.' It was held that despite the evidence of a mental disorder, the defendant had known that his actions were contrary to the law. The defendant's statement indicated that he was aware that his actions were illegal. His inability to fully appreciate that he ought not to have killed his wife was irrelevant, the court holding that such moral considerations were beyond its purview.

8.8 Irresistible Impulse

The M'Naghten Rules permit a defendant to plead insanity where he suffers from a cognitive disorder, i.e. he did not understand what he was doing. Volitional disorders, or those that affect the defendant's ability to control his behaviour, are not explicitly included in the Rules. So, if X suffers from a disease of the mind that makes it impossible for him to stop himself from committing an offence (a so-called irresistible impulse), can he plead insanity? The English courts have taken a very literal view of the Rules, and have excluded irresistible impulses from the ambit of the Rules (although it is now possible for some forms of irresistible impulse to be considered by English courts under the concept of diminished responsibility – see section 8.11). Despite some authority to the contrary, *R v. Kopsch* (1925) firmly removed any possibility of irresistible impulse as a form of insanity. In that case, the defendant strangled his aunt. In his defence, he argued that when he acted, he did so under the control of his subconscious mind, and was powerless to stop himself. It was held that this was a 'fantastic and subversive' theory that was unrecognised by the law. In *R v. Haynes* (1859), it had been argued that where such a powerful impulse existed to commit an offence, it was imperative that the law had an equally powerful deterrent to act as a safeguard. The same argument was put more colourfully in *R v. Creighton* (1909), when it was said, 'if you cannot resist an impulse in any other way, we will hang a rope in front of your eyes, and perhaps that will help.' A further argument advanced against the recognition of irresistible impulse as a form of insanity is that it would be difficult to distinguish between an impulse that was irresistible due to a disease of the mind and one that was irresistible due to greed or revenge.

The Irish courts have rejected this approach. In a number of cases, the courts implicitly accepted that irresistible impulse is a form of insanity. In *The People (Attorney General) v. McGrath* (1960), for example, the defendant committed an assault from which the victim later died. The defence appealed against conviction on the basis that the killing was due to an uncontrollable impulse. The defence was rejected solely on the basis that there was no evidence of such an impulse. Eight years later, however, the matter was finally decided on its merits. In *The People (Attorney General) v. Hayes* (1967), the defendant argued that he had killed his wife due to an impulse that he could not control. Henchy J. held that the M'Naghten Rules were based on knowledge, i.e. the defendant did not know the nature and quality of his action or that it was wrong, but did not take account of a person's inability to act or refrain from acting despite that knowledge. Henchy J. went on to hold that even though the defendant knew what he was doing and knew that it was illegal, it would be unjust to deny a defence of insanity where the impulse to kill could not be controlled due to some mental illness. In *Doyle v. Wicklow County Council* (1974), an abbatoir owned by the plaintiff had been burned by a seventeen-year-old youth, and the plaintiff sought compensation from the defendant under the malicious damage scheme. The youth had been suffering from a mental condition that led him to believe that because he loved animals so much, he was entitled to burn the abattoir without fear of any legal penalty. If his actions were insane, they could not be considered to be criminal, and the plaintiff would be denied compensation. If they were not insane, however, the actions would be criminal and the defendant would be liable to pay compensation to the plaintiff. The Supreme Court held, upholding an earlier decision in *The People (Attorney General) v. O'Brien* (1936), that the M'Naghten Rules were not the 'sole and exclusive test' of insanity. Further, the court explicitly endorsed the ruling in *Hayes* by stating that it would be unjust to deny a defence of insanity where an irresistible impulse to commit an offence was created through some mental illness.

8.9 Proving Insanity

The onus of proving insanity rests on the defendant, and can be discharged on a balance of probabilities. This will usually be done through the introduction of medical evidence from expert psychiatrists, although it is not essential – the defendant may prefer to rely on his own testimony. However, where the defence is that the defendant has no recollection of the events, as in *R v. Quick* (1973), there will be obvious difficulties in doing so. As McAuley notes, there are no reported cases in the recent past where a defence of insanity was successfully raised in the absence of medical evidence.[2]

The Court of Criminal Appeal in *The People (DPP) v. Abdi* (2004) has recently emphasised the central importance of the jury in determining whether or not the defendant should be acquitted on the grounds of insanity:

2 McAuley, *Insanity, Psychiatry and Criminal Responsibility*, Dublin: Round Hall Press, 1993, p. 97.

> It is essential that every [decision on insanity] be taken by a properly informed jury in a public forum. Equally it is important that where a person does not suffer a criminal conviction on the ground of insanity, such insanity should be clearly and publicly established to the satisfaction of the general public as represented by the jury. The role of the expert witness is not to supplant the tribunal of fact, be it judge or jury, but to inform that tribunal so that it may come to its own decision.

Thus, it is a question of fact for the jury, not doctors, to determine whether or not the defendant was insane. In doing so, the jury must consider all the evidence, medical and non-medical, and are entitled to reject medical evidence. Thus, in *The People (Attorney General) v. McGrath* (**1962**), medical evidence suggested that the defendant was an aggressive psychopath who, in killing the deceased by a series of blows, would not have known what he was doing at the time he struck the fatal blow. The Court of Criminal Appeal upheld the defendant's conviction of murder despite this evidence on the basis that there was non-medical evidence which tended to show rationality on the part of the defendant, due to which the jury could legitimately have rejected the medical evidence. Similarly, in *Arnott & Co. (Dublin) Ltd v. Dublin Corporation* (**1951**), the defendant was attempting to show that the criminal damage for which the plaintiff was claiming compensation was prompted by insanity on the part of the perpetrator. While there was medical evidence that indicated a delusion on the part of the perpetrator, there was also evidence that he had been arrested with an iron bar in his hand and that he went willingly with the arresting garda. The court ruled that this evidence showed that the perpetrator knew that what he had done was illegal. Further, the court indicated that had the perpetrator been on trial, he would have been convicted of causing criminal damage.

8.10 Disposition of Insane Offenders

Section 2 of the Trial of Lunatics Act 1883 requires a verdict of 'guilty but insane' to be passed on a defendant found by the jury to have been insane at the time he committed the offence charged. In *Gallagher v. DPP* (**1991**), the Supreme Court held that this verdict, despite its formulation, was a finding of acquittal. However, unlike acquittals generally, a defendant who has been acquitted on the grounds of insanity is not free to leave. Section 2(2) of the 1883 Act requires that such a defendant be detained in a psychiatric facility during the government's pleasure. In practice, this order means that the defendant will be detained in the Central Mental Hospital in Dundrum, established under the Central Criminal Lunatic Asylum Act 1845. In *O'Halloran v. Minister for Justice* (**1999**), the High Court confirmed that it has been understood for over a century that all offenders found to be insane are to be detained in Dundrum, and that the Minister does not have the power to order such an offender's detention in a psychiatric hospital controlled by a health board. The detention under the 1883 Act is for an indeterminate period of time, possibly for longer than would have been the case had the defendant been convicted. For this reason alone, the insanity defence is not likely to be very popular, even with defendants who could raise it successfully. Insanity tends to be a defence of last resort; as Lawton L.J. noted in *R v. Quick* (1973), insanity is a 'quagmire of law seldom entered nowadays save by those in desperate need of some kind of defence.' In practice, the defence arises only in murder cases; Courts' Service Annual Reports show that from 2000 to 2004, there were twelve findings of insanity out of 208 homicide trials. It is possible that there are some defendants whose criminal acts are prompted by mental disorders who regard conviction and punishment as preferable to acquittal and mandatory indeterminate detention in the Central Mental Hospital. There is some evidence from England that granting the trial courts more discretion in dealing with insane offenders might result in the insanity defence becoming more attractive. Prior to 1991, the Criminal Procedure (Insanity) Act 1964 mandated indeterminate detention in a psychiatric facility for all offenders found to have been insane at the time of committing the offence. In 1991, the Criminal Procedure (Insanity and Unfitness to Plead) Act was enacted by the British Parliament, which gave trial courts a number of options in dealing with those offenders found to be insane (unless the charge was murder, in which case detention remained mandatory): guardianship orders, supervision and treatment orders, admission to hospital or absolute discharges. Mackay and Kearns reported that in the first five years of the operation of this new legislation, the frequency of insanity verdicts doubled compared to the last five years of the previous regime, i.e. 1992–1996 compared with 1987–1991. The authors speculate that criminal lawyers now realise that the 1991 Act removed 'the more glaring disincentives inherent' in the previous regime.[3]

While the detention period is indeterminate, it is clear that insane detainees have the right to apply for release. In *Gallagher*, the Supreme Court held that because the verdict of guilty but insane is one of acquittal, the decision as to release from the Central Mental Hospital is not a judicial matter, but rather lies with the executive. However, McCarthy J. held that all insane detainees have the right to apply for release on the grounds that they are no longer suffering from any mental disorder warranting continued detention in the public and private interest. In *Gallagher v. Director of Central Mental Hospital* (1996), Geoghegan J. expressed his view, *obiter*, that if the detainee's mental disorder no longer existed, the detention could not be continued on the grounds that the detainee was still considered to be dangerous. To hold otherwise would be to permit an unconstitutional form of preventative detention. When an application for release is received, the government must hold a full and fair enquiry before coming to a decision. In so doing, the government must exercise its powers in a quasi-judicial manner; it must act only on evidence and, in particular, must not

---

3 R.D. Mackay, and G. Kearns, 'More Fact(s) About the Insanity Defence', [1999] *Crim. LR* 714.

be swayed by the wishes of the victim's family. The practice at present is for the Minister for Justice to establish an ad hoc Advisory Committee to review the application, and the applicant is entitled to participate in this process according to the rules of natural justice. Thus, in *Kirwan v. Minister for Justice* (**1994**), the High Court held that the detainee must be in a position to put his case and to do so it was not unreasonable that he would need the assistance of a solicitor. If the detainee could not afford a solicitor, he was entitled to apply for legal aid. Once the enquiry has been properly held, the decision as to the detainee's release lies with the government and is not reviewable by the courts.

8.11 Diminished Responsibility

Diminished responsibility is a lesser form of insanity introduced into English law by section 2 of the Homicide Act 1957. It operates as a partial defence to murder only, and, if successful, reduces murder to manslaughter. If the defendant can show that at the time he committed the murder he was suffering from an abnormality of the mind that substantially impaired his mental responsibility for his acts, he will be convicted of manslaughter. In *R v. Byrne* (1960), the defendant was a violent sexual psychopath who strangled a young woman and then mutilated her corpse. The medical evidence disclosed a long history of violent perverted desires that were stronger than the normal sexual desires. It was suggested by the defence that the defendant found it difficult, and at times impossible, to resist those urges. It was held that an 'abnormality of the mind' is not the same as a 'defect of reason':

> Abnormality of mind … means a state of mind so different from that of ordinary human beings that the reasonable man would term it abnormal. It appears to us to be wide enough to cover the mind's activities in all its respects, not only the perception of physical acts and matters and the ability to form a rational judgement whether an act is right or wrong, but also the ability to exercise willpower to control physical acts in accordance with that rational judgement. The expression 'mental responsibility for his acts' points to a consideration of the extent to which the accused's mind is answerable for his physical acts which must include a consideration of the extent of his ability to exercise willpower to control his physical acts.

It is noteworthy that Lord Parker expressed this definition in terms that a jury could easily understand. The test is objective, and as set out by Lord Parker, is wide enough to include irresistible impulse. However, the jury should approach the matter in a commonsensical way, considering all of the evidence, not just the opinions of medical experts. This should be enough to allow the jury to distinguish between an irresistible impulse and one that the defendant did not want to resist due to greed or revenge.

Irish law does not recognise the defence of diminished responsibility. In *The People (DPP) v. O'Mahony* (**1985**), the defendant had been convicted of murder, despite a long history of in-patient psychiatric care. In his appeal, he argued that diminished responsibility was part of Irish law. He argued that the English Homicide Act 1957 was merely declaratory in that it simply codified a defence that already existed in English common law. Therefore, the Irish courts would have precedent on which to allow the defence in Irish law. It was held, however, that the 1957 Act was more than just declaratory; it had altered the common law by introducing a new defence. If the defendant could show some psychological condition that made it impossible for him to resist the impulse to kill, he could plead insanity. However, the defence of diminished responsibility did not form part of Irish law, and the courts had no power to introduce the defence. This would have to be done by the legislature. This decision was reaffirmed by the Court of Criminal Appeal in *The People (DPP) v. Reddan and Hannon* **(1995)**, rejecting the defendant's attempt to argue that even if he had not been fully insane at the time, his intent with respect to the killing was flawed and therefore did not meet the level of intention required for murder by the Criminal Justice Act 1964. A similar attempt was made more recently in *The People (DPP) v. Willoughby* **(2005)**. There, the defendant argued that even if the jury rejected the insanity defence, they should still have received special instructions concerning the defendant's mental state and his ability to form the intention required for a murder conviction. The Court of Criminal Appeal rejected the argument, holding that it was unnecessary to 'sub-divide and compartmentalise' the instructions on intention as suggested.

8.12 Reform

The insanity defence is under pressure from two sources. First, a finding of guilty but insane, together with the subsequent right to seek release due to recovery of sanity, can appear to the public as a mechanism for allowing killers to literally get away with murder. Following the *Gallagher* case, for example, the media has reported that juries are reluctant to issue guilty but insane verdicts: an article in *The Irish Times* in 1998 indicated that juries are unwilling to enter guilty but insane verdicts for fear that killers will later be released.[4] If this situation is true, it can hardly have been helped by Gallagher absconding to Britain in 2000 while on temporary release from the Central Mental Hospital, or by the fact that he could not then be extradited as he had been acquitted of the charges against him. Similar public disquiet came to the fore in the US following the acquittal on the grounds of insanity of John Hinckley for the attempted murder of President Ronald Reagan in 1981. The level of disquiet was such that one state, Idaho, actually abolished the insanity defence, limiting the relevance of evidence of mental illness on the part of the defendant to the sentencing stage.[5]

---

4   See, for example, C. Coulter, 'Juries are Unlikely to Bring in "Guilty but Insane" Verdicts', *The Irish Times*, 26 February 1998, p. 6.
5   See C.V. Clarkson, *Understanding Criminal Law*, London: Sweet & Maxwell, 2001, pp. 101–2.

Despite feelings of disquiet on the part of the public, it is clear that the insanity defence is not a popular option for defendants; we have already noted that the requirement of mandatory detention in the Central Mental Hospital surely dissuades defendants from raising the defence, especially in non-homicide cases. Indeed, in *R v. Sullivan* (1984), the epileptic defendant went all the way to the House of Lords in an attempt to avoid the insanity defence. Thus, rather than being taken advantage of, it is probably more likely that the insanity defence is not being used as often as it should be. Further, the ***Gallagher*** case illustrates that being released from the Hospital is not a straightforward matter: Gallagher spent nearly twelve years in the Hospital before absconding. Consequently, the public belief that multiple killers are able to avoid justice by claiming insanity seems to have more to do with perception than with reality.

The second challenge to the insanity defence comes from Ireland's obligations under the European Convention on Human Rights. Article 5(1)(e) of the Convention allows for the detention of persons of unsound mind, but in the leading decision on this provision, *Winterwerp v. The Netherlands* (1979), the European Court of Human Rights imposed conditions on any such detentions:

> The individual concerned should not be deprived of his liberty unless he has been reliably shown to be of 'unsound mind'. The very nature of what has to be established before the competent national authority – that is, a true mental disorder – calls for objective medical expertise. Further, the mental disorder must be of a kind or degree warranting compulsory confinement. What is more, the validity of continued confinement depends upon the persistence of such a disorder.

However, the Court later accepted in *Luberti v. Italy* (1984) that national authorities have a 'certain margin of appreciation since it is in the first place for the national authorities to evaluate the evidence adduced before them in a particular case.'

It seems certain that the operation of the insanity defence in Ireland is open to challenge under the Convention in at least three respects. First, *Winterwerp* requires that the finding of insanity should be based on objective medical expertise. We have already noted that the legal concept of insanity differs markedly from the medical definition, and has been held to include physical conditions such as arteriosclerosis and epilepsy. No mental health professional would ever consider an epileptic to be insane and in need of confinement in a secure psychiatric facility. Further, the decision as to whether a defendant is insane is made by non-medically trained people (either a judge or a jury); it is reasonable to question the extent to which such a decision is based on objective medical expertise, especially as medical evidence as to insanity carries no greater weight than any other kind of evidence. Second, confinement in a psychiatric facility is permissible under the Convention only where such confinement is required by the nature of the mental illness. However, as we have seen, the Trial of Lunatics Act 1883 mandates detention in all cases; there is at present no facility open to the Irish courts to determine whether such confinement is actually necessary. Further, there are no options other than detention available to the Irish courts under existing legislation even if such a determination could be made. The legality of this situation under the Convention is made worse by the opinion of the European Court of Human Rights in *Varbanov v. Bulgaria* (2000) to the effect that the assessment as to the need for confinement should be based on the person's state of mind at the time of the assessment. The order of an Irish court under the 1883 Act, by contrast, is based on the defendant's state of mind at the time he committed the offence. Third, continued detention is justified under the Convention only where the mental condition persists. Under existing Irish practice, detainees in the Central Mental Hospital are entitled to apply for release and the government is required to treat the application fairly and come to a timely decision. However, this practice places on the detainee the obligation to initiate the review and release procedure; there is at present no system of automatic review for the criminally insane as there is for civil commitments following the enactment of the Mental Health Act 2001. Thus, it seems certain that the insanity defence as it now stands in Irish law is in breach of the Convention.

An attempt was made to reform the insanity defence in 1996, but the Bill foundered. A second attempt, the Criminal Law (Insanity) Bill 2002, has at the time of writing been passed by the Seanad and is being considered by the Dáil. The expressed purpose of the Bill is to bring Irish law on the insanity defence up to date and in line with the jurisprudence of the Convention. The Bill makes several important changes. The Criminal Lunatics Act 1800 and the Trial of Lunatics Act 1883 will be repealed in their entirety. The basis of the insanity defence will be mental disorders, defined in section 1 to include mental illness, mental handicap, dementia or any disease of the mind but does not include intoxication. It is unclear whether the phrase 'disease of the mind' will continue to have the same meaning as it does today. Assuming this to be the case, physical conditions will continue to be included as forms of insanity if they affect the working of the mind, and this accords with the phrase 'mental disorder', of which diseases of the mind will be a part. The existing defence of insanity as encompassing lack of knowledge of the nature and quality of the act, its illegality or the irresistibility of an impulse is given statutory effect in section 4. It is curious, however, that there is no provision dealing directly with the burden of proving insanity, especially as the burden of proving the partial defence of diminished responsibility is explicitly placed by section 5(2) on the defence. It seems unlikely that the legislature intends to place the burden on the prosecution, and it is unfortunate that in a Bill designed to comprehensively restate the defence of insanity, this issue is not dealt with more explicitly.

Section 4 will also require that the court or jury be presented with evidence from a consultant psychiatrist as to the defendant's mental condition. The drafters of this provision clearly had in mind the requirement in *Winterwerp* that a finding of insanity be based on objective medical expertise. The section does not, however, indicate any change in the current practice of not according such evidence any special weight. The jury must hear the psychiatrist's evidence, but will still be able to reject it if they so choose. Section 4 will also change the current illogical form of the special verdict to be returned; instead of 'guilty but insane', the verdict will be 'not guilty by reason of insanity'. The Bill also proposes in section 7 to give a right of appeal to a defendant who has been found not guilty by reason of insanity on one of three grounds: that he did not commit the act in question, that he was not suffering from a mental disorder or that the court should instead have found that he was unfit to be tried.

There are considerable changes contemplated to the disposition of those found not guilty by reason of insanity. Under section 4(2), the trial court will be obliged to assess the defendant's state of mind after the verdict is announced to determine the need for in-patient care, and for that purpose the court may direct that the defendant be committed to a designated centre, i.e. the Central Mental Hospital or other facility so designated, for up to fourteen days for examination. This examination period may be extended, but the total examination period cannot last for more than six months. The court must receive a report from the designated centre within the examination period as to whether the defendant is suffering from a mental disorder as defined in the Mental Health Act 2001 and needs to be committed for in-patient care. 'Mental disorder' is defined in section 3 of this Act as mental illness, severe dementia or intellectual disability causing a likelihood either of serious and imminent danger to the person or to others or a deterioration in the person's condition where treatment could benefit or alleviate that condition. If the court concludes on foot of this report, and any other evidence adduced, that the defendant is suffering from such a mental disorder and is in need of in-patient care, the court will be required to order that the defendant be detained in a designated centre. These measures should address the *Winterwerp* requirements as to ordering detention, and should also end the current requirement of detaining people suffering from physical conditions in psychiatric facilities. However, the options available to the courts under the Bill in dealing with insane offenders will be limited to either ordering detention if required or granting a complete discharge. It is regrettable that the drafters of the Bill did not take this opportunity to provide the courts with the range of intermediate options available in England since 1991.

The Bill proposes to establish a permanent Mental Health Review Board to replace the current ad hoc Advisory Committees. The Board will be chaired by a lawyer who is either a practitioner with at least ten years' experience or is a judge of the Circuit, High or Supreme Courts. At least one member of the Board must be a consultant psychiatrist. The Board will be required to ensure that all detentions under the Bill are reviewed at least every six months, and the clinical director of the designated centre in question will be obliged to comply with all requests from the Board in connection with such reviews. If the clinical director forms the opinion that the patient is no longer in need of in-patient care, the Board must be notified immediately. The Board must then arrange for a hearing to determine whether the detention should continue and will have the power to make the order it thinks fit in each case. Alternatively, any person detained under the Bill will be able to apply to the Board for a review of his detention, and the Board is required to hold a hearing as soon as possible. Finally, the Board may initiate a review of any detention on its own authority. These provisions should give effect to the *Winterwerp* requirement that the detention of persons of unsound mind can continue only where such detention is medically necessary.

Finally, the Bill proposes to create the partial defence of diminished responsibility in Irish law. Under section 5, this defence will be available only on a murder charge, and the burden of proof will rest with the defendant. The defence will be available when the court is satisfied that the defendant was suffering from a mental disorder at the time of the act, which carries the same meaning here as it does for insanity under section 4. This definition expressly excludes intoxication, thus preventing any consideration of this defence in cases involving intoxicated offenders. The mental disorder, while insufficient for a finding of not guilty by reason of insanity, must have been sufficient to substantially diminish the defendant's responsibility for the act. On making such a finding, the court should convict the defendant of manslaughter.

8.13 Further Reading

Binchy, 'Mental Retardation and the Criminal Law', (1984) 2 *ILT* 111.

Boland, 'Diminished Responsibility as a Defence in Irish Law', (1995) 5 *ICLJ* 173.

————, 'Diminished Responsibility as a Defence in Irish Law: Past English Mistakes and Future Irish Directions', (1996) 6 *ICLJ* 19.

Mackay, R.D. and Kearns, G., 'More Fact(s) about the Insanity Defence', [1999] *Crim LR* 714.

McAuley, *Insanity, Psychiatry and Criminal Responsibility*, Dublin: Round Hall Press, 1993.

————, 'The Civilian Experience of the Insanity Defence', (1989) 24 *Ir Jur (ns)* 227.

O'Hanlon, 'Not Guilty Because of Insanity', (1968) 3 *Ir Jur (ns)* 61.

Osborough, 'M'Naghten Revisited', (1974) 9 *Ir Jur (ns)* 76.

Yeo, 'Rethinking the Incapacities of Insanity', (2001) 36 *Ir Jur (ns)* 275.

CHAPTER NINE

INTOXICATION

9.1 Introduction

The necessity for the prosecution to establish the existence of *mens rea* has already been explored in Chapter 4. However, in some cases, a defendant may have committed the offence while under the influence of an intoxicant. The issue arises as to the effect intoxication should have on the imposition of criminal liability. With this issue, the law faces a serious conflict between principle and policy. In principle, the prosecution must prove the *mens rea* required by the definition of the charge. If the defendant was unable to form the required *mens rea* due to intoxication, he should logically be acquitted on any charge. However, there are two policy issues that cast doubt on the foregoing statements of principle. First, there is a public safety issue. In *R v. Doherty* (1887), Stephen J. observed that if drunkenness was an excuse for criminality, 'you might as well shut up the criminal courts, because drink is the occasion of a large proportion of the crime which is committed.' Thus, to allow the effect of the ingestion of intoxicants as a defence would result in the removal of any semblance of protection of the public from a large proportion of violent offenders. Second, unlike insanity, which affects a person through no fault of his own, the effects of intoxication are almost always entirely self-inflicted. It is unsettling that an offender could engineer an escape from the consequences of his actions because of a self-inflicted mental impairment. As Lawton L.J. put it in the Court of Appeal's decision in *DPP v. Majewski* (1976), it would be strange if 'the more drunk a man became, provided he stopped short of making himself insane, the better chance he had of an acquittal.'

The law has struggled to balance the requirements of principle and policy. Traditionally, the common law made no allowance for intoxication; Hale, writing in the eighteenth century, for example, wrote that an intoxicated offender shall 'have the same judgment as if he were in his right senses.' Thus, even where the defendant was totally incapable of knowing what he was doing because he was so intoxicated, he was treated as if he were fully sober. However, as the *mens rea* requirement assumed greater importance, it was realised that there was a logical contradiction between treating an intoxicated man who could not form *mens rea* as if he had *mens rea*. The modern approach in England, which has recently been adopted in Ireland, is something of a compromise between principle and policy. The basic premise is that intoxication offers no answer to a criminal charge unless the offence in question requires proof of intention. If the jury finds that the defendant did not have the required intention, then he should be acquitted.

Charges involving offences supported by negligence or recklessness cannot be defended on the basis of intoxication.

9.2 Definition of Intoxication

While most intoxication cases have arisen as a result of alcohol, it was held in *R v. Lipman* (1969) that the same principles should apply to intoxication as a result of the ingestion of drugs. This is a sensible conclusion, and accords with the definition of an intoxicant given in the Road Traffic Act 1961, section 50(1)(b), as amended by section 11 of the Road Traffic Act 1978: 'alcohol and drugs and any combination of drugs or of drugs and alcohol'. This definition was endorsed by the Law Reform Commission in its *Consultation Paper* and *Report on Intoxication*, both published in 1995. The Commission went on to adopt the definition of intoxication given by the American Law Institute in its Model Penal Code: 'a disturbance of mental or physical capacities resulting from the introduction of substances into the body.'

It is important to bear in mind that intoxication in this respect means far more than mere drunkenness. Drunkenness is never a defence to any charge, and may indeed be an aggravating factor resulting in the imposition of a heavier sentence. In *The People (DPP) v. Sheedy* (2000), for example, the Court of Criminal Appeal, in upholding a sentence of four years' imprisonment for causing death by dangerous driving, listed as an aggravating factor the fact that the defendant had consumed four pints of beer prior to driving. Intoxication as a possible defence arises where the defendant was so intoxicated that he was unable to form the necessary *mens rea*.

The law has traditionally distinguished between two types of intoxication: voluntary and involuntary. The former arises where the defendant deliberately ingested alcohol or drugs, whereas the latter arises where the defendant was unaware of doing so. If the defendant deliberately took an intoxicant but was unaware of its strength, he will be considered to have voluntarily intoxicated himself. This point was considered by the Court of Appeal in *R v. Allen* (1988). The defendant had been convicted of buggery and indecent assault, and one of his arguments was that if he had committed the offences, he had done so while intoxicated. He claimed that he had been given some wine by a friend, and that he had not realised its alcoholic content. He claimed that this established involuntary intoxication. It was held that he had known that he was drinking alcohol, and that such drinking does not become involuntary simply because he had underestimated the strength of the alcohol involved.

9.3 Voluntary Intoxication

The starting point for the modern defence of intoxication is the decision of the House of Lords in *DPP v. Beard* (1920). The defendant raped a girl and then suffocated her to death. He argued that intoxication is a defence to any criminal charge, and this submission was accepted by the Court of Appeal. However, on appeal again to the House of Lords, it was held that this contention was too broad and did not represent the law as it was not based on authority. It was held, restoring the original murder conviction, that there is a distinction between drunkenness and intoxication. The former is never a defence, while the latter may be if the defendant was incapable of forming the specific intent required to constitute the offence.

The operative phrase in *Beard* was 'specific intent', and has become all-important in English case law. In *DPP v. Majewski* (1976), *Beard* was considered and explained. The defendant had been convicted of three counts of assault occasioning actual bodily harm and three counts of assaulting a police officer, all arising out of a brawl. His defence was that prior to the incident, he had consumed a considerable quantity of alcohol and drugs, and that he therefore had no *mens rea*, nor indeed any memory of the incident. This case therefore raised the conflict between principle and policy alluded to above (section 9.1). It was held by the House of Lords that the basic common law rule that intoxication is never a defence still existed, but was no longer applied absolutely, with some exceptions having been allowed. These exceptions were crystallised into one proposition: where an offence required proof of specific intent, intoxication could operate as a defence if it negatived that specific intent.[1] Where, however, the offence required proof of basic intent, intoxication was irrelevant. This decision was essentially policy-based, with two policies to the forefront:

(a) where a person causes himself to be in a position where his self-control is removed, he should not be permitted to benefit from it; and
(b) one of the purposes of the criminal law is to protect people from unjust attack; if intoxication were to be a general defence, the public's level of protection would necessarily be reduced.

The Lords acknowledged that the distinction between specific and basic intent was illogical, but it was an attempt to balance policy with principle. Lord Russell, in particular, noted that 'logic in criminal law must not be allowed to run away with common sense', sentiments echoed by Lord Salmon.

One of the core difficulties with *Majewski* is that it rests on the distinction between specific intent and basic intent. However, at least three different definitions of specific intent were offered. It was not until *MPC v. Caldwell* (1981) that the House of Lords settled, by a majority, on a definition of a crime of specific intent as one that requires proof of intention. Thus, offences such as murder, theft, robbery, burglary and all attempts are offences of specific intent to which intoxication can offer an answer. Offences of basic intent are those that require proof of recklessness: manslaughter, rape, assault, etc. In *Majewski*, the

---

1 Another exception is where the defendant, through his drinking, induces a disease of the mind. In such cases, the matter falls to be decided under the M'Naghten Rules.

Lords ruled that intoxication can never offer an answer to such charges. The reasoning here was explained by Lord Elwyn-Jones: 'By allowing himself to get drunk and thereby putting himself in such a condition as to be no longer amenable to the law's commands, a man shows such recklessness as amounts to *mens rea* for the purposes of all ordinary crimes.' However, the Court of Appeal has refined this position since *Majewski*.

In *R v. Quick* (1973), the defendant was a diabetic who had suffered a hypoglycaemic episode, i.e. low blood sugar levels, from taking insulin and then going out drinking having eaten very little. During the episode, he committed an assault and wanted the jury to consider a plea of non-insane automatism rather than insanity. When the trial judge refused permission to allow this defence, the defendant changed his plea to guilty and appealed. The Court of Appeal ruled that the root cause of the defendant's hypoglycaemic episode was the external factor of taking the insulin rather than the internal factor of the underlying diabetes. Accordingly, the insanity defence was inappropriate. However, the court also ruled that non-insane automatism was not available when the automatism was caused through the ingestion of drink or drugs, or by doing something the effect of which the defendant ought to have foreseen. However, this decision was handed down before the House of Lords had decided *Majewski*. In *R v. Bailey* (1983), the Court of Appeal accepted, on the basis of *Majewski*, that self-induced intoxication does offer a defence to charges involving specific intent. Further, the court ruled that self-induced intoxication may sometimes offer a defence to a charge involving an offence of basic intent depending on the defendant's awareness of the effects of the substance he was ingesting. If the intoxication occurred through the ingestion of drink or dangerous drugs, the effects of which are well known, then the defendant can be presumed to have known the risk that he was running by ingesting such substances. Consequently, he acted recklessly in consuming those substances, and recklessness is sufficient for offences of basic intent. However, if the intoxication occurred due to the ingestion of intoxicants other than drink or dangerous drugs, the effect of the substances consumed might not be so well known and therefore cannot be presumed. Accordingly, awareness of the risk of intoxication, and therefore recklessness, could not be presumed. In such cases, the prosecution would have to prove that the defendant was aware of the effect of the substance he was consuming and was therefore reckless. If the prosecution was unable to discharge this burden, the intoxication should be considered inadvertent and the defendant would have a defence to a charge involving an offence of basic intent. The Court of Appeal indicated that the effects of not eating after taking insulin, as had occurred in this case, would not be well known. Thus, it could not be presumed that a diabetic would be aware of the risk that he was running and this would have to be proven.

There is an apparent conflict between these decisions in relation to cases involving basic intent offences. *Quick* held that the issue of self-induced intoxication should be decided objectively, i.e. persons using drink or dangerous drugs ought to know the effects of those substances, while *Bailey* held that the issue should be decided subjectively, i.e. intoxication only fails as a defence if the defendant actually knew of those effects. However, if *Quick* is limited to situations involving drink and dangerous drugs, as suggested in *Bailey*, then the conflict can be resolved. Thus, if the intoxication was induced through the consumption of drink or dangerous drugs, there is no defence to a charge involving offences of basic intent. In all other situations, however, self-induced intoxication may offer a defence to such charges if the defendant was unaware of the effects of the substances that he was consuming. Thus, in *R v. Hardie* (1984), the defendant took valium tablets following the break-up of a relationship with a woman. Some time later, he set fire to the apartment in which the woman and her daughter were living. The trial judge told the jury that because the valium had been taken deliberately and not on prescription (the tablets belonged to a friend of the defendant), the intoxication defence was not available. The Court of Appeal ruled that this was a misdirection. The jury should have been directed to consider whether the defendant had acted recklessly in taking the valium, i.e. had the defendant foreseen the effect that the valium might have, bearing in mind that valium is a sedative which is different from drugs likely to cause aggression.

9.4 *Majewski* in the Commonwealth

The decision in *Majewski* has received considerable criticism from courts throughout the Commonwealth for allowing convictions for offences of basic intent. Two clear themes emerge from these criticisms. First, on principle, the Lords in *Majewski* were wrong to assume that drinking could necessarily supply the fault requirement necessary for conviction. As Cory J. explained in the Canadian case of *Daviault v. R* (1994), a sexual assault case, the 'consumption of alcohol simply cannot lead inexorably to the conclusion that the accused possessed the requisite mental element to commit a sexual assault, or any other crime. Rather, the substituted *mens rea* rule has the effect of eliminating the minimal mental element required for sexual assault.' Thus, it cannot be said that an intent to drink equates with the intent to commit a sexual assault. Indeed, in the Australian case of *O'Connor v. R* (1980), Barwick C.J. noted that voluntary intoxication might occur inadvertently, and gave the example of a person at dinner who might not notice the frequency with which his glass is replenished with wine. Further, even if voluntary intoxication should be considered an evil, it is not a crime, and nor is it related to the criminal act. Thus, *Majewski* created difficulties with the contemporaneity requirement of criminal liability: in a sense, an intoxicated offender who is convicted of a crime of basic intent has been convicted for becoming intoxicated.

Second, the Commonwealth courts have been unimpressed by the policy arguments cited by the Lords in *Majewski*. Barwick C.J. indicated that juries would be unlikely to be indulgent to intoxicated offenders, and indeed they might conclude that the defendant was responsible for everything that flowed from the condition he got himself into. In *O'Connor*, Cory J. pointed to scientific evidence that the Lords' fears of opening the floodgates to intoxicated offenders were groundless. One study of over 500 trials in New South Wales found only one case in which there was any certainty that intoxication brought about an acquittal. As the author of that study commented, allowing a full defence of intoxication 'far from opening any floodgates has at most permitted an occasional drip to escape from the tap.' Further, Barwick C.J. argued that if the public required protection from violent offenders, do they not also require protection from robbers and burglars whose crimes might also be motivated by alcohol? Yet, due to the manner in which the distinction between specific and basic intent operates, robbery and burglary are crimes of specific intent to which intoxication is a full answer. Accordingly, these Commonwealth courts declined to follow *Majewski*.

9.5 Irish Law

Until recently, there was no Irish authority on the status of *Majewski* in Ireland. In *The People (Attorney General) v. Manning* (1953), the defendant had been charged with murder and raised two defences: insanity and absence of *mens rea* due to intoxication. The Court of Criminal Appeal accepted that intoxication was no defence unless the defendant had consumed so much alcohol 'as to render him incapable of knowing what he was doing at all, or if he appreciated that, of knowing the consequences or probable consequences of his actions.' In *The People (DPP) v. McBride* (1997), the same court accepted as a general statement defence counsel's contention that while drunkenness was no defence to any charge, it would be relevant to a consideration of whether or not the defendant was capable of forming the *mens rea* of murder. It is interesting in light of these decisions that the Law Reform Commission took the view in its 1995 *Report on Intoxication* that in practice, intoxication is not a defence to a criminal charge, and recommended that this position should not be altered.

The issue of intoxication as a defence to a criminal charge arose directly before the Court of Criminal Appeal in *The People (DPP) v. Reilly* (2004). In this case, following the consumption of a massive quantity of alcohol – one expert witness suggested that the quantity was so great as to leave the defendant almost anaesthetised – the defendant went to sleep in a friend's house in a room in which the friend's eighteen-month-old son was sleeping. During the night, the defendant stabbed the child several times, but the following morning he had no recollection of doing so and was in a very dazed state. At trial, the defendant was acquitted of murder but convicted of manslaughter, and it was against this conviction that the defendant appealed. The Court of Criminal Appeal ruled that the decision in *Manning* did not create a general defence of intoxication; rather, *Manning* allowed an intoxicated defendant charged with murder to be convicted of manslaughter. Having reviewed *Majewski* and its principal judicial critics, McCracken J. ruled that for all its logical problems, the policy issue of protecting the public should override strict logic, and that the decision in *Majewski* represents Irish law:

> However, whatever may be the logic, the Court is here concerned with the commission of actions of violence by one person against another. It is not sufficient to make decisions on such issues in a purely theoretical manner. The Court must have regard to the rights of an accused person, but it must also have regard to the interest of the public at large who are entitled to be protected from acts of violence. If a person by consuming alcohol induces in himself a situation in which his likelihood to commit acts of violence is increased, particularly to the stage where he commits an act which he would not have committed had he not consumed the alcohol, then surely the Courts would be failing in their obligations to the public if they allowed the cause of his violence, namely the alcohol, to excuse his actions. The reasoning behind the *Majewski* decision appears to this Court to achieve the balance between the rights of the accused, who would be entitled to be acquitted if the jury found automatism which was, in the words of the trial Judge, *'Free standing',* as against the rights of the public to ensure that the Applicant will be held liable for actions which were induced by alcohol voluntarily consumed.

Accordingly, the defendant's manslaughter conviction was affirmed. It is not clear whether the refinements to the *Majewski* test developed by the Court of Appeal in *Bailey* and *Hardie* also apply in Ireland. However, the logic behind these decisions is impeccable, and it is submitted that if *Majewski* is incorporated into Irish law, so too must the refinements.

9.6 Dutch Courage

The position where a defendant deliberately drinks in order to give himself the courage to commit an offence is relatively straightforward, and Irish law undoubtedly follows English law. In *Attorney General for Northern Ireland v. Gallagher* (1961), the defendant wanted to kill his wife. He bought a knife and a bottle of whiskey. He drank the whiskey to give himself the courage to go through with the killing, and then stabbed his wife to death. The House of Lords held that his conviction for murder should be upheld. Lord Denning held that where the defendant forms the intention to kill and prepares to do so, and then drinks alcohol to give himself courage, he cannot then claim to have been incapable of forming *mens rea*. Indeed, Lord Denning felt that such a man was far more deserving of condemnation than a man who only decides to kill after getting drunk. However, as Smith and Hogan point out, *mens rea* and *actus reus* must coincide in terms of time. Where the defendant forms the *mens rea* and then drinks himself into an intoxicated state before committing the *actus reus*, there is no necessary coincidence between the two. It is possible that at the time the *actus reus* is committed, the defendant cannot form *mens rea*, and therefore should be acquitted.[2] However, the fact that he went through with the killing could just as easily be evidence of a continuing intent. Whichever is true, under *Gallagher* the defendant has no defence. Whether or not the Irish courts would accept the *Gallagher* decision regarding Dutch courage has not yet been decided. On purely policy grounds, the decision is better than allowing a defendant to, quite literally, get away with murder.

9.7 Involuntary Intoxication

Involuntary intoxication arises where a defendant ingests an intoxicant without his knowledge, usually because his drink was 'spiked'. Where he knew of the spiking, the intoxication that resulted was not involuntary. Until recently, it seemed that where involuntary intoxication was shown, the defendant would not be held responsible for his actions. In 1994, however, this position was explained and narrowed somewhat. In *R v. Kingston* (1994), the defendant was a man with paedophiliac tendencies. Another man planned to blackmail him and to this end he lured a fifteen-year-old boy back to his flat, spiked the defendant's drink and invited him to abuse the boy. Both the defendant and the blackmailer were charged with indecent assault. The defendant argued that his actions were brought about by the spiked drink, and that he therefore should not be held accountable. The trial judge directed the jury that the defendant could only be acquitted where the intoxication negatived *mens rea*, and the defendant was convicted. On appeal, the Court of Appeal quashed the conviction on the grounds that the defendant's actions had been brought about by the fraud of another person. This decision was appealed by the DPP. The House of Lords ruled that the original conviction should be reinstated. The House of Lords unanimously rejected the defendant's assertion that absence of moral fault equated with absence of *mens rea*. Lord Mustill, who delivered the judgment of the House, pointed out that a 'drugged intent is still an intent', and that the mere fact that the involuntary intoxication caused the defendant to lose his inhibitions did not mean that his actions were unintended. Consequently, the defendant had the necessary *mens rea*. If the defendant was unable to form the required *mens rea*, then he would have a complete answer to any charge.

There is no existing Irish authority on this issue. However, the Law Reform Commission considered it during their consideration of the wider context of intoxication as a defence to criminal charges. The Commission suggested that involuntary intoxication should be a defence to any charge where the level of intoxication is such that the defendant could not form the necessary *mens rea*. As the Commission noted, the defence would be available where the intoxication caused the offence rather than merely facilitated it, as in *Kingston*.[3] Additionally,

---

2 Smith and Hogan, *Criminal Law*, 11th ed., Oxford: Oxford University Press, 2005, p. 285.
3 Law Reform Commission, *Report on Intoxication*, LRC 51–1995, p. 11.

the concept of involuntary intoxication should be expanded to include situations where the defendant took a drug for medicinal purposes either on medical advice and according to directions, or while unaware that it would or might create aggressive or uncontrollable behaviour. In this respect, the Commission endorsed the position already reached by the English courts.

9.8 Further Reading

Boland, 'Intoxication and Criminal Liability', (1996) 60 *JCL* 100.

Clements, 'After *R v. Kingston*: Is there Scope for a New Defence', (1995) 59 *JCL* 305.

Law Reform Commission, *Consultation Paper on Intoxication as a Defence to a Criminal Offence*, 1995.

————, *Report on Intoxication*, LRC 51–1995.

McAuley, 'The Intoxication Defence in Criminal Law', (1997) 32 *Ir Jur (ns)* 243.

O'Leary, 'Lament for the Intoxication Defence', (1997) 48 *NILQ* 152.

————, 'Post-Mortem on the Special Position of the Innocently Intoxicated Person', (1996) 6 *ICLJ* 72.

O'Malley, 'Intoxication and Criminal Responsibility', (1991) 1 *ICLJ* 138.

CHAPTER TEN

DURESS

10.1 Introduction

In most cases, if a defendant commits a proscribed act with the specified level of *mens rea*, a conviction will follow. In some situations, however, the defendant may still escape criminal liability on the basis that he was coerced into committing the act. Such an argument forms the core of the defence of duress. If the jury is satisfied that the defendant's actions were prompted by threats, then he has a complete answer to most charges. The rationale for allowing the defence of duress could have been framed in terms of voluntariness, but the courts have instead viewed the defence as a 'concession to human frailty' (*R v. Howe* (1987)). There is no question that a defendant who committed an illegal act under duress lacked *mens rea*; on the contrary, he knew what he was doing and indeed consciously chose to commit the act. However, the fact that the defendant was effectively forced by threats to commit the act renders the defendant morally innocent, and it would therefore be 'impossible for a civilised system of criminal law to hold him fully responsible' (*Lynch v. DPP for Northern Ireland* (1975)). The basis for the defence of duress has traditionally been threats of serious injury or death proffered by individuals. However, the English courts have extended the defence to dangerous circumstances; in *Howe*, Lord Hailsham indicated that he could see no reason to treat threats arising from circumstances any differently to threats from individuals – the distinction between them was a 'distinction without a relevant difference'. In *R v. Pommel* (1995), the Court of Appeal ruled that the two forms of duress followed the same contours and were based on the same test. The Irish courts accepted in *The People (Attorney General) v. Whelan* (**1934**) that 'threats of immediate death or serious personal violence so great as to overbear the ordinary power of human resistance should be accepted as a justification for acts which would otherwise be criminal.'[1] As yet there is no clear Irish authority as to duress by circumstance, but Lord Hailsham's logic seems impeccable: if a person can be excused because his will was overborne by a threat from another person of serious injury, there is no rational reason to treat differently the effect of a threat of serious injury from a situation. Accordingly, if a suitable case should arise, it is submitted that the Irish courts should follow their English brethren.

---

1   As an aside, this is one of the few areas of law in which the English courts have developed their jurisprudence in reference to an Irish authority.

10.2 The Test

The crucial element in duress is that the defendant's will was overborne by the threats made against him. There is, however, an immediate issue with this requirement: suppose X is particularly weak willed, and his will collapses in the face of an innocuous threat that would not concern a person of ordinary firmness. Should X be allowed to escape liability on account of his own subjective fear, or should the law demand a reasonable degree of courage? In *Whelan*, Murnaghan J. referred to the 'ordinary power of human resistance', which is an objective test. The jury must be satisfied that the defendant acceded to threats that would have overborne the will of a reasonable person. However, it is not clear whether the jury should have regard to the particular infirmities of the defendant. In *The People (DPP) v. O'Toole* (2003), the Court of Criminal Appeal endorsed the trial judge's instructions to consider how they would have reacted in a situation similar to that in which the defendant found himself. On this basis, it would be no defence for the defendant to argue that he was unusually susceptible to threats that a reasonable person would have shrugged off. However, in *The People (DPP) v. Dickey* (2003), the Court of Criminal Appeal made no comment on the following passage from the judge's charge to the jury:

> When you are considering this you have to consider it from the powers that you perceive the accused to have; it is not what you would do in the situation but what you perceive the accused's powers were, and take into account the particular circumstances and human frailties of the accused specifically.

This charge injects a certain degree of subjectivity into the test and does not sit well with the objective test suggested in *Whelan*. Marginal as it is, the weight of Irish authority suggests that the charge in *Dickey* was unduly lenient to the defendant.

The English courts have developed the test for duress to a greater degree of precision than the Irish courts. The House of Lords in *R v. Howe* (1987) was specifically asked to determine whether or not the test for duress was objective. On policy grounds, the House held that the test did indeed contain an objective element. The House compared a situation of duress with a situation of provocation: just as the law of provocation requires a defendant to have reasonable self-control, so too the law demands that a defendant who pleads duress to have a reasonable level of steadfastness. The House approved a formulation set out by the Court of Appeal in *R v. Graham* (1982):

> (1) was the defendant, or may he have been, impelled to act as he did because, as a result of what he reasonably believed [the threatener] had said or done, he had good cause to fear that if he did not so act [the threatener] would kill him or (if this is to be added) cause him serious physical injury? (2) if so, have the prosecution made the jury sure that a sober person of reasonable firmness, sharing the characteristics of the defendant, would not have responded to whatever he reasonably believed [the threatener] said or did by taking part in the killing?

In *R v. Hegarty* (1994), it was held that the kind of characteristics that the sober person of reasonable firmness could share are age, gender and state of physical health. The existence of a mental condition that made the defendant more susceptible to threats was irrelevant, as it was incompatible with the concept of reasonable firmness. This approach must now be considered suspect, as the law on provocation in England is currently in a state of flux. The House of Lords in *Howe* (and the Court of Appeal in *Hegarty*) developed this test by comparison with the law of provocation, in which the test for provocation allowed for the reasonable person to share certain of the defendant's characteristics. However, in *R v. Smith (Morgan)* (2000), the House of Lords radically altered the test for provocation to one in which the defendant is required to exercise the degree of self-control that society can reasonably expect from him bearing in mind his characteristics. This alteration has since been called into question by a subsequent decision of the Privy Council in *Attorney General of Jersey v. Holley* (2005) (see section 18.13). However, if the English courts follow *Smith (Morgan)*, then logically, the second strand of the test for duress should also be altered to whether the defendant exercised the degree of firmness that society could reasonably expect from him bearing in mind his characteristics.

10.3 The Nature of the Threat

The kind of threat that will justify a plea of duress will depend on the kind of duress being pleaded. It is clear that the only threats that will suffice for a successful plea of duress by threats are those of imminent serious injury or death. Thus, in *R v. Steane* (1947), the defendant was an Englishman caught in Germany at the outbreak of World War Two. He agreed to make propaganda broadcasts for the Germans following repeated beatings and threats to his family from the Gestapo. After the war, he was tried and convicted of assisting the enemy, which is a form of treason. On appeal, the Court of Appeal accepted that the defendant's actions were not as a result of his free will, but had instead been brought about through violence and serious threats. The conviction was quashed. However, in *R v. Rodger and Rose* (1998), it was held that no plea could arise from threats from the defendant to harm himself. Threats to a person's property or a threat to cause embarrassment also will not be sufficient. In *R v. Valderrama-Vega* (1985), it was held that threats to reveal the defendant's homosexual proclivities were insufficient for a plea of duress, although the cumulative effect of such a threat could be considered in conjunction with threats of serious harm.

In cases in which duress of circumstances is pleaded, there must have been some kind of emergency in which the defendant felt so threatened that he had no reasonable alternative but to break the law. Given the English authority that both forms of duress should follow the same path, presumably the plea of duress by circumstance will be limited to emergencies that threaten death or serious harm. So, in *DPP v. Rogers* (1998), the defendant argued that he had been speeding trying to avoid a car that was following him; he claimed that he thought he was being followed by an aggressive neighbour and was in serious danger. The court ruled that even if this version was true, there was no necessity for the defendant to drive on a main road in the way he had been driving.

As *Steane* suggests, it is not necessary that the threat be directed at the defendant himself, and this point was confirmed by the Court of Appeal in *R v. Pommell* (1995). However, the Court of Appeal in *R v. Wright* (2000) and the House of Lords in *R v. Hasan* (2005) indicated that only threats made against the defendant, the defendant's family or to another person for whom the defendant could reasonably believe that he was responsible will suffice for a plea of duress. This seems unduly restricted; the degree of relationship is certainly a factor relevant to an assessment of the actor's reaction to the perceived threat, but such a relationship is hardly conclusive. While a threat to a loved one is likely to have greater impact than a threat to a stranger, it is certainly conceivable that a person's will might be overborne by threats to strangers. The High Court of Justiciary in Scotland in *Lord Advocate's Reference No.1 of 2000* (2001), discussing the related defence of necessity, noted that if this restriction was accepted, then a person who took ostensibly illegal action to prevent a runaway vehicle hitting a crowd of people would have a defence only if he happened to have had a companion in the crowd. If the crowd were all strangers, the actor would be without a defence. The court ruled that there was 'no acceptable basis for restricting rescue to the protection of persons already known to and having a relationship with the rescuer at the moment of response to the other's danger.' This more open approach has more to commend it than the position of the English courts: a person whose will has been overborne by threats to a stranger is no more morally guilty than a person whose will has been overborne by threats to a loved one. Accordingly, the availability of the duress defence should not be dependent on the relationship to the actor of the threatened person.

Perception of what constitutes a threat will obviously vary, and the question arises as to whose perspective of the threatening conduct should be taken: the defendant himself or the reasonable person. English case law is mixed, but the House of Lords in *Lynch* and *Howe* were firmly of the view that the defendant must have reasonably believed that he was being threatened with death or serious injury. The objective nature of the duress defence has been further underlined by the recent decision of the House in *R v. Hasan* (2005) that the defence is precluded where a defendant ought reasonably to have known that his association with the group might lead to coercion. Thus, an honest belief that a threat of death or serious harm has been made is not sufficient; there must also be good reason to believe that such a threat exists.

Whether the duress arises from threats or from circumstances, the threat facing the defendant must be imminent, but it is clear that imminent does not mean immediate. In *R v. Hudson and Taylor* (1971), the defendants had been called as prosecution witnesses but perjured themselves as a result of threats made against them. The Court of Appeal held that it was irrelevant that the threat could not be carried out immediately in the courtroom; it was enough that the threats were present and could be carried out shortly after the trial. However, it is clear that the threats must be capable of being carried out within a short period of time; in *R v. Hasan* (2005), Lord Bingham indicated that threats due to be carried out the following day would not be sufficiently imminent. With duress of circumstances, the threatening situation must be present at the time of the unlawful act. However, it seems that there does not have to be any specific threat. In *R v. Abdul-Hussain* (1999), the defendants, Shia Muslims, hijacked an aircraft to take them to Britain in order to avoid serious religious persecution in Iraq. The Court of Appeal rejected the argument that the threats against them lacked imminence, and gave the following example: 'if Anne Frank had stolen a car to escape from Amsterdam and been charged with theft, the tenets of English law would not, in our judgment, have denied her a defence of duress of circumstances, on the ground that she should have waited for the Gestapo's knock on the door.'

10.4 Effect of the Threats or Circumstances

The mere fact that threats were made is not in itself sufficient for a successful plea of duress; in **Whelan**, the Court of Criminal Appeal stressed that the defendant's will must have been overborne by the threats. However, in *Valderrama-Vega*, the Court of Appeal confirmed that the mere existence of other motivations on the defendant's part would not necessarily defeat the defence. In *R v. Ortiz* (1986), the defendant was a Colombian involved in the fashion industry who acted as a courier for Columbian drug lords. He pleaded duress on the basis that he had received threats against his family from Colombian drug lords. However, the prosecution was able to point to considerable financial benefits that the defendant had enjoyed as a result of his involvement with the drugs business, and argued that this involvement came about through greed rather than fear. The Court of Appeal confirmed that the defendant's actions must have been brought about by the threats, and it was unlikely in practice that the jury would conclude that a person such as the defendant had acted out of fear.

Duress will only provide a defence in situations in which the threat was operating on the defendant's will. This has two implications. First, once the threat ceases, so too does the duress, but the fact that the defendant continued to act unlawfully for some time after the duress ceased may not be fatal to the defence if he provides a reasonable explanation. In *R v. Pommel* (1995), the defendant had taken possession of a firearm from another man in order to prevent that other man from using the weapon. However, he was in possession of the weapon for a number of hours, and the prosecution argued that once the defendant was in possession of the weapon the threat had passed. As he had not turned in the weapon immediately, he was precluded from pleading duress. The Court of Appeal ruled that the jury must consider the defendant's actions in the light of all the circumstances, including the fact that the defendant had taken possession of the weapon early in the morning. The jury was entitled to conclude that it was not unreasonable that the defendant had merely waited until a more reasonable hour before bringing the weapon to the police. Second, in **Whelan**, the Court of Criminal Appeal ruled that if the defendant had an opportunity to escape from the duress and failed to avail of it, the plea should fail. In *Hudson and Taylor*, the prosecution argued that as the threats made against them were not going to be carried out immediately, the defendants could have escaped from the duress by going to the police. The Court of Appeal ruled that whether the defendants had foregone an opportunity to escape was a matter of fact for the jury, although the court did observe that it would not always be possible for the police to offer effective protection. By extension, if there was a reasonably effective alternative option available that did not involve breaking the law, the defendant will have no excuse for his unlawful behaviour.

10.5 Self-induced Duress

The rationale for the defence of duress is that a person who commits an offence due to threats from another person or from the circumstances in which he finds himself is morally innocent and this innocence should be recognised by the law. It follows that a person who voluntarily exposes himself to such threats by his own choice has helped to bring about the dangerous situation and is not morally innocent. The law is reluctant to allow such people to escape liability: as was said in *R v. Fitzpatrick* (1977), those who have voluntarily associated with violent people cannot wear 'the breastplate of righteousness' when it suits them. The question then arises as to the degree of exposure required to preclude the defence of duress: must the defendant have foreseen the risk that he would be coerced into committing a crime? In *R v. Sharp* (1987), the defendant was a member of a gang that committed a number of robberies, during one of which a person was killed. The defendant claimed that he had participated in the robberies only out of fear of the gang leader. Lord Lane ruled:

> Where a person has voluntarily, and with knowledge of its nature, joined a criminal organisation or gang which he knew might bring pressure on him to commit an offence and was an active member when he was put under such pressure, he cannot avail himself of the defence of duress.

However, this issue has recently been reviewed by the House of Lords in *R v. Hasan* (2005). The defendant worked for a woman who ran an escort agency and was involved with a man named Sullivan who, the defendant claimed, had a reputation for violence and drug-dealing. The defendant claimed that he committed an aggravated burglary out of fear of Sullivan, who had threatened the defendant and his family. Lord Bingham, giving the judgment for the majority on this point, summarised the law as follows:

> The policy of the law must be to discourage association with known criminals, and it should be slow to excuse the criminal conduct of those who do so. If a person voluntarily becomes or remains associated with others engaged in criminal activity in a situation where he knows or ought reasonably to know that he may be the subject of compulsion by them or their associates, he cannot rely on the defence of duress to excuse any act which he is thereafter compelled to do by them.

It is irrelevant that the defendant did not foresee the kind of offence that he might be compelled to commit, or even that he would be compelled to engage in criminal activity at all. If he, or a reasonable person in his circumstances, was aware of the risk of compulsion to do anything, the defence of duress will not be available. The House was clearly concerned that duress was being pleaded too frequently and was turning into a 'charter for terrorists, gang-leaders and kidnappers' (*per* Lord Simon of Glaisdale in *Lynch v. DPP for Northern Ireland* (1975)). Thus, anyone who voluntarily risks compulsion of any kind through association with criminal groups must fully accept the consequences of exposing himself to that risk.

One last point needs to be made concerning the degree of association required for the defence of duress to be precluded. The cases just discussed involve defendants who joined criminal groups, but duress can be precluded even where the defendant did not join such a group. In *R v. Heath* (2000), the defendant borrowed money from a drug dealer and claimed that the drug dealer had forced him to collect a consignment of drugs. The Court of Appeal noted that the defendant in his own evidence had accepted that he had placed himself in a situation in which he might suffer compulsion, and accordingly, he could not raise the defence of duress.

10.6 Scope of the Defence

Duress is a general defence that may be pleaded to meet most charges. In *R v. Pommell* (1995), the Court of Appeal ruled that the defence was available to meet any charge other than murder, attempted murder and some forms of treason, although the court did not specify which forms of treason could not be met by a plea of duress. In **Whelan**, the Court of Criminal Appeal specifically left the precise scope of the defence open, holding only that it did not apply to murder. However, it seems likely that the Irish courts will allow the defence of duress to the same extent as the English courts. Why is the defence not available to meet a charge of murder, especially if the threat to the defendant is such that a reasonable person might have acceded to it? In *Lynch*, Lord Morris asked whether it is just to expect in a courtroom a level of heroism that even a reasonably brave person would have difficulty in meeting. He suggested that recognising the agony of the coerced person 'is not to make the law weak but to make it just'. This is particularly so given that no allowance is made by the law to a situation in which a person's family is threatened – thus, individuals are expected not only to sacrifice their own lives rather than to kill an innocent, but also to sacrifice the lives of their families.

The policy of the law with respect to duress and murder is based on the principle of the sanctity of human life and the need to protect it – there can be no excuse for the taking of an innocent life. Further, the courts have been concerned to ensure that the law retains its ability to effectively deal with violence from organised criminal and terrorist groups. If a murder charge could be met with a plea of duress, then the more vicious and brutal the leaders of these groups were, the more successful the defence of duress – and the more impotent the law – would become. The concession to human frailty offered by the defence of duress could then be used by these criminal groups to build an experienced and untouchable organisation: in *Abbott v. R* (1976), Lord Salmon argued that having released a person who took innocent lives on the grounds of duress, the criminal group would then be free to coerce that person into doing it again, and this time he would be more experienced and therefore more dangerous. Additionally, in *Howe*, Lord Hailsham doubted that heroism is beyond the reach of ordinary people:

> I have known in my own lifetime of too many acts of heroism by ordinary human beings of no more than ordinary fortitude to regard a law as either 'just or humane' which withdraws the protection of the criminal law from the innocent victim and casts the cloak of its protection on the coward and the poltroon in the name of a 'concession to human frailty'...

Lord Hailsham also noted that a range of executive measures exists by which clemency could be granted to a person who has been coerced into killing an innocent life. Accordingly, the preclusion of the duress defence in murder cases 'in order to emphasise to all the sanctity of a human life is not an excessive price to pay'.

Finally, with respect to attempted murder, the House of Lords in *R v. Gotts* (1992) held that duress could not be a defence where the murderous attempt failed. The defendant was a sixteen-year-old boy who tried to kill his mother on his father's orders. There was evidence that the father had threatened to kill the defendant if he disobeyed. The House noted that duress was not available in a murder case in which proof of an intention to kill was unnecessary: an intention merely to cause serious harm was sufficient. Thus, if X had intended only to cause serious injury but went too far and killed his victim, X would be precluded from pleading duress. The House held that it would be illogical to allow a defence to a person who intended to kill but failed when that defence was not available to a person who did not intend to kill anyone. As Lord Jauncey put it in *Gotts*:

> The intent required of an attempted murderer is more evil than that required of a murderer and the line which divides the two offences is seldom, if ever, of the

deliberate making of the criminal. A man shooting to kill but missing a vital organ by a hair's breadth can justify his action no more than can the man who hits that organ. It is pure chance that the attempted murderer is not a murderer ...

10.7 Further Reading

Alldridge, 'Duress and the Reasonable Person', (1983) 34 *NILQ* 125.

Kewley, 'Murder and the Availability of the Defence of Duress in the Criminal Law', (1993) 57 *JCL* 298.

McAuley, 'Necessity and Duress in Criminal Law: The Confluence of Two Great Tributaries', (1998) 33 *Ir Jur (ns)* 120.

Smith, 'Duress and Steadfastness: In Pursuit of the Unintelligible', [1999] *Crim LR* 363.

CHAPTER ELEVEN

NECESSITY

11.1 Introduction

Necessity is one of the most controversial areas of the criminal law. Typically, the invocation of the defence of necessity involves a claim by the defendant that he broke the law in order to secure some higher value. What makes this claim so controversial is that the defendant's claim is that despite committing a proscribed act with the required *mens rea*, his acts were *justified* by the need to secure this higher value and so were not criminal. A claim of necessity is therefore distinct from an act of civil disobedience in which the actor knowingly breaks the law, not out of a belief that the act was not wrong, but rather to draw attention to some perceived injustice. In other words, an act of civil disobedience is a political act in which the infliction of criminal punishment is accepted, if not desired, by the actor in order to make a political point. A claim of necessity, on the other hand, is predicated on the actor's belief that his action was not unlawful due to a supervening circumstance. Typically, the defendant will claim that this circumstance constituted some sort of emergency and that as a result he had no option but to commit a proscribed act.

The necessity defence is controversial because in putting his defence, the defendant admits that he deliberately chose to ignore the enacted law of the land but claims that he should not be punished for doing so because his actions were right in the circumstances, and not merely excused as with a claim of duress. The danger inherent in such a claim for the rule of law was explained by Dickson J. in the Canadian case of *Morgentaler v. R* (1976):

> No system of positive law can recognize any principle which would entitle a person to violate the law because on his view the law conflicted with some higher social value ... To ... hold that ostensibly illegal acts can be validated on the basis of their expediency, would import undue subjectivity into the criminal law. It would invite the courts to second guess the Legislature and to assess the relative merits of social policies underlying criminal prohibitions.

More succinctly, Edmund Davies L.J. pointed out in *Southwark London Borough Council v. Williams* (1971) that 'necessity can very easily become simply a mask for anarchy.' Such sentiments were visible in **The People (DPP) v. Kelly (2004)**. There, the defendant had caused damage to a warplane belonging to the US Navy on the grounds that she was trying to protect human life in Iraq. Permission to develop this line of argument was refused by the Circuit Court in order to prevent the trial turning into a political debate on the legitimacy of the US invasion of Iraq. Specifically, Judge Moran stated that 'society at large expects me as a judge to stop and prevent the social anarchy that would prevail if people were allowed to take the law into their own hands.'

On the other hand, the law must accept that there will be occasions in which a higher value really can be secured by breaching a legal obligation. Suppose X sees a child drowning in a river and breaks a window to get a rope to save the child. Ostensibly, X has committed the offence of causing criminal damage to the window, but it would be outrageous to bring charges against him. For that reason, the Criminal Damage Act 1991, as amended by the Non-Fatal Offences Against the Person Act 1997 (see section 27.3), specifically allows a necessity defence for people like X providing the actions were reasonable in the circumstances as he believed them to be and were necessary to prevent harm occurring. However, suppose this provision does not apply in a particular case – could X avoid criminal liability on the basis of a general defence of necessity?

In England, the courts have been reluctant to define the parameters of a general defence of necessity, preferring instead to extend the defence of duress to threats arising from circumstances (see Chapter 10). In most cases, duress of circumstances will provide a full answer to a criminal charge. A similar position pertains in Ireland, on the assumption that the Irish courts will accept in an appropriate case that duress of circumstances is a legitmate defence in Irish law. It is important to note, however, that duress of circumstances is not the same as necessity. Duress of circumstances provides an excuse when the defendant's will has been overborne by a dangerous situation, but necessity provides a justification when the defendant made a conscious decision to break the law to prevent danger.

In Scotland, the High Court of Justiciary has recently provided some guidance on the contours of the necessity defence. In *Lord Advocate's Reference No.1 of 2000* (2001), the respondents were anti-war activists who caused damage to a naval vessel involved in the Trident nuclear weapons programme. The respondents argued that their acts were not unlawful in that they were a necessary response to the alleged illegal actions of the British government in deploying Trident nuclear weapons. The High Court ruled that an otherwise illegal act can be justified only if it is carried out to prevent danger to the actor or to others. The court stressed that individuals are not entitled to take the law into their own hands, and so cannot commit illegal acts for the purpose of preventing crime; it is the prevention of danger only that justifies otherwise illegal acts. The danger must be so immediate as to make the actor's breach of the law realistically unavoidable; in other words, the breach of the law must have been forced upon the actor. If the danger was not immediate, then the actor would have had time to take lawful measures or to notify the appropriate authorities. Further, drawing on duress precedents, the court ruled that the defence is available only if a sober person of reasonable firmness sharing the characteristics of the defendant would have acted similarly: the court was clearly concerned to exclude the defence if a person simply overreacted to a situation. The actor must have had reasonable grounds to believe that his action was necessary, and the act must have had some prospect of successfully preventing the danger. If these conditions were met, the actor's actions would be justified and hence lawful.

As the Criminal Damage Act 1991 allows for a necessity defence in relation to causing criminal damage, and duress of circumstance will excuse criminal liability for breaking the law in most other circumstance, the principal issue that arises with respect to the necessity defence is whether the taking of innocent lives to prevent even more loss of life can ever be justified, i.e. does necessity extend as a defence to homicide charges? This issue was not considered in *Lord Advocate's Reference*. Suppose an aircraft with 100 passengers has been hijacked and is being directed by the hijackers towards a building containing 1,000 people. If X makes a deliberate decision to shoot down that aircraft, he has killed 100 innocent people but has also saved 1,000 innocent people. It is usually no defence on a murder charge to argue that the deceased was going to die anyway; the *actus reus* of murder is established when the defendant's actions are shown to have accelerated the deceased's death (see section 18.4). Thus, by shooting down the aircraft, X has ostensibly murdered the 100 innocent people on board the aircraft. The defence of duress of circumstances is of no assistance to X: we have seen that the courts have refused on policy grounds to extend the defence of duress to homicide charges (see section 10.6). The only possible defence available to X is that his actions were necessary and saved more people than were lost. This is a distinctly utilitarian argument, an argument that seems at odds with the principle of the sanctity of each human life. Nevertheless, there are grounds to believe that, at least in limited circumstances, necessity might be available as a defence to a murder charge.

11.2 Necessity and Homicide

The leading authority on necessity and homicide is *R v. Dudley and Stephens*. The defendants, another man and an injured youth were cast adrift with few supplies following a shipwreck. After many days without food or water, the defendants killed the youth and all three men ate his body and drank his blood. A few days later, the survivors were rescued and on their return to England, the defendants were charged with murder. The defendants argued that their actions had been necessary (and, apparently, permitted by the custom of the sea): by killing one person they had saved three lives. On the facts, the jury evidently agreed: they found as a matter of fact that the youth would probably have died anyway and that the defendants would probably also have died had they not acted as they did. However, the jury was not permitted to render verdict in the case; instead, their findings of fact were considered by a Divisional Court which ruled that the defendants were guilty of murder. Lord Coleridge C.J., speaking for the court in highly moralistic language, grounded his opinion on two major points. First, he suggested that allowing the temptation to commit murder as a defence would represent a total divorce of the law from morality. While there is generally a moral duty to preserve one's own life, in some extreme circumstances such as war and emergencies there will be a moral duty to sacrifice one's life. Therefore, it is not true that a person has a legal right to do what is necessary to save himself, regardless of the method adopted for choosing who was to die. Thus, Lord Coleridge rejected the American decision of *United States v. Holmes* (1842), in which it was suggested that as long as those who are to die are selected fairly by casting lots, it is permissible to kill some to save others. Second, there were practical reasons to disallow a necessity defence in these circumstances:

> Who is to be the judge of this sort of necessity? By what measure is the comparative value of lives to be measured? Is it to be strength, or intellect, or what? It is plain that the principle leaves to him who is to profit by it to determine the necessity which will justify him in deliberately taking another's life to save his own.

In this case, Lord Coleridge pointed out, the defendants had chosen as their sacrifice the person who was the weakest, youngest and least able to resist. The Chief Justice accepted that the standard being set by the court was one of heroism that was beyond the reach of many, but also noted that if an injustice was done in a particular case, a petition for clemency could be addressed to the Crown. Setting a legal principle under which murder could be permitted if deemed necessary was too dangerous and 'might be made the legal cloke for unbridled passion and atrocious crime.'

For many years, this decision was taken as authority for the proposition that necessity is never a defence to a charge of murder, although the decision seems eminently distinguishable. In *Dudley and Stephens*, the defendants not only decided who was to die but also benefited by their own decision; effectively, they acted as judge, executioner and beneficiary. However, what about a situation in which the decision is made by a person who does not benefit by it, or alternatively, a situation in which the person who is to die has already been chosen by fate? In *Re A (Conjoined Twins)* (2000), the Court of Appeal was faced with conjoined twins – Mary and Jodie – who were sharing one set of body organs. Medical evidence established that if they were not separated, both would die. However, the separation would certainly result in the death of Mary. Thus, doctors were faced with either intentionally killing Mary (within the meaning of intention as decided by the House of Lords in *R v. Woollin* (1998) – see section 4.3) or intentionally breaching their duty to save Jodie; effectively, the doctors were faced with a choice of kill one or kill both. The Court of Appeal decided that the separation should proceed, thereby allowing a necessity defence to what would otherwise have been an unlawful killing by the doctors. The parameters of the defence as a result of this decision are unclear. Ward L.J. was at pains to limit the precedential value of the decision to similar cases in which one patient cannot be saved but is by her very existence killing another patient who can be saved. On this basis, killing out of necessity would be limited to cases of medical necessity. However, Brooke L.J. took a wider view. He concluded that as Mary could not be saved, she had been designated for death and was alive only by virtue of the fact that she had been, 'fortuitously, deriving oxygenated blood from her sister's bloodstream'. In other words, the person to die had been pre-selected by circumstances and not by the decision of a beneficiary. The third judge, Robert Walker L.J., also extended the necessity defence to cover this case and referred to the fact that Mary was bound to die regardless (although he did not use the phrase 'designated for death'), but based his concurrence on other factors. The 'designated for death' test, if adopted in subsequent decisions, is clearly wide enough to cover non-medical situations such as the hijacked aircraft scenario discussed above: the passengers on board the hijacked aircraft have been designated for death and are beyond saving, but the people in the building can be saved. Therefore, if X shoots down the plane, he should be able to avail of the necessity defence.

The application of necessity to homicide has not been directly discussed by an Irish court, but the decision of the Supreme Court in *Attorney General v. X* **(1992)** could be taken as indirect authority for allowing necessity to meet a homicide charge. In that case, the Supreme Court decided that abortions are not to be permitted under Irish law unless performed to save the life of the mother. At common law, an unborn child does not have the status of a human being, but this view may not have survived the Eighth Amendment to the Constitution, which specifically guarantees the right to life of the unborn on equal terms with that of the mother. There are indications (see section 18.5) that a majority of the Supreme Court took the view that the Constitution rejected the common law view of an unborn child. That being the case, by holding that an abortion was permitted by Irish law to save the life of the mother, the Court effectively ruled that one person could be killed to save the life of another. This was most certainly not the *ratio* of the case, and the Supreme Court was considering the offence of abortion rather than the offence of murder. However, this interpretation could be taken as a basis on which a necessity defence to a murder charge could be developed in Ireland.

11.3 Further Reading

Bennum, 'Necessity – Yet Another Analysis', (1986) 21 *Ir Jur (ns)* 186.

Clarkson, 'Necessary Action: A New Defence', [2004] *Crim LR* 81.

Glazebrook, 'The Necessity Plea in English Criminal Law', (1972) *Cambridge LJ* 87.

Rogers, 'Necessity, Private Defence and the Killing of Mary', [2001] *Crim LR* 515.

Walker, 'Mary and Jodie – The Case of the Conjoined Twins', (2002) 53 *NILQ* 195.

CHAPTER TWELVE

INFANCY

12.1 Introduction

From the earliest times, common law has recognised that children should not be fully accountable for their actions. In particular, because of their youth, children will not always be capable of fully realising the consequences or the moral character of their actions, and therefore would not be able to form the required *mens rea*. The law has therefore always tried to shield children from the full rigours of the criminal justice system. However, the law also recognised that a child's understanding increased with age, so the protection given to children diminished as the child got older. Where it was shown that the child defendant did understand the nature of what he had done, he was fully liable and would suffer the consequences. Blackstone records cases in which an eight-year-old boy was hanged for arson, while a thirteen-year-old girl was burned for murder (at the time, hanging was the standard punishment for males, while burning was the standard punishment for females).[1] While the modern law has altered its view on the punishment of children, the rules relating to the criminal responsibility of child offenders have remained virtually static for centuries.

12.2 Juvenile Justice System

In *R v. Home Secretary, ex parte Venables and Thompson* (1997), Lord Hope of Craighead stressed the importance of viewing the criminal responsibility of children in the context of the overall juvenile justice system:

> The age of criminal responsibility in England and Wales is lower than it is in most other European countries, but that in itself does not seem to me to be a ground for criticism. One has to look at the whole picture, including the nature of the sentences which the court can impose and the way in which they are administered, in order to see whether the effect of placing criminal responsibility on children as young as the applicants are in this case is objectionable.

Accordingly, a brief survey of the main points of the juvenile justice system that operates today in Ireland will provide the framework within which child offenders are dealt.

The Children Act 1908 established for the first time a separate judicial scheme for dealing with juvenile offenders. At the time, this legislation was regarded as a highly enlightened advance, and was referred to as the 'Children's

---

1 Blackstone, *Commentaries on the Laws of England*, Book IV (1783), London: Garland, 1978, p. 23.

Charter'. However, the 1908 Act was rooted in the ideas of the later Victorian period and by the end of the twentieth century was in need of reform. A new Children Act was enacted in 2001 to update the juvenile justice system. Its broad thrust is directed to the rehabilitation of juvenile offenders, i.e. those under eighteen years of age, and contemplates the use of various techniques (family conferences, diversion schemes, specialised courts) to attain this goal. The Act is being brought into force on a phased basis to give the various authorities an opportunity to prepare for the new regime. However, progress has been slow, and to date about half of the Act remains to be implemented.

Garda Juvenile Diversion Programme

In 1963 the Garda Síochána initiated a diversion scheme to provide an alternative method of dealing with young offenders that did not involve formal prosecutions through the judicial system. Run by Juvenile Liaison Offices (JLOs), the scheme was characterised by the use of a caution followed by garda supervision for a period of twelve months. However, the scheme lacked statutory authority until Part 4 of the Children Act 2001 was brought into force in May 2002, which put the scheme on a statutory footing. The overriding principle on which the programme operates is that any juvenile offender of responsible age and under eighteen should be considered for admission to the programme if he has admitted his offence. In practice, however, the gardaí will also consider the nature of the offence committed and the offender's criminal history. The views of the victim will also be considered, although section 23 makes it clear that admission to the programme is not dependent on the victim's consent.

Prosecution of Juveniles

If a juvenile offender is not admitted to the Diversion Programme, the alternative is a formal prosecution through the courts. Part 6 of the Act, in force since May 2002, provides specific procedures for the treatment of juvenile suspects in garda stations. The gardaí are required at all times to act with due respect for the rights and dignity of the suspect and to bear in mind that juvenile suspects are more vulnerable than their adult counterparts. Juvenile suspects are to be kept apart from adult suspects, and their parents or guardians must be notified as soon as possible. As a general rule, the suspect should not be questioned in the absence of a parent or guardian, although this requirement may be dispensed with if there is reasonable cause to believe that any delay might result in harm to others or the destruction of property or evidence. A parent or guardian may also be excluded if he or she is being charged or if he or she would obstruct the questioning. At all times, the juvenile and his parents or guardians must be kept properly informed of the charges against the juvenile.

Since the foundation of the courts system in 1924, there has been recognition that juvenile offenders should be dealt with in separate courts. The 2001 Act continues that tradition in Part 7, under which Children Courts are established. Section 71 provides that any District Court that is hearing charges against a child will be considered a Children Court. Such courts are given the jurisdiction to deal summarily with any charges against juveniles other than those reserved for trial in the Central Criminal Court or manslaughter. In so far as possible, the affairs of the Children Court will be arranged so that juvenile offenders will not be in contact with other persons attending sittings of the court, and that any waiting periods are kept to a minimum. There are a series of measures contained in Part 8 of the Act concerning the procedures of the Children Court, especially with respect to the involvement of health boards, probation officers and family conferences, but for the most part these provisions have yet to be brought into force. In the event of the juvenile being found guilty, the penalties that have been brought into force at the time of writing include ordering a conditional discharge, the payment of a fine, a compensation order against the juvenile or the juvenile's parents, or what amounts to a curfew under section 133.

Detention is also possible at one of five certified schools in the State, with room for 210 boys and sixteen girls: Trinity House, Lusk, County Dublin; Finglas Children Centre, Dublin 11, which comprises St Michael's Assessment Centre and St Lawrence's Special School; St Joseph's Special School, Clonmel, Co. Tipperary; and Oberstown Boys and Girls Centres, Oberstown, Lusk, County Dublin. When Part 10 of the 2001 Act is brought into force, these schools will be redesignated Children Detention Schools with a primary purpose of providing training and education with a view to ultimately preparing the detainees for reintegration into society. There has been regular judicial criticism of the shortage of appropriate detention facilities for juvenile offenders, a shortage that has required the courts to accept inappropriate arrangements. For example, in *The People (DPP) v. DE* (1991), the Court of Criminal Appeal had to order the release of a fifteen-year-old boy rather than acquiesce in sending him to prison. The court was of the view that detention in a special school was the most appropriate course of action, but there were no places available for him.

12.3 Age of Responsibility

The foregoing provides an overview of the main points of the juvenile justice system, which in turn provides the context for a discussion of the age of responsibility in Ireland. Part 5 of the 2001 Act makes changes to this area of the law, but at the time of writing, Part 5 has not been brought into force. Accordingly, the age of criminal responsibility is still governed by common law rules. Common law recognises three categories of child offenders:

(a) those aged under seven,
(b) those aged between seven and fourteen, and
(c) those aged fourteen and over.

By virtue of section 4(1) of the Age of Majority Act 1985, the first category lasts until the child turns seven, the second category until the child turns fourteen, and full criminal responsibility is attributed to a child on his fourteenth birthday.

12.4 Children under Seven

There is a conclusive presumption that children under seven are incapable of distinguishing between right and wrong, and are therefore incapable of forming the *mens rea* for any crime. They are said to be *doli incapax* (incapable of crime). As a result, a child under seven can effectively commit any offence in plain view of a member of the gardaí, and he cannot, as a matter of law, be prosecuted. This is a common law presumption that still represents the law in Ireland. However, in England, the age limit has been increased twice. The Children and Young Persons Act 1933 raised it to eight, while the Children and Young Persons Act 1963 raised it again to ten. The Children and Young Persons Act 1969 made provision for the age to be increased again to fourteen, but this has not been implemented by the British government.

The effect of the principle of *doli incapax* was illustrated in *Walters v. Lunt* (1951). The defendants took possession of a tricycle from their seven-year-old son, knowing full well that it was not his property. They were charged with receiving stolen property. It was held that as the child could not steal, the tricycle could not be treated as stolen property, and the defendants therefore could not have received stolen property. This decision must be treated with some caution. The fact that a child is *doli incapax* does not mean that if he commits an act that is prohibited by law that no crime has been committed; rather, the child will simply be excused from responsibility for the crime due to his age and lack of understanding. We have seen (section 6.6) that the fact that a person is excused from responsibility for an offence does not mean that no offence was committed. Hence, it is submitted that the child in *Walters v. Lunt* was merely excused from responsibility for his theft, but the theft still occurred. Accordingly, as the child's parents knew that the tricycle did not belong to their son, they knowingly received stolen property and should have been convicted. Further, if a parent sends his child out to steal hoping that he can shelter behind his child's immunity, the parent should be charged as a principal offender. The child in such circumstances should be treated as an innocent agent.

12.5 Children Aged between Seven and Fourteen

Children aged between seven and fourteen are also presumed to be *doli incapax*. However, this presumption may be rebutted by showing that the child knew the difference between right and wrong. This rebuttable presumption was severely criticised by the English courts in *C v. DPP* (1995), in which the High Court ruled that it was no longer part of English law. On appeal, however, the House of Lords reinstated it on the basis that only Parliament could abolish a common law rule of such long standing.

In *R v. Gorrie* (1919), it was held that it must be shown that the child knew that what he was doing was seriously wrong, a test endorsed by the Irish High Court in *KM v. DPP* **(1994)**. Obviously, the closer the child is to his fourteenth birthday, the easier this will be. Therefore, while the protection of all children in this category is theoretically the same, in practice, those aged closer to seven will receive a greater degree of protection than those aged closer to fourteen.

In earlier times, rebutting the presumption was considerably easier. In *R v. York* (1748), a ten-year-old boy was convicted of murdering a five-year-old girl because he lied about what he had done and had hidden the body. The court accepted that these actions indicated that the boy knew that he had done wrong. In recent years, however, rebutting the presumption seems to have become more difficult. In *C v. DPP* (1995), the House of Lords held that the prosecution cannot rely solely on the nature of the crime to prove knowledge that the action was seriously wrong. For example, if X brutally murdered a younger child, the prosecution cannot argue that the crime was so horrific that X must have known that it was seriously wrong. In *IPH v. Chief Constable of South Wales* (1987), an eleven-year-old child had caused damage to a van, and was convicted of causing criminal damage on the basis that the nature of the offence was such that any child would know that it was seriously wrong. On appeal, the conviction was quashed because such knowledge cannot be presumed, irrespective of how horrific the offence might be. The prosecution must introduce evidence to prove this knowledge. Irish authorities, however, seem to disagree. In *Green v. Cavan County Council* **(1959)**, it was stated that if a crime was committed deliberately by a child, the deliberate nature of the crime could be used as evidence from which it could be inferred that the child knew that what he was doing was seriously wrong. Likewise, in *Monagle v. Donegal County Council* **(1961)**, it was held that evidence that an offence had been committed deliberately and with planning was sufficient to rebut the presumption of *doli incapax*. However, these decisions must be regarded with suspicion since the adoption of the *Gorrie* test in *KM v. DPP* **(1994)**. A planned and deliberate action does not of itself indicate that the child knew that what he was doing was seriously wrong. For example, a child may plan to burn his house and then deliberately do so without realising that he has done anything wrong.

The evidence must show that the child knew that his actions were *seriously* wrong. A belief that the action was merely naughty will not be sufficient. As a result, many decisions have emphasised that any action that is equally consistent with knowledge of mere naughtiness as with knowledge that the action was seriously wrong will not rebut the presumption. Therefore, evidence that the child lied or ran away will not be enough, as these actions are consistent with the child knowing that he has merely done something naughty. In *IPH v. Chief Constable of South Wales* (1987), it was suggested that the child should be asked directly if he knew that what he was doing was seriously wrong, and that his answer and demeanour would be of great importance. The court did not, however, indicate what should happen if the child simply lied about his knowledge. However, in *KM*, the High Court accepted that evidence that a child threatened his victim in order to secure her silence could rebut the presumption. In some respects, it is difficult to reconcile this decision with the *Gorrie* test as threatening a victim is much the same as lying or running away: it could simply be an indication that the child thought he had done something naughty. However, if the threat is serious enough, it might indicate that the child knew that his actions were more than naughty.

Proof of prior convictions for similar offences used to be a mainstay of the prosecution. It was believed that as the child had been in trouble before for a similar offence, he could hardly claim that he did not know that his actions were seriously wrong. However, in *C v. DPP* (1995), the House of Lords ruled that such evidence was unduly prejudicial to the defendant, and should not be admitted unless it came within a recognised rule of evidence, such as the similar fact rule. Irish authorities, however, seem to accept such evidence. In *Monagle v. Donegal County Council* (**1961**), Murnaghan J. noted that the child suspected of causing fire damage to the plaintiff's shed had been punished by his mother on previous occasions for similar actions. While it is not clear how much weight was placed on this evidence, no objection was made to it being admitted. Whether an Irish court would follow this approach today, or would follow the House of Lords in *C*, is unclear.

12.6 Children Aged Fourteen and Over

Once a child turns fourteen, the law conclusively presumes that he is able to distinguish between right and wrong, unless there is evidence of insanity, in which case the matter will be dealt with under the M'Naghten Rules (see Chapter 8). Accordingly, such a child may be prosecuted in the same way as an adult. In *R v. Fitt* (**1919**), the defendant committed a murder while aged sixteen. He was not able to claim *doli incapax*, and was accordingly convicted and sentenced to death.

12.7 Reform

The age of responsibility has been reviewed in a number of official reports, the most important of which are the following:

(a) *Reformatory and Industrial Schools Systems Report* (1970) (better known as the *Kennedy Report*);
(b) *Report of the Task Force on Child Care Services* (1980); and
(c) *First Report of the Dáil Select Committee on Crime: Juvenile Crime – its causes and its remedies* (1992).

Invariably, the common law rules came in for stinging criticism, with all but the 1980 Task Force Report recommending that the age for the conclusive presumption of *doli incapax* be raised from seven to twelve.

Part 5 of the Children Act 2001 enacted a number of changes to the age of responsibility, none of which have been implemented at the time of writing. Accordingly, the law regarding the age of responsibility at present continues to be governed by the common law principles discussed above. When Part 5 is brought into effect, the age below which there is a conclusive presumption of *doli incapax* will be raised to twelve. Thus, anyone under the age of twelve will effectively be exempted from the application of the criminal law, but anyone (excluding another under-age child) who aids, abets, counsels or procures the commission of the offence committed by the under-age offender can be prosecuted under section 54 as a principal offender. The target of this provision is adults who use children to commit crimes for them; such adults are deemed to be principal offenders themselves and cannot hide behind the children's lack of responsibility to evade criminal liability.

Offenders below the age of twelve who commit offences will in the first instance be brought home by the gardaí to their parents. However, if the garda forms a reasonable opinion that the offender is not receiving adequate care and protection at home, he must inform the local health authorities, who are empowered to seek care or supervision orders under the terms of the Child Care Act 1991. Offenders over the age of twelve but under the age of fourteen are also protected by the presumption of *doli incapax* on the basis that such offenders lack the capacity to know that their acts were wrong. The wording of this provision suggests that rebutting the presumption of *doli incapax* in respect of these offenders should be somewhat easier than is presently the case. The current rebuttal test, set out in *Gorrie*, requires that the offender knew that what he was doing was *seriously* wrong; the test in the 2001 Act appears to be knowledge that the act was merely wrong – apparently a lighter standard. If this is true, then many of the current practical difficulties in overturning the presumption should be avoided.

12.8 Further Reading

First Report of the Dáil Select Committee on Crime: Juvenile Crime – its causes and its remedies (1992).
Hanly, 'The Defence of Infancy', (1996) 6 *ICLJ* 72.
Reformatory and Industrial Schools Systems Report (1970).
Report of the Task Force on Child Care Services (1980).

CHAPTER THIRTEEN

MISTAKE

13.1 Introduction

It is axiomatic that to err is human, and that people sometimes commit actions while under a mistaken view of the facts. For example, if X comes across Y and Z engaging in a pretend sword fight and he sees that Y is losing, he may conclude that Y is in serious danger, because he is not aware that the fight is not real. If he charges in to 'save' Y, and in doing so kills Z, has he committed a homicide? In principle, it would seem that he should be acquitted – on his view of the situation, he acted reasonably to save another person who appeared to be in serious danger. If his view of the facts had been real, he would be able to plead lawful use of force, and could be acquitted. Is it just, therefore, that his genuine mistake should make him guilty of murder? On the other hand, it would hardly be in the best interests of the public for a defendant to simply claim that he made a mistake and that he should therefore be excused from liability. The law must consequently try to balance these two competing principles.

The example above is of a mistake of fact. A person might also make mistakes as to the law. For example, X might be a foreign national from a country that does not recognise the concept of theft. If he walks into a shop in Ireland and helps himself to various goods, can he avoid liability by saying that he did not know that taking other people's property was illegal? In other words, should he be excused on the basis of a mistaken view of the law? It could be argued that because he is a foreign national, he could not reasonably be expected to know the provisions of Irish law. However, the primary purpose of criminal law is to protect people from wrongdoing, a function that would be seriously undermined if ignorance of the law was a defence.

The basic rule adopted in Irish law in relation to a mistake is summed up in the Latin maxim *ignorantia facti excusat; ignorantia juris non excusat*. In other words, a mistake of fact will be excused, while a mistake of law will not be excused. However, even where the defendant made a mistake as to a fact, the jury must still be satisfied that the defendant did not have the required *mens rea* as a result of the mistake. The burden of proving that the defendant was not acting under a mistaken view of the facts rests upon the prosecution.

13.2 Mistake of Fact

In all cases, before a mistake can excuse liability, it must be relevant to a definitional element of the offence charged. So, if X shot and killed Y but claimed that he made a mistake and had intended to shoot Z, the mistake is irrelevant as the *mens rea* of murder is an intention to cause death or serious injury to any person. The *mens rea* of the offence is fulfilled despite the mistake. However, if X shot Y while out hunting and thought he was shooting a deer, the mistake negates the required *mens rea* and X will be acquitted. The principal question that has arisen is whether the mistake must be reasonable. Until the 1970s, the leading case was *R v. Tolson* (1889), in which the defendant, honestly and reasonably believing that her husband was dead, remarried even though her husband was in fact alive. On a charge of bigamy, Cave J. held that 'at common law an honest and reasonable belief in the existence of circumstances which, if true, would make the act with which the defendant is charged an innocent act has always been held to be a good defence.' Thus, it seemed that a mistake must be one that any reasonable person could have made before it would excuse criminal liability. The basis for this ruling might have been a perceived need to restrict the circumstances in which liability could be excused due to a mistake. However, it is noteworthy that none of the judges in *Tolson* actually held that reasonableness was a prerequisite for such an excuse; they merely stated that an honestly held reasonable mistake would excuse liability. Nevertheless, for nearly 100 years, *Tolson* was taken as authority that mistakes had to be reasonable before they could excuse, a view that was not challenged until the House of Lords' decision in *DPP v. Morgan* (1975).

In *Morgan*, the defendants had sexual intercourse with the complainant at the urging of the complainant's husband. Charged with rape, they argued that they had been convinced by the complainant's husband that she enjoyed having rough sexual intercourse with strangers, and had honestly believed that the complainant was consenting. They did not claim that their mistake was reasonable, merely that it was honest and that this was sufficient to excuse them from criminal liability. By a narrow majority, the House of Lords agreed with their contention, although the convictions were upheld. Lord Hailsham, delivering the leading opinion, held that the *mens rea* of rape was subjective: the prosecution had to prove that the defendant intended to have sexual intercourse regardless of the woman's consent. If the jury concluded that the defendants had honestly though mistakenly believed that the woman was consenting, then it 'followed as a matter of inexorable logic' that the prosecution had failed to prove the required *mens rea* and the defendants must be acquitted. Further, the fact that the defendants' mistake was unreasonable was irrelevant in itself; providing there was an honest belief as to consent, the required *mens rea* by definition could not be present. However, Lord Hailsham pointed out that the jury could have regard to the reasonableness of the mistake in determining whether or not the mistake was genuine. Thus, the more outrageous the mistake, the less likely the jury would be to believe that it was honestly held.

The *Morgan* decision was highly controversial; there were suggestions that all a defendant had to do to avoid a rape conviction was to claim that he made a mistake. That this is not so can be seen from the facts of *Morgan* itself: the convictions were upheld on the grounds that no jury, properly instructed, could have believed that the defendants' claim was genuine. Nevertheless, the *Morgan* ruling was considered by an expert group chaired by Mrs Justice Heilbron, which concluded that the decision was correct. The decision was given statutory effect in the UK and also in Ireland in section 2 of the Criminal Law (Rape) Act 1981. However, in the UK, the Sexual Offences Act 2003 has redefined the offence of rape such that only a reasonable belief in consent will now excuse the defendant from liability.

The Lords in *Morgan* did not overrule *Tolson*, but rather distinguished it. An offence supported by objective *mens rea* such as negligence can still look to *Tolson* as authority. In such a case – for manslaughter, for example – the defendant's mistake must be reasonable: an unreasonable mistake by definition constitutes a failure to reach the standard of a reasonable person. Hence, an unreasonable mistake is itself evidence of the *mens rea* of the offence. In a manslaughter case, however, the mistake must have been grossly negligent: in *The People (Attorney General) v. Dwyer* (**1972**), Walsh J. indicated that a manslaughter conviction could be sustained where the defendant acted in self-defence and 'honestly believed what he did [was] necessary but that was a belief resulting from a grossly negligent over-assessment of the situation.' So in *R v. Foxford* (1974), the defendant was a British soldier accused of the manslaughter of a twelve-year-old boy in Northern Ireland. The defendant argued that he had shot and killed the boy mistakenly believing him to be armed. The Northern Ireland Court of Appeal upheld the manslaughter conviction on the basis that the defendant's mistake, even if it was genuine, was grossly negligent, and gross negligence constituted the *mens rea* of the charge.

Mistakes offer an answer to a criminal charge in that their existence negates *mens rea*. However, if proof of *mens rea* is not required anyway, it follows that the mistake will be irrelevant. For example, the Criminal Law Amendment Act 1935 makes it an offence for a man to have sexual intercourse with a girl under the age of seventeen. In *The People (Attorney General) v. Kearns* (**1949**), the Court of Criminal Appeal confirmed that *mens rea* as to the girl's age was not required. Consequently, the fact that the defendant made an honest and reasonable mistake as to her age was irrelevant.

One final matter needs to be mentioned. Suppose X shoots Y under the mistaken impression that he has shot an animal, and the mistaken impression was caused by a disease of the mind. In these circumstances, the defendant should be dealt with under the M'Naghten Rules (see Chapter 8). Similarly, if the mistaken impression was caused by X's intoxication, X should be dealt with under *Majewski* and *Reilly* (see Chapter 9).

13.3 Mistake as to the Law

Generally, a mistake as to the law provides no excuse. A mistake as to the law arises where a person either does not know that something is illegal or makes a mistake as to the effect of a legal provision. In *R v. Bailey* (1800), the defendant, a ship's captain, was convicted under a statute that had been passed while he was away at sea. As a result, he had no chance of knowing that his conduct was now illegal. His conviction was upheld despite this, largely on policy grounds. In *Kiriri Cotton Co. v. Dewain* (1960), Lord Denning stated:

> It is not correct to say that everyone is presumed to know the law. The true position is that no man can excuse himself from doing his duty by saying that he did not know the law on the matter.

This statement was adopted by the Supreme Court in **Rogers v. Louth County Council (1981)**. Were it to be otherwise, every defendant would have a simple and effective defence that the prosecution would find next to impossible to rebut. Additionally, such a defence would amount to an incentive to turn a blind eye to the law. As was said by the Supreme Court in **The People (DPP) v. Healy (1990)**, 'if it were otherwise, there would be a premium on ignorance'.

The one exception to this general rule arises in situations in which absence of a mistake is an element of the offence. In such a case, if the jury concludes that the defendant did indeed make this mistake, then the defendant's conduct is excluded from the definition of the offence and he must be acquitted. For example, the Criminal Justice (Theft and Fraud Offences) Act 2001 defines theft as the dishonest appropriation of property belonging to someone else. Dishonesty in this context excludes taking the property under a claim of right, i.e. a belief by X that he has a right to take property owned by Y. In **The People (DPP) v. O'Loughlin (1979)**, the Court of Criminal Appeal held that even if such a belief turned out to be incorrect in law, as long as it was genuinely held, the defendant's act of taking the property did not constitute stealing.

13.4 Further Reading

McAuley, 'The Grammar of Mistake in Criminal Law', (1996) 31 *Ir Jur (ns)* 56.

CHAPTER FOURTEEN

ENTRAPMENT

14.1 Introduction

Entrapment as a defence to a criminal charge has been largely developed in America. In essence, it arises where a defendant was induced to commit a crime by a police officer or someone working on behalf of the police. The crucial element of the defence is that the defendant was tempted to commit an offence that he would not otherwise have committed. Where the defendant was already going to commit the offence anyway, whether or not the police tempted him to do so, no issue of entrapment arises. In *Sherman v. US* (1958), the defendant had been asked on several occasions by a man working for the government to buy him some heroin. Despite some reluctance, he did so, and was arrested. It was held, quashing the defendant's conviction, that the police had effectively created the crime. The Supreme Court accepted that stealthy police undercover work was necessary for the prevention and punishment of crime. However, such work 'manifestly . . . does not include the manufacturing of crime', which is precisely what the police had done in this case.

14.2 English Law

The common law in England has traditionally rejected the concept of entrapment. In *R v. Sang* (1979), the defendant had been induced by an agent of the police to become involved in the forgery of US dollars. In rejecting a substantive defence of entrapment, Lord Diplock noted that all of the elements of the offence were present, including *mens rea*: an induced intent is still an intent. It was no defence to argue that someone else procured the defendant's involvement in the offence. This other person might well be guilty of incitement, but incitement by a citizen is not a defence and the Lords ruled that incitement by a police officer or by a police agent was no different. The Lords also ruled that there was no discretion to exclude evidence obtained as a result of entrapment. Such evidence would likely represent the bulk of the prosecution's case, and its exclusion would therefore constitute a procedural form of an entrapment defence. The Lords endorsed the statement in *R v. Leatham* (1861) that 'it matters not how you get [the evidence]; if you steal it even, it would be admissible.'

Since *Sang*, English law has altered its position on entrapment. Section 78 of the Police and Criminal Evidence Act 1984 gives courts the power to exclude prosecution evidence if, in all the circumstances, the admission of that evidence would have an unduly adverse effect on the fairness of the proceedings. Further, in *R v. Latif, R v. Shazard* (1996), the House of Lords confirmed that the courts have the power to stay a prosecution altogether if there has been a serious abuse by the executive of its power, and this power can be exercised in respect of a case brought on foot of entrapment. The movement of the English courts away from *Sang* was further emphasised by the House of Lords in *R v. Looseley, Attorney General's Reference No.3 of 2000* (2001). There, the House unanimously ruled that entrapment is an abuse of executive power, and that a prosecution brought on foot of such an abuse would constitute 'an affront to the public conscience'. Accordingly, the House ruled that where such an abuse occurred, a stay on the prosecution should be deemed the most appropriate response. However, the Lords were also at pains to point out that some latitude must be given to the police in their investigative techniques; offences such as drug trafficking, in which there is no immediately identifiable victim to make a complaint, would be impossible to police without the involvement of undercover police officers or agents. Such undercover agents would have to become actively involved in the criminal project, and such active involvement should not constitute entrapment. Thus, the courts must carefully consider all of the circumstances, including the nature of the crime being investigated, the reason for the police operation, whether the police had a reasonable suspicion that the defendant was involved in criminal activity and the nature of the police inducement. Of particular, though not conclusive, importance is evidence that the defendant was already predisposed to commit the crime, and the fact that the police behaved as would a normal customer of the trade in question. Thus, a police officer who approaches a drug dealer and asks to buy a quantity of cocaine is acting normally in the context of the sale of illegal drugs and there is no entrapment if the dealer complies with the request. If, however, the police officer induces the dealer to manufacture a quantity of cocaine, he has gone beyond the actions of a normal customer and has effectively created a different offence. If the dealer is then prosecuted for the manufacture of cocaine, the prosecution might well be stayed on the grounds of entrapment.

14.3 Irish Law

The issue of entrapment has not yet been the subject of a definitive ruling by the Irish courts. In ***Dental Board v. O'Callaghan*** **(1969)**, the defendant was suspected of practising as a dentist without a proper licence. The Dental Board sent an investigator who asked the defendant to repair a set of dentures, which the defendant duly did. The District Court dismissed the evidence of the investigator as he was an accomplice to the offence and his evidence could not be relied upon. In the High Court, Butler J. ruled that the investigator's evidence could be accepted: the general belief in the unreliability of accomplice testimony did not arise in this case as the investigator was not seeking to paint himself in a better light. Furthermore, despite a general judicial dislike of the actions of *agents provocateur*, Butler J. accepted that investigative work by undercover agents would sometimes be necessary if crime was to be detected and punished. If there was no reasonable alternative to such operations, Butler J. indicated that the evidence of such undercover agents was admissible. An alternative way of looking at this case is that the investigator acted as would a normal customer of the trade: he merely requested that a set of dentures be repaired. The defendant was not induced to do anything that he would not otherwise have done. Thus, the High Court's decision was fully in line with that of the House of Lords in *Looseley*: no issue of entrapment arose and there was consequently no reason to exclude the investigator's evidence. Similarly, **in *The People (DPP) v. Van Onzen and Loopmans* (1996)**, the defendants were involved in the importation into Ireland of nearly 2,000 kilos of cannabis resin. The gardaí had intercepted a mobile phone being used by drug traffickers and when contacted by the defendants had not revealed their true identity. As a result, the defendants brought the drugs into Irish waters and were arrested. The defendants argued that they had been lured or entrapped into entering Irish waters, but the Court of Criminal Appeal ruled that the gardaí's actions did not constitute entrapment. On the contrary, the court ruled that the gardaí had carried out their duties 'absolutely properly'. Again, the gardaí had not gone beyond what might be expected of people involved in the drug-trafficking trade; indeed, if actions such as these were deemed by the courts to be improper, it is likely that drug trafficking would be impossible to combat.

In both of these cases, there was no evidence that the State agents had in fact created the crime that was being prosecuted. Suppose, however, that the gardaí had truly incited a person to break the law and then sought to have that person prosecuted. It seems that in such a case, the Irish courts would have the power to exclude any evidence derived from entrapment. In *King v. Attorney General* **(1981)**, Henchy J., commenting on the constitutional guarantee of personal liberty not being removed except in due course of law, stated that 'due course of law' excluded investigative operations that 'stoop[ed] to methods which ignore the fundamental norms of the legal order postulated by the Constitution.' The collection of evidence through true entrapment would seem to breach such fundamental norms, and the courts have a discretion to exclude such evidence. In *The People (Attorney General) v. O'Brien* **(1965)**, the defendant's larceny conviction had been brought about through the use of a defective search warrant. The Supreme Court accepted that the defect was unintentional, and thus the search was not unconstitutional – had it been, the courts would have been under a duty to exclude the evidence. Instead, the evidence had been illegally obtained, and the courts could exclude it if the public interest so required. The courts in such cases must balance the public interest in having crime investigated and punished with the public interest in preventing 'illegal and inquisitorial' methods of investigation. Thus, the Irish courts have a power to exclude evidence gained through entrapment. However, in *DPP v. McCutcheon* **(1986)**, the High Court ruled that before a court can exercise this discretion, the court must have a proper basis for believing that the circumstances that require the exercise of the court's discretion actually exist. In other words, the court must have evidence that the public interest balance, referred to in *O'Brien*, is in issue. It is not open to a court to exclude the evidence of an *agent provocateur* simply because he is an *agent provocateur*.

There is as yet no indication that an Irish court will issue a stay on a prosecution brought on foot of entrapment. Nor is it entirely clear whether entrapment can be raised in an Irish court as a substantive defence, as in the United States. In *Quinlivan v. Conroy (No.2)* **(2000)**, the defendant had escaped from Brixton Prison in the UK while awaiting trial on explosives charges. The UK sought his extradition to face these charges as well as others resulting from the escape. One of the factors involved in extradition requests is the so-called 'correspondence principle'. The charges faced by the person being extradited in the requesting country must correspond to charges known to Irish law. The defendant argued that he had been entrapped into escaping from prison by a prison officer whom the defendant alleged was working with the British security services. He argued that no Irish court would convict him of escaping from prison in these circumstances, and that consequently the UK request lacked sufficient correspondence. The High Court rejected this argument, partly on the absence of evidence of any entrapment. However, the court also noted that the defendant's contention 'invite[d] the court to consider, not the constituents of an offence, but rather a *defence* which may be open to the applicant in respect of the offence charged' (italics added). The court refused the invitation on the grounds that it was not the function of an Irish court in dealing with an extradition request to inquire into the innocence or guilt of the person whose extradition was being sought. The description of entrapment as a defence that goes to a person's innocence or guilt is strongly suggestive of a substantive defence that goes beyond a mere procedural remedy. The procedural approach to entrapment adopted by the English courts 'assumes the defendant's guilt and is concerned with the standards of behaviour of the law enforcement officers' (*per* Lord Hoffman in *Looseley*). Thus, the High Court in *Quinlivan* may have taken a tentative first step towards the approach of the American federal courts.

14.4 Further Reading

Allen, 'Judicial Discretion and the Exclusion of Evidence in Entrapment Situations in Light of the House of Lords Decision in *R v. Sang*', (1982) 33 *NILQ* 105.

Choo, 'A Defence of Entrapment', (1990) 53 *MLR* 453.

Robertson, 'Entrapment Evidence: Manna from Heaven, or Fruit of the Poisoned Tree', (1994) *Crim LR* 805.

PART III

INCHOATE OFFENCES

CHAPTER FIFTEEN

ATTEMPTS

15.1 Introduction

There are three types of inchoate offences: attempts, conspiracy and incitement. They are offences ancillary to other more substantive offences; for example, attempted murder is ancillary to murder, incitement to rape is ancillary to rape, and conspiracy to commit arson is ancillary to arson. All inchoate offences are, however, offences in their own right. The law on attempts forms the basis of this chapter, while conspiracy and incitement are considered in Chapters 16 and 17, respectively.

In England, attempts are covered by the Criminal Attempts Act 1981. In Ireland, attempts were covered by common law rules, under which they were all considered to be misdemeanors irrespective of the substantive offence in question. However, with the abolition of felonies and misdemeanors by the Criminal Law Act 1997, this situation has changed. By virtue of section 2 of that Act, arrestable offences are defined as any offence that carries a penalty of five years' imprisonment or more, or any attempt to commit such an offence. Some attempts are therefore considered to be arrestable offences for which offenders may be arrested without warrant, while others are non-arrestable offences requiring a warrant.

15.2 The *Actus Reus*

The modern law on attempts grew from the decision in *R v. Eagleton* (1855). In that case, the defendant supplied bread to a Poor Law Authority that was below the contracted weight. He was convicted of attempting to obtain money by false pretences. The court explained that:

> The mere intention to commit a misdemeanor is not criminal. Some act is required, and we do not think that all acts towards committing a misdemeanor are indictable. Acts remotely leading towards the commission of the offence are not to be considered as attempts to commit it, but acts immediately connected with it are . . .

This statement contains the basic principles that are still applicable to the *actus reus* of a criminal attempt. Indeed, the *actus reus* was described in nearly identical terms by the Court of Criminal Appeal in *The People (Attorney General) v. Thornton* (1952):

> . . . an act done by the accused with a specific intent to commit a particular crime; that it must go beyond mere preparation, and must be a direct movement towards the commission after the preparations have been made; that some such act is required.

Thus, in *R v. Campbell* (1991), the defendant was seen 'lurking around' outside a post office, and was found in possession of an imitation firearm. He was arrested one yard from the post office. His conviction for attempted robbery was overturned on the grounds that he had merely prepared for the crime, but had not yet made any attempt. The Court of Appeal made particular reference to the fact that the defendant had not even entered the premises, and suggested that in circumstances such as these, a person could rarely be said to have made an attempt. Contrast that case with *R v. Jones* (1990), in which the defendant got into the victim's car with a sawn-off shotgun, levelled the gun and told the victim to drive. The victim, however, grabbed the gun and threw it out of the car. The defendant was convicted of attempted murder, but appealed on the grounds that the safety catch was still on and his finger was not on the trigger. He argued that this indicated that his actions were too remote from completing the offence of murder to constitute attempted murder. His conviction was upheld, however, on the grounds that getting into the car and pointing the gun were more than merely preparatory acts. The fact that the safety catch was on, meaning that the gun was not capable of being fired there and then, was irrelevant. Had he simply purchased the gun and shortened it, he would not have been convicted, as these acts would have been merely preparatory.

15.3 Proximity

At what point preparations become an actual attempt is unclear, a situation that is unsatisfactory as this issue goes to the heart of criminal attempts. Indeed, this was noted by the Court of Criminal Appeal in *The People (Attorney General) v. England* (1947), in which it was said that 'the extreme difficulty of attaining precision in the conception of an attempt at crime has baffled many a court and this is one of the rare offences that has defied scientific definition in exact terms.' In that case, it was held that words on their own could not constitute an attempt; they would have to be accompanied by some positive action. Further guidance was given by the Supreme Court in *The People (Attorney General) v. Sullivan* (1964), which endorsed a proximity test. In other words, the acts charged must be proximate, or close, to the commission of the complete offence. In that case, the defendant was a midwife who was paid a basic salary for up to twenty-five cases, but was entitled to an allowance for every extra case she dealt with. She created a number of fictitious patients with a view to crossing the twenty-five threshold and thereby making extra money fraudulently. It was held that an action must be sufficiently proximate to the commission of the substantive offence in order to be considered as an attempt. Furthermore, as in this case, where an action is 'the first of a series of similar acts intended to result cumulatively in the crime', such an action will be sufficiently proximate to justify a conviction for an attempt. Therefore, each and every fictitious claim made by the defendant constituted a separate attempt to defraud.

The proximity test begs the very question it is designed to answer: at what point is an act sufficiently proximate to the full offence to constitute an attempt? Most cases on this point suggest that the defendant must come very close to committing the offence. Indeed, in *R v. Stonehouse* (1978), Lord Diplock suggested that there must be evidence that the defendant had 'crossed the Rubicon and burnt his boats' before he could be convicted. This does not necessarily mean that the defendant had been at the point of committing the full offence, but he must have been close to it.

15.4 The *Mens Rea*

The *mens rea* of all attempts is intention; the defendant must be shown to have intended to commit the complete substantive offence. It is not sufficient to show recklessness even where recklessness is sufficient for the complete offence. For example, if X is charged with attempted rape, it must be shown that he intended to rape, even though the *mens rea* of rape is intention or recklessness. In other words, the defendant must be shown to have intended to succeed in committing the offence. In the case of attempted murder, this requirement leads to an unusual situation: only an intent to *kill* will suffice. In *The People (DPP) v. Douglas & Hayes* (1985), the defendants were convicted of shooting with intent to commit murder, contrary to section 14 of the Offences Against the Person Act 1861 (a particular form of attempted murder). It was held that an intent to kill had to be proven. This was so even though the *mens rea* of the complete offence of murder is an intent to kill *or to cause serious injury*. This latter form of *mens rea* – an intention to cause serious injury – is not sufficient for attempted murder. In determining the defendant's state of mind, the jury is entitled to draw inferences from the defendant's actions. In *The People (DPP) v. BK* (2000), the Court of Criminal Appeal confirmed that the jury should be instructed that once the defendant's actions had been proven by the prosecution, the jury were entitled to draw inferences from those proven actions as to the defendant's intentions. However, if there was more than one inference that could reasonably be drawn, and one such inference favoured the defendant, then the defendant was entitled to the benefit of the doubt. So, if X was charged with attempted rape and the facts established by the prosecution led either to a reasonable inference that the defendant intended to penetrate the complainant regardless of her consent, or to another reasonable inference that the defendant was not going to penetrate the complainant without consent, then the jury should adopt the second inference. In such circumstances, the jury must, by definition, have a reasonable doubt as to the defendant's intention.

There is, however, a complicating point to be considered. As noted in the previous paragraph, the defendant must intend to commit the complete offence. That is the *mens rea* of attempt. However, the complete offence has its own *mens rea* which must also be proven by the prosecution on a charge of attempt. For example, suppose X is charged with attempted rape. As far as *mens rea* is concerned, the prosecution must prove two things: first, it must prove that X intended to have intercourse with the victim, and second, it must prove that X had the *mens rea* for rape, i.e. knowledge that the victim was not consenting or recklessness as to her consent. To put it another way, the only difference between an attempt and the complete offence is the fact that the attempt failed; the *mens rea* requirement is the same. Consequently, the prosecution must prove that the defendant intended to succeed and had the *mens rea* required for the offence. This is called a distinction between consequences and circumstances. *Mens rea* as to consequences requires intention, while *mens rea* as to circumstances may consist of recklessness or intention, depending on the offence. In *R v. Khan* (1990), the defendant had been convicted of attempted rape. The trial judge had directed the jury that recklessness as regards the lack of consent was sufficient for a conviction. It was held on appeal that intention was only required in respect of completing the offence, i.e. as to consequences. However, the complete offence could be established by recklessness as to consent. Therefore, the trial judge's direction was correct. Similarly, in *Attorney General's Reference No.3 of 1992* (1994), the defendants had thrown a petrol bomb at a stationary car. The bomb missed and exploded against a wall. The defendants were charged with, and convicted of, attempted arson with intent to endanger life or being reckless as to whether life was endangered. It was held that the prosecution must prove an intention to commit the full offence. However, the full offence may be established by proving that the defendant was reckless as to whether life would be endangered. Therefore, proof of recklessness, as far as circumstances are concerned, was also sufficient for attempting the offence.

15.5 Impossibility

What is the position where a defendant attempts to commit an action that he believes to be a crime, but could not in reality amount to a crime? In other words, can a defendant be convicted of attempt even where it is impossible for a complete offence to be committed? In *Haughton v. Smith* (1973), the House of Lords decided that impossibility is generally a defence to a criminal charge. This applies where a crime is physically or legally impossible to commit. A physical impossibility is where, for example, X attempts to murder Y who is already dead. A good example of a legal impossibility is provided by the facts of *Haughton v. Smith* itself. The police had intercepted a quantity of stolen corned beef, but allowed it to continue as a ruse. The defendant took possession of the beef and was charged with attempting to handle stolen property. It was held that the beef was at that point under police control, and had therefore, by law, been returned to lawful custody. Consequently, the beef was at that point no longer stolen, and therefore, the defendant's conviction could not be maintained.

There is one exception to the defence of impossibility. A person may be convicted where the impossibility relates to the method used. For example, suppose X wishes to kill Y by poisoning, but mistakenly uses a non-lethal drug. In the circumstances, it would be impossible for the attempt to succeed, but X could still be convicted of attempted murder, as he intended to kill Y and it was possible for him to do so. Thus, in *R v. White* (1910), the defendant had tried to kill his mother with poison, but had used a dose that would have been insufficient. His conviction for attempted murder was upheld.

15.6 Abandonment

Whether or not a defendant can avoid liability for an attempt by abandoning it is the subject of some disagreement in the common law world. In *Haughton v. Smith* (1973), the House of Lords suggested that the crucial point about abandonment is when it occurs. If it occurs prior to the proximate act, then there is no liability on the defendant. If it occurs after the proximate act has been committed, it is irrelevant, and the defendant may be convicted. This decision indicates that there is no defence of abandonment; it does not apply where the proximate act has been committed, and where the proximate act has not yet been committed, liability cannot be imposed anyway. Likewise in Ireland: abandonment is irrelevant, and liability can be imposed once a person has committed a proximate act. In *The People (Attorney General) v. Sullivan* (1964), Walsh J. said:

> ... even if there was evidence that [the defendant] had in fact changed her mind it would not amount to a defence because the offence charged is that of having the intent at the time the act constituting the attempt is carried out. [A charge of attempt] cannot be answered by evidence of a subsequent abandonment of the intent.

While this approach seems to be logically correct, it does suggest that there is no advantage to the defendant in having a change of heart, other than avoiding a charge for the full offence. It would appear, therefore, that once a defendant has committed a proximate act, he is by law committed to his course of action.

15.7 Further Reading

Glazebrook, 'Should We Have a Law of Attempted Crime?', (1969) 85 *LQR* 27.
Smith, 'Proximity at Attempt: Lord Lane's Midway Course', [1991] *Crim LR* 576.

CHAPTER SIXTEEN

CONSPIRACY

16.1 Introduction

The essence of a conspiracy is an agreement between two or more people to commit an unlawful action. In *R v. Parnell* (1881), the defendant and others were charged with eighteen counts of conspiracy arising out of the efforts of the Land League to persuade tenant farmers not to pay their rents and to intimidate landlords and their agents by means of boycotts. Fitzgerald J., in his charge to the jury, explained that there were three forms of conspiracy:

> Conspiracy has been aptly described as divisible under three heads – where the end to be attained is in itself a crime; where the object is lawful, but the means to be resorted to are unlawful; and where the object is to do injury to a third party or to a class, though if the wrong were effected by a single individual it would be a wrong but not a crime.

The first two are self-explanatory and require little discussion. The third arises where the conspirators agree to do something that is actionable by civil remedy, in this case, persuading tenant farmers not to pay rents. What turns the matter into a crime is the fact that it is done by more than one person. The justification given by Fitzgerald J. was that a person might be able to defend his interests against an individual, but it would be considerably more difficult against a group, thus requiring the intervention of the State.

Unlike attempts, conspiracies do not require any act towards the commission of the substantive offence; the mere making of an agreement is sufficient. The law recognises a number of different categories of conspiracies: to commit a crime, to defraud, to pervert the course of justice, to effect a public mischief, to corrupt public morals, to commit a tort or to outrage public decency. In *DPP v. Withers* (1974), it was held that a conspiracy must fall into one of these categories, otherwise no criminal conspiracy has been committed. In each of the different categories, the elements that constitute the conspiracy are the same.

16.2 The *Actus Reus*

The essential element in a conspiracy is an agreement between two or more parties. Who the parties are is irrelevant, unless they are married. In *Mawji v. R* (1957), the Privy Council held that spouses could not enter into a criminal conspiracy with each other. This decision was based on the idea that a husband and wife were one, and one person cannot enter into a conspiracy with himself. While this concept is somewhat outdated, the Irish courts' attitude to it is unclear. The conviction for murder of the husband and wife defendants in *The People*

(DPP) v. Murray **(1977)** on the basis of a common design would indicate a willingness to treat spouses independently. However, the rule was specifically endorsed in England in section 2 of the Criminal Law Act 1977. The rationale for doing so was to preserve the stability of marriage, which would also be in accord with Irish public policy. On balance, it is likely that the Irish courts will continue to regard conspiracies between husband and wife as being outside the definition of criminal conspiracy, although their rationale would probably follow that of the English 1977 Act.

There does not have to be a formal agreement or contract. All that is required is that the parties pursue a common aim in combination. In *R v. Walker* (1962), the defendant had a discussion with others about stealing a payroll. It was held that it would be unreasonable to regard this as conspiracy. Therefore, a negotiation or similar preparatory measures will not constitute an agreement. Additionally, there is no requirement that the conspiracy be a secret. In **Parnell**, Fitzgerald J. noted that in many cases, the conspiracy would be hatched behind closed doors, but held that this was not a necessary element of the offence. So, in that case, the fact that the meetings of the Land League, at which the alleged conspiracy was planned, were open did not defeat the charge.

It is essential that a distinction be made between an agreement to commit a crime on the one hand, and, on the other, independent actions by two or more persons acting towards the same unlawful objective. For example, no conspiracy is committed if X and Y both work independently towards killing Z, as there has been no agreement between them. If, however, X and Y agree to co-operate in killing Z, there is a conspiracy. Furthermore, even if X and Y are working independently, but X sees that Y has a better chance of succeeding and offers to help, they may be found to have conspired to commit murder once X accepts the offer. If the offer is rejected, however, there is no conspiracy.

Whether or not an agreement has been reached is a matter of fact for the jury to decide in each case. In the absence of a confession, this will usually be done by showing that the defendants' actions were concerted, leading to an inference that the actions must have been co-ordinated beforehand. In *R v. Porter* (1980), a Northern Ireland decision, the defendant was charged with conspiracy to make available materials which might be useful to terrorists. He received a telephone call from a man claiming to be involved in Loyalist welfare. This man asked the defendant, who was a lorry driver, to pick up a parcel in England and bring it back with him to Northern Ireland. The defendant asked whether the package contained weapons, and the man told him to make no comment on it if he knew what was good for him. The defendant, by his own admission, made a number of efforts to locate the package in order to bring it back to Northern Ireland, but the package had already been picked up by another driver. The Court of Appeal noted that there was no evidence of an agreement, but held that there was sufficient evidence from which an inference could be drawn that the defendant had joined the conspiracy. It must, however, be stressed that the conspiracy does not lie in the concerted acts: it lies in the prior agreement that is inferred from the acts. As was stated in *R v. Bolton* (1991), 'it is what was agreed to be done and not what was in fact done which is all important.'

Finally, once the agreement is made, the crime of conspiracy has been committed. It is irrelevant that the conspiracy is not implemented, or even that the conspirators abandon their agreement; the moment the agreement is made, the crime has been committed. By extension, if the conspiracy is implemented but fails, the parties to the agreement can still be prosecuted for conspiracy. In *The People (DPP) v. O'Brien* (2002), the defendant and others set up a company with the object of defrauding others. A number of individuals were then informed that they were the beneficiaries of a large amount of money that could be released only if the individuals in question paid an advance fee to the defendant's company. There was of course no money, and the individuals became suspicious and did not hand over any money. The object of the conspiracy therefore failed. Nevertheless, in the Court of Criminal Appeal, Keane C.J. pointed out that 'the fact that the conspiracy failed to achieve its object of defrauding the two people concerned did not make it any the less a conspiracy for the purpose of the criminal law.' The crime had been committed from the moment the parties to the conspiracy made their agreement; what happened after that moment was irrelevant as far as their guilt of conspiracy was concerned.

16.3 The *Mens Rea*

As with attempts, it must be shown that the conspirators intended to commit the substantive offence. To intend to commit the offence, the conspirator must know what the conspiracy is about. How much knowledge is required was explored in *Porter*. It was argued that the defendant did not know what the package contained, and that therefore there was insufficient evidence that he had agreed to join the conspiracy. The Court of Appeal noted, however, that a co-conspirator will rarely have absolute knowledge of all the steps to be taken by the other conspirators, and such knowledge was not required to support a conspiracy charge. The defendant, by his own admission, had known that the package contained something like guns or ammunition, although he may not have known the precise nature of the contents. Where a defendant deliberately shut his eyes to the truth, he will not be allowed by the law to argue that he did not know. Thus, the position in conspiracy would appear to be similar to that in secondary participation: the defendant must be shown to have known the nature of the agreement, even though he did not know the precise details.

As always, there must be a distinction between intent and motive. In *Wai Yu-tsang v. R* (1991), it was held in relation to a conspiracy to defraud that the defendants' purpose is irrelevant; all that matters are their intentions. Where two people have agreed to carry out a crime, that is their intent although it may not be their precise purpose or motive. So, the defendants in that case were fraudsters acting with an intent to defraud, but their purpose was to enrich themselves. This was still held by the Privy Council to be a conspiracy. Finally, as a conspiracy is committed solely by the making of an agreement, the distinction made by the law on attempts between consequences and circumstances does not arise.

16.4 Co-conspirators

A conspiracy, by definition, necessarily involves at least two people. However, does a conviction for conspiracy against one of them depend on convictions against the others? In *DPP v. Shannon* (1974), the respondent and another were jointly tried for conspiracy to handle stolen goods. The respondent pleaded guilty, but the other defendant contested the matter, with the result that the jury was hung. In a later retrial, he was acquitted. The respondent then appealed on the grounds that as his co-conspirator had been acquitted, his conviction could not stand. The conviction was quashed by the Court of Appeal, and the prosecution appealed. It was held by the House of Lords that where the defendants are tried separately, the acquittal of one does not prejudice the conviction of the other. The fact that the respondent had pleaded guilty was irrelevant against the co-accused; likewise, the co-accused's acquittal was irrelevant in the respondent's case. The conviction was therefore reinstated. However, it was also suggested by two of the Lords that where co-conspirators are tried jointly, it would probably never be right to convict one and acquit the other. That this is so was explained by the Court of Appeal in *R v. Coughlan* (1976). The appellant and another had been tried jointly for conspiracy to cause explosions while acting as members of the IRA. The trial judge had directed the jury that they must find both defendants guilty or find them both not guilty; it was not open to them to convict one and acquit the other. The appellant appealed on the basis that, as the evidence against his co-defendant was stronger than against him, by tying his verdict to that of the co-defendant, the trial judge had unfairly deprived him of a chance of an acquittal. In doing so, he used *dicta* from *Shannon* as support. The Court of Appeal rejected this submission, noting that *Shannon* did not in fact provide support for this contention. The court endorsed the direction and noted that where the evidence against one defendant is stronger than the evidence against the other, there is an option to request separate trials. This request will be decided by the trial judge according to the weight of evidence against each party.

This matter has been addressed in England: section 5 of the Criminal Law Act 1977 provides that the acquittal of one conspirator will not prejudice the convictions of the other conspirators, irrespective of how they are tried. In Ireland, the common law position still applies. Consequently, where X and Y are both prosecuted separately for a conspiracy, the fact that X is acquitted does not of itself mean that Y should also be acquitted, although the justice of the case may demand that this be done. Where they are tried jointly, it would seem that their verdicts should generally be the same.

16.5 Impossibility

Impossibility is a defence to a charge of conspiracy, providing the agreement is to engage in a specific course of conduct. In *DPP v. Nock and Alsford* (1978), the defendants conspired to produce cocaine. They obtained a powder which they thought contained cocaine, and they planned to separate it from the other elements of the powder. Unknown to them, however, the powder did not in fact contain cocaine, thereby rendering their plan impossible to carry out. It was held by the House of Lords that the agreement was only for a specific purpose, and that as that purpose was impossible to achieve, the defendants should be acquitted. The answer would have been different had the conspiracy been of a more general nature and would not thereby have been defeated by impossibility. For example, if the defendants had conspired to supply cocaine, they could have been convicted as they could have obtained supplies of the drug from sources other than the powder. The conspiracy would therefore not have been impossible.

What about the situation where the defendants conspire to commit a crime that is possible at the time the conspiracy is entered into, but subsequently becomes impossible? Suppose, for example, that X and Y conspire to kill Z, and prepare to do so. However, two weeks after the conspiracy is made, Z dies from natural causes. As the conspiracy is specific, do X and Y have a defence of impossibility? In principle, it would seem that they do not. The offence of conspiracy is complete once the agreement has been made; no further actions are required. Therefore, X and Y have committed a conspiracy from the moment they agree to kill Z, and it is not impossible to do so at that point. Consequently, the decision in *Nock* does not seem to apply, and the fact that Z dies before the plan can be implemented would appear to be irrelevant.

16.6 Further Reading

Hocking, 'Conspiracy as a Very Enduring Practice, Part I', (1998) 8 *ICLJ* 1.
———, 'Conspiracy as a Very Enduring Practice: Part II', (1998) *ICLJ* 121.

CHAPTER SEVENTEEN

INCITEMENT

17.1 Introduction

It is an offence to incite a person to commit an indictable or summary crime. The incitement will usually be by persuasion, but may also be by duress such as threats or pressure. Consequently, if X threatens to kill Y's wife unless he assists in a bank robbery, X can be convicted of incitement. There are also some statutory forms of incitement, the most important being contained in the Prohibition of Incitement to Hatred Act 1989. Under this Act, it is an offence to utter threatening, abusive or insulting words, or publish, display, distribute or broadcast threatening, abusive or insulting material that is intended or is likely to incite hatred.

17.2 The *Actus Reus*

The *actus reus* of incitement comprises any action that seeks to influence another person to commit an offence. In *R v. Goldman* (2001), the Court of Appeal adopted the following comments from a South African judge, Holmes JA.:

> An inciter ... is one who reaches and seeks to influence the mind of another to the commission of a crime. The machinations of criminal ingenuity being legion, the approach to the other's mind may take many forms, such as a suggestion, proposal, request, exhortation, gesture, argument, persuasion, inducement, goading or the arousal of cupidity.

Typically, an incitement will involve one of the these actions coupled with an explicit or implied promise of a reward (*R v. Fitzmaurice* (1983)), although in *RRB v. Applin* (1974), Lord Denning indicated that incitement also could be brought about through the use of threats or pressure. However it comes about, incitement is more than a mere desire that some crime be committed; the defendant must take some steps towards recruiting another person to commit the offence. Thus, suppose X has just had an argument with his wife, and goes straight to the local pub where he tells his friend Y about the argument. He wishes aloud in the local pub that she would fall under a bus, and the next day Y pushes X's wife in front of a bus, killing her instantly. In these circumstances, X is not guilty of incitement. If, however, X had suggested to his friend that there might be a reward for anyone who brought this about, he can be convicted. In both cases, X could be said to have solicited the death of his wife, but the first instance is merely an expression of a desire, whereas in the second instance, he has actively sought his friend's involvement. Consequently, while all forms of incitement involve solicitation of some kind, not all solicitations can constitute incitement. In *The People (Attorney General) v.*

Capaldi **(1949)**, the defendant brought a pregnant woman to a doctor and asked that something 'be done for' her, referring to an illegal abortion. The defendant also said that he had plenty of money to pay the doctor's fees. The doctor refused and asked the defendant to leave. The defendant argued that his words and conduct amounted to no more than an expression of a desire that an offence be carried out, rather than an incitement. It was held by the Court of Criminal Appeal that a mere expression of a desire or a wish would not be sufficient to constitute incitement. However, in this case the specific request coupled with the financial incentive offered went beyond a mere desire and was an attempt by the defendant to convince the doctor to perform the abortion. Consequently, the defendant's actions were sufficient to constitute incitement.

The solicitation, in whatever form it takes, must be communicated in some way to the person or persons being incited. Indeed, it is possible for the incitement to be addressed to all and sundry. Thus, in *R v. Most* (1881), the publication of a newspaper article urging revolutionaries around the world to assassinate their Heads of State was found to be sufficient communication to establish incitement to commit murder. If the communication fails to reach the person(s) being incited, or is intercepted by the gardaí, the inciter can still be prosecuted for an attempted incitement: *Chelmsford Justices, ex parte Amos* (1973). However, once the communication occurs, the offence of incitement has been established. It is not necessary that the incitement succeed. In *The People (DPP) v. Murtagh* **(1990),** the defendant had brought false charges against a garda and had asked a woman to give false evidence on his behalf. The defendant was charged with attempting to pervert the course of justice by inciting another to commit perjury. The Court of Criminal Appeal commented that 'such an offence is completed when the words of incitement are uttered, and so the offence is committed even though the incitement fails.'

Once the incitee agrees, both he and the inciter become conspirators. Thus, in the example given above, once Y agrees to push X's wife in front of the bus, the incitement becomes a conspiracy to commit murder involving X and Y. Once Y pushes X's wife in front of the bus, he may be convicted of murder, and X may be convicted as an accessory to murder.

One last point should be made. The person being incited must be capable in law of committing the complete offence. A good example of this is the somewhat tortuous case of *R v. Whitehouse* (1977). The defendant was accused of inciting his fifteen-year-old daughter to commit incest with him. However, under the Sexual Offences Act 1956, incest (of the female variety) was defined as occuring when a woman over the age of sixteen allows a man whom she knows to be her father to have sexual intercourse with her. A woman under the age of sixteen could not commit incest, the law conclusively presuming that such a woman was a victim rather than an offender. Thus, the prosecution was alleging that the defendant had incited his daughter to commit a crime that by law she could not commit. The prosecution accepted this point, but suggested that the charge could be amended to incitement by the defendant of his daughter to aid and abet in the commission of incest on her by him. It was held that there is a general rule of law that a person over the age of criminal responsibility can aid and abet the commission of a crime that he or she cannot commit as a principal offender. However, in this case, the daughter would be aiding and abetting the commission of a crime upon herself. The Court of Appeal held that the daughter belonged to a class that is protected by the law and not punished by it. Accordingly, the prosecution's convoluted amended charge resulted in the same conclusion as the original charge: it was not possible for the girl in question to commit the offence, and the defendant's conviction could not stand.

17.3 The *Mens Rea*

The *mens rea* of incitement is quite straightforward. As with all inchoate offences, it must be shown that the defendant intended the person incited to commit the substantive offence. Additionally, the defendant must know of all the elements of the offence incited. Where the defendant is aware that the incitee lacks capacity to commit the offence, as in *Whitehouse*, there is no incitement as the defendant is not inciting the commission of a crime. So, if X asks a six-year-old boy to deliver drugs for him, X cannot be prosecuted for incitement to supply controlled drugs. If, however, the boy actually delivers the drugs, X can be prosecuted as the principal offender; the boy will be an innocent agent. Finally, the defendant's liability is limited to the act incited. So, if X incites Y to steal from Z's house, but Y actually kills Z, X is not guilty of incitement to murder.

17.4 Impossibility

As with all inchoate offences, impossibility is a general defence. In *R v. Fitzmaurice* (1983), the defendant was asked by his father to recruit others into a robbery plan. He duly approached another man and brought him into the scheme. Unknown to him, however, there was no plan; the father intended to inform on the 'plan', and claim a reward for preventing a robbery. The defendant was convicted of inciting a robbery. It was held by the Court of Appeal that the evidence must be analysed carefully to decide the actual offence incited. The approach taken in *DPP v. Nock and Alsford* (1978) in connection with conspiracy was specifically endorsed – liability will depend on the nature of the incitement. If the offence incited is of a general nature, impossibility is not a defence. If, however, the incitement is specific and the specific object is impossible, the impossibility will be a defence. In this case, the object of the incitement had been to commit *a* robbery, and was therefore of a general nature. Consequently, it could not be said that the object of the incitement was impossible to carry out, notwithstanding the fact that the whole project was in essence a charade.

Fitzmaurice sets out the basic principle, but it can become more complex. For example, it is possible for a person to incite the commission of an offence in general terms. If the incitee agrees, a conspiracy is born. However, if the conspiracy then focuses on a specific action which is impossible to achieve, the conspirators will be acquitted, but the inciter can still be convicted of incitement. Thus, X incites Y to join him on a killing spree, and Y agrees. They then conspire to kill Z, who, unknown to them, is already dead. A conspiracy charge will fail, because the specific object of the conspiracy is impossible. However, X can still be convicted of incitement because the object of the incitement, i.e. the killing spree, was of a general nature and could not be defeated by impossibility. If, however, X had incited Y specifically to kill Z, the incitement charge would fail due to impossibility. This also indicates that, as with conspiracy, impossibility is not a defence where the offence incited becomes impossible to commit after the incitement has occurred.

17.5 Further Reading

Holroyd, 'Incitement, A Tale of Three Agents', (2001) *JCL* 515.
Leng, 'Incitement – An Objective Approach to the Definition of Crime', (1978) 41 *MLR* 725.

PART IV

OFFENCES AGAINST THE PERSON

CHAPTER EIGHTEEN

HOMICIDE

18.1 Introduction

Homicide is a general catch-all category that encompasses virtually every conceivable way of killing, but in general parlance refers only to murder and manslaughter. The modern law grew from the early common law concept of homicide, which effectively combined murder and manslaughter in one offence. It was only later that the modern concept of murder began to develop, which required a highly specific form of *mens rea*: malice aforethought. The early connection between the two offences is maintained and reflected in the fact that murder and manslaughter are alternatives. In other words, if X is charged with murder, but the jury is not satisfied beyond reasonable doubt that he is guilty, it has the option of returning a verdict of guilty of manslaughter.

This chapter is a long one, and covers most of the offences known to Irish law that involve the killing of human beings. Of central importance are murder and manslaughter, two of the most serious offences in Irish law. Provocation is also considered here as it is a defence that is only available to murder and reduces murder to manslaughter. Other forms of killing are also considered: suicide, euthanasia, infanticide and death by dangerous driving.

MURDER

18.2 Introduction

Murder is the most serious offence known to Irish law, and many of the general principles of law have been developed in murder cases. The law on murder is not, however, entirely coherent, which is surprising for such an important offence. As Lord Mustill stated in *Attorney General's Reference No.3 of 1994* (1996):

> One could expect a developed system to embody a law of murder clear enough to yield an unequivocal result based on a given set of facts, a result which conforms with apparent justice and has a sound intellectual base. This is not so in England, where the law of homicide is permeated by anomaly, fiction, misnomer and obsolete reasoning.

These comments are equally applicable to Irish law on the subject. Indeed, this case is interesting not only for its own content, but also because it contains a detailed discussion on the general rules applicable to murder.

The general law on murder is based on the common law offence, with some amendments introduced by statute dealing with *mens rea* and punishment. The classic definition of murder was given by Chief Justice Coke in 1640 and is still generally applicable today:

> Murder is when any man of sound memory, and of the age of discretion, unlawfully killeth within any country of the realm any reasonable creature *in rerum natura* under the King's Peace [*with malice aforethought either expressed by the party or implied by law*], so as the party wounded, or hurt, etc. die of the wound or hurt, etc. [*within a year and a day after the same*].

The italicised portions of the quotation contained within square brackets concern the common law *mens rea* of murder and the year and a day rule, respectively, neither of which apply today. The common law *mens rea* requirement of malice aforethought was replaced by section 4(1) of the Criminal Justice Act 1964 (see section 18.7), while the year and a day rule was abolished by the Criminal Justice Act 1999 (see section 18.6). The balance of the quotation accurately describes the *actus reus* of murder. It contains a number of elements that should be considered in turn. It should also be noted that the *actus reus* of murder is identical to that of manslaughter; the difference between the two offences lies in their respective *mens rea* requirements.

18.3 Sound Memory and the Age of Discretion

This element simply requires that the defendant should be legally sane and over the age of criminal responsibility. Both of these concepts have already been explored in detail (see Chapters 8 and 12, respectively). For present purposes, it is sufficient to note that if a person is legally insane at the time of the killing, he will not be guilty of murder. In these circumstances, a special verdict of 'guilty but insane' will be returned, which is technically an acquittal. As far as the age of responsibility is concerned, Irish law currently follows the common law view that a child under the age of seven cannot commit an offence, while a child under fourteen is presumed to be incapable of so doing, but this presumption can be rebutted by showing that the child knew that his actions were seriously wrong. As long as the child has reached his seventh birthday, therefore, he is over the age of responsibility and may be charged with murder. The Children Act 2001 has made provision for the age of responsibility to be raised to twelve, but at the time of writing this provision has not yet been brought into force.

18.4 Unlawful Killing

In any murder case, there must be proof of death. Such a seemingly obvious point belies the difficulty that has arisen in practice in defining the point at which death occurs. The accepted practice is to regard the cessation of brain stem activity as the point of death. In *Airedale NHS Trust v. Bland* (1993), the House of Lords considered the case of a young man who was in a persistent vegetative state. The medical evidence showed that brain stem activity was continuing, and therefore

Lord Goff ruled that 'in the present state of medical science, [the young man] is still alive and should be so regarded as a matter of law.' Lords Keith and Browne-Wilkinson made comments to similar effect. However, in a Canadian case, *R v. Green and Harrison* (1988), the Supreme Court of British Columbia ruled that for the purposes of the criminal law, the cessation of brain stem activity was an impractical test. In this case, the defendants were charged with murder. The evidence showed that the second defendant shot the deceased in the head and the first defendant followed suit, firing two shots. There was a conflict as to which of the defendants had actually killed the deceased, and Wood J. ruled that the brain stem test could only work in this case if 'someone had happened along with an EEG monitor and applied same to [the deceased] either before or immediately after the two shots allegedly fired by Green.' Accordingly, Wood J. stated that he would instruct the jury that 'as a matter of law Mr. Frie was alive so long as any of his vital organs – which would include his heart – continued to operate.' However, as explained earlier, under Irish law, if two or more parties are involved in a killing either as joint principals or as principal and secondary parties, it does not matter which of the parties is actually responsible for the killing (see Chapter 6). If it is a case of common design, then each party is fully responsible for the acts of the other; if it is a case of secondary liability, the secondary participant is indicted, tried and punished as a principal. Thus, the situation facing Wood J. in *Green and Harrison* would not arise in Ireland, and Charleton indicates that the brain stem test is the one that operates in Ireland.[1]

The act of killing comprises any action (or omission) that brings a person to the point of death as just defined. It is no answer to a murder charge to argue that the deceased was going to die shortly anyway. If X falls from a great height and has only moments to live, but Y shoots and kills X before he strikes the ground, Y is precluded from arguing that his actions made no real difference to X's fate and merely hastened his death by perhaps a second or two. So, in *R v. Dyson* (1908), Lord Alverstone ruled that if the defendant accelerated the deceased child's death, the 'fact that the child was already suffering from meningitis from which it would in any event have died before long, would afford no answer to the charge of causing its death.' Similarly, in *Attorney General's Reference No.3 of 1994* (1996), the House of Lords was faced with a child who was born prematurely as a result of an assault on its mother before it was born. The child lived for 121 days, and then died as a result of the premature birth. As Lord Mustill noted, 'in a narrow perspective, she died from natural causes'. In other words, there was no direct action on the part of the defendant that caused death. However, Lord Mustill accepted that the child would have lived longer had it not been for the assault prior to its birth. This was sufficient for a finding of manslaughter. Thus, the *actus reus* of murder is any action on the part of the defendant that hastens the deceased's death, no matter how slightly.

---

1 Charleton, *et al.*, *Criminal Law*, Dublin: Butterworths, 1999, para. 7.83.

Finally, the killing must have been unlawful. This requirement excludes any killings in which the killer acted out of justification, such as self-defence. So, if X kills Y in self-defence, a murder has not been committed providing the force used was reasonable in the circumstances (see Chapter 7). A similar reasoning could be applied to necessity if the Irish courts accept that killings done in situations of extreme emergency are justified (see Chapter 11). The unlawfulness requirement also excludes legitimate killings such as those carried out by soldiers in wartime or by executioners acting on foot of a court-imposed death sentence.

18.5 Any Reasonable Creature *In Rerum Natura*

In short, this element requires that the person killed be a human being. Homicide cannot be committed against an animal. Additionally, at common law, homicide could not be committed against a foetus who was regarded as not yet alive; a potential human being rather than an actual human being. Protection was given, however, to the foetus in the form of a prohibition on abortion in sections 57 and 58 of the Offences Against the Person Act 1861, which has since been lifted in England under certain circumstances, by the Abortion Act 1967. It is not entirely clear whether the common law view of the status of the foetus has survived the enactment of the Constitution in Ireland, especially the Eighth Amendment. The Eighth Amendment does not specifically grant the status of a human being to the foetus. It does, however, guarantee to protect the right to life of the unborn, on equal terms with that of the mother (see section 21.1). In *Attorney General v. X* **(1992)**, Hederman J. specifically stated that 'the terms of the Constitution totally exclude any possible suggestion that the unborn life is any less a human life than a life which has acquired an existence independent of its mother.' In the same case, however, McCarthy J. referred to the mother as a 'life in being', while the unborn child was a 'life contingent'. This distinction equates with the common law view of the status of the unborn child. However, it was expressly disavowed by Finlay C.J., and the general view seems to be that McCarthy J.'s judgment was the most liberal from the perspective of allowing abortion. Could a homicide prosecution therefore be taken following an abortion? If the Eighth Amendment has altered the common law to the extent that a foetus is now regarded as a human being, then such a prosecution is possible. Even if this is the case, it is difficult to see such charges being laid, although this would have more to do with policy considerations than with legal principles. If, however, the common law view that a foetus is not a human being is unaffected by the Constitution, such a prosecution could not be taken. On the strength of the judgments in *X*, it would seem that the former position is the most likely.

One complicating situation has arisen: suppose X assaults Y, a pregnant woman. The child, Z, is born alive, but is suffering from some injury as a result of the assault and later dies. Is X guilty of murder? In a Hong Kong decision, *R v. Kwok Chak Ming* (1963), a pregnant woman was stabbed during an assault.

Her child was born alive, but died soon after from the stabbing. It was held by the Hong Kong Court of Appeal that, providing all of the other elements of the offence existed, the defendant could be convicted of murder or manslaughter, depending on his intention. In England, in *Attorney General's Reference No.3 of 1994* (1996), the House of Lords considered a similar situation, except the child died after 121 days from a premature birth brought on by a stabbing, rather than from the stabbing itself. It was held that where the intention of the defendant was directed solely towards the pregnant woman, the defendant could not be convicted of murder because the doctrine of transferred intent did not apply in these circumstances (see section 4.3). The defendant could, however, be convicted of manslaughter. Presumably, where the defendant intended to kill or seriously injure the foetus, a murder conviction could be obtained.

18.6 Causation

Murder is a result offence; the prosecution is therefore required to prove that the defendant's action caused the deceased's death. The rules of causation have already been discussed (see section 3.4) and need not be repeated here. However, some specific points in relation to murder need to be made.

The defendant apparently does not have the right to expect the victim to mitigate his loss. Therefore, if X intentionally assaults Y, causing a serious injury, and Y refuses medical care for whatever reason and dies as a result, X is still guilty of murder. In *R v. Flynn* (1867), the deceased had been involved in a fight with the defendant, after which the defendant had thrown a stone which hit the deceased on the head. The deceased went to a local pub with some family members, then went to the police station, and then rode four miles home the following morning despite being very weak. It was only two days after the fight that the deceased called a doctor, but died the following day. It was held that the deceased's neglect of his wound would not exonerate the defendant unless the deceased's actions could be regarded as creating a new cause of death. In other words, if the deceased went out of his way to make the injury worse, the defendant would not be liable. The deceased's actions would effectively constitute a *novus actus interveniens*. In this case, the defendant had done nothing that he would not ordinarily have done; consequently, it could not be said that he had made the wound worse, and the conviction was upheld. Where the refusal of treatment is based on religious grounds, the defendant will also be convicted of murder: *R v. Blaue* (1975) (see section 3.4).

It seems that where the defendant caused the deceased to act in a dangerous manner, resulting in his death, then the defendant may be liable. For example, if X attacks Y and Y, in trying to save himself, jumps out of a third-storey window and dies from the fall, X may be convicted of murder. Lord Coleridge noted, in *R v. Halliday* (1889):

When a man creates in another man's mind an immediate sense of danger, which causes such person to try to escape, and in doing so injures himself, the person who creates such a state of mind is responsible for the injuries.

This point was explained in *R v. Williams and Davis* (1992), in which the deceased was a hitch-hiker who was given a lift by the defendants who intended to rob him. In trying to escape, the deceased jumped from the car and was killed. It was argued that the escape attempt was a *novus actus interveniens*. The Court of Appeal held, however, that an attempt to escape from a threat will not interfere with causation if it is a response that could have been foreseen by reasonable people. However, in deciding the issue of foreseeability, the jury should also consider the nature of the threat. If the threat was life-threatening, then foreseeability will not be much of a problem. If, however, the threat is not so serious, the jury must consider whether the deceased's action was 'so daft as to make it his one voluntary act which amounted to a *novus actus interveniens* and consequently broke the chain of causation.' However, the jury should also bear in mind that in the heat of the moment, the deceased may not have acted with much thought or deliberation. On this basis, even suicide can be included in the chain of causation, as shown by the unusual American judgment in *Stephenson v. State* (1933). The defendant raped the deceased, who committed suicide as a result. It was held that the defendant, by his actions, had rendered the deceased 'distracted and mentally irresponsible', and that her suicidal actions while in that condition were directly attributable to him. Therefore, the chain of causation was not broken.

The Year and a Day Rule

Until 1999, the common law required proof that the deceased died within a year and a day of the defendant's actions before a murder prosecution could succeed. If a death occurred outside this period, the law conclusively presumed that the death was not caused by the defendant's action. This presumption originated at a time when medical and forensic science were in their infancy, and linking a death to a specific cause could be problematic. The longer the gap between the defendant's act and the deceased's death, the greater the chance that errors in the attribution of criminal liability would be made. Thus, the common law judges developed this year and a day requirement as the functional equivalent of the doctrine of remoteness in tort: a death that occurred outside this period was too remote from the defendant's actions, and it was therefore too risky to attribute blame for the death to the defendant. However, by the twentieth century, the rule became increasingly anachronistic and began to cause practical difficulties, especially with the deliberate infliction of HIV. Suppose X stabbed Y with a blood-filled syringe, causing Y to contract the HIV virus. Y would then be in great danger of developing AIDS, which is incurable. However, the incubation period of AIDS is measured in years, and Y could conceivably live for a long time before the disease claimed his life. Y's death would therefore fall outside the year and a day period, but it could not reasonably be denied that X was responsible for Y's death.

Charleton notes a Pennsylvania case – *Commonwealth v. Ladd* (1960) – in which it was held that the year and a day rule would not apply where adequate proof of causation could be tendered.[2] However, no similar authority existed on this side of the Atlantic, and the legislatures in both England and Ireland removed the year and a day rule by statute. In England, the rule was abolished by the Law Reform (Year and a Day Rule) Act 1996, which requires the permission of the Attorney General for a homicide prosecution to be taken in cases where the death occurred more than three years after the defendant's action or where the defendant has already been convicted of another offence in respect of the initial action. In Ireland, section 38 of the Criminal Justice Act 1999 abolished the rule without any such proviso. Thus, homicide charges may now be laid against a defendant regardless of the delay between the defendant's act and the deceased's death, subject to the normal rules of causation.

18.7 *Mens Rea*

Until 1964, the *mens rea* of murder was described in the traditional common law terminology as being 'malice aforethought'. Since the Criminal Justice Act 1964, however, the common law terminology has been dropped. Section 4 of the 1964 Act provides:

1. Where a person kills another unlawfully the killing shall not be murder unless the accused person intended to kill, or cause serious injury to, some person, whether the person actually killed or anyone else.
2. The accused person shall be presumed to have intended the natural and probable consequences of his conduct; but this presumption may be rebutted.

Proof of an actual intention to kill or to cause serious injury is essential; proof of recklessness is not sufficient for murder. It is in this respect that murder differs from manslaughter; the latter offence can be established by proof of recklessness or gross negligence.

Section 4(1)

Section 4(1) requires proof of intention before a defendant can be convicted of murder. The meaning of intention has already been discussed in detail in Chapter 4 (see section 4.3), and that discussion need only be summarised here. In essence, there are two forms of intention, direct and oblique. A direct intention arises where the defendant intended to bring about a certain result. An oblique intention arises

---

2 Charleton, *et al.*, *op. cit.*, para 7.22.

where the defendant acted intentionally, but brought about a result that he did not specifically desire. A direct intention will always be sufficient for a conviction, but the position of an oblique intention is less clear. In *R v. Nedrick* (1986), the Court of Appeal held that an oblique intent is sufficient for murder if the defendant foresaw death or serious injury as a virtually certain result of his actions. This test has now been confirmed by the House of Lords in *R v. Woollin* (1998). In Ireland, the most recent direct authority is that of the Court of Criminal Appeal in *The People (DPP) v. Douglas & Hayes* (1985) in which it was held that that a deliberate action with recklessness as to the consequences of an action may be sufficient for an inference of intention. As already discussed (see section 4.3), this test sets the threshold too low for murder; the English test, set out in *Woollin*, is more appropriate.

Section 4(1) also provides that where the defendant intends to kill or seriously injure any person, he is guilty of murder, whether or not the person actually killed was the intended victim. So, if X intends to kill Y, but kills Z instead, X is still guilty of murder. This is a statutory form of the doctrine of transferred intent which has also already been discussed (see section 4.3) and needs only to be summarised here. The malice or intention that a defendant bears one person can be transferred to another in certain circumstances. However, for such a transfer to be made, the *mens rea* of the intended offence must be the same as that of the actual offence. Thus, if X tries to shoot Y but hits Z instead, his intent to harm Y can be transferred to Z. If, however, X misses Y and smashes a window in Z's house, X's intent cannot be transferred from attempted murder to causing criminal damage.

Finally, it is noteworthy that an intention merely to cause serious injury is sufficient for a murder conviction. As Lord Mustill commented in *Attorney General's Reference No.3 of 1994* (1996), 'it is possible to commit a murder not only without wishing the death of the victim but without the least thought that this might be the result of the assault.' So, if X assaults Y intending only to give him a good beating, and Y dies, X is guilty of murder. This is something of an anomaly in that, as explained in Chapter 4, intention normally requires either a direct intention to do something, or an oblique intention in which the result is foreseen as a virtual certainty. Lord Mustill's explanation for this anomaly is that it is something of a relic, developed from other rules that have long since been discarded.

Section 4(2)

Section 4(2) of the 1964 Act places upon a statutory footing in the case of murder the common law rule that people are presumed to intend the natural and probable consequences of their actions. This presumption has already been considered in Chapter 4 (see section 4.8), and needs only a summary here. In *The People (DPP) v. Hull* (1996), the Court of Criminal Appeal held that the jury should approach this presumption in a two-stage process. First, the jury should consider whether death or serious injury was a natural and probable consequence of the defendant's actions. If the answer to this question is in the affirmative, the jury should then consider whether there is an alternative explanation, and whether the prosecution has proven beyond reasonable doubt that the presumption has not been rebutted by the defence. Consequently, the presumption does not alter the burden of proof, despite the wording used in the provision.

Law Reform Commission Proposals

The Law Reform Commission has made a number of provisional recommendations in its *Consultation Paper on Homicide: The Mental Element in Murder* (LRC CP17-2001). The Commission began with the assumption that the murder/manslaughter distinction should be retained, and then considered where the appropriate dividing line should be drawn. The Commission's proposals, if adopted, would permit two alternate forms of *mens rea* to support a murder conviction. The first form is the traditional requirement that the defendant cause the death of another intending to kill or to cause serious injury. At present, the only guidance given by the Irish courts as to the meaning of intention is the decision of the Court of Criminal Appeal in **Douglas & Hayes**. However, the Commission concluded that this decision set the threshold for intention at a level too low for a murder conviction, and recommended that the *Woollin* conception of intention be formally adopted into Irish law. Thus, a person would intend to bring about a result if either bringing about that result was his object or purpose, or if he was aware that his actions were virtually certain to cause the result or would be virtually certain to cause the result if he succeeded in bringing about another result. The Commission further recommended that an intention to cause serious injury continue to be sufficient for a murder conviction, principally on the grounds that anyone who intends to cause a serious injury must be aware that he is risking a life and therefore has sufficient moral culpability for a murder conviction.

However, the Commission was also concerned that limiting the fault element of murder to intention as defined above would exclude some homicidal incidents that are morally indistinguishable from an intentional killing. In moral terms, there is but a slight distinction between a person who wants to cause serious harm only and a person who acts with an extreme indifference to human life. In the former case, there is sufficient fault to ground a murder conviction, and the Commission could see no reason why the latter case should be treated differently. Accordingly, the Commission recommended that the *mens rea* of murder should encompass killings committed recklessly under circumstances that manifest an extreme indifference to human life. Recklessness in this context was defined subjectively: the defendant should have consciously disregarded a substantial and unjustifiable risk that death would occur as a result of his actions.

18.8 Absence of a Body

The existence of a body, together with all the forensic evidence that can be gathered from the body, is obviously of tremendous importance for the prosecution. However, the body is not a prerequisite for a prosecution. It is possible for a conviction for murder to be obtained in the absence of a body. In *The People (Attorney General) v. Ball* (1936), the defendant was charged with the murder of his mother. In his defence, he argued that his mother had committed suicide, and that he had put her body in the sea to prevent embarrassment. However, the gardaí had found a blood-stained hatchet in the house, together with a large amount of blood splashed around. It was held that the absence of a body was not fatal to the prosecution, and the circumstantial evidence was sufficient for a conviction. In *The People (Attorney General) v. Cadden* (1957), however, the Court of Criminal Appeal emphasised that a conviction based on circumstantial evidence could only be sustained where the jury was satisfied, and had been warned by the judge, that the circumstances of the incident were not only consistent with the defendant having committed the act, but also that they were inconsistent with any conclusion other than his guilt.

18.9 Punishments

At common law, murder was a felony, and attracted the usual punishments for a felony: a death sentence and forfeiture of all property. Forfeiture for all felonies was removed as a penalty by the Forfeiture Act 1870, but the death penalty was retained as the mandatory punishment. The Criminal Justice Act 1964 abolished the death penalty for murder except in the case of capital murder. In its place, a mandatory sentence of life imprisonment was imposed (section 2). However, the Criminal Justice Act 1990, section 1, abolished the death penalty for any offence, thereby effectively abolishing capital murder (see section 18.10). The penalty for any form of murder is now life imprisonment. Murder is one of the very few offences in which a judge has no discretion in the choice of a penalty. The Law Reform Commission, in its *Report on Sentencing* (1994), recommended the abolition of this mandatory penalty and its replacement with a penalty that allows the trial judge some discretion.

18.10 Capital Murder

Capital murder was created as an offence by the Criminal Justice Act 1964 when the death penalty was abolished for murder – until then, all murders were capital in that they all attracted the death penalty. Under the 1964 Act, capital murder applied to the killing of gardaí or prison officers acting in the course of their duties, or the murder for political reasons of foreign Heads of State or diplomats, or murders committed in furtherance of certain subversive objectives under the Offences Against the State Act 1939. The rationale for creating this new offence, punishable by the death penalty, was to protect certain people who, by virtue of their duties, were in a very exposed and dangerous position. Gardaí, for example, are required to put themselves in danger when dealing with criminals. To compensate for this, an extra level of protection was required in the form of a more severe penalty.

That capital murder was an offence distinct from murder was demonstrated by the Supreme Court in *The People (DPP) v. Noel and Marie Murray* **(1977)**. The defendants, a husband and wife, had robbed a bank. In making their escape in their car, they collided with a car being driven by an off-duty garda. The garda gave chase in his car, eventually forcing the defendants to try to escape on foot. Again, the garda gave chase, and was about to catch the first defendant when the second defendant shot the garda at point blank range, killing him. The defendants were both charged with, and convicted of, capital murder. On appeal to the Supreme Court, it was held that capital murder was distinct from murder. In other words, a capital murder charge required more than proof of the killing of a person who happened to be a member of the gardaí. It required an extra element of *mens rea*: the defendants had to be shown to have either known that their victim was a garda or to have been reckless as to this possibility (reckless in the subjective sense). Further, it followed that a common design as to murder would not be sufficient proof of a common design as to capital murder. The first defendant's conviction was therefore quashed and replaced with a conviction for murder. The second defendant's conviction was also overturned, and a retrial was ordered.

The Criminal Justice Act 1990 abolished the death penalty for all offences (section 1). As this effectively abolished capital murder, special provisions were enacted in section 3, which created a new form of murder. For the sake of convenience, this new offence can be referred to as murder under section 3. This new kind of murder has the same application as the offence of capital murder under the 1964 Act, i.e. gardaí and prison officers acting in the course of their duties, etc., and is to all intents and purposes capital murder without the death penalty. Section 3(2)(a) provides that this is an offence distinct from murder which is not committed unless it can be shown that the defendant 'knew of the existence of each ingredient of the offence ... or was reckless as to whether or not that ingredient existed.' Thus, the Supreme Court decision in *Murray* has now been placed on a statutory footing. In place of the death penalty, section 4 provides that a mandatory life sentence should be imposed, with a requirement that the defendant serve at least forty years. Furthermore, the power to commute or remit the punishment contained in the Criminal Justice Act 1951 cannot be exercised until after this period has expired (section 5(1)). Remission for good conduct is, however, allowed under section 5(2). Temporary release is also prohibited unless for 'grave reasons of a humanitarian nature'. Finally, where a person is accused under section 3, but the evidence is found to be insufficient (as in the *Murray* case), section 6 provides for alternative verdicts of guilty of murder or manslaughter as the case may be.

Indeed, section 2(b) provides that the same procedure should be followed for murder under section 3 as for ordinary murder.

18.11 Attempted Murder

Attempted murder follows the same general rules on attempts discussed in Chapter 15. It is accordingly unnecessary to repeat them. Nevertheless, two points should be made here. First, as with all attempts, only proof of intention will satisfy the *mens rea* requirement. However, there is an anomaly here in that for murder, an intention to kill or to cause serious injury is sufficient, whereas for attempted murder, an intention to kill is required. Thus, if X attacks Y with the intention of only causing serious injury, and Y dies, X is guilty of murder. If, however, Y does not die, X is not guilty of attempted murder. There is no justification for this anomaly, and none was attempted by the Court of Criminal Appeal in *The People (DPP) v. Douglas & Hayes* (1985).

Second, the Criminal Justice Act 1990 contains special provisions for attempts to commit a murder under section 3. Attempts to commit such murders are special offences distinct from ordinary attempted murder and follow the same scheme as for murder under section 3, i.e. sentences cannot be commuted until the minimum period has been served, etc. The punishment is a mandatory sentence of at least twenty years' imprisonment, and in no case may less than twenty years be served.

PROVOCATION

18.12 Introduction

In Irish law, and indeed in the laws of most other common law jurisdictions, provocation exists only as a defence to a charge of murder. For this reason, it is convenient to consider provocation under the heading of homicide instead of the general defences. On all other charges, such as for assault, provocation is relevant only to the issue of sentence rather than guilt. Even on a murder charge, it is only a partial defence in that it reduces murder to manslaughter – irrespective of the severity of the provocation, an acquittal will never be justified.

In essence, the defence of provocation relates to a sudden and temporary loss of self-control that makes the defendant incapable of preventing himself or herself from committing a homicide. As Charleton notes, it is 'a concession to human frailty'.[3] The common law rule was well defined by Devlin J. in *R v. Duffy* (1949) in the following terms:

> Some act, or series of acts, done by the dead man to the accused, [*which would cause in any reasonable person*], and actually causes in the accused a sudden loss of self-control, rendering the accused so subject to passion as to make him or her for the moment not the master of his mind.

---

3 Charleton, *et al. op.cit.,* para. 14.01.

This definition is essentially correct from the perspective of Irish law, with two caveats. First, the italicised portion of the quotation contained within square brackets imposes an objective element on the test. Irish law has rejected this element, preferring a completely subjective approach, although this has led to serious criticism. It would appear that English law is also moving towards a more subjective test. Second, Irish law seems to recognise that words can constitute a provocation, a recognition that also exists in England by virtue of the Homicide Act 1957.

It is important to note at the outset that provocation, when successful, does not mean that the defendant did not have the *mens rea* for murder. On the contrary, if X, having been provoked, explodes in rage and kills Y, he quite clearly intended to kill or cause serious injury. The point is that the *mens rea* was caused by the provocation, and the law makes an allowance for that. The law thus recognises the cause of the killing rather than excuses it. As McAleese notes, to suggest otherwise would render the defence useless. If the defendant was required not to have the necessary *mens rea* for murder before a plea of provocation would be successful, the defence would not be needed as the defendant could not be convicted of murder anyway.[4] This is indeed the approach of the Irish courts; in *The People (DPP) v. MacEoin* **(1978)**, the Court of Criminal Appeal held that the provocation is in fact at least one of the causes of the formation of the intent. Thus, arguing that provocation must negative an intent to kill or cause serious injury is incorrect and confuses cause and result.

The jury must be satisfied that the killing was carried out by the defendant while he was so under the influence of the provocative conduct that he had completely lost his self-control or, in the *Duffy* formulation, the provocation rendered him not the 'master of his mind'. It is essential if the plea of provocation is to succeed that the defendant's actions were induced by provocative conduct; in *The People (DPP) v. Davis* **(2001)**, the evidence showed that the defendant was already angry and intent upon causing harm to the deceased long before any provocation occurred. As a result, the defendant could not claim that his violence was brought about by the deceased's conduct.

It is not precisely clear what is meant by phrases like 'complete loss of self-control' or 'he was not the master of his mind', but it is clear that they must be approached with caution. Taken literally, these phrases suggest a situation akin to automatism which offers a complete defence to any charge (see section 3.3). Thus, if such a state of mind was required in order to successfully raise the issue of provocation, the defence would be superfluous as the defendant could not be convicted of murder anyway due to an absence of *mens rea*. So, in *R v. Richens* (1993), the Court of Appeal ruled that a direction to the jury that they must find that the defendant had lost his self-control to the extent that he did not know what he was doing overstated the required effect of the provocation. Nevertheless, a

---

4 McAleese, 'The Reasonable Man Provoked?', (1978) *DULJ* 53.

successful plea of provocation requires the jury to find more than that the defendant was angry; as the Court of Appeal put it in *Richens*, the test is loss of self-control rather than loss of temper. However, the fact that the defendant was very angry would be evidence from which a loss of self-control could be inferred. What is most important is that there is no evidence of deliberation on the part of the defendant; thus, in *The People (DPP) v. Kelly* **(2000)**, the Court of Criminal Appeal stressed that for a plea of provocation to succeed, the defendant must not have acted out of a 'calculating mind'. The law is concerned to prevent the plea of provocation being used to mitigate planned or vengeful killings. A person who reacts out of anger to a provocation has not entirely chosen to act as he did; rather, he has merely responded out of human weakness to a situation that was not of his own making. In such circumstances, the person is not fully responsible for the incident, and a degree of mitigation seems appropriate. People who engage in planned or revenge killings, however, are in a different position. They have not merely reacted out of weakness to a situation, but instead have taken the time to choose a reaction. This choice renders such people fully responsible for their acts and makes mitigation inappropriate.

18.13 The Objective Requirement

In its original conception, the law of provocation focused on the nature of the provocative conduct. In the leading case of *R v. Mawgridge* (1706), Lord Holt C.J. set out four circumstances in which provocation could be pleaded: a grossly insulting assault, witnessing an attack on a relative, finding one's wife in bed with another man and witnessing an Englishman being unlawfully deprived of his liberty. In any of these circumstances, the defendant's lethal retaliation would be mitigated regardless of the nature of the retaliation. However, by the nineteenth century, the law's focus shifted away from the provocation towards the retaliation. In particular, the law began to demand that a person exercise a reasonable level of restraint before retaliating. The decisive shift occurred in *R v. Welsh* (1869) when Keating J. made the following statement:

> The law is, that there must exist such an amount of provocation as would be excited by the circumstances in the mind of a reasonable man and so as to lead the jury to ascribe the act to the influence of that passion.

The purpose of this requirement was to prevent the defence from acting as a shield for unusually excitable and aggressive individuals who failed to exercise a reasonable degree of self-control. This requirement became embedded in the law of provocation and formed an integral part of the definition of provocation given by Devlin J. in *Duffy*, set out above, which contains subjective and objective elements. Thus, a jury would have to be satisfied not only that the defendant himself had been provoked, but also that a reasonable person would have reacted in a manner similar to the defendant before allowing a plea of provocation.

For example, if X taunted Y about his sexual prowess, causing Y to explode in rage and kill X, an English court would instruct the jury to decide (a) did the taunt cause Y to lose his self-control, *and* (b) would the taunt have caused any reasonable person to lose his self-control? If the answer to both questions was in the affirmative, then the defence would succeed. If the answer to either of the questions was no, then the defence would fail. The classic example of this approach is *Bedder v. DPP* (1954). The defendant was eighteen years old and sexually impotent. A prostitute mocked him for his inability to have intercourse and kicked him in the groin, causing him to attack and kill her in a blind rage. It was held by the House of Lords that the defendant's impotence was not to be taken into account in assessing the reaction of a reasonable person. If the jury was to take into account the peculiarities of the defendant, the objective test would, by definition, be made a nonsense. In other words, the defendant in this case should be judged according to the standard of a sexually healthy person.

Not surprisingly, the *Bedder* decision attracted a great deal of criticism. In particular, it is difficult to see the logic of a purely objective approach, in that people's emotions and temperaments vary considerably, and are intimately connected with their own attributes. To divorce the reasonable person from these attributes is to judge the defendant by an alien standard. To take the facts in *Bedder*, for example, an ordinary sexually healthy man would not be subjected to the same kind of taunts, and even if he was, the taunts would be meaningless. Judging the defendant by this standard is therefore absurd.

English law has now changed to some degree since the Homicide Act 1957 was passed. Section 3 of that Act requires the jury to consider whether the defendant was provoked to the degree that he lost his self-control, and also what effect the provocation would have had on a reasonable person bearing in mind what was said and done. This provision was considered in *R v. Camplin* (1978). The defendant, a fifteen-year-old boy, was buggered by the deceased against his will, causing him to feel ashamed. The deceased laughed and jeered at him, causing the defendant to lose his self-control. He picked up a pan and attacked the defendant, killing him. He was convicted of murder on the basis of the judgment in *Bedder*, and appealed. The House of Lords was asked to decide whether the defendant should be judged against the standard of a reasonable adult or that of a reasonable fifteen-year-old boy. It was held that section 3 had effectively overruled *Bedder*. The standard of the reasonable person was still that of an ordinary person with ordinary powers of self-control, but who also has the characteristics of the defendant which the jury thought relevant to the gravity of the provocation. In effect, therefore, the objective test had been qualified with some subjective elements. Thus, if *Bedder* had been decided under the *Camplin* formulation, the jury would have been asked to decide whether a reasonable eighteen-year-old man suffering from sexual impotence would have reacted in a similar manner.

The House of Lords in *Camplin* held that only some of the defendant's characteristics could be taken into account, including age and gender. The issue of which other characteristics can be taken into account by the jury in deciding whether a reasonable person would have been provoked has been the subject of numerous conflicting decisions. In *R v. Newell* (1980), the Court of Appeal ruled that only permanent characteristics such as race, ethnicity and disability could be taken into account, but only if such characteristics were relevant in the sense that the provocation was aimed at them. However, in *R v. Morhall* (1996), the House of Lords indicated that the *Newell* formulation was too strict, and that even a discreditable characteristic such as a drug addiction could be properly taken into account. The Privy Council suggested in *Luc Thiet Thuan v. R* (1996) that only the characteristics that impacted on the gravity of the provocation could be attributed to the reasonable person; characteristics that impacted on the defendant's ability to control herself could not be shared. Thus, a mental condition that rendered the defendant more violent and aggressive could not be shared by the reasonable person as this condition went to the defendant's ability to control herself rather than to the gravity of the provocation. Somewhat confusingly, however, the jury could still take account of such a condition in deciding the subjective question of whether the defendant himself had been provoked. Thus, the jury could consider the condition for one part of the test but would have to ignore it in relation to the other part. Further, such a condition could be considered in relation to the objective test if the condition itself was the subject of the provocation – if the provocation consisted of taunts about the defendant's mental abnormality, for example.

The decision in *Luc Thiet Thuan* seemed to be at odds with the general drift of decisions from the Court of Appeal and an authoritative decision was required. This was apparently provided by the House of Lords in *R v. Smith (Morgan)* (2000). There, as part of his provocation defence, the defendant sought to introduce evidence that he suffered from a depressive illness but the evidence had been deemed irrelevant by the trial judge (although it was relevant to a defence of diminished responsibility). Overruling this decision, a majority of the House of Lords abandoned the traditional 'reasonable person having the defendant's characteristics' test on the grounds that it was inherently confusing for juries and unworkable. Instead, the majority recast the objective requirement in terms of societal expectations of personal self-control. Lord Hoffman explained:

> [T]he fact that something caused [the defendant] to lose self-control is not enough. The law expects people to exercise control over their emotions. A tendency to violent rages or childish tantrums is a defect in character rather than an excuse. The jury must think that the circumstances were such as to make the loss of self-control sufficiently *excusable* to reduce the gravity of the offence from murder to manslaughter. This is entirely a matter for the jury. In deciding what should count as a sufficient excuse, they have to apply what they consider to be appropriate standards of behaviour; on the one hand making allowance for human nature and the power of emotions but, on the other hand, not allowing someone to rely upon his own violent disposition. In applying these standards of behaviour, the jury represent

the community and decide … what degree of self-control 'everyone is entitled to expect that his fellow citizens will exercise in society as it is today'.

Lord Hoffman went on to hold that while generally everyone should be held to the same standard of behaviour regardless of their psychological state, there may be occasions when it would be unjust for the jury to be instructed to ignore a particular psychological condition. The jury should be left to determine for themselves which factors were relevant in determining whether the defendant had displayed the 'degree of control which society could reasonably have expected of him'.

The authority of the decision in *Smith (Morgan)* must now be doubted as a result of the subsequent decision of the Privy Council in *Attorney General for Jersey v. Holley* (2005). There, a nine-judge panel of Law Lords considered the conflict between *Smith (Morgan)* and the Council's own previous decision in *Luc Thiet Thuan*. By a majority of six to three, the Council ruled that *Smith (Morgan)* did not represent English law and constituted an unauthorised departure from the law as established by section 3 of the Homicide Act. Strictly speaking, this decision is not binding upon English courts, but nine Law Lords decided the case and it seems likely that the English courts will now follow the approach outlined by the Privy Council in *Luc Thiet Thuan*.

The Irish courts have apparently rejected the objective element of the common law definition given in *Duffy*. In **The People (DPP) v. MacEoin (1978)**, the defendant and the deceased had been friends since their time in Mountjoy Prison. On leaving prison, they maintained their friendship, and eventually the defendant moved into the deceased's flat. Both were heavy drinkers, especially the deceased, who also tended to become very loud and aggressive when drunk. One night the defendant went home having consumed a considerable amount of alcohol (fourteen to twenty pints of stout), and went to bed. The deceased, who had also been drinking, attacked him with a hammer. After a struggle, the defendant had the hammer in his hand, but the deceased kept on hitting him. The defendant lost control and struck the deceased over the head, knocking him down, and continued to hit him up to six more times, killing him. He was convicted of murder, and appealed. The Court of Criminal Appeal noted that the objective test was 'profoundly illogical' in that it required a defendant to be judged according to a standard that would not necessarily bear any relationship to his own temperament and knowledge. Consequently, it was held that the objective standard should no longer form part of Irish law. The jury should therefore be instructed to decide only whether or not the defendant was actually provoked to the point that he lost his self-control. The effect that the provocation would have had on a reasonable person was irrelevant.

Every decision since **MacEoin** has emphasised the subjective nature of the test for provocation. A number of objections can be made to this approach, not least of which is the apparent absence of any requirement of self-control on the defendant's part before he can qualify for the mitigation offered by the plea of provocation. Further, a fully subjective test is difficult for the prosecution to counter effectively. In *The People (DPP) v. Davis* **(2001)**, the Court of Criminal Appeal indicated that the plea of provocation is constrained in that it can be raised only when there is evidence of provocative conduct, and that accordingly the plea is not as open as some commentators have suggested. As will be seen shortly, this constraint has become rather limited (see section 18.14). However, the court also accepted that policy considerations might require limits to be placed on the availability of the defence at some point in the future. Giving the example of a killing occurring during an incident of 'road rage', the court said:

> There is, it seems to us, a minimal degree of self-control which each member of society is entitled to expect from his or her fellow members: without such a threshold, social life would be impossible. It appears to this Court that the development of 'road rage' and of cognate types of socially repugnant violent reaction, with an incidence sufficiently great to have attracted a special name, emphasises factors which were perhaps not so common at the time of *MacEoin*. This however will be for another Court to address authoritatively.

This comment, while made *obiter*, is a welcome recognition that the Irish courts may have allowed the subjectivity of the test to extend the plea of provocation too far, but to date no steps have been taken to limit the application of the defence.

18.14 Provocative Conduct

In *MacEoin*, the Court of Criminal Appeal confirmed that before a plea of provocation can go to the jury, the judge must be satisfied that there is some evidence of provocative conduct that might have caused the defendant to lose his self-control, bearing in mind the defendant's temperament, character and circumstances. Without such evidence, the plea cannot be presented to the jury. This requirement was identified in *The People (DPP) v. Davis* **(2001)** as one of the constraints upon the availability of the defence that made the fully subjective test manageable for the prosecution. However, the existing authorities demonstrate that this constraint is not exacting; in *Davis*, the court accepted that 'even weak or limited' evidence of provocation would be sufficient to satisfy this preliminary requirement. The authorities also show that the concept of provocative conduct has been progressively expanded to the point that it now encompasses virtually all kinds of conduct.

Traditionally, the defence of provocation was confined to acts that would have been considered by society as disreputable at least. In *R v. Mawgridge* (1706), Lord Holt C.J. ruled that provocation could be pleaded in one of four circumstances only: a grossly insulting assault, an assault upon a friend, relative or kinsman, finding one's wife engaged in an adulterous act with another man or witnessing an Englishman being unlawfully deprived of his liberty. In the later case of *R v. Fisher* (1837), a further circumstance was added: finding a man engaged in unnatural acts with one's son. In each of these cases, the defendant's violent reaction was deemed to be an almost justified response to what would have been seen as a slight to the defendant's honour or that of his family. Today, the defence of provocation is not so confined, and it seems that conduct does not have to be discreditable in any sense in order to constitute provocation. In *Duffy*, Devlin J. referred to 'any act or series of acts', which would suggest that any kind of act could give rise to provocation. In *R v. Doughty* (1986), the defendant father smothered his baby child in order to stop the child's incessant crying. The trial judge had ruled that a baby's crying could not legally amount to a provocation – it was simply something that had to be put up with. However, the Court of Appeal ruled that section 3 of the Homicide Act 1957 encompassed any action that could loosely be termed provocative, and that could include a baby's crying. What was important was the impact of the baby's crying on the defendant; if the defendant had lost his self-control as a result of the crying, he should be able to plead provocation. Almost certainly, the Irish courts would take a similarly broad view. In *MacEoin*, Kenny J. used the phrase 'wrongful acts', but it is not clear whether this phrase meant unlawful acts or simply the acts in question that lead to the killing. Given that the focus of modern Irish law is on the impact of the provocation on the defendant, it seems likely that the latter interpretation is the more likely and this has been borne out by subsequent case law. In *The People (DPP) v. McDonagh* (**2001**), the Court of Criminal Appeal accepted that even an innocuous act such as the clicking of one's fingers could constitute a provocation. Further, a seemingly innocuous action might also constitute provocation on the basis that it formed part of a chain of events whose cumulative effect was to cause a person to lose his self-control: *R v. Thornton* (1992). Thus, in *The People (DPP) v. O'Donoghue* (**1992**), the defendant had suffered physical and verbal abuse from her husband for a number of years, and had obtained a barring order against him. However, she allowed him to return home because she felt sorry for him. He then verbally abused her again, causing the defendant to snap and kill him with a hammer. She was charged with murder but was convicted of manslaughter and received a suspended sentence.

At common law, words could not generally constitute a provocation unless they were of a threatening nature and were accompanied by physical blows of some kind. In *R v. Holmes* (1946), the defendant had suspected his wife of having an affair, and when she admitted that this was true, he struck her with a hammer and killed her. The Court of Criminal Appeal upheld the defendant's murder conviction, holding that words could not legally constitute a provocation unless they constituted a sudden admission (by a wife) of adultery. The rationale for this exception appears to have been that such a sudden admission would cause as much a shock to a man as actually finding his wife engaged in adultery with another man; as the latter constituted provocation, so too should the former.

However, in this case, the defendant had already suspected that his wife was having an affair, and her admission therefore could not have come as a shock to him. The effect of this decision has now been overtaken by statute. Section 3 of the Homicide Act 1957 now allows the jury to find that the defendant had been provoked 'by things done or by things said or by both together.' In Ireland, the Court of Criminal Appeal in *MacEoin* expressly referred to 'conduct or words' as being sufficient to constitute a provocation. In *The People (DPP) v. Davis* **(2001)**, the defendant appealed his murder conviction on the grounds that there was evidence that he had lost his self-control as a result of certain statements made to him by the deceased. While denying the defence of provocation on the facts of the case, the Court of Criminal Appeal specifically noted with approval that the trial judge's charge to the jury had included a passage in which the possibility of words constituting a provocation had been covered.

The common law did not recognise circumstances or Acts of God as provocative conduct. Thus, if X killed Y out of frustration at being stuck in traffic, X would be precluded from pleading provocation. In England, this remains the case as the Homicide Act 1957 requires evidence of things done or things said. In *R v. Acott* (1997), the defendant had been convicted of the murder of his mother. The defence of provocation had not been raised, but the defendant appealed on the grounds that the prosecution had raised the possibility that he had committed the killing having lost his self-control, and thus the issue of provocation should have been put to the jury. The House of Lords ruled that there was no evidence that anything had been done or said that might have provoked the defendant to lose his self-control. In the absence of such evidence, the trial judge had been correct not to allow the issue of provocation to go to the jury. In Ireland, the position is less clear. In *The People (DPP) v. Kehoe* (1992), the defendant met his former girlfriend for a drink and then returned with her to her apartment. In the apartment, the defendant found his former best friend, with whom the woman was now having a relationship. In a rage, the defendant picked up a knife from the kitchen and killed the other man. There was no evidence that the defendant said or did anything; indeed, the evidence suggested that the deceased was asleep at the time. Nevertheless, the Court of Criminal Appeal, while upholding the defendant's murder conviction, did not preclude the plea of provocation in these circumstances. This suggests that, at least in some circumstances, even a mere circumstance may qualify under Irish law as a provocation.

Finally, in *Duffy*, Devlin J. made it clear that the provocation must have been done by the deceased to the defendant. In other words, the defence was available only where the defendant had been provoked by the person against whom he retaliated, thus limiting the availability of the defence to situations in which the person responsible for the incident was killed. Where the defendant had retaliated against anyone else, the defence was not available. However, in

England, the Homicide Act 1957 appears to have removed this restriction. In *R v. Davies* (1975), the defendant became jealous of his wife's relationship with another man and the marriage had broken down. The defendant observed this other man walking towards his wife's place of employment, and when his wife came out of the building, the defendant walked up to her and shot her. The Court of Appeal ruled that under the 1957 Act, words or acts capable of constituting provocation should not be disregarded simply because they came from someone other than the deceased. Consequently, it should have been open to the jury to consider whether the defendant had been provoked into losing his self-control by the conduct of the other man. In Ireland, the Irish courts have adopted a similar position. In *The People (DPP) v. Doyle* (2002), the appellant argued that he should not be precluded from raising the provocation defence because the provocation had come from someone other than the deceased. While rejecting the argument on the facts of the case, the Court of Criminal Appeal accepted that 'no doubt cases can arise in which, for example, during a mêlée A is provoked to such a degree by B that he loses control of himself and mistakenly kills C, in which case a defence of provocation could be properly left to the jury.' This statement is consistent with the subjective test that has been endorsed by the Irish courts, a test that focuses entirely on the effect of the provocation on the defendant (see section 18.13). In the light of such a focus, the source of the provocation logically becomes irrelevant. However, the Court of Criminal Appeal's comment in *Doyle* refers to a mistaken killing of an innocent person; it is unclear whether a plea of provocation would be permitted where such a killing was not mistaken. It can be argued on policy grounds that the mitigation offered by the defence should not be available where the defendant has killed someone who was innocent of the provocation.

18.15 In the Heat of the Moment

In general, the retaliation must be done in the heat of the moment; the greater the time between the provocation and the retaliation, the less likely it is that the defence will be successful. In *Mancini v. DPP* (1941), Lord Simon stated that 'it is of particular importance to consider whether a sufficient interval has elapsed since the provocation to allow a reasonable time to cool.' Similarly, in *R v. Duffy* (1949), Devlin J. stated:

> Circumstances which induce a desire for revenge are inconsistent with provocation, since the conscious formulation of a desire for revenge means that a person has had time to think, to reflect, and that would negative a sudden temporary loss of self-control which is the essence of provocation.

So, if X punches Y, and Y immediately retaliates, the defence is available. If, however, Y waits until the following day before retaliating, his actions will be viewed as simple revenge, and the defence of provocation will not be available.

As indicated by Devlin J. in *Duffy*, this requirement exists principally to distinguish between acts committed in revenge and those committed in the heat of passion.

How long exactly the cooling-off period is before retaliation becomes revenge is unclear, but it is likely to be very short. This point was brought sharply into focus in a series of cases in which wives had killed their husbands having suffered continual domestic abuse. That the law recognises the concept of cumulative provocation is beyond doubt. The fact that a long period of abuse has been suffered by the defendant may explain why she exploded over a seemingly trivial incident. Thus, in *R v. Thornton* (1992), the Court of Appeal held that cumulative provocative acts may be relevant in considering the background against which the defendant's reaction to the provocative conduct had to be judged. Similarly, in **The People (DPP) v. O'Donoghue (1992)**, the defendant had suffered physical and verbal abuse from her husband for a number of years, and had obtained a barring order against him. However, she allowed him to return home because she felt sorry for him. He then verbally abused her again, causing the defendant to snap and to kill him with a hammer. She was convicted of manslaughter and received a suspended sentence. However, in all cases, as in **O'Donoghue**, the cumulative provocation must still result in a sudden and temporary loss of control. The difficulty is that in a number of cases, the defendant waited for some time before reacting, which on the face of it would defeat the claim of provocation. In *Thornton*, the defendant had suffered abuse from her husband for years. Following one bout of intense verbal abuse, the defendant went to the kitchen to calm down. While there, she picked up a knife and sharpened it, then went back to her husband. He threatened to kill her while she was sleeping, to which she replied that she would kill him before he got the chance. She lowered the knife slowly, thinking that he would defend himself, but he made no move. She stabbed and killed him, but later claimed that she had only intended to frighten him (at the time, however, she told the police that she had wanted to kill him). It was held by the Court of Appeal that provocation must result in a sudden loss of control. However, on the defendant's own statement of the circumstances, there was no sudden loss of self-control, so her conviction for murder was upheld.

In *R v. Ahluwalia* (1992), the defendant had entered into an arranged marriage to a man who turned out to be violent towards her. On one occasion, she had a row with her husband, during which he threatened to beat her up the following morning. She waited until her husband was asleep, collected some petrol that she had bought some time earlier, threw the petrol into the room and set it on fire. The husband died as a result of the burns he received. Again, it was held that there was a cooling-off period and that there was no loss of self-control. On appeal, the defendant claimed, arguing that the trial judge had incorrectly summarised the law, that the long history of abuse that she had suffered amounted to a provocation, and that 'battered woman syndrome' was a factor to be taken into account in assessing the provocation. The Court of Appeal held, as in *Thornton*, that there must be a sudden loss of self-control. 'Battered woman syndrome' could be a relevant factor, but as there was no evidence of it at trial, the trial judge's summary could not be faulted. However, the Court of Appeal also modified the sudden loss of control requirement:

> We accept that the subjective element in the defence of provocation would not as a matter of law be negatived simply because of the delayed reaction in such cases, provided that there was at the time of the killing a 'sudden and temporary loss of self-control' caused by the alleged provocation. However, the longer the delay and the stronger the evidence of deliberation on the part of the defendant, the more likely it will be that the prosecution will negative provocation.

Hence, the word 'sudden' does not necessarily mean 'immediate'. However, the defendant had argued that such cumulative provocation would cause a 'slow burn' reaction rather than a sudden loss of control, and that the defence of provocation should be modified to accomodate this. By endorsing the sudden loss of control requirement, the court specifically rejected this argument. In the circumstances, therefore, it was held that the trial judge had correctly interpreted the law, and the jury's decision was upheld (although the conviction was quashed on other grounds). Following the decision in *Ahluwalia*, a fresh appeal was permitted in Thornton's case (*R v. Thornton (No.2)* (1996)), and the Court of Appeal, while admitting the possible relevance of 'battered woman syndrome', restated this principle:

> A defendant, even if suffering from that syndrome, cannot succeed in relying on provocation unless the jury consider she suffered or may have suffered a sudden and temporary loss of self-control at the time of the killing.

Thus, the English courts have accepted that a sudden loss of control at the time of the killing is an essential element of the defence of provocation, even if the loss of control does not occur immediately following the provocation.

The Irish courts have not definitively ruled on this issue, but in *The People (DPP) v. Kelly* (2000), the Court of Criminal Appeal stated that the 'loss of self-control must be total and the reaction must come suddenly and before there has been time for passion to cool ... there must be a sudden unforeseen onset of passion which, for the moment, totally deprives the accused of his self-control.' These statements do not necessarily preclude a delayed reaction coming within the defence of provocation, providing the defendant had lost her self-control at the time of the killing. The jury in an Irish court is required to consider only whether the defendant suffered a sudden and total loss of self-control as a result of the provocation at the time of the killing. Further, the level of provocative conduct required to establish the defence seems to be very low. Thus, if an Irish defendant suffered a sudden loss of self-control sometime after a provocative act, especially if that act was the latest in a cumulative series of provocative acts, and there was no evidence of deliberation on her part, it seems highly unlikely that an Irish court would deny her the defence of provocation.

18.16 Proportionality

At common law, there was also a requirement of proportionality similar to that required in self-defence. In essence, for the defence of provocation to succeed, the jury had to be satisfied that the retaliation bore some reasonable relationship to the provocation. This seems to be an objective test, the purpose being to ensure that a person who totally overreacts to a situation will not be able to use his over-reaction to escape liability. So, for example, if X provokes Y with fists, and Y draws a gun and shoots X, Y's plea of provocation may fail. This principle was accepted by the Court of Criminal Appeal in *MacEoin*, which held that 'if the prosecution prove beyond reasonable doubt that the force used was unreasonable and excessive having regard to the provocation, the defence of provocation fails.' It has, however, apparently been dropped by the English courts, which seems to be a preferable approach. The proportionality requirement seems illogical in two respects. In the first place, the whole point of the defence of provocation is to offer a partial defence to a person who loses his self-control on foot of another person's conduct. This premise does not sit easily with a requirement that the defendant must also retain sufficient control to prevent an excessive reaction. An attempt at reconciliation can be made by recalling that the law of provocation does not require that the defendant go completely berserk to the extent that he did not know what he was doing. Such a requirement would render the provocation defence superfluous in that a person who did not know what he was doing could not be convicted of murder anyway on the grounds of insufficient *mens rea*. Thus, the provocation defence contemplates retention by the defendant of some degree of self-awareness. Nevertheless, any such reconciliation between these two requirements should not be overstated: there is an inherent tension between requiring a person to totally lose his self-control while at the same time requiring him to objectively measure his response. Secondly, proportionality requires an objective assessment of the retaliation in the light of the provocation, but the Irish courts have made it clear that the test of the provocation defence in Irish law is exclusively subjective.

The Irish courts have struggled to explain how these two apparently contradictory standards can co-exist, and the most recent attempt to do so by the Court of Criminal Appeal has resulted in yet another modification of the common law formulation of the defence. In *The People (DPP) v. Kelly* (2000), doubts were expressed about the *MacEoin* formulation to the extent that it was suggested that trial judges should not quote from the *MacEoin* decision in their charges to juries. The Court essentially ruled that the proportionality requirement was no more than an issue of credibility:

The question [the jury] have to decide is not whether a normal or reasonable man would have been so provoked by the matters complained of as totally to lose his self-control but whether this particular accused with his peculiar history and personality was so provoked. At the same time they are entitled to rely upon their common sense and experience of life in deciding this as in deciding all other matters. If the reaction of the accused in totally losing his self-control in response to the provocation appears to them to have been strange, odd, or disproportionate that is a matter which they are entitled to take into consideration in deciding whether the evidence on which the plea of provocation rests is credible.

Thus, it would be open to a jury to conclude that the defendant's reaction was so excessive in relation to the alleged acts of provocation that his claim must be false. However, intuition suggests that it is more likely that a jury would accept that the more excessive the reaction, the more likely it was that the defendant had indeed lost his self-control. In either case, the decision in *Kelly* represents a considerable alteration to the law on provocation. Under *MacEoin*, proportionality was a substantive requirement about which the jury had to be satisfied before allowing the plea of provocation; following *Kelly*, the proportionality of the defendant's response is no more than an evidential matter of credibility.

On a related point, if the killing was unusually barbarous or cruel, the provocation plea would fail at common law. So, in *Halloway's Case* (1629), the defendant had caught a boy stealing wood from a forest and in punishment he tied the boy to a horse's tail, struck the horse so that it galloped off, and the boy was killed while being dragged along behind it. The defendant was convicted of murder largely on the basis that the defendant's cruel punishment indicated a degree of deliberation which in turn indicated malice aforethought. Thus, the defence failed, not so much because it was disproportionate, but because the very cruelty involved indicated that the defendant had acted deliberately rather than out of a loss of self-control.

18.17 Self-induced Provocation

Where the defendant's own conduct caused the deceased to provoke him, the defence generally will not succeed. Suppose, for example, that X insults Y, and Y retaliates by insulting X's mother. As a result, X develops a blind rage and kills Y. If X tries to plead provocation, he will fail. In *Edwards v. R* (1973), the defendant had followed the deceased to Hong Kong with the intention of blackmailing him. As a result, the deceased confronted the defendant with a knife. Following a struggle, the defendant stabbed the deceased with the knife, killing him. It was held that on principle the defendant should not succeed even where he was able to establish a sudden loss of self-control. The one possible exception to this might be where the deceased's actions were completely excessive in relation to the defendant's conduct. In the circumstances of this case, it was held that the deceased's reaction was excessive, i.e. threatening to kill, and actually attacking the defendant with a knife as opposed to the threat of blackmail. Therefore, the issue was suitable for the jury to decide. However, in *R v. Johnson* (1989), it was held by the Court of Appeal that the issue of provocation should be put to the jury even where it was self-induced. Thus, to that extent, *Edwards* has been over-ruled. Irish law on this issue is unclear. In *The People (DPP) v. Hennessy* (2000), the defendant had been suspended from his job on suspicion of embezzlement. He admitted this to his wife, and in the course of an ensuing argument, the defendant beat his wife to death with a car-jack. The trial judge, Finnegan J., accepted the jury's finding of provocation, but also noted that the defendant had been the author of his condition in that he had embezzled money from his employer. In other words, the trial judge explicitly recognised this as a self-induced situation, yet the plea of provocation was still allowed to go to the jury. However, in *The People (DPP) v. Kelly* (2000), the Court of Criminal Appeal stated that the provocation 'must be genuine in the sense that the accused did not deliberately set up the situation which he now invokes as provocation.' The defendant in *Hennessy* certainly did not engage in embezzlement so as to have a partial excuse for later killing his wife, and to that extent he did not set up the situation which he later invoked as mitigation. Nevertheless, the incident that led to his wife's death still came about as a result of the defendant's own deliberate and dishonest actions. Thus, the propriety of allowing the provocation defence to go to the jury in *Hennessy* must be doubted, and it is submitted that the comments in *Kelly* should be taken as the policy of the law in Ireland.

18.18 Proof of Provocation

Whether or not the defendant was actually provoked to the extent that he completely lost his self-control is a matter to be left entirely in the hands of the jury. As with all other defences except insanity, the prosecution bears the burden of proving beyond reasonable doubt that the defendant was not provoked. In *The People (DPP) v. Ceka* (2004), the Court of Criminal Appeal confirmed that 'once the issue [of provocation is left to the jury] by the trial judge, the issue is subject to the orthodox rule regarding the burden of proof. The legal burden remains with the prosecution.' In other words, the defendant does not have to establish the defence, the prosecution has to negative it. Further, while the defendant does bear an evidential burden to raise the defence, if the prosecution's case indicates that an issue of provocation might arise, then the trial judge must instruct the jury on it. The judge is not required to raise the issue, however, where it has not been raised by the defence or by the facts. Accordingly, in practical terms, the defence must, in the words of the Supreme Court in *O'Laoire v. Medical Council* (1997), 'set forth circumstances of provocation (if that is his case) and then the prosecution must satisfy the jury beyond reasonable doubt that the killing was unprovoked.'

Whether or not the defendant was sufficiently provoked is a matter of fact for the jury alone to determine. The evidence of the defendant is of critical importance. In *The People (DPP) v. Kehoe* **(1992)**, the defendant called a psychiatrist to support his contention of provocation. The Court of Criminal Appeal held that the evidence of a psychiatrist as to the defendant's state of mind at the time of the killing could add nothing to the defendant's own evidence. As a result, this was not the kind of case in which such evidence was appropriate, and it should not have been entered. His conviction for murder was upheld.

18.19 Law Reform Commission Proposals

The Law Reform Commission, in its *Consultation Paper on Homicide: The Plea of Provocation* (LRC CP27-2003), was clearly unhappy with the current state of Irish law on provocation. The Commission's overriding concern was to limit the application of the defence, and to this end the Commission argued that the current focus of the defence on the defendant's loss of self-control is misplaced; rather, the focus should be on the provocative conduct of the other party, as it was in *Mawgridge*. Such a refocus would necessitate the restructuring of the provocation defence as a partial justification rather than a partial excuse, as it is at present. However, the Commission was also concerned that the law should not revert to the purely objective model as set out in *Bedder*, and argued that some regard must be had of the defendant's own characteristics. Accordingly, the Commission proposed that the jury be posed two issues. First, the jury would have to consider whether there was provocative conduct that deprived the defendant of the power of self-control and thereby induced him to commit a homicide. The Commission was concerned to take account of the difficulties posed by the heat of the moment requirement, and recommended that a plea of provocation should be permitted even though the killing did not follow immediately upon the provocation. In effect, this proposal would enact the Court of Appeal's ruling in *Ahluwalia*. The Commission proposed to limit the scope of provocative conduct by excluding self-induced provocation or conduct committed in the lawful exercise of a power conferred by law. Thus, it would not be possible under this proposal for a person to claim that he was provoked by a person attempting to serve a court summons. The Commission was also willing to allow the defence to be raised where the provocation arose from someone other than the deceased on the ground that limiting the defence to retaliation against the provoker alone might be unduly restrictive. However, provocation could only be pleaded where an innocent party had been killed if the killing occurred by mistake or by accident. Thus, if X was provoked by Y but focused his retaliation on Z, the provocation defence would be precluded. Finally, the Commission recommended the resurrection of the proportionality requirement as a substantive element of the defence, thereby effectively overturning the decision in *Kelly*. The illogicality that lay at the heart of that decision would be avoided by the removal of the emphasis upon a *total* loss of self-control, and also by the inclusion of an objective element in the second part of the test.

The second issue would require the jury to decide whether the provocation would have had sufficient gravity in the circumstances of the case to deprive an ordinary person of the power of self-control. To avoid the problems that became apparent in *Bedder*, the Commission recommended that the jury should bear in mind any of the defendant's characteristics it thinks relevant, except for the defendant's temperament, state of intoxication or mental disorder. The defendant's temperament should not be considered because of the Commission's insistence that the defence be regarded as a partial justification, and an unlawful killing committed due to the undue pugnacity of the defendant could not be justified in any way. A similar point could be made in relation to the exclusion of the defendant's intoxication; a further point is that intoxication can also be considered in its own right following the Court of Criminal Appeal's decision in *The People (DPP) v. Reilly* **(2004)** (see Chapter 9). As to mental disorder, the Commission argued, surely correctly, that this evidence should be considered not as part of a provocation defence but rather as part of a defence of diminished responsibility. The Commission noted that the absence of such a defence in Irish law has resulted in the plea of provocation being used as a substitute, and recommended that reforms to the law in relation to diminished responsibility should precede any reforms to the law of provocation. Thus, this second element of the proposed provocation test would permit the jury to consider the defendant's response in the context of generally accepted standards of behaviour, thereby incorporating some degree of objectivity into the provocation defence. At the same time, the excesses apparent in the *Bedder* decision could be avoided along with the difficulties experienced by the English courts in deciding which of the defendant's characteristics could be taken into account and which could not.

MANSLAUGHTER

18.20 Introduction

The offence of manslaughter is huge and encompasses all unlawful killings of human beings that do not rise to the level of murder; as O'Flaherty J. pointed out in *The People (DPP) v. Mullane* **(1997)**, manslaughter is 'capable of such a variety of manifestations, ranging from a case which will border on murder to one which will come nearer to misadventure than to homicide.' The *actus reus* of the offence is identical to that of murder, the difference between the two offences relating solely to *mens rea*. Manslaughter is an automatic alternative in a murder case, so if a jury in such a case is not convinced that the defendant intended to kill or cause serious harm to the deceased, it can return a verdict of not guilty of murder but guilty of manslaughter. For ease of consideration, it is common to divide manslaughter into two categories: voluntary and involuntary. Voluntary manslaughter occurs in one of two ways: (a) a killing arising out of provocation, or (b) where a defendant kills in self-defence using more force than was reasonably necessary, but no more than he genuinely believed to be necessary. Both of these issues have already been dealt with – see sections 18.12–18.19 and section 7.7, respectively. Additionally, if the Criminal Justice (Insanity) Bill 2002 is enacted, a further category of voluntary manslaughter will be added, namely a killing carried out while the defendant was suffering from diminished responsibility. This has already been considered in Chapter 8, on insanity.

Involuntary manslaughter is something of a misnomer in that it does not arise involuntarily in the sense of automatism. It simply refers to a killing that does not amount to murder due to a lack of *mens rea*. Accordingly, this form of manslaughter arises where the defendant kills another person, but does so recklessly or with gross negligence. It can be conveniently analysed as arising in one of three ways: (a) by an unlawful and dangerous act, (b) by a wilful failure to perform some legal duty, and (c) by a lawful act performed with gross negligence. Each category will be considered in turn.

18.21 An Unlawful and Dangerous Act

An act done with the intent of causing physical harm that results in death will be manslaughter. It is important that the intent is to cause physical harm only; an intention to cause serious harm will result in a murder charge. For manslaughter, it appears that only minor harm is required. An old English case is a good illustration of this point. In *R v. Wild* (1837), a guest of the defendant had outstayed his welcome. In trying to get him to leave, the defendant gave him a kick which resulted in his death. The defendant had not intended any real harm to come to him, but as the act was unjustifiable, his conviction for manslaughter was upheld. The court noted that a kick was not an acceptable way to ask a guest to leave! However, force may be used to evict a trespasser in appropriate circumstances – section 18, Non-Fatal Offences Against the Person Act 1997 (and see section 7.2).

This rule has been amended to incorporate two elements: the act must be dangerous *and* unlawful. In *R v. Larkin* (1943), the defendant threatened another man, who was seeing the defendant's mistress, with an open 'cut-throat' razor. The defendant's mistress was also present and was drunk. She swayed against the defendant and accidentally cut her own throat on the open razor. It was held that for a manslaughter conviction, it must be shown that the defendant's actions were unlawful and dangerous. In this case, the defendant's action was clearly dangerous, and it constituted an assault. Both elements of the test were therefore satisfied, and the conviction was upheld. In *R v. Church* (1966), Lord Edmund-Davies gave a further explanation of what constitutes a dangerous act:

> An unlawful act causing the death of another cannot, simply because it is an unlawful act, render a manslaughter verdict inevitable. For such a verdict inexorably to follow, the unlawful act must be such as all sober and reasonable people would inevitably recognize must subject the other person to, at least, the risk of some harm resulting therefrom, albeit not serious harm.

Whether an act was dangerous is therefore to be judged from an objective perspective.

The decision in *Larkin* was specifically adopted in Ireland by the Court of Criminal Appeal in *The People (Attorney General) v. Crosbie and Meehan* **(1966)**. The defendants were neighbours and friends, and dock-workers in Dublin. Meehan's two sisters worked in a café, where another dock-worker named Meier was offensive to them. All the parties went to the 'read room' in the Dublin docks, where the dock-workers went to find out who would be getting work. Crosbie carried a knife, and Meehan a spanner, to the read room, intending, with others, to assault Meier. A fight developed involving at least eight men. During the mêlée, the deceased, Noel Murphy, was stabbed by Crosbie and later died as a result. The Court of Criminal Appeal specifically approved the formulation in *Larkin*, holding that it was not sufficient to show that a death arose from an unlawful act; it also had to be shown that the act was dangerous. Whether or not the act was dangerous is a question of fact for the jury to decide objectively; it is irrelevant that the defendant thought the act was not dangerous. The conviction for manslaughter was upheld. This point was reaffirmed by the Court of Criminal Appeal in *The People (DPP) v. Hendley* **(1993)**. The defendant killed his wife during a row. In the course of the row, the defendant gripped his wife's neck while also kneeling on her to restrain her. It was the act of kneeling on her that caused death due to the pressure on her liver. The defendant argued that this action was accidental, and that he did not even remember it. The trial judge directed the jury that it was sufficient for the prosecution to prove that the defendant was engaged in an unlawful act. On appeal, it was held that this was not enough; the prosecution also had to show that the act was deliberate and dangerous.

Hendley also illustrates a further point, namely causation. There was no question that an assault had occurred. However, the assault *per se* was not responsible for the deceased's death. Rather, it was the pressure applied to her liver that was the cause. This was the act that the jury had to consider: was it deliberate, unlawful and dangerous? The fact that the defendant was clearly guilty of an assault was irrelevant to the manslaughter charge.

Thus, a person can be convicted of manslaughter even though he did not intend to kill or cause any serious harm. Nor is it necessary for death to have been foreseeable by a reasonable person. This form of manslaughter is consequently often referred to as constructive manslaughter, i.e. the charge of manslaughter is constructed on the basis of an underlying non-lethal offence. The UK Law

Commission, in its 1996 *Report on Involuntary Manslaughter*, argued that permitting the conviction of a person for manslaughter in a situation in which the possibility of death could not be foreseen even objectively is unprincipled. For example, if X pushes Y during a fight, causing Y to stagger backwards, X will be guilty of some form of assault at most. If, however, Y staggers backwards and loses his balance and falls, perhaps due to uneven paving stones, striking his head on the ground and suffering fatal head injuries, then X is guilty of manslaughter. However, in the latter scenario, X's conduct is morally no worse than in the former scenario; Y's death was caused, arguably, by bad luck, certainly by factors beyond X's control. The Commission recommended that manslaughter should not be found unless the defendant acted with a level of *mens rea* appropriate to a homicide charge.

Where the act is neither dangerous nor unlawful in itself, a manslaughter charge will not be upheld. In *R v. Arobieke* (1988), the deceased had been electrocuted on a railway line. There had been a long history of hostility between the defendant and the deceased. On the day in question, the deceased had just boarded a train which was standing at the station. The defendant was on the platform and looked into the train. The deceased saw him, and tried to flee by jumping from the train onto the tracks, and was electrocuted. The defendant was convicted of manslaughter, and appealed. It was held that the conviction could not be sustained; the defendant's act of looking into the train was neither dangerous nor unlawful. The conviction was therefore quashed. Furthermore, as shown in **Hendley**, the act must also be deliberate; an action done accidentally should result in an acquittal.

18.22 A Wilful Failure to Perform a Legal Duty

Where a defendant is under a positive duty to act, a failure to do so that causes a death may result in a conviction for manslaughter. Such duties can arise in a number of ways: a special relationship, a voluntary assumption of the duty, a contractual duty, a statutory duty or a duty arising from prior conduct. In each case, the principle is the same: the person's failure to act which causes death is considered to be a breach of duty. The death therefore constitutes manslaughter. A number of examples can be given, many of which have already been considered in section 3.2. In *R v. Instan* (1893), the defendant lived with her elderly aunt, who was suffering from a disease that made her incapable of moving. As a result, she was entirely dependent on the defendant. The defendant, however, refused to supply the aunt with food or medicine. As a result of this neglect, the aunt died. It was held that the defendant was under a clear moral obligation to assist her aunt; her refusal to do so at least accelerated the death of the deceased, and so constituted manslaughter. In a similar vein, in *R v. Senior* (1899), the defendant was a member of a religious sect which believed that accepting medical assistance amounted to a lack of faith in God. His eight-month-old child developed pneumonia, for which treatment was readily available. In line with his religious beliefs, however, he refused to allow the treatment to go ahead, as a result of which the child died. This was found to be manslaughter. More recent examples also illustrate the point. In *R v. Stone and Dobinson* (1977), the first defendant lived with his elderly sister (the deceased) and his partner (the second defendant). The sister refused to eat, and became seriously ill. The defendants failed to obtain medical help and even failed to mention the sister's plight to a visiting social worker. It was held that the defendants were under a duty to find help for the deceased. This duty arose from a number of sources: a blood relationship; the fact that both defendants were aware of her condition because she lived in their house; and because the second defendant had undertaken the duty of washing the deceased. It is, however, clear that a blood relationship is not necessary: in *R v. Taktak* (1988), an Australian decision, the defendant brought a prostitute to a party and, when he returned for her, found her in a state of unconsciousness. He removed her from the party but failed to seek professional medical help until it was too late. The court accepted that in these circumstances, the defendant could be found to have assumed responsibility for the deceased, not least because in removing her from the party, he had prevented anyone else from coming to her assistance. His failure to discharge this assumed duty could justify a manslaughter conviction (although the conviction was quashed on other grounds).

This area of the law was criticised by the UK Law Commission in its 1996 *Report on Involuntary Manslaughter* for its inherent ambiguity, not least in determining the boundaries of criminal liability for failures to act. This is a criticism of particular relevance to Irish law given the constitutional requirement here (and that contained in the European Convention on Human Rights) that the criminal law be defined with some precision (see section 2.2). However, the Commission was unable to offer any suggestions for codification, believing that the scope of omission of liability could not be reduced to statutory form. Instead, the Commission endorsed an opinion expressed by the UK Criminal Law Revision Committee in 1980 that the courts ought to continue to apply the common law to omission liability.

18.23 A Lawful Act Performed With Gross Negligence

In *R v. Larkin* (1943), it was stated that a person could be convicted of manslaughter for engaging in a lawful action where that action is performed negligently. It was stressed, however, that the negligence in question would have to be of a high degree. Consequently, proof of negligence that would merely satisfy the civil standard would not be sufficient. The prosecution would have to show that the defendant had acted in such a way that he was reckless as to the consequences of his action. The same point was discussed by the House of Lords in *R v. Adomako* (1994). The defendant was an anaesthetist who failed to notice that a tube had become disconnected during an operation. The patient suffered a cardiac arrest and died. The House of Lords held that the jury should approach such cases in a three-stage process. First, the jury should decide whether the defendant had been negligent according to the ordinary principles of civil negligence. If so, the jury must then consider whether that negligence caused the death of the deceased. Finally, where this causation is established, the jury must consider whether the defendant's negligence was so great as to constitute gross negligence. In doing so, the jury should consider the extent of the defendant's departure from the expected standard of care. Only where the jury is satisfied that the defendant's negligence was of a very high degree could a conviction for manslaughter be justified.

This general point has also been accepted in Irish law, although reservations have been expressed as to using a test that refers to recklessness. In *The People (Attorney General) v. Dunleavy* **(1948)**, the defendant was a taxi-driver who knocked down and killed a cyclist. The evidence showed that the deceased was within six or seven feet of the kerb at the time of the impact. The prosecution's case was that the defendant was driving too close to the kerb, i.e. within seven feet on a stretch of road over forty feet wide, at night and without lights. The point under appeal concerned the degree of negligence required for a manslaughter conviction. The Court of Appeal discussed the use of the word 'reckless' and concluded that, while it could be useful, it could also be misleading. The court stated that the better formulation would be to relate the negligence to the risk of harm to others. In essence, therefore, a defendant may be convicted of manslaughter where he acts in a way that a reasonable person would realise would run a very high degree of risk of causing substantial personal injury to another person. It is noteworthy that the test in *Dunleavy* involves an objective test; it is irrelevant that the defendant himself did not appreciate the risk.

The construction of liability for manslaughter on the grounds of gross negligence is open to the immediate charge that it involves a degree of circularity: the jury can convict the defendant of the crime charged only if they find that his negligence was criminal. Furthermore, given the lack of precision in the definition of gross negligence, as opposed to ordinary negligence, the possibility of inconsistent application of the law by different juries is very real. The Court of Appeal in England has recently determined that this form of ambiguity does not contravene the requirement of clarity in the European Convention on Human Rights, as the ambiguity relates more to the method of determination of the case rather than the definition of the offence (see section 2.2). Whether the European Court of Human Rights will agree remains to be seen.

18.24 Corporate Manslaughter

A new form of manslaughter developed during the twentieth century, namely manslaughter committed by corporate entities. The common law had traditionally taken the view that homicide could be committed only by human beings, and even as late as 1927, Finlay J. accepted in *R v. Cory Brothers* (1927) that indictments for manslaughter could not be laid against a corporation. It was not until the development of the controlling mind doctrine in the 1940s that formal manslaughter prosecutions against companies became possible. This test, explained in detail already (see section 6.3), allows the company to be identified with the person who controls the company; if that person has sufficient culpability, then so too does the company. On the basis of this approach, in *R v. HM Coroner for East Kent, ex p. Spooner* (1989), Bingham L.J. felt sufficiently confident to state that in principle a manslaughter indictment could properly be laid against a company. However, it has become apparent that the controlling mind theory has limited utility in attributing criminal liability to companies. Unless it is possible for the prosecution to identify an individual who is at once sufficiently senior to be considered the controlling mind, while at the same time is sufficiently involved in the actual direction of the company's day-to-day activities to be actually culpable himself, the prosecution will fail. In effect, the prosecution would fall between two stools. This was demonstrated in *R v. P & O Ferries (Dover) Ltd* (1991), a prosecution against P & O Ferries in respect of the Zeebrugge disaster in which the ferry, *Herald of Free Enterprise*, capsized, causing the deaths of 192 people. The ferry had left port with its bow doors open, causing seawater to flood the vessel. The trial court ruled that a manslaughter indictment could be brought against the defendant company, but ruled that there was no culpable controlling mind and accordingly directed the acquittal of the defendant company. A determined effort to expand the reach of corporate manslaughter failed in *Attorney General's Reference No.2 of 1999* (2000) when the Court of Appeal rejected the aggregation of individual negligent acts of the employees of a defendant company as a basis for attaching liability to the company for gross negligence. Instead, the court reiterated the need to find a culpable employee of sufficient seniority to be considered a controlling mind of the company. It was not until 1994 that a manslaughter conviction was successfully brought against a company, and that company was essentially a one-man concern in which there could be no doubt of the identity of the controlling mind (*R v. Kite and OLL Ltd* (1994)). Since then, only seven successful prosecutions for manslaughter have been brought against companies in England, out of thirty-four attempts.[5] No efforts have yet been made in the Irish courts to prosecute a company for manslaughter, but it seems unlikely that an Irish court would push the boundary of corporate manslaughter any further than the English courts have. An attempt to place corporate manslaughter on a statutory footing was made with the Corporate Manslaughter Bill 2001, introduced as a Private Member's Bill, but it was not debated and lapsed.

---

5   C.M.V. Clarkson, 'Corporate Manslaughter: Yet More Government Proposals', [2005] *Crim LR* 677.

18.25   Reform of Manslaughter

The offence of manslaughter was considered by the Law Commission in the UK in 1996, which concluded that the principal problem with the offence was its sheer size. The offence stretches from almost murder to almost accidental death, and the Commission was concerned at the possibility that some of the more serious forms of manslaughter might be undervalued through association with less serious forms. Broadly, the Commission recommended the abolition of much of the present law of manslaughter, and the creation of two new statutory offences: reckless killing and killing by gross carelessness. In this way, only defendants who were morally culpable for the death of the deceased could be convicted of homicide. The only part of the present law that would be retained would be manslaughter by omission. Reckless killings would arise when X's conduct caused the death of Y, and X was aware of a risk that his conduct might cause death or serious injury and that his conduct was unjustified in the circumstances as he believed them to be. This proposal, if adopted, would effectively end any form of constructive liability for homicide. Killing by gross carelessness would arise if X causes Y's death in a situation in which the risk of X's conduct causing death or serious injury would have been obvious to any reasonable person, X was capable of appreciating that risk, and X's conduct fell far short of what could reasonably have been expected of him in the circumstances. The Commission was particularly concerned to avoid any reference in its formulation of this offence to the language of negligence, which it felt was unduly confusing. Liability for killing by omission would continue to be dealt with under existing common law principles.

The Law Commission also proposed the creation of a new offence of corporate killing that would broadly correspond to the proposed offence of killing by gross carelessness. The offence would be committed by a corporate entity if, through a failure in the way in which its activities were organised or managed, the corporation's conduct fell far below what could reasonably have been expected of it and led to the death of the deceased. In Ireland, the Law Reform Commission has also published proposals to reform the area of corporate manslaughter in its *Report on Corporate Killing* (2005). The Commission recommended that undertakings, whether or not incorporated, should be made amenable to charges of homicide through the enactment of a statutory offence of corporate manslaughter which would broadly equate to the existing common law offence of manslaughter by gross negligence. The negligence of the undertaking should be assessed by looking at the entity as a whole. Negligence for the purposes of this offence should arise on ordinary common law principles: the undertaking owed the deceased a duty of care, breached that duty and the breach caused the death. A breach of duty would occur when the undertaking failed to take all reasonable measures to anticipate and prevent risks of death or serious harm, having regard to the undertaking's size and circumstances. Particular regard should be had to the regulatory framework in which the undertaking operated, and the way in which its activities are managed or organised by its high managerial agents, including the allocation of responsibility of decision making and the training and supervision of staff. To convict an undertaking of corporate manslaughter, this breach of duty would have to be shown to have been of a sufficiently high degree to be characterised as 'gross' and therefore to warrant criminal sanction. To satisfy this criterion, the negligence must have been of a very high degree such that it involved a significant risk of death or serious personal harm. The Commission recommended that the courts be given the power to impose an unlimited fine for corporate manslaughter, but should receive a pre-sanction report on the undertaking before doing so. The courts should also be given the power to issue remedial orders and community service orders.

Additionally, the Commission was concerned in its recommendations to allow prosecutions to be brought against individuals connected to incidents of corporate killing. Thus, anyone within the undertaking who was connected to such an incident should be prosecuted for gross negligence manslaughter according to normal principles. The Commission also recommended that a new personal offence be created of grossly negligent management causing death. This offence would be committed if a high managerial agent knew or ought to have known of the existence of a substantial risk of serious personal harm or death and failed to take reasonable steps to eliminate that threat, and this failure fell far below what could reasonably have been expected in the circumstances and contributed to the commission of the corporate offence. High managerial agents are defined as directors, managers or other similar officers of the undertaking, or persons purporting to act in that capacity. In assessing the agent's actions, regard should be had of his power to take steps to eliminate risks of serious harm or death, but even where the agent in question did not have the power to take these steps, he could still be culpable if he failed to pass information relevant to the risks to those who did have such power. The Commission recommended that the maximum penalty for this offence should be twelve years' imprisonment and an unlimited fine. The courts should also have the power to preclude any high managerial agent who has been convicted of this offence or of manslaughter in relation to a corporate killing from acting in such a managerial capacity for such period as the court thinks fit.

DEATH BY DANGEROUS DRIVING

18.26 Introduction

Dangerous driving causing death is an offence under section 53 of the Road Traffic Act 1961, as amended, which provides as follows in sub-section 1:

> A person shall not drive in a public place in a manner (including speed) which having regard to all the circumstances of the case (including the condition of the

vehicle, the nature, condition and use of the place and the amount of traffic which then actually is or might reasonably be expected to be therein) is dangerous to the public.

Sub-section 2 provides two means of prosecution: on indictment in the event that the dangerous driving caused death, or on indictment or by summons in any other case. In *Attorney General (Ward) v. Thornton* **(1964)**, the Supreme Court held that this provision does not create two distinct offences. Rather, there is one offence – that of dangerous driving – which may be prosecuted in one of two ways depending on the consequences of the dangerous driving. So, a charge of dangerous driving causing death must be prosecuted on indictment, although in the alternative a charge of dangerous driving *simpliciter* may be brought by summons even if a death was caused. Thus, if the facts of a case disclose a death caused by dangerous driving, a number of prosecutorial options are available, depending on the evidence:

(a) murder (if there is evidence that the car was used to intentionally kill or cause serious injury to another person), with a mandatory sentence of life imprisonment;
(b) manslaughter, with a maximum sentence of life imprisonment;
(c) dangerous driving causing death, charged on indictment, under section 53 of the Road Traffic Act 1961, with a maximum sentence of ten years' imprisonment (Road Traffic Act 1994, section 49) and a fine of up to €15,000 (Road Traffic Act 2002, section 23);
(d) dangerous driving, charged by summons under section 53 of the Road Traffic Act 1961, with a maximum sentence of six months' imprisonment and a fine of up to €2,500 (Road Traffic Act 2002, section 23).

The choice as to which charge to bring lies almost exclusively in the hands of the prosecution; the Supreme Court has held that judicial review of such prosecutorial decisions will lie only if there is evidence of improper conduct on the part of the Director of Public Prosecutions: *State (McCormack) v. Curran* **(1987)** and *H v. DPP* **(1994)**.

To establish a charge under section 53 of the 1961 Act, the prosecution must be able to prove that the defendant was driving in a manner that was dangerous to the public. The leading decision in Ireland on what constitutes dangerous driving is from the Circuit Court in *The People (Attorney General) v. Quinlan* **(1962)**. There, it was held that the offence under section 53 would be established if the defendant was driving 'in a manner which a reasonably prudent man, having regard to all the circumstances, would clearly recognize as involving a direct and serious risk of harm to the public.' This statement was subsequently endorsed by the Court of Criminal Appeal in *The People (DPP) v. Connaughton* **(2001)**. Thus, the test for dangerous driving is objective in that it is not necessary to prove that the defendant appreciated the risk that his driving was causing.

Indeed, in *R v. Gosney* (1971), the Court of Appeal stated that dangerous driving could be found even if the driver was merely inexperienced and 'while straining every nerve to do the right thing, falls below the standard of a competent and careful driver.' However, drivers cannot be faulted under section 53 for risks that a reasonable person would not have appreciated; as the Court of Appeal pointed out in *R v. Loukes* (1996), it would not be sufficient to show that if the driver 'had examined the vehicle by going underneath it, he would have seen the defect.' So, in *R v. Spurge* (1961), the Court of Criminal Appeal accepted that a driver should be held no more accountable for losing control of the car due to a defect in the car than for losing control of the car due to an affliction of the person. However, if the driver was aware of the defect in the car – in this case, the brakes tended to cause the car to swerve while going around a bend – he could be convicted if the defect caused a dangerous situation on the road.

The wording of section 53 lists some of the factors that a court should take into account: the speed and condition of the vehicle, the condition, nature and use of the place where the incident occurred, and the amount of traffic in or reasonably expected in the place. Further, section 53(3), as inserted by section 13 of the Road Traffic Act 2004, provides that it is no defence for the defendant to merely show that he had not breached the speed limit 'applying in relation to the vehicle or the road, whichever is the lower' (the 2004 Act gave the government the power to specify different speed limits to different categories of vehicle). Another factor that may be relevant is the consumption of intoxicants. In *The People (Attorney General) v. Regan* (**1975**), the defendant had collided with and killed a pedestrian who had been walking in the middle of a narrow road. The defendant had consumed seven pints of beer but, when examined some hours later, he was found not to be unfit to drive. However, his condition may have been different at the time of the accident. It was argued that as there was no evidence that the defendant's drinking had had any relationship to the accident, his drinking was irrelevant and should have been excluded. The Court of Criminal Appeal held that the evidence of the defendant's consumption of alcohol could be admitted to show that the quantity of drink consumed would affect any driver. The quantity of alcohol would have to be significant, and in this case, it was held that seven pints of beer was a significant quantity. In *The People (Attorney General) v. Moore* (**1964**), it was held that the consumption of three pints of beer was also significant. Pierse comments that consuming enough alcohol to place the driver over the legal limit would probably be considered significant.[6]

Finally, on a charge of dangerous driving causing death, it will be essential for the prosecution to prove that the deceased's death was in fact caused by the defendant's dangerous driving. The principles of causation have already been considered (see section 3.4) and need not be considered in detail here. Suffice it

---

6 Pierse, *Road Traffic Law*, 2nd ed., Dublin: Butterworths, 1995, p. 257.

to say that the prosecution does not have to prove that the defendant's dangerous driving was the sole cause of the deceased's death; as long as the driving was more than a minimal cause, the prosecution has discharged its burden. If the prosecution fails to prove causation, the charge will fail and the defendant cannot later be charged with dangerous driving *simpliciter*: this is the effect of the Supreme Court's decision in **Thornton** that section 53 creates one offence that may be prosecuted in one of two ways. However, section 53(4) provides that it is open to a court to convict a defendant charged under section 53 of an offence under section 52 (careless driving) if the court believes that the evidence is sufficient to establish careless driving and not dangerous driving or dangerous driving causing death.

SUICIDE AND EUTHANASIA

18.27 Introduction

At common law, suicide was a felony, being regarded as self-murder. This position was best summarised by Blackstone:

> And also the law of England wisely and rigorously considers that no man hath a power to destroy life, but by commission from God, the author of it, and as the suicide is guilty of a double offence; one spiritual, in evading the prerogative of the Almighty, and rushing in to his immediate presence uncalled for; the other temporal, against the King, who hath an interest in the preservation of all its subjects; the law has therefore ranked this among the highest crimes, making it a peculiar species of felony, a felony committed on oneself. A [suicide] therefore is he that deliberately puts an end to his own existence, or commits any unlawful malicious act, the consequence of which is his own death.[7]

Furthermore, under the doctrine of transferred intent, if a person attempted to kill himself, but accidentally killed someone else, he was guilty of murder, i.e. the intent that he bore himself was transferred onto the deceased.

While it seems somewhat strange at first sight, the punishment for a successful suicide was severe. The suicide was buried in the public highway with a stake through the body. Furthermore, as suicide was a felony, all of the suicide's possessions were forfeit to the Crown. These punishments remained in place until 1882 and 1870, respectively, when they were repealed, thus effectively leaving suicide as a crime with no penalty. This remained the position until the Criminal Law (Suicide) Act 1993 was passed, which is almost a carbon copy of the English Suicide Act 1961. By virtue of section 2(1), suicide is no longer an offence. Furthermore, as Smith and Hogan point out, the doctrine of transferred intent can no longer have any application to suicide: by law, suicide no longer involves malice towards oneself; consequently, if in the attempt the would-be

---

7 Blackstone, *Commentaries on the Laws of England*, Book IV, 1783, p. 189.

suicide kills another person, there is no malice to transfer to the victim. Consequently, the would-be suicide could not be convicted of murder.[8] The purpose of this decriminalisation was to remove the stigma attached to suicide, with a view to bringing it out into the open. Once it was in the open, it was felt that treatment would be more effective. Offences ancillary to suicide (such as aiding and abetting) are still offences under the 1993 Act.

Attempted suicide has also been abolished, it not being possible to criminalise the inchoate offence when the complete act is not an offence. This is indicated by section 3, which repeals section 9 of the Summary Jurisdiction (Ireland) Amendment Act 1871. Section 9 of the 1871 Act allowed a person who admitted to attempting suicide to be imprisoned for up to three months by the District Court, providing he consented to his case being heard in the District Court.

18.28 Aiding and Abetting a Suicide

Under section 2(2), any person who aids, abets, counsels or procures a suicide or an attempted suicide by another person is guilty of an offence and is liable to up to fourteen years' imprisonment. The reason for such a severe penalty is to cover situations in which one person tries to engineer the suicide of another for their own gain. For example, suppose X stands to inherit a large amount of money from his uncle, Y, who is feeling depressed. It is obviously in X's interests to have Y die as soon as possible, and as Y is depressed anyway, he might be open to manipulation. The severity of the penalty is designed to deter X from taking advantage of his uncle.

The offence under this section is based on the same words used in the Criminal Law Act 1997 to define secondary participation. It is not clear that they will be interpreted as having a separate and distinct meaning, as suggested in *Attorney General's Reference No.1 of 1975* (1975) (see section 6.5). In *Attorney General v. Able* (1984), the Court of Appeal seemed to take the four words together, and gave them the meaning of 'to help'. The defendant, a member of an unincorporated society that advocated voluntary euthanasia and suicide, published a booklet that gave advice to people contemplating suicide on how to do so quickly and painlessly. It was held by the Court of Appeal that this did not of itself amount to an offence under an identical English provision. For such an offence, it would have to be shown that the defendant: (a) intended the pamphlet to be used by, and to be of assistance to, someone contemplating suicide, (b) that with such an intent, he distributed the pamphlet, and (c) that the recipient derived some assistance from the pamphlet in making an attempt to commit suicide.

Under section 2(3), if a person is charged with murder, murder under section 3 of the Criminal Justice Act 1990, i.e. murder of a garda or prison officer acting

---

8 Smith and Hogan, *Criminal Law*, 11th ed., Oxford: Oxford University Press, 2005, p. 494.

in the course of their duties, etc. (see section 18.10), or manslaughter, and it appears from the evidence that he is guilty of an offence under section 2(2) in respect of the person killed, he may be convicted under that section. Section 2(3) therefore provides for an alternative verdict in circumstances in which it might be difficult to distinguish between murder and secondary participation in a suicide.

Finally, under section 2(4), prosecutions for offences under section 2(2) may only be brought by or with the consent of the DPP. The purpose of this provision is apparently to try to ensure consistency in the application of section 2(2), and effectively removes, or at least severely restricts, the right of a common informer to initiate a private prosecution.

18.29 Euthanasia

Euthanasia is more commonly referred to as mercy killing, and involves the killing of another person who wishes to die, usually in order to end suffering. While a number of jurisdictions have legalised the practice, it is illegal in the UK and in Ireland. Section 2(2) of the 1993 Act makes it an offence to aid or abet a suicide or an attempted suicide, punishable by up to fourteen years' imprisonment. Furthermore, if a person actually kills another person at the request of that person, he is guilty of murder. Put another way, consent is no defence to a charge of murder.

It must be emphasised that while a person may not assist in another person's death or perform the killing, it is permissible for doctors to withdraw life-saving treatment to allow death to occur naturally. In *Re a Ward of Court* (1995), the Supreme Court considered a request from the parents of a young woman, who was in a coma, to allow her to die. In 1972, the young woman underwent an operation under a general anaesthetic. While unconscious, she suffered three heart attacks which caused severe brain damage. She was left spastic, unable to move, feed or care for herself. Her nutritional requirements were supplied by means of a tube inserted into her stomach. Two years later, she was declared a ward of court. In 1994, her mother applied to the High Court to have all nutritional assistance removed. This application was opposed by the hospital in which the woman had been looked after for over twenty years. The High Court held that while the woman was not in a completely persistent vegetative state, in that she had some cognitive ability, she was not far from it. There was no prospect of improvement, and whether or not the application should be granted should depend on the best interests of the woman. The court accepted that if she was able, the woman would refuse the treatment that she was undergoing. The family's application was therefore granted. On appeal, the Supreme Court agreed and upheld the High Court order. The Supreme Court held that the right to life implied a right to die naturally and with dignity. This implied a right to refuse medical treatment that would have the effect of artificially maintaining life. Where the person was not in a position to make that decision as a result of a severe medical condition, the decision could be made by her guardian, which in this case was the courts. The test adopted by the High Court, i.e. the best interests of the woman, was correct, and there was ample evidence to support the High Court conclusion that the woman's best interests would be served by the withdrawal of treatment. The Supreme Court was at pains to point out, however, that its decision did not amount to the legalisation of euthanasia. In doing so, it adopted the reasoning of the House of Lords in a similar case, *Airedale NHS Trust v. Bland* (1993). Euthanasia was defined in both cases as the taking of positive steps to cause death. In both cases, there were no such positive steps; rather, what was being proposed was the removal of means by which life was being artificially maintained, which would allow death to occur naturally. Hamilton C.J. specifically stated that 'the court can never sanction steps to terminate life.'

INFANTICIDE

18.30 Introduction

At common law, the killing by a mother of a child while suffering from some mental condition was considered to be a form of murder, and was treated as such. Alternatively, if an intention to kill or to cause serious injury could not be shown, then a verdict of manslaughter could be returned. Thus, no allowance was made by the law for post-natal depression. A slight concession, however, was made in the area of punishment in that the mandatory death sentence was always commuted to life imprisonment. In England, the position was altered by the Infanticide Act 1922, which was repealed and replaced by the Infanticide Act 1938. Smith and Hogan note that the 1922 Act was introduced due to the impossibility of getting convictions against the defendant mother as a result of public opinion.[9] However, the purpose of the Act was frustrated by its own terms which limited the offence of infanticide to newly born children. In *R v. O'Donoghue* (1927), the Court of Appeal held that a child killed thirty-two days after birth was not a newly born child. The defendant mother was therefore convicted of murder. The 1938 Act was introduced to remedy this situation, and provides the basis of the Infanticide Act 1949 enacted into Irish law.

18.31 The Infanticide Act 1949

The 1949 Act provides, at section 1(3), that the offence of infanticide is committed where a mother causes the death of her child within twelve months of its birth in

---

9   Smith and Hogan, *op.cit.*, p 498.

circumstances that would otherwise have made her guilty of murder, providing that at the time of the killing, the balance of her mind was disturbed as a result of the effects of childbirth or lactation. In these circumstances, the offence should be tried and punished in the same way as manslaughter. The Act also makes two further provisions in respect of alternative charges and verdicts. First, under section 1(1), where a woman is charged with the murder of her child (under twelve months of age), the District Justice may alter the charge to infanticide during the *prima facie* hearing. Second, under section 1(2), if a jury is satisfied that a defendant mother charged with the murder of her child is guilty of infanticide as defined in section 1(3), it may return a verdict of guilty of infanticide.

The burden of proof is on the prosecution. In other words, it is for the prosecution to prove beyond reasonable doubt that the defendant's actions do not fit within the definition of infanticide. The crucial factor is whether or not the balance of the defendant's mind was disturbed by childbirth or lactation. Charleton argues that this test is sufficiently wide to allow for a wide variety of conditions and causes, such as the stress of a greater burden for poor families, a failure of bonding between the mother and child, or stress caused where the mother is unable to cope with the child.[10]

18.32 Further Reading

Bacik, 'If it Ain't Broke – A Critical View of the Law Reform Commission's Consultation Paper on Homicide: The Mental Element', (2002) 12(1) *ICLJ* 6.

Biggs, 'Euthanasia and Death with Dignity: Still Poised on the Fulcrum of Homicide', (1996) *Crim LR* 878.

Carey, 'The Year and A Day Rule in Homicide', (2001) 11(1) *ICLJ* 5.

Carney, 'Decriminalising Murder?', (2003) 8 *Bar Review* 254.

Charleton, 'Causation in the Law of Homicide', (1991) 1 *ICLJ* 68.

Costello, 'The Terminally Ill: The Law's Concerns', (1986) 21 *Ir Jur (ns)* 35.

Donnelly, 'Battered Women Who Kill and the Criminal Law Defences', (1993) 3 *ICLJ* 40.

Feenan, 'Death, Dying and the Law', (1996) 14 *ILT* 90.

Keane, 'Murder, The Mental Element', (2002) 53 *NILQ* 1.

Keown, 'The Law and Practice of Euthanasia in the Netherlands', (1992) 108 *LQR* 51.

Law Reform Commission, *Consultation Paper on Corporate Killing*, LRC CP26-2003.

———, *Consultation Paper on Homicide: The Mental Element in Murder*, LRC CP17-2001.

———, *Consultation Paper on Homicide: The Plea of Provocation*, LRC CP27-2003.

---

10 Charleton, *et al.*, *op. cit.*, para. 7.72.

————, *Report on Corporate Killing*, LRC 77-2005.

Maier-Katkin and Ogle, 'A Rationale for Infanticide Laws', (1993) *Crim LR* 903.

McAleese, 'The Reasonable Man Provoked', (1978) 1 *DULJ* 53.

Newman, 'Reforming the Mental Element of Murder', (1995) 5 *ICLJ* 194.

Nicolson and Sanghui, 'Battered Women and Provocation: The Implications of *R v. Ahluwalia*', (1993) *Crim LR* 728.

O'Malley, 'Sentencing Murderers: The Case for Relocating Discretion', (1995) 5 *ICLJ* 31.

Stannard, 'Making Sense of *MacEoin*', (1998) 8 *ICLJ* 20.

————, 'Medical Treatment and the Chain of Causation', (1993) 57 *JCL* 88.

CHAPTER NINETEEN

NON-FATAL OFFENCES AGAINST THE PERSON

19.1 Introduction

Until recently, the law on non-fatal offences was contained in a combination of common law rules and statutes, principally the Offences Against the Person Act 1861 (OAPA). This area has always been diverse, and covers a wide variety of offences. Indeed, the OAPA has been described as a 'ragbag of offences'.[1] This is undoubtedly as a result of the historical development of the law. Originally, the law treated non-fatal offences, even attempted murder, as misdemeanours punishable with imprisonment and fines. Such leniency is surprising given the ferocity of punishments available for other offences. Statutory intervention began to change this, but only in a piecemeal fashion. The OAPA was the first real attempt at a codification of non-fatal offences. This Act, in combination with the common law rules, remained the mainstay of the law until 1997. In that year, prompted by the Law Reform Commission's *Report on Non-Fatal Offences Against the Person* (1994), virtually all of the substantive provisions of the OAPA, except for those relating to abortion, were repealed, and the common law offences of assault, battery and false imprisonment were abolished. In replacement, and to reform the law, the Oireachtas enacted the Non-Fatal Offences Against the Person Act 1997. However, as the Act is, in many cases, simply a codification or reform of the common law rules, much of the pre-1997 case law is still relevant in interpreting the new legislative provisions.

ASSAULT

19.2 Introduction

At common law, there was a distinction between the *actus reus* of assault and that of battery. An assault was an action that caused the victim to fear the immediate infliction of force, while a battery was the actual infliction of force. Despite the technical distinction, both offences were usually referred to collectively as 'common assault', punishable under the OAPA by a fine of up to £50 and/or six months' imprisonment if convicted summarily (section 42), or up to twelve months' imprisonment if convicted on indictment (section 47). In terms of *mens rea*, both offences were similar in that proof of intention or recklessness was sufficient. Therefore, the *mens rea* of assault was an intention to raise a fear of immediate violence or recklessness as to whether that fear was created. The *mens*

---

1 Smith, 'Commentary on *R v. Parmenter*', (1991) *Crim LR* 41, 43.

rea of battery was an intention to inflict force upon another person or recklessness as to whether force was inflicted. Some confusion existed as to whether recklessness should be defined subjectively or objectively, with considerable conflicts in the authorities. In *R v. Spratt* (1991), for example, the Court of Appeal held that it should be subjective, while in *DPP v. K (a minor)* (1990), it was held that recklessness should be objective. The law of assault was considered by the House of Lords in *R v. Savage; Parmenter* (1991), but the issue of recklessness as such was not dealt with. That case was concerned with the meaning of the word 'maliciously' in statutory assault, so it was unnecessary to decide the meaning of recklessness. There were, however, suggestions that it should be subjective, and this appears to have been the accepted view.

The Law Reform Commission, in its *Report on Non-Fatal Offences Against the Person* (1994), felt that the law of assault worked fairly well and recommended that it should be retained. However, it recommended that the distinction between assault and battery be abolished, incorporating both elements into one statutory offence of assault. Words should be capable of constituting an assault if, judged by an objective standard, they could cause a fear of immediate personal violence. Additionally, the Commission recommended that the *mens rea* of assault should be intention or recklessness, with recklessness being defined subjectively. Finally, consent should remain a defence to minor assaults.

19.3 Definition of Assault

Section 28 of the 1997 Act abolished the common law offences of assault and battery. In their place, section 2 created a new offence of assault, which is defined as follows:

> 2(1) A person shall be guilty of the offence of assault who, without lawful excuse, intentionally or recklessly:
> (a) directly or indirectly applies force to or causes an impact on the body of another, or
> (b) causes another to believe on reasonable grounds that he or she is likely immediately to be subjected to any such force or impact,
> without the consent of the other.

Recklessness is not defined in the Act, but it seems certain that the common law interpretation of subjective recklessness will continue to apply under the Act. The offence of assault may be tried only summarily, thereby removing the right of election enjoyed by prosecutors under section 47 of the 1861 Act. The effect of section 2 is to combine the common law offences of assault and battery into one offence. The elements of the two forms of assault require further consideration.

19.4 The Infliction of Force

The first form of the offence of assault is the direct successor to the common law offence of battery and involves the infliction of force or the causing of an impact upon another person. To constitute the offence, the force must be inflicted or the impact caused without the consent of the other person.

Direct and Indirect Actions

As regards the first form of assault, i.e. the infliction of force or an impact, at common law, the force inflicted upon the victim had to be inflicted directly. Therefore, if X dug a hole into which he hoped that Y would fall, X committed no battery. However, in *DPP v. K (a minor)* (1990), the defendant, a fifteen-year-old schoolboy, was engaged in a chemistry class at school, when he spilled some sulphuric acid onto his hand. He was given permission to go to the toilet to wash it off. Unknown to the teacher, however, he brought a tube of acid with him which he proceeded to pour onto a piece of toilet paper to test the reaction. He heard footsteps, panicked, and poured the sulphuric acid into a hand dryer in the school toilets in order to conceal it. He then returned to the classroom, intending to return later to remove the acid. Some time later, however, another schoolboy used the dryer and suffered permanent scarring as a result of the acid. At trial, the defendant was acquitted, and the prosecution appealed. The Court of Appeal held that while the defendant's action was clearly an indirect act, he was as guilty of assault as if he had turned on the machine himself, and the appeal was allowed. The Law Reform Commission, however, doubted the accuracy of the judgment on the grounds that it went contrary to the great weight of authority. Under the new provision, such an indirect act is expressly brought within the concept of assault. Thus, while *DPP v. K* may have been contrary to the weight of common law authority, it may be taken as a good illustration of the new provision.

Force

The essence of the first form of assault is the use of force or the causing of an impact. Force is defined in section 2(2) as including the application of heat, light, electricity, noise, any other form of energy or any other thing in solid, liquid or gaseous form. Causing an impact is not defined, but it presumably refers to actions such as throwing an object at another person. There is no minimum force requirement, indicating a continuation of the common law rule that any degree of force, no matter how slight, was sufficient to constitute the offence. So, if X kisses Y lightly on the cheek, an assault under section 2 has occurred. Furthermore, as apprehension of the force is not required, the fact that Y is asleep at the time of the kiss, and therefore is unaware of the assault, is irrelevant. This approach reflects the concern of the law to respect the personal autonomy of the individual. If autonomy is to have any real meaning, then the

251

body of each person must be considered inviolate and any form of molestation, regardless of how serious, must be prohibited. So, in *R v. Thomas* (1985), the defendant touched the bottom of a woman's skirt and rubbed it. This was held to constitute a battery, despite the fact that the woman did not feel the contact. Indeed, the court held that touching a person's clothes while they were being worn is the equivalent of touching the person.

19.5 Apprehension of Force

The second form of the offence of assault is the direct successor to the common law offence of assault and involves the creation of apprehension of suffering the infliction of force or an impact. As with the first form of the offence, the apprehension must be caused without the consent of the other party in order for the offence to be committed.

Apprehension

The essence of the second form of assault is a reasonable apprehension of the immediate infliction of force, and this follows the old common law. No contact of any kind is required as apprehension alone is sufficient. So, if X advances towards Y while swinging a stick, an assault is committed. If, however, Y is asleep at the time, no assault is committed, as Y is not in a position to apprehend the possibility of force. It is not necessary that the victim is actually afraid of the force; indeed, he may be supremely confident of his ability to defend himself and still be the victim of an assault. All that is required is that he recognises that the defendant will immediately inflict force upon him, providing that recognition is reasonable, which is an objective requirement. It must be shown by the prosecution that a reasonable person would also have believed that force or an impact was imminent. Thus, if the victim is unusually nervous and overreacts to the defendant's actions, no assault is committed.

Immediacy

The common law requirement that the apprehension must be of immediate violence is retained in the second form of the offence. The purpose of the requirement is, as suggested by the Commission, to exclude threats that are too remote in terms of time. Immediacy is not defined by the Act, but it is likely that the common law rule will continue in operation. The courts did not require that 'immediate' mean there and then, and developed what amounted to a flexible proximity test. In *R v. Horseferry Road Magistrates' Court, ex parte Saidatan* (1991), it was held that the word required proximity in time and causation; that violence will result within a reasonably short period of time. This interpretation accords with the interpretation of the immediacy requirement in the defence of duress (see section 10.3). However, even with such a generous interpretation, the decision in *R v. Ireland* (1997) is difficult to comprehend. The defendant made a large number of telephone calls to three women during which he remained silent when the women answered the phone. All of the women suffered psychological injury as a result. It was held by the Court of Appeal that the act of making a phone call, resulting in psychological damage, was sufficient to establish an assault. However, as Smith and Hogan point out, an assault requires an action that creates fear of immediate violence, not simply fear itself.[2] It is difficult to see how a fear of immediate violence could be caused when the defendant is far away from the victim.

Words

It is not clear whether words can now form the basis of an assault. At common law, mere words alone, no matter how threatening, could not constitute an assault; there had to be some threatening action of any kind that would create a fear of immediate violence. Thus, in a Canadian decision, *R v. Byrne* (1968), the defendant went up to the ticket office at a theatre with a coat over his arm. He said: 'I've got a gun, give me all your money or I'll shoot.' It was held that no assault had been committed. However, while words could not constitute an assault, they could negative one. In the famous case of *Tuberville v. Savage* (1669), the defendant put his hand on his sword and said: 'If it were not assize time, I would not take such language.' It was held that by placing his hand on his sword, the defendant had committed an assault in that the victim could reasonably have been put in fear of an immediate battery. However, the defendant's words negatived any such fear; therefore no assault had occurred. This common law rule that words cannot constitute an assault was universally condemned by commentators and by the Law Reform Commission. There is no reason why words that would cause a person to reasonably fear the infliction of immediate force cannot come within the new formulation of the second form of the offence. Thus, if a case with the facts of *Byrne* were to come before the Irish courts, it is submitted that the defendant could be convicted of assault. However, the rule that words can negative an assault, as in *Tuberville v. Savage*, is not affected by the new provision.

19.6 Minor Contacts

Any non-consensual contact can constitute an assault under section 2. However, some unwanted physical contact is probably inevitable given the proximity to others that is characteristic of modern society. Walking along a crowded street on a Saturday afternoon, for example, will result in a certain amount of jostling from other people. This contact is non-consensual in that specific consent to it has not

---

2 Smith and Hogan, *Criminal Law*, 11th ed., Oxford: Oxford University Press, 2005, p. 520.

been given, but it would be absurd if these slight contacts were treated as criminal assaults. The common law developed a concept of implicit consent to deal with these circumstances. In *Collins v. Wilcock* (1984), the Court of Appeal said that:

> [M]ost of the physical contacts of ordinary life are not actionable because they are impliedly consented to by all who move in society and so expose themselves to the risk of bodily contact. So nobody can complain of the jostling which is inevitable from his presence in, for example, a supermarket, an underground station or a busy street nor can a person who attends a party complain if his hand is seized in friendship, or even if his back is (within reason) slapped ...

The Court went on to say that these situations are more commonly regarded as 'falling within a general exception embracing all physical contact which is generally acceptable in the ordinary conduct of daily life.' An identical approach is adopted in section 2(3) of the 1997 Act, which provides as follows:

> No ... offence is committed if the force or impact, not being intended or likely to cause injury, is in the circumstances such as is generally acceptable in the ordinary conduct of daily life and the defendant does not know or believe that it is in fact unacceptable to the other person.

Suppose that X wishes to speak to Y, and touches Y's arm to attract his attention. Such an action would be considered quite normal in ordinary daily life, and also was not intended or likely to cause injury. In these circumstances, X's action, while strictly speaking an assault, would not be considered unlawful. However, if X knows or believes that Y dislikes being touched by others, then X has deliberately invaded Y's autonomy, and his actions will constitute a criminal assault.

AGGRAVATED ASSAULTS

19.7 Introduction

The OAPA 1861 contained a wide variety of aggravated assault offences, all of which have now been abolished. Even before their formal abolition, many of them were expressed in terms that were clearly outdated, not having been altered since 1861. The most important forms of aggravated assault were contained in sections 18, 20 and 47. Section 18 prohibited the unlawful and malicious causing of a wound or grievous bodily harm (GBH), or shooting at another person, with the intent to maim, disfigure or disable any person, or to do some other GBH to any person, or to resist the arrest of any person. Section 20 was a slightly less serious form of aggravated assault than section 18. It prohibited the unlawful and malicious wounding of, or infliction of GBH upon, any other person with or without a weapon. Section 47 was the least serious of the aggravated assaults and prohibited assaults occasioning actual bodily harm. The Law Reform

Commission recommended the enactment of a new scheme of aggravated assaults that would remove all the technical limitations surrounding the older terminology. The Commission's proposals were adopted in the 1997 Act; the aggravated assault offences contained in the 1861 Act were repealed and new offences enacted in sections 3 and 4.

19.8 The 1997 Scheme

Section 3 makes it an offence to assault another person causing harm. Unlike assault under section 2, an offence under section 3 can be prosecuted summarily or on indictment. On summary conviction, the maximum penalty is a fine of €1,905 or twelve months' imprisonment, or both. A conviction on indictment carries a maximum penalty of a fine or five years' imprisonment, or both. Section 4 makes it an offence to intentionally or recklessly cause serious harm to another person. The penalty for a conviction on indictment under this section is a fine or imprisonment for any term up to life.

Actus Reus

The formulation of sections 3 and 4 is considerably less complex than that of sections 18, 20 and 47 of the OAPA 1861. Those provisions created highly technical distinctions between actual bodily harm, grievous bodily harm and wounding. These distinctions have all been removed for the purposes of assault and subsumed into the concepts of harm and serious harm.

Section 3 requires proof of an assault that causes harm. Consequently, the prosecution must prove all the elements of assault as defined in section 2, and show that the assault caused harm. Harm is defined in section 1 as 'harm to body or mind and includes pain and unconsciousness'. This definition appears to include the infliction of psychological distress of the sort inflicted in *Ireland* (although as noted earlier, it is difficult to see how the making of a telephone call could fit within the definition of assault (see section 19.5)). This is a continuation of the position reached by the common law. In *R v. Miller* (1954), the defendant physically forced his estranged wife to have sexual intercourse with him, during which the woman was thrown to the ground three times. It was claimed on a charge of assault occasioning actual bodily harm that the woman had suffered no bodily harm, although there was evidence that the incident had caused her to suffer a hysterical and nervous condition. Lynskey J. held that if a 'person is caused hurt or injury resulting, not in any physical injury, but in an injury to the state of his mind for the time being, that is within the definition of "actual bodily harm".'

Section 4 requires proof that the defendant caused the complainant serious harm. There is no requirement that the prosecution must prove an assault as defined in section 2, although in practice section 4 charges are likely to involve assaults. All that is *required* is proof of serious harm caused by the defendant to the complainant. This formulation removes the need to engage in convoluted and unconvincing reasoning – whether the defendant's actions fit the definition of an assault is irrelevant providing serious harm was caused. Serious harm is defined in section 1 as an injury that causes a substantial risk of death, serious disfigurement, the substantial loss or impairment of the body's mobility as a whole, or the substantial loss or impairment of the function of any organ or body member. This definition is exhaustive; therefore, for a conviction under section 4, an injury must come within this definition.

Mens Rea

Under the 1861 Act, assault occasioning actual bodily harm under section 47 could be committed recklessly and the weight of opinion suggested that foresight, or subjective recklessness, was required. Sections 18 and 20 required proof of malice, and malice required proof of subjective recklessness: *R v. Cunningham* (1957). Under the 1997 Act, section 4 explicitly requires proof of intention or recklessness. Section 3 is silent as to *mens rea*; however, section 3 requires proof of an assault which in turn requires proof of intention or recklessness. Presumably, the same meaning will be applied to the concept of recklessness for the three assault provisions, and almost certainly subjective recklessness will be required.

One particularly difficult issue that arose under the old provisions, which also has relevance under the new provisions, was whether the defendant had to foresee the precise kind of injury contemplated by the section. For example, suppose X attacks Y with a bottle, intending only to hit Y on the arm and not foreseeing any risk of seriously injuring him. However, the bottle breaks and causes a deep wound in Y's arm. In other words, X foresaw only a risk of causing actual bodily harm (as in section 47), but actually caused grievous bodily harm and a wound (as in section 20). Could X be convicted under section 20, or should it be necessary to show that the defendant foresaw a risk of causing a wound or GBH, the harm required under section 20? It would seem that a conviction for the more serius offence was possible in these circumstances. In *R v. Mowatt* (1967), the victim had been robbed by a person who had been in the company of the defendant. The victim demanded that the defendant tell him where the robber had gone. The defendant knocked the victim down, sat on him and punched him in the face a number of times. He was convicted under section 20 and appealed. It was held by the Court of Appeal that it was irrelevant that he had not foreseen that his actions might cause GBH or a wound. It was sufficient that he had foreseen that some minor physical harm would be done to the victim. Despite some confusion in later cases, the House of Lords confirmed this decision in *R v. Savage; Parmenter* (1991). Lord Ackner stated that it was sufficient that the defendant 'should have foreseen that some physical harm to some person, albeit of a minor character, might result.' This decision can be criticised because, as Charleton notes, by providing separate offences, the legislature clearly intended to distinguish between them. By allowing the *mens rea* required for the lesser offence to support the more serious offence, this intention was effectively subverted.[3] Whether or not the Irish courts would have followed the English approach is unclear; the matter does not appear to have come before them. However, there is nothing to suggest that this reasoning cannot be applied under the new scheme in the 1997 Act if the Irish courts are so willing. Indeed, the Law Reform Commission appears to have accepted this possibility. Therefore, where a defendant realises that there is a risk of harm but not of serious harm and decides to run the risk anyway and actually causes serious harm, it would seem that he can be convicted under section 4.

DEFENCES TO ASSAULT

19.9 Introduction

All of the general defences discussed in Part III can be used to defend a charge of assault. It is accordingly not necessary to review them here. Two defences of particular application to assault must, however, be considered: consent and lawful discipline.

19.10 Consent

One of the guiding principles of the modern criminal law is respect for the autonomy of the individual. If this principle is to be given effect in the context of assault, the State should not, as a rule, be permitted to override the consent of an individual to the infliction of force upon himself. Therefore, in principle, the consent of the party harmed should provide a complete answer to any assault charge. This is broadly the approach of the 1997 Act, an approach that differs somewhat from the position at common law. However, whether under the Act or at common law, the law demands that consent flows from the will of the person giving it in order to provide an answer to an assault charge. Thus, consent obtained through force, fear or fraud will not constitute true consent (this issue is discussed more fully in the context of rape; see section 20.5). Further, the party giving the consent must also be competent to do so in terms of age and mental ability. There is no statutory guidance as to the age a person would need to be to give consent to an assault; each case must be judged according to its own circumstances. However, as a general rule of thumb, the more serious or dangerous the assault in question, the greater the maturity and understanding of the person purporting to give consent will need to be before a court will regard that consent as an answer to the charge. In *R v. Sutton* (1977), the defendant was

---

3 Charleton, *et al., Criminal Law,* Dublin: Butterworths, 1999, para. 9.11.

a coach for an under-age soccer team. He photographed three boys from the team, all aged under thirteen, in various states of undress, intending to sell the photographs to Scandinavian magazines. He touched the boys only on the arms and legs to indicate the positions they were to adopt. In quashing the defendant's conviction for indecent assault, the Court of Appeal held that the facts of the case did not disclose an indecent assault, and that the boys' consent to the touching was valid, which thereby precluded any suggestion of assault. Presumably, if the boys had been younger – say, seven or eight – the court would have been more willing to find an incapacity to understand what was happening or to give proper consent.

Pre-1997

Consent can provide an answer to a charge either as a defence or by its absence being a constituent element of the offence. In the case of assault before 1997, the relevance of consent was considered by the House of Lords in *R v. Brown* (1993). The defendants had been charged with a number of counts of aggravated assault under sections 20 and 47 of the 1861 Act arising out of episodes of consensual homosexual sadomasochism, during which injuries had been inflicted upon each other. The defendants argued that the consent of all the participants should provide them with a complete answer to the charges. A majority of the House decided that absence of consent was not an element of assault; rather, consent provided a complete defence to a person charged with assault. Accordingly, while the prosecution bore the legal burden of negating the issue of consent if it had been raised, the defendant would be under an evidential burden to raise the issue if he wished to rely on it. Further, the majority ruled that consent provided a defence to an assault charge on the basis of public policy, and that public policy also limited the extent of the defence. In particular, the majority decided that public policy generally dictated that people should not cause injury to each other. Hence, on public policy grounds, consent to the infliction of injury would not be operative. If injury was not inflicted, then public policy would not interfere with the participants' consent. A similar public policy approach has rendered consent irrelevant to participation in a prize-fighting contest (*R v. Coney* (1882)), fighting (*Attorney General's Reference No.6 of 1980* (1981)) and sexual assault causing injury (*R v. Donovan* (1934)).

Despite the general rule set out in *Brown*, the common law has always recognised a number of instances where consent could legitimately be given to the infliction of injury. Thus, a person can consent to rough and undisciplined horseplay, a situation which effectively removed from the law of assault injuries received during children's playground games such as the 'bumps' (*R v. Jones* (1986)). However, this principle has been extended to conduct of an exceptionally serious kind carried out by adult RAF officers. In *R v. Aitken* (1992), a group of officers held a party to celebrate the end of their flight training, during which a number of them attempted to set each other alight. One of the group suffered serious burns, but the consent of the participants to the rowdy behaviour was held capable of offering a complete answer to any assault charges. Consent to any form of body art such as tattooing will be an effective defence, as will consent to branding (*R v. Wilson* (1996)). Consent is also a full defence at common law to surgery. Finally, consent will operate in respect of participation in dangerous exhibitions, and also in violent sports. In the case of sports, the Court of Appeal has given further guidance in *R v. Barnes* (2004). The court accepted that people who engage in contact sports implicitly consent to a certain degree of risk of incurring injury, and this degree will vary from one sport to another. The accepted rules of the sport can provide a good indication of the limit of a participant's consent, and generally actions that fall within those rules will not be criminal. However, the opposite will not necessarily be true: the fact that an action contravenes the rules, even where the contravention results in a sanction such as being sent off, does not necessarily make the act criminal. Even acts that are illegal under the rules of the game must reach a certain objective threshold of seriousness before they can be considered to be criminal. In particular, the court must be satisfied that the act was not an 'instinctive reaction, error or misjudgement in the heat of the game.' Whether this threshold was reached would depend on a variety of factors:

> The type of the sport, the level at which it is played, the nature of the act, the degree of force used, the extent of the risk of injury, the state of mind of the defendant are all likely to be relevant in determining whether the defendant's actions go beyond the threshold.

The 1997 Act

Section 2 of the 1997 Act makes it clear that the absence of consent is now an element of the offence of assault. Accordingly, the prosecution must prove in all cases that consent was not given, and the defendant no longer carries an evidential burden to raise the issue of consent. As an assault as defined in section 2 is an essential element of the offence prohibited by section 3 (assault causing harm), the same situation arises in all section 3 charges. Further, the 1997 Act clearly contemplates individuals being able to consent to the infliction of harm, which is a considerable alteration from the common law position. As noted above, common law only permitted an individual to consent to assault as long as injuries were not inflicted unless the situation fell into one of the recognised public policy exceptions. Because absence of consent is an element of the offence covered by section 3, it follows that individuals may now consent to the infliction of harm as defined for the purposes of the Act (see section 19.4). Thus, if *R v. Brown* (1993) arose before an Irish court today, the defendants would almost certainly be acquitted. It also follows that as far as the infliction of harm is concerned, the common law public policy exceptions have now become redundant.

In relation to section 4, the position is different. As noted earlier (section 19.7), a charge under section 4 does not incorporate the offence of assault; section 4 prohibits the intentional or reckless infliction of serious harm. There is no indication that absence of consent is an element of the offence and there is no defence of consent applicable to section 4. Accordingly, it seems that the consent of the party who suffered the injury generally will be irrelevant if charges are brought under section 4. However, section 22 of the 1997 Act provides that the provisions of the Act – including section 4 – have effect subject to any existing defence. Consequently, there seems to be room for a defendant to defeat a section 4 charge by showing that the serious harm was inflicted in circumstances that fit within one of the common law public policy exceptions. Suppose X causes Y to suffer permanent brain damage as a result of some heavy punches thrown legitimately during a boxing match. Under the definition of serious harm contained in section 1 of the Act, X has inflicted serious harm upon Y, but X should have a complete defence to any section 4 charge on common law public policy grounds. The same situation should apply where serious harm is inflicted during any of the other public policy exceptions, including – controversially – an episode of rough and undisciplined horseplay.

19.11 Lawful Chastisement of Children

Common Law

At early common law, a very wide concept of lawful discipline existed. For example, a husband had the right to physically discipline his wife in order to maintain domestic discipline. Additionally, a master had the right to administer discipline to servants and apprentices, and the master of a ship could inflict corporal punishment on sailors under his command. All of these rules have fallen into disuse, and are now obsolete.

The infliction of corporal punishment upon children, however, is still permitted. This power exists primarily in parents and legal guardians. The common law extended this right of discipline to teachers, although the Department of Education prohibited the use of physical punishment in schools in 1982. A breach of this prohibition might have given rise to disciplinary proceedings against teachers, but teachers would still have been entitled to raise the defence of lawful chastisement at common law if prosecuted for assault. However, this defence was abolished by section 24 of the Non-Fatal Offences Against the Person Act 1997, following a recommendation to this effect from the Law Reform Commission in its 1994 *Report on Non-Fatal Offences Against the Person*. Thus, the power to inflict physical punishment on children is now vested only in parents and legal guardians. The punishment inflicted has to be reasonable and for the sole purpose of discipline. What constitutes reasonable discipline is a matter of fact for the jury to decide in each case, and tends to vary over time. The basic rule, however, has remained unaltered for well over a century. In *R v. Hopley* (1860), Cockburn L.C.J. said that punishment will be unlawful:

> if [the punishment] be administered for the gratification of passion or rage or if it be immoderate or excessive in its nature or degree, or if it be protracted beyond the child's power of endurance or with an instrument unfit for the purpose and calculated to produce danger to life and limb ...

Thus, in *R v. Smith* (1984), two strokes with a belt was found to be unreasonable. Similarly, in *R v. Taylor* (1983), the throwing of an exercise book by a teacher at a student was said to be unreasonable. On the other hand, in *A v. United Kingdom* (1998), an English jury found a beating with a garden cane that caused extensive bruising around the child's buttocks to be reasonable. The European Court of Human Rights held, however, that the infliction of physical punishment upon children could constitute a violation of Article 3 of the Convention, which prohibits torture, inhumane and degrading treatment, if the punishment reached a certain level of severity. Whether a particular punishment reached this level would need to be judged according to 'all the circumstances of the case, such as the nature and context of the treatment, its duration, its physical and mental effects and, in some instances, the sex, age and state of health of the victim.' The court found that the punishment in this case reached the required level of severity and because English law had failed to vindicate the child's rights, English law was found to violate the Convention. Strictly speaking, the decision in *A* applied only to the infliction of punishments that were sufficiently severe to constitute torture, inhumane or degrading punishment within the meaning of Article 3; punishments that did not reach that level of severity are beyond the reach of Article 3. However, in *R v. H* (2002), the Court of Appeal indicated that juries should be directed to take account of the factors suggested by the European Court of Human Rights in *A* in deciding whether a punishment was reasonable. By so doing, the Court of Appeal indicated that the common law could be reconciled with the Convention, and it seems certain that this reinterpretation of the common law defence will apply regardless of the severity of the punishment inflicted.

Reform

The Law Reform Commission was clearly unhappy at any person having the power to inflict physical punishment upon children. As noted above, the Commission recommended that the common law immunity of teachers in respect of corporal punishment be abolished, and this was accomplished by section 24 of the Non-Fatal Offences Against the Person Act 1997. The Commission further recommended that corporal punishment be abolished as a court-ordered sanction – until then, courts had a formal power to order a juvenile offender to be whipped as a punishment for a crime. The Commission's recommendation was enacted in section 12 of the Criminal Law Act 1997. Furthermore, section 201 of the Children Act 2001 will specifically prohibit the imposition of corporal punishment in any Children Detention School, along with the deprivation of food or water, and the infliction of any cruel, inhumane or degrading treatment or any punishment that would be detrimental to a child's psychological, emotional or physical well-being. At the time of writing, section 201 has not been brought into force.

Regarding the parental right to discipline children, the tenor of the Commission's discussion leaves no doubt that it would have preferred that such a right be abolished. However, the Commission noted that this right was so widely accepted in Irish society that change would need to be gradual rather than immediate. Accordingly, the Commission recommended that parents continue to have the legal right to physically discipline their children, but also recommended that parents be 're-educated' without delay. Since then, however, the issue became the focus of a case brought against Ireland under Article 17 of the European Social Charter, which requires States through their laws to protect all children and young persons from violence (*World Organisation against Torture v. Ireland* (2005)). The complainant, a French human rights group, claimed that the right of parents under Irish law to physically punish their children was in breach of Article 17. The European Committee of Social Rights ruled in January 2005 that Article 17 obliges all States to legislatively prohibit all forms of violence against children, 'regardless of where it occurs or of the identity of the alleged perpetrator. Furthermore the sanctions available must be adequate, dissuasive and proportionate.' Accordingly, Irish law was found to breach Article 17. However, the Committee's decision has no binding legal force, and there is no indication as yet that the right of parents to chastise their children is going to be abolished.

SYRINGE OFFENCES

19.12 Introduction

Until 1997, the use of a syringe in an assault was not an offence in itself, being dealt with simply as a form of aggravated assault or robbery. However, due to the apparent increase in the use of syringes as weapons, pressure increased for the creation of a specific offence to deal with such attacks. The Opposition introduced the Punishment of Aggravated Robbery Bill 1997, which proposed to make it an offence to use a syringe to effect a robbery. It also proposed a graded system of punishment of at least five years' imprisonment for a first offence, at least seven years for a second offence and life imprisonment for a third offence. This Bill lapsed following the enactment of the 1997 Act, which addresses the use, possession and disposal of syringes in sections 6, 7 and 8. For the purposes of these sections, syringes are defined in section 1 as including any part of a syringe or a needle or any sharp instrument capable of piercing skin and passing on to another person blood or a blood-like substance. Section 6 is the main provision and creates four distinct offences.

19.13   Section 6(1) – Stabbing or Threats to Stab

It is an offence to injure or threaten to injure another person by piercing their skin with a syringe, either with the intent of causing that person to believe that he or she may have been infected with a disease, or where there is a likelihood of causing such a belief. The maximum punishment is a fine, ten years' imprisonment or both. Presumably, a threat to stab with a syringe will ordinarily attract a lesser punishment than an actual stabbing.

An offence under section 6(1) can arise in one of two ways: either an actual stabbing with a syringe or a threat to do so. The stabbing offence is established by proof that a syringe pierces another person's skin, which presumably means that the whole skin must be pierced, as opposed to merely being scratched. Threatening to stab someone with a syringe is self-explanatory. There is no requirement for either form or the offence that the syringe is filled with blood or a blood-like substance. It is sufficient that the attack was intended or was likely to cause a fear of infection; the lack of infected material within the syringe is irrelevant in itself (although an empty syringe may be evidence from which it can be inferred that such an intention was not present, nor was there any likelihood of a fear of infection).

The *mens rea* of the offence is in two parts. The defendant must act intentionally or recklessly as regards the stabbing or threat to stab. It is likely that subjective recklessness will be required for this element of the *mens rea*, as with the aggravated offences under the OAPA 1861. However, this must be accompanied by another element of *mens rea*, which can be established in two ways. Either the defendant must act with the intent of causing a belief in the victim that he or she may have been infected with a disease, or the circumstances must be such that there is a likelihood of causing such a belief. Thus, this extra element of *mens rea* can be established with proof of either intention or recklessness. Recklessness in this context appears to be objective – there must be a likelihood of causing a belief that the victim may be infected with a disease. There is no requirement that the defendant actually adverted to the risk that such a belief might be caused. Consequently, where X stabs Y with a syringe and, in the circumstances of the attack, a reasonable person would have appreciated the risk of causing such a belief, *mens rea* is established. It is not necessary that the belief is actually caused; it is sufficient to show that causing the belief was the defendant's intention, or was the likely result.

19.14   Section 6(2) – Spraying or Threats to Spray Blood

It is an offence to spray, pour or put blood or a blood-like substance onto another person, or to threaten to do so, with an intention to cause a belief of infection in the victim, or where there is a likelihood of causing such a belief. The *actus reus* of the offence is self-explanatory, while the *mens rea* is the same as under section 6(1).

19.15   Section 6(3) – Transferred Intent

Where a person attempts to commit or is in the process of committing an offence under sections 6(1) or (2), but either pierces the skin of a third party or sprays, etc. blood or a blood-like substance onto a third party, an offence is committed under section 6(3), providing the third party believes that he or she may become infected with a disease. This section effectively places on a statutory footing the doctrine of transferred intent (see section 4.3). Therefore, if X tries to stab Y with a syringe but stabs Z instead, X is guilty under section 6(3), and may be sentenced as if he had succeeded in stabbing Y. The same considerations apply where X tries to throw blood at Y but misses and hits Z instead. There is no *mens rea* requirement as such; the *mens rea* required for X's attack on Y will be transferred to Z. Thus, it must be shown that X had the *mens rea* necessary for section 6(1) or (2) as appropriate. Finally, unlike under sections 6(1) and (2), for an offence under section 6(3), it must be shown that the person actually stabbed or sprayed, etc. developed a belief that he or she may be infected. That the belief turns out to be unfounded or unreasonable is irrelevant, but the belief must have been caused.

19.16   Section 6(5) – Stabbing with a Contaminated Syringe

It is an offence to injure another person by intentionally piercing his or her skin with a contaminated syringe, or to intentionally spray, pour or put contaminated blood onto another person, or to do either to a third party while committing or attempting to commit this offence. Anyone convicted of this offence on indictment is liable to life imprisonment. A contaminated syringe is one that has contaminated blood or fluid on or in it. Contaminated blood or fluid is blood, fluid or a substance that contains any disease, virus, agent or organism that could cause a life-threatening or potentially life-threatening condition to another person if passed into his or her bloodstream. This is by far the most serious offence in section 6, which is reflected in the punishment. The offence exists mainly to deal with situations in which a defendant deliberately infected another person with a serious disease such as the HIV virus. Given the absence of a cure for this virus, the defendant's actions could be seen as tantamount to homicide, albeit death would not occur for a considerable period of time after the infection occurred. Under the law of homicide as it stood in 1997, a prosecution for homicide was precluded by the year and a day rule (see section 18.6), leaving a defendant in a situation such as this exposed to a charge of aggravated assault at most. The offence in section 6(5) allowed for a charge that more correctly reflected the consequences of the defendant's actions, although much of the original rationale for this offence was removed by the abolition of the year and a day rule by the Criminal Justice Act 1999. Thus, if a defendant now infects a person with a deadly disease which will result in death considerably later in time, a prosecution for murder could be brought when the victim eventually dies. It is essential, however, for this offence that the defendant knows that the syringe or blood is contaminated. It is not sufficient to show that the defendant could not care less whether there was contamination, i.e. recklessness; there must be an intention.

19.17 Possession and Disposal of Syringes

Sections 7 and 8 criminalise the possession of syringes and their careless disposal, respectively. Section 7(1) makes it an offence to be found in possession in a public place of a syringe or a blood container with intent to cause or threaten to cause an injury to, or to intimidate, another person. The definition of a public place in section 1 is wide, and includes any street, seashore, park, land, field or highway, or any other place to which the public has access. The construction of the offence (requiring an intent) is such that the defendant must know that he is in possession of the syringe or blood container. In *Minister for Posts and Telegraphs v. Campbell* (1966), it was made clear that possession was impossible unless the defendant had knowledge of the article in question. Thus, if X puts a syringe into Y's pocket without Y's knowledge, Y is not guilty under this section, even where he would have accepted the syringe had he known of it. Finally, where a person is charged under section 7(1), it is not necessary that the prosecution prove an intent with respect to any particular person. Additionally, if the court thinks fit bearing in mind all of the circumstances, it may regard the mere possession of the syringe or blood container as evidence in itself of an intent to injure, etc. Particular circumstances that might be taken into account include the contents of the syringe, the time of the day or night at which the offence is committed or the place where the offence is committed.

Under section 7(2), a member of the gardaí may stop, question and search any person in a public place whom he has reasonable cause to suspect is in possession of a syringe or a blood container with intent to injure, threaten to injure or to intimidate. Any syringe or blood container found may be seized unless the suspect has a reasonable excuse to be so in possession. If the suspect refuses to stop or to give his name and address, or attempts to obstruct a search, he may be arrested without warrant and may be charged under section 7(4).

Under section 8(1), it is an offence to place or abandon a syringe in any place in such a manner that it is likely to injure another person and does in fact injure another person, or where it is likely to injure, cause a threat, or frighten another person. The offence is established by recklessness only, and it seems that it is not necessary to prove subjective recklessness. Therefore, if X leaves a syringe lying on a seat in a children's playground, he will be convicted under section 8(1) if a reasonable person would have foreseen a risk of injury, etc. Anyone who is administering or assisting in lawful medical, dental or veterinary procedures is not liable to prosecution under this section. Additionally, it is a defence, where the syringe was placed in his normal residence, for the defendant to show that he did not intentionally place the syringe in such a manner that it injured, or was likely to injure or cause a threat or to frighten another person.

Where the defendant intentionally disposes of the syringe in such a manner that it injures another person, he commits a distinct offence under section 8(2). Anyone convicted of such an offence on indictment is liable to life imprisonment. This is a considerably more serious offence, and its seriousness is reflected in the maximum penalty available.

THREATS AND COERCION

19.18 Introduction

At common law, a threat to kill or cause injury at some point in the future was generally not actionable: it could not be considered to be an assault because the threat was not of immediate violence. One exception to this was contained in section 16 of the OAPA 1861. This section made it an offence to maliciously send written death threats to any person. The *mens rea* of the offence was intention or recklessness, although it is hard to see how a person could write such a letter with anything less than an intention. It was also unnecessary to show that the person who received the letter was the victim, providing the recipient believed the threat to be real. Therefore, if X wrote to Y threatening to kill Z, the offence had been committed. Furthermore, a person who merely acted as a courier could also be convicted under this section if he knew the contents of the letter. The Law Reform Commission was unimpressed with the provision, noting that it was limited in two ways: to written threats, and to threats to kill. It recommended the repeal of this section, replacing it with a provision that would cover any threat to kill or to cause serious harm to any person, howsoever made. Under the Commission's proposal, it would also be unnecessary to show that the recipient was the intended victim, providing the recipient was intended to believe the threat. This proposal was enacted in section 5 of the 1997 Act.

Coercion and harassment were virtually unknown to Irish criminal law. The exception was section 7 of the Conspiracy and Protection of Property Act 1875. This provision prohibited the use of violence or intimidation against any person or his family, following that person alone or with others (while acting in a disorderly manner), watching his house or place of business or hiding any of his property, with a view to forcing him to do something or to restrain him from doing something. Intimidation included any action for which a court would bind the defendant to the peace. The Commission was generally happy with this provision but did recommend that the punishment be increased. It also recommended that any other acts of harassment should be criminalised. It gave stalking as an example of the conduct that was not covered by Irish law. In essence, it recommended that any act that seriously interfered with another person's peace and privacy should be an offence. These proposals were enacted in sections 9 and 10 of the 1997 Act. The legislature also created, in section 11, a new offence of demands for payment of bills that cause alarm. However, the Commission's proposal that a specific offence of making terrorist-type threats was not implemented.

19.19 Section 5 – Threats

Under section 5, it is an offence to make a threat to kill or to cause serious harm to any person and to communicate that threat by any means to any person, whether the person so threatened or not, providing the defendant intended that the recipient believe the threat. It is, however, a defence to show that the person making the threat did so with a lawful excuse. The terms of this section are identical to those proposed by the Commission. Serious harm has the same meaning as under section 4 (see section 19.8). It would seem, therefore, that a threat to cause harm is not actionable. Additionally, as it is a requirement that the person making the threat intends the recipient to believe the threat, it would not be an offence if X jokingly told Y that he intended to kill Z, even if Y believed the threat to be real. The issue is not Y's belief, but X's intent.

19.20 Section 9 – Coercion

Section 9 effectively recreates, with a few minor amendments, section 7 of the Conspiracy and Protection of Property Act 1875. It is an offence to use any of the following means without lawful authority to compel a person to refrain from doing something that he or she is legally entitled to do, or, alternatively, to do something that he or she is legally entitled not to do:

(a) using violence or intimidation to that person or his or her family;
(b) injuring or damaging his or her property;
(c) persistently following him or her from place to place;
(d) watching or besetting his or her place of residence or business, or the approaches thereto, or any other place where that person happens to be; or
(e) following him or her with others in a disorderly fashion.

Property, for the purposes of (b), is defined in section 1 to exclude intangible property, but includes money and animals. Therefore, if X maims Y's cattle intending to force Y to do something, he is guilty of an offence. If, however, he interferes with a right of way that Y uses to get to work, he has committed no offence under this section. The other terms are self-explanatory. Section 9(2) provides a defence where the defendant was at the person's home or place of work under (d) merely to obtain or to communicate information. It is unlikely that this defence would apply where the defendant repeatedly approached the victim at home or at work on a pretext of communicating with him.

19.21 Section 10 – Harassment

Section 10 of the 1997 Act creates a new offence of harassment by any means, including the telephone. The provision is aimed at people who, without lawful authority or reasonable excuse, persistently follow, watch, pester, beset or communicate with another person. Section 10(2) provides that harassment occurs where the defendant by his acts 'intentionally or recklessly, seriously interferes with the other's peace and privacy or causes alarm, distress or harm to the other', providing that a reasonable person would realise that the acts in question would so interfere or cause alarm, distress or harm to the other person. Thus, whether or not the defendant has engaged in harassment must be judged from both an objective and a subjective standpoint. This dual requirement effectively prevents the definition of harassment from being decided by a particularly sensitive person; if a reasonable person would not regard the defendant's conduct as harassment, then the complainant's own view of the conduct will be an insufficient basis for the charge. Further, section 10 can be invoked only where the defendant has acted persistently. So, in *The People (DPP) v. Woods* (2002), the defendant had made over 2,000 telephone calls to a woman. Such conduct clearly constituted harassment; indeed, the Court of Criminal Appeal commented that labeling this behaviour as harassment was 'a very mild way to express it'. Section 10 does not penalise one-off contacts, no matter how unwanted they might be, and it is not clear from the Act at what point the threshold for harassment is reached. The requirement of persistent contact suggests that the defendant must have engaged in the prohibited conduct on at least two occasions but it is unclear how many such occasions are required before a court would accept that harassment has occurred. In *The People (DPP) v. Ramachchandran* (2000), the defendant sent a book entitled *Murder and Homicides* to the mother of a young woman in whom he was interested. The Court of Criminal Appeal accepted that this action 'clearly caused great distress and fright, and understandably so, to the [woman's] mother.' However, this was one action on the defendant's part, and on its own probably could not have amounted to harassment. When viewed in the context of a three-year campaign of unwanted contacts, however, a single act can be viewed as an example of harassment. If the defendant's conduct is especially serious or invasive, presumably a court would be more willing to label that conduct as harassment with relatively little repetition; more minor conduct would need to be repeated more often to constitute harassment. Ultimately, the decision will depend on the factors in each particular case and will be judged objectively.

In addition to a maximum sentence of seven years' imprisonment, section 10 empowers the courts to grant what amounts to an injunction to prevent any further contact between the parties under section 10(3). A breach of this order is an offence subject to the same penalties as a breach of section 10 itself. Further, this order can be granted whether or not the defendant was convicted of harassment, and is potentially unlimited in its scope. In *Ramachchandran*, the Court of Criminal Appeal quashed the defendant's conviction and refused to order a retrial. However, the court granted an order under section 10(3) to protect the complainant from being contacted again by the defendant at home or at work. The defendant was prohibited from contacting the complainant in any way for a period of ten years. More specifically, the defendant was prohibited from coming within a radius of five miles of Ardrahan village and three miles from the centre of Eyre Square in Galway for ten years.

19.22 Section 11 – Demands for Payment

Under section 11, it is an offence to use any of the following means to enforce the payment of a debt:

(a) frequent demands which, by reason of their frequency, are calculated to cause the debtor or a member of his or her family alarm, distress or humiliation;
(b) false representations that the debtor will be prosecuted;
(c) falsely impersonating an official with the authority to enforce payment; or
(d) use of a document that is falsely represented to be official in character.

The offence is committed even though the debt is genuine and legally enforceable; the purpose of the provision is only to regulate procedures for the enforcement of debts. The *mens rea* required is unspecified, but it appears to be intention or knowledge. In (a), intention is clearly required as the demands must be calculated to cause alarm, distress or humiliation. In the other three cases, the defendant must have been shown to have engaged in false representations; it is difficult to see how a person could do this unintentionally.

POISONING

19.23 Introduction

Poisoning was an offence under sections 23 and 24 of the Offences Against the Person Act 1861, which together made it an offence to unlawfully and maliciously administer to or cause to be administered to or taken by another person any poison or any other destructive or noxious thing. A poison was defined in *R v. Cramp* (1880) as a substance that is injurious to health or life once administered. A noxious thing was defined in *R v. Marcus* (1981) as a substance that, in terms of quantity or quality, is injurious, hurtful, harmful or unwholesome. The *mens rea* of the offences, as indicated by the word 'maliciously', was entirely subjective. Thus, the prosecution had to prove that the defendant intentionally administered a poison, etc. or that he foresaw the risk that a poison, etc. would be administered and consciously ran that risk. However, both offences had extra elements of *mens rea*: section 23 made it an offence to administer the poison, etc. with the intent to endanger life or to inflict grievous bodily harm, while section 24 made it an offence to administer the poison, etc. with the intent to injure, aggrieve or annoy the other person. The Law Reform Commission was of the view that its proposals on the infliction of harm and serious harm would render these poisoning offences largely redundant in practice. Accordingly, the Commission recommended that section 23 be abolished and that section 24 be replaced by a new offence of poisoning while knowing that the poison would interfere with the victim's bodily functions. The 1997 Act abolished section 23 of the 1861 Act, and section 12 of the 1997 Act created a new offence of poisoning that is substantially in line with the Commission's recommendations.

19.24 Section 12 – Poisoning

Section 12 of the 1997 Act makes it an offence to intentionally or recklessly administer to, or cause to be taken by, another person without that other person's consent a substance which the defendant knows is capable of substantially interfering with the other person's bodily functions. The *actus reus* of the offence is similar to that which existed under the 1861 Act: the defendant must be shown to have either administered the substance to another person or caused the substance to be taken by the other person. The concept of 'administration' of a substance in ordinary speech suggests an injection or some such method of delivery, but it seems that the concept might be wider for the purposes of section 12. In *R v. Gillard* (1988), the Court of Appeal considered whether spraying CS gas into a man's face could be considered to be an administration of a noxious thing for the purposes of section 24 of the 1861 Act. The Court of Appeal reversed the trial judge's ruling that this conduct did not constitute an administration of a noxious thing; instead, the court ruled that administration 'includes conduct … which brings the noxious thing into contact with [the other person's] body.' The court also indicated that causing a noxious thing to be 'taken' required some form of ingestion by the victim.

There is no requirement in section 12 that the substance be a poison as such; the prosecution is required to show only that the substance was capable of interfering with the victim's bodily functions. Section 12(2) provides that a substance capable of inducing unconsciousness or sleep is a substance within the meaning of section 12. There is no requirement that the substance actually has the effect of interfering with the other person's bodily functions; it is sufficient that the defendant is aware that the substance is capable of producing that effect.

So, if X administers a sleeping pill to Y knowing that it is a sleeping pill, the offence is committed even if the pill has no effect on Y due to his tolerance of sleeping medication. Similarly, if X surreptitiously puts alcohol into Y's non-alcoholic drink, X can be prosecuted under section 12, as alcohol is clearly capable of interfering with a person's bodily functions.

Finally, the prosecution must show that the recipient of the substance did not consent to what was being done. The purpose behind section 12 is to protect against invasions of a person's bodily integrity; a person who decides to ingest a substance – even an illegal substance – which can affect his bodily functions has suffered no invasion. Thus, the conscious ingestion of drugs by, for example, a patient as part of medical treatment will not generally constitute poisoning for the purposes of section 12. If the patient has not consented to take the substance, however, then the person who administers it may be convicted of poisoning even if he was acting in the interests of the patient: there is no requirement that the administration of the substance be done for malicious purposes. Further, if the true nature and effect of the substance is concealed from the recipient of the substance, charges under section 12 may be brought; a person who does not know what he is taking cannot truly be said to have consented to what was being done. So, if X induces Y to agree to swallow a sleeping pill by describing it as a vitamin pill, X is open to a charge of poisoning.

ENDANGERMENT

19.25 Introduction

Endangerment arises when an unjustifiable risk is taken that endangers the health or property of another person. Such an offence was unknown to common law, and there was no general provision made for it in the OAPA 1861. The 1861 Act, while containing no specific endangerment offences, did contain a number of endangerment-type provisions – section 17 (impeding persons trying to save themselves from shipwrecks) and section 31 (the laying of traps), for example.

Providing for an offence of endangerment can be criticised as it is inherently uncertain, subjective and anticipatory. However, as the Commission pointed out, there is no reason why the law must wait for an actual injury to occur before acting. For example, attempt, incitement and conspiracy are offences even though no injury has occurred. Additionally, as noted above, Irish criminal law already recognised a number of endangerment-type offences. Consequently, there would be no reason in principle why a general endangerment offence could not be created. Furthermore, the Commission noted that, by doing so, the constitutionally recognised right to bodily integrity (see *Ryan v. Attorney General* (**1965**)) could be given greater protection. The Commission was aware of the possibility of their proposals being misused, and for that reason recommended that the proposed offence of endangerment be limited to acts that create a substantial risk of which the actor was aware. The Commission also recommended the creation of a specific offence of endangering traffic. These proposals were adopted by the legislature in sections 13 and 14 of the 1997 Act, respectively.

19.26 Section 13 – Endangerment

Section 13 makes it an offence to intentionally or recklessly engage in conduct which creates a substantial risk of death or serious harm to other people. The offence mirrors almost exactly the recommendations of the Law Reform Commission. The offence is limited to a risk of death or serious harm, with serious harm having the same meaning as for offences under section 4 (see section 19.8). There is no limitation on the kinds of conduct encompassed by the offence. In *The People (DPP) v. Cagney* (2004), the Court of Criminal Appeal noted that section 13 created 'a general offence of endangerment. It is not a particularized offence. As it is a general offence its applicability will not be limited to any specific areas.' So, in *Cagney*, the court held that a jury was entitled to view an aggressive pursuit of another person with shouts and threats directed at that other person as conduct that created a risk of death or serious harm. The court also accepted, *obiter*, that the offence could arise through the contamination of a building, or a water supply or blood, or on a sport's field. Further, providing the defendant's conduct created a substantial risk of death or serious harm, the fact that death or serious harm actually occurred was irrelevant to the issue of guilt (although it would presumably be highly relevant to the issue of punishment). As the Court of Criminal Appeal pointed out in *Cagney*, a wanton disregard for the safety of others 'is itself deserving of condemnation and sanction as a serious infringement of basic values.'

To prove the *mens rea* of the offence, the prosecution must show that the defendant either intentionally or recklessly engaged in conduct that created a substantial risk of death or serious harm. Thus, a defendant may be convicted of endangerment in a situation in which he had no intention of creating a substantial risk of death or serious harm. However, the prosecution must be able to show that the defendant was aware that such a risk might be created and consciously chose to run that risk: in *Cagney*, the Court of Criminal Appeal adopted the subjective definition of recklessness put forward by Henchy J. in *The People (DPP) v. Murray* (1977) (see section 4.5). The required subjective state of mind on the part of the defendant can be shown by drawing reasonable inferences from his conduct. In *Cagney*, the court held that the evidence of the defendant 'pursuing, shouting at and threatening [the victim] is such that an intent may be inferred from it as to whether he intentionally or recklessly engaged in conduct which creates a substantial risk of death or serious harm to [the victim].' What would happen, however, if the jury concludes that X foresaw a substantial risk only of harm being caused as opposed to such harm? The Law Reform Commission's recommendations make it clear that they intended the offence to be limited to situations in which the defendant either intentionally risked causing serious harm or at least foresaw the possibility of serious harm. On this construction, X should be acquitted, but it is far from clear whether that section is limited in this manner. The decision of the House of Lords in *R v. Savage; Parmenter* (1991), on a similar point in relation to statutory assault, would appear to be relevant here. The Lords decided that, on a charge under section 20 (causing grievous bodily harm or wounding), it was not necessary that the defendant foresaw grievous bodily harm or wounding as a result of his actions; it was sufficient that he foresaw any form of physical harm. The Commission seemed to endorse this approach in relation to assault, and there seems to be no reason why the reasoning in *Savage; Parmenter* should not apply to endangerment as well. That being the case, in the example given above, X should be convicted. Such a conclusion would, however, expand the offence beyond the Commission's recommendations.

19.27 Section 14 – Endangering Traffic

The offence under this section is limited to endangering any form of traffic. The defendant must know, when committing any of the following actions, that his actions may cause injury or damage, or must be reckless in that regard:

(a) intentionally placing or throwing any dangerous obstruction upon a railway, road, street, waterway or public place;

(b) intentionally interfering with any machinery, signal, equipment or other device for the direction, control or regulation of traffic upon that railway, etc.;

(c) intentionally interfering with or throwing anything at or on any conveyance used or to be used on the railway, etc.

A conveyance is a vehicle designed or adapted for the carriage of goods or people by land or water, thereby encompassing all motor vehicles, trains, trams, ships, boats, barges, etc. It does not include aircraft. 'Railways' includes a tramway or a light railway, while 'waterway' means any water-based route used by any conveyance.

In many respects, this offence is similar to the offences under sections 33 and 34 of the 1861 Act, which penalised actions intended to interfere with railways and trains. In *R v. Pearce* (1966), it was held that it was an offence in itself under section 34 to cut overhead signal wires. It was not necessary to show that the cutting of the wires caused an accident, as the offence consisted only of intending to create a source of danger. Whether the danger was actually realised was irrelevant. This analysis appears to be relevant to the new offence under section 14. The defendant must intentionally place some form of an obstruction across a land- or water-based route, either knowing that an injury or damage may result, or being reckless as to the result. Once this has been done, the offence is committed; there is no requirement that an injury or damage actually occur as a result of the defendant's actions.

KIDNAPPING AND ABDUCTION

19.28 Common Law Offences

Until the 1997 Act was enacted, the deprivation of liberty could have been punished in a variety of ways: common law false imprisonment or some specific statutory abduction offences against children and women. False imprisonment and kidnapping were felonies by virtue of the Criminal Law (Jurisdiction) Act 1976, section 11. False imprisonment occurred where a defendant intentionally or recklessly deprived another person totally of his or her liberty for any amount of time. The deprivation of liberty ('imprisonment') could take place anywhere as long as it was total; in *McDaniel v. State* (1942), a Texas State decision, it was held that driving a car so fast that the victim dare not try to get out could amount to false imprisonment. Similarly, in *Ludlow v. Burgess* (1971), it was held that it was possible to falsely imprison a person in the middle of a public street. It was not, however, possible to imprison a person by continual surveillance: **Kane v. The Governor of Mountjoy Prison (1988)**. By implication, it was not necessary that the victim be physically detained or detained within a confined area. Indeed, a person could be detained by words alone, but in this case, the victim would have to submit to the detention. In effect, the victim would have to consider himself to be detained. So, if X fraudulently told Y, 'I am a police officer; don't move, you are under arrest', and Y believed him, X could be found guilty of false imprisonment. Furthermore, there was no temporal requirement for an imprisonment; if X was unlawfully totally detained even momentarily, the offence was committed.

Kidnapping was a more serious form of false imprisonment that involved an element of abduction. In *R v. D* (1984), the House of Lords found four distinct ingredients in the offence:

(a) the taking and carrying away of one person by another;
(b) force or fraud on the part of the kidnapper;
(c) the absence of consent by the victim; and
(d) the absence of a lawful excuse.

In **The People (Attorney General) v. Edge (1943)**, however, a majority of the Supreme Court accepted that kidnapping was a colloquial term only, and was not an offence known to the law. It was in effect merely a term that referred to a species of false imprisonment. As a result of this decision, the law on kidnapping effectively fell into disuse. Thus, where a person was confined against his will, the charges brought were framed in terms of false imprisonment.

19.29 Statutory Offences

Child stealing was an offence under section 56 of the 1861 Act. Under this section, it was an offence to unlawfully, with force or fraud, take a child under fourteen away from its guardian with intent either to deprive the guardian of possession of the child or to steal any article from the child, whether owned by the child or not. Anyone receiving a child knowing him to have been so taken was guilty of an offence. The section did not, however, apply to certain kinds of people: anyone who had claimed a right of possession of the child, the mother of the child or the father of an illegitimate child.

A related offence was created under section 55 of the 1861 Act. An offence was committed where a person unlawfully took an unmarried girl under the age of sixteen away from her mother or father without their consent. In *R v. Prince* (1875), the defendant abducted a girl who was under sixteen but who looked older. It was held that *mens rea* was not required for the age element of the offence. Consequently, the defendant's honest belief that the girl was over sixteen was no defence.

Finally, section 54 of the 1861 Act and section 7 of the Criminal Law Amendment Act 1885 (as amended by section 20 of the Criminal Law Amendment Act 1935) created offences involving the abduction of women and unmarried girls under eighteen, respectively, for the purpose of marrying or having intercourse with them. In the latter offence, the *Prince* reasoning applied; therefore a genuine belief that the girl was over eighteen was irrelevant to the issue of guilt.

19.30 Reform Proposals

The Law Reform Commission noted the particular importance of this area of the criminal law in the light of the constitutional guarantee of personal liberty expressly contained in Article 40.4.1, and implied in Article 40.3.2. The Commission was unhappy with the uncertainty in the area of kidnapping in particular, caused largely by the Supreme Court's decision in *Edge*. The Commission was also of the view that false imprisonment should be codified, and that the statutory offences in the 1861 Act required updating. The Commission proposed that kidnapping should be abolished, noting that a codified offence of false imprisonment would cover kidnapping as well. The Commission also felt that its false imprisonment proposal would render redundant those statutory offences concerning the abduction of women and girls for sexual purposes (sections 53 and 54 of the 1861 Act, and section 8 of the Criminal Law Amendment Act 1885). As far as the remaining statutory offences were concerned (sections 55 and 56 of the 1861 Act, and section 7 of the 1885 Act – abduction of girls under sixteen), the Commission recommended that they be updated. These proposals were accepted and enacted in sections 15, 16 and 17 of the 1997 Act.

19.31 Section 15 – False Imprisonment

The 1997 Act abolished the common law offences of false imprisonment and kidnapping in section 28, and replaced them with a new composite offence in section 15. This provision codifies the offence of false imprisonment in line with the recommendations of the Law Reform Commission. Section 15(1) provides as follows:

> A person shall be guilty of the offence of false imprisonment who intentionally or recklessly –
> (a) takes or detains, or
> (b) causes to be taken or detained, or
> (c) otherwise restricts the personal liberty of,
> another person without that other's consent.

By section 15(2), consent must be real and freely given. Therefore, if a person consents out of fear or fraud, that consent will not operate to provide the defendant with a defence. Fraud in this case means situations in which the defendant caused the victim to believe that he had a legal duty to consent to being detained.

The new offence covers both of the old offences of false imprisonment and kidnapping, and extends their application. It is not necessary that a person be totally detained; it is sufficient that a person's personal liberty is restricted. Clearly, however, the greater the degree of restriction, the more serious the offence, and the greater the penalty that will be imposed. The rest of the section appears to be a codification of the common law.

19.32 Section 16 – Abduction of a Child by a Parent

Section 16(1) provides as follows:

> (1) A person to whom this section applies shall be guilty of an offence, who takes, sends, or keeps a child under the age of 16 years out of the State or causes a child under that age to be so taken, sent or kept –
> (a) in defiance of a court order, or
> (b) without the consent of each person who is a parent, or guardian or person to whom custody of the child has been granted by a court unless the consent of a court was obtained.
> (2) This section applies to a parent, guardian or a person to whom custody of the child has been granted by a court but does not apply to a parent who is not a guardian of the child.

Under section 16(3), it is a defence to any such charge if the defendant was unable to communicate with each of the child's parents, guardians or custodians, as required under section 16(1)(b), but believed that they would consent had such communication been possible. Alternatively, if the defendant did not intend to deprive others who had guardianship or custody rights over the child, he will also have a full defence. Private prosecutions cannot be brought by virtue of subsection 5, which requires that all prosecutions should be brought by, or with the consent of, the DPP.

The requirement that the child be removed from Ireland indicates that the offence is intended to apply to situations in which one of the parents has a foreign home, and decides to take the child to that home despite the wishes of the other parent. In such cases, the limited defences allowed under section 16(3) will be unlikely to be of much use to the defendant. Clearly, the legislature took the view that where a child is taken by a parent, but remains within the jurisdiction of the Irish courts, there is no need for a separate offence as the courts can order the return of the child. Where the child has been sent abroad, however, such a solution would not be possible. The offence will not apply, however, to a parent who is not the guardian of the child. Such parents can be dealt with under section 17, dealing with child abduction by others.

19.33 Section 17 – Abduction of a Child by Others

Section 17 only applies to persons not covered by section 16 (essentially, anyone who has not been granted custody of the child). Section 17 provides:

> (1) A person, other than a person to whom section 16 applies, shall be guilty of an offence who, without lawful authority or reasonable excuse, intentionally takes or detains a child under the age of 16 years or causes a child under that age to be so taken or detained –
>   (a) so as to remove the child from the lawful control of any person having lawful control of the child; or
>   (b) so as to keep him or her out of the lawful control of any person entitled to lawful control of the child.
> (2) It shall be a defence to a charge under this section that the defendant believed that the child had attained the age of 16 years.

This offence is wider than that in section 16 in that there is no requirement that the child be removed from the jurisdiction. It is intended to apply only to 'ordinary' kidnappings involving people who do not have custody of the child. The taking of the child must, however, be a deliberate act; proof of recklessness is not sufficient. This is not likely to cause any problems in practice as it is hard to conceive of a kidnapping occurring without intention. The defence allowed – that the defendant believed the child to be sixteen – effectively reverses the decision in *R v. Prince* (1875), which had decided that the old offence of child-stealing was an offence of strict liability in that proof that the defendant knew that the child was under sixteen was irrelevant.

19.34 Further Reading

Allen, 'Consent and Assault', (1994) 58 *JCL* 183.
Bacik, 'Striking a Blow for Reform?', (1997) 7 *ICLJ* 48.

Bamforth, 'Sado-Masochism and Consent', [1994] *Crim LR* 661.

Foley, 'Boxing, the Common Law and the Non-Fatal Offences Against the Person Act 1997', (2002) 12(1) *ICLJ* 6.

Law Reform Commission, *Report on Non-Fatal Offences Against the Person*, LRC 45–1994.

McCutcheon, 'Kidnapping Reconsidered', (1985) 3 *ILT* 146.

———, 'Sports Violence, Consent and the Criminal Law', (1994) 45 *NILQ* 267.

———, 'The Abductive Element in the Offence of Kidnapping', (1993) 3 *ICLJ* 1.

Roberts, 'The Philosophical Foundations of Consent in the Criminal Law', (1997) 17 *Ox JLS* 389.

Rogers, 'A Criminal Lawyer's Response to Chastisement', [2003] *Crim LR* 98.

CHAPTER TWENTY

SEXUAL OFFENCES

20.1 Introduction

Sexual offences encompass some of the most serious offences known to Irish law. They are also the area of law most beset with conflicts of ideology. As O'Malley notes, the study of sexual offences is a study in social values.[1] As values change, so too does society's conception of sexual offences. Thus, rape was originally regarded as a crime against property. The female victim was the property of the man who owned her; consequently, the rapist was seen to have committed a crime against him. In later times, even though the law had recognised the importance of the woman's consent, as often as not, if a rape went to trial, it was the woman who was effectively 'in the dock'. Indeed, in *PC v. DPP* (**1999**), it was stated by McGuinness J. in the High Court that:

> In years gone by, accusations of rape or any kind of sexual assault were treated with considerable suspicion. The orthodox view was that accusations of rape and sexual assault by women against men were 'easy to make and hard to disprove'... No one today would support this orthodoxy of the past and there has been a great increase in the psychological understanding of sexual offences generally.

While much, though not all, of this has now changed, Irish law on rape, and on most sexual offences, is still heavily influenced by nineteenth-century legislation. However, many changes have been made: statutory changes to the law of rape, the creation of aggravated sexual assaults and the decriminalisation of homosexual activity. These changes were made to reflect changed social values and to recognise changed realities.

RAPE

20.2 Introduction

Rape is a common law offence that is made punishable by section 48 of the Offences Against the Person Act 1861. However, the crime of rape is now defined in section 2 of the Criminal Law (Rape) Act 1981, as amended by the Criminal Law (Rape) (Amendment) Act 1990, in the following terms:

(1) A man commits rape if:
    (a) he has sexual intercourse with a woman who at the time of the intercourse does not consent to it; and

---

1 O'Malley, *Sexual Offences: Law, Policy and Punishment*, Dublin: Round Hall Sweet & Maxwell, 1996, p. 1.

(b) at the time he knows that she does not consent to the intercourse or he is reckless as to whether she does or does not consent to it . . .

Paragraph (a) therefore contains the *actus reus* of rape, while paragraph (b) contains the *mens rea*.

In *The People (DPP) v. Tiernan* (**1988**), the Supreme Court discussed the nature of rape, noting that it is one of the most serious offences known to Irish law, causing long-term emotional damage as well as physical harm. The court noted that any attempt to view it as a minor offence would be unconstitutional, particularly as it represented an attack upon the human dignity of the woman. For these reasons, section 48 of the OAPA 1861 allows for a penalty of up to life imprisonment for those convicted of rape.

20.3 Capacity

Section 2 of the 1981 Act maintains the traditional explicitly gender-biased formulation of the crime: rape can be committed only by a man against a woman. At common law, three categories of males were considered incapable of committing rape. First, boys under the age of fourteen were conclusively presumed to be physically incapable of committing any penetrative act, although they could commit an indecent assault. This presumption was abolished by section 6 of the Criminal Law (Rape) (Amendment) Act 1990. Notwithstanding section 6, however, boys under the age of fourteen still receive protection from the second common law immunity, that created by the presumption of *doli incapax*. This issue has been discussed in Chapter 12. Thus, a boy aged under seven is immune from prosecution, while a boy aged between seven and fourteen can be prosecuted only if the prosecution can show that he knew that what he was doing was seriously wrong. Once the relevant provisions of the Children Act 2001 are implemented, boys up to the age of twelve will be immune from prosecution for rape. Finally, there was a conclusive presumption that a husband was incapable of committing rape upon his wife; this was the so-called 'marital exemption'. The rationale for the exemption was that a woman gave her consent to sexual relations as part of her marital vows, a consent that was presumed to continue for the duration of the marriage. In *R v. Miller* (1954), the defendant was charged with raping his wife, who had left him and had petitioned for a divorce decree. Lynskey J. considered whether these facts would indicate the revocation of the complainant's implied consent to sexual relations. He ruled that the issue of a petition for divorce had no effect on the marriage, not least because the petition could be rejected. Accordingly, Lynskey J. ruled that 'the defendant cannot be guilty of the crime of rape, and I shall direct the jury that there is no evidence on which they can convict him of rape.' However, the defendant was convicted of assault occasioning actual bodily harm. This case demonstrated the absurdity of the marital exemption; the facts showed that the defendant succeeded in having intercourse with the complainant by assaulting her, yet she was deemed to have consented to the intercourse but not to the assault. This legal position was untenable, and section 5 of the 1990 Act abolished the marital exemption. However, section 5(2) provides that a prosecution against a man for raping his wife must be brought by or with the consent of the Director of Public Prosecutions. While it is true that in practice all rape cases are brought by the Director in the name of the People of Ireland, the restriction in section 5(2) has no counterpart in respect of any other rape complaint, and it is not clear what useful purpose is served by the restriction.

The gender-biased formulation in section 2 can be justified in that it is a reflection of the fact, established by all official and non-official statistics, that women face a vastly greater threat of rape than men. However, the formulation as it stands could also cause difficulties in rare cases involving a post-operative transsexual. To establish the *actus reus* of rape, the prosecution must prove that a *man* had sexual intercourse with a *woman* without the woman's consent. In *Corbett v. Corbett* (1970), the Court of Appeal confirmed that for the purposes of marriage, i.e. the union between one man and one woman, gender was determined according to three biological criteria assessed at childbirth: chromosomes, gonads and genitalia. If these three criteria were congruent and indicated that a child was, say, male, then the male gender would be assigned to that child and in the eyes of the law he would remain male for the rest of his life, regardless of any subsequent gender reassignment procedures. Further, in *R v. Tan* (1983), the Court of Appeal ruled that 'common sense, and the desirability of certainty and consistency' demand that the test for gender for the purposes of marriage should also be applied to criminal charges relating to a man living off the earnings of prostitution. In Ireland, the High Court endorsed a similar biology-based test for gender in **Foy v. Registrar for Births, Deaths and Marriages (2002)** in refusing to order the applicant's birth certificate to be altered to reflect her post-operative female identity. These decisions mean that men who have undergone gender reassignment to become women remain men for the purposes of the criminal law, even though they possess surgically constructed vaginas. Consequently, if a post-operative female is non-consensually penetrated by a man in her artificial vagina, the logical legal conclusion is that the man has penetrated the vagina of another man. Similarly, if a post-operative male uses a surgically constructed penis to penetrate a woman's vagina, the law must logically conclude that the perpetrator was a female with a penis. In either case, the definition of rape is not fulfilled, and the offences could be prosecuted as sexual assault at most. This position is logically and morally untenable. However, in *Goodwin v. UK* (2002), the European Court of Human Rights ruled that the failure of the UK to recognise the applicant's new gender for a variety of purposes, including marriage, was in breach of the European Convention on Human Rights. Irish courts are now bound to interpret

Irish law in accordance with the Convention, and following the logic expressed in *Tan* that the test for gender for the purposes of marriage should be extended into the criminal law, a modern Irish court should be in a position to declare that a transsexual's post-operative gender is his or her gender for the purposes of section 2 of the 1981 Act.

20.4 Sexual Intercourse

There must be proof that the defendant had sexual intercourse with the complainant. Section 1 of the 1981 Act defines sexual intercourse in the same way as carnal knowledge under section 63 of the OAPA 1861, in so far as it relates to natural intercourse. Natural intercourse has been repeatedly defined to mean the penetration of a woman's vagina by a man's penis; penetration of a woman's anus cannot legally amount to rape: *R v. Gaston* (1981). Section 63 of the OAPA 1861 provides that it is unnecessary to prove emission in order to establish that natural intercourse occurred. Thus, penetration is all that must be proven, and it is clear that any degree of penetration will be sufficient. In *The People (Attorney General) v. Dermody* (1956), the young victim gave evidence that the defendant had 'put his private part a wee bit into mine'. Medical evidence established that the girl's hymen had not been ruptured. The Court of Criminal Appeal ruled that once it was proven that the defendant's penis had entered the opening of the complainant's vagina, natural sexual intercourse had occurred for the purposes of rape.

It is not clear whether penetration by an artificial penis or of an artificial vagina will constitute sexual intercourse for the purposes of the offence of rape. In *S v. S* (1963), Willmer L.J. held that legal consummation of a marriage is possible where the woman's vagina required surgical intervention to permit full penetration. In so holding, Willmer L.J. commented that were it otherwise, 'such a woman might be to a considerable extent beyond the protection of the criminal law, for it would seem to follow that she would be incapable in law of being the victim of a rape.' However, Ormrod J. cast some doubt on these comments in *Corbett v. Corbett* (1970) when he suggested that intercourse with a woman whose vagina was entirely artificial was 'the reverse of ordinary and in no sense natural'. More recently, a Crown Court judge ruled in *R v. Matthews* (1996) that there was no public policy reason why non-consensual penetration of an artificial vagina should be legally incapable of constituting the crime of rape. In the UK, section 79(3) of the Sexual Offences Act 2003 now makes it clear that artificial body parts have the same status as natural body parts, but the matter has not yet arisen in Ireland.

20.5 Consent

The crucial element of the *actus reus* of rape is lack of consent; the prosecution must prove that the woman did not consent to sexual relations. In *R v. Dee* (1884), Palles C.B. described consent in the following terms:

Consent is the act of man [sic], in his character of a rational and intelligent being, not in that of an animal. It must proceed from the will, not when such will is acting without the control of reason, as in idiocy or drunkenness, but from the will sufficiently enlightened by the intellect to make such consent the act of a reasoning being.

More recently, in *The People (DPP) v. C* **(2001)**, Murray J. said:

Consent means voluntary agreement or acquiescence to sexual intercourse by a person of the age of consent with the requisite mental capacity. Knowledge or understanding of facts material to the act being consented to is necessary for the consent to be voluntary or constitute acquiescence.

The consent of the woman must therefore reflect a conscious choice on her part. If the woman is not in a position to give consent, then sexual intercourse with her may amount to rape. In *R v. Mayers* (1872), the defendant tried to have intercourse with a woman while she was asleep. It was held that the inability of the woman to give consent could render the defendant guilty of rape. In *R v. Camplin* (1845), the defendant caused the victim to become very drunk, and later had sex with her. He was convicted of rape, because the girl was incapable of giving real consent due to the level of her intoxication. However, in *R v. Lang* (1975), the Court of Appeal made it clear that it is not the drink that is important, but the effect of the drink on the woman's state of mind. Where her state of mind is so affected by alcohol that she is incapable of exercising judgment, she cannot be taken to have given consent. However, in this case, the woman, by her detailed evidence, demonstrated that her judgment had not been impaired. A similar rationale applies with respect to age. In *Gillick v. West Norfolk and Wisbech AHA* (1985), the House of Lords ruled that a child may consent to medical treatment providing she has sufficient understanding of what is proposed to be able to choose among different alternatives. This ruling applies equally to the case of a child purporting to consent to sexual intercourse (although, if the child is under the age of seventeen, the defendant will still be convicted of statutory rape regardless of the child's consent – see section 20.15).

Fraud

Consent should represent the will of the woman in order to be effective, and fraud on the part of the defendant may have the effect of negating any such consent. However, it was made clear in *R v. Clarence* (1888) that the mere presence of fraud does not of itself lead to this conclusion. It is only when the woman is unaware, as a result of the fraud, that she will be participating in a sexual act that her consent will be negated. In *R v. Flattery* (1877), the defendant had intercourse with a girl while pretending to perform surgery. The girl submitted, but the defendant was still convicted due to fraud. Similarly, in *R v. Williams* (1922), the defendant had sex with the victim on the pretext that he was improving her singing voice by making an air passage. Although she did not refuse or resist, he was convicted of rape. In both cases, the women had consented to the procedure that the defendants had said they were going to carry out, rather than to those that were actually carried out. Other cases have involved fraud of a different nature in which the woman gave consent to intercourse on the strength of an extraneous fraudulent promise. In these cases, the defendant generally is not guilty of rape, because the woman was fully aware of the defendant's intentions. Thus, in *R v. Linekar* (1995), the defendant fraudulently offered to pay the complainant for sexual intercourse. The complainant agreed on this basis, but afterwards the defendant refused to pay the money. The prosecution case was that the complainant was induced to give her consent on foot of a fraudulent promise; if this promise had not been given, she would not have agreed to have intercourse. The Court of Appeal held that the mere presence of fraud was insufficient to negate the complainant's consent to sexual intercourse. The complainant had agreed to have intercourse, a fact that was not changed because her agreement had been induced by a false pretence. Similarly, in *R v. Dica* (2004), the Court of Appeal commented, *obiter*, that the defendant's deliberate failure to inform his sexual partners that he was HIV positive did not change the fact that they had agreed to have sexual intercourse with him. But, in *R v. Tabussum* (2000), the Court of Appeal ruled that consent given by a number of women to a breast examination was negated by the fact that the man giving the examination was not medically qualified, as he had claimed to be. The court ruled that the women had consented to the nature of the act, but not to its quality and the defendant was therefore guilty of an indecent assault. This was precisely the argument that had been rejected in *Dica*, and it is difficult to see how these two decisions may be reconciled. However, the decision in *Tabussum* marks a substantial departure from established case law and accordingly should be treated with some caution.

A particular instance of fraud arises where the defendant impersonates a woman's husband. In doing so, he is guilty of rape by virtue of section 4 of the Criminal Law Amendment Act 1885. Until this Act was passed, the English courts had held that such impersonators were guilty of assault only. The Irish courts, however, seem to have rejected such an approach. In *R v. Dee* **(1884)**, a woman went upstairs to her bedroom and fell asleep while her husband was out fishing. A man came into her room, waking her. She spoke to him, but he made no answer. He penetrated her, and at that point, she realised that the man was not her husband as she had assumed. The defendant tried to rely on the English decisions, but the court rejected them as being 'revolting to common sense'. The 1885 Act therefore codified the position already reached by the Irish courts. It does not, however, apply to non-married partners. So, if X is cohabiting with her boyfriend Y, and Z has intercourse with X while pretending to be Y, can Z be convicted of rape? In *The People (DPP) v. C* **(2001)**, the Court of Criminal Appeal rejected a contention by the defendant that a 'person who consents to sexual intercourse with A believing that she is having sexual intercourse with B, has consented to that sexual intercourse if there is no active attempt at personation by A.' If the defendant knows that consent was given by the complainant because she thought the defendant was her boyfriend, then he knows that she has not consented to have sexual intercourse with him, and therefore he has sufficient *mens rea* for rape. However, it is open to the defendant to argue that he had no such knowledge, and that he thought the complainant wanted to have intercourse with him, an argument that, if accepted by the jury, would result in an acquittal due to lack of *mens rea*.

Resistance

At one time, there had to be evidence that the intercourse had occurred with force against the resistance of the woman. It is now well established that the *actus reus* of rape is made out by proving only that the woman did not consent. It is not necessary to prove that the woman resisted. Indeed, section 9 of the Criminal Law (Rape) (Amendment) Act 1990 explicitly provides as much:

> It is hereby declared that in relation to an offence that consists of or includes the doing of an act to a person without the consent of that person any failure or omission on the part of that person to offer resistance to the act does not of itself constitute consent to the act.

Such a failure may, of course, be taken into account by a jury as evidence from which consent may be inferred, but the failure is not sufficient in itself. However, from an evidential perspective, evidence of resistance is useful in convincing a jury that consent was not given.

Submission

It is possible for a woman to submit, perhaps out of fear, to intercourse while not consenting to it. In such circumstances, a conviction is possible if the jury is satisfied that the submission did not amount to consent. This issue was considered by the Court of Appeal in *R v. Olugboja* (1981). The defendant, a Nigerian studying at Oxford, had intercourse with a sixteen-year-old girl, J, at a friend's bungalow following a disco. J had already been raped by the friend, and she had asked that she be left alone. Nevertheless, the defendant told J that he intended to have intercourse with her, and insisted that she remove her trousers, which she did out of fear. He proceeded to have intercourse with her, and she did not resist. The defendant later told the police that while J had not initially consented to intercourse, he had persuaded her. The Court of Appeal held that a jury in a rape trial should be told that submission and consent are not the same; every consent involves submission, but not every submission involves consent. A submission brought about by threats should not be equated with consent. This concept would not be difficult for a jury to grasp where the submission was brought about by force or threats of force. However, a submission could be brought about by different forms of threats not involving force. In such cases, a jury should take into account the complainant's state of mind, and should also have regard to the events leading up to the incident. Looking at such factors, the jury should use its own common sense and experience in deciding whether the submission constituted consent.

Reforms in the UK

In the UK, consent is defined in section 74 of the Sexual Offences Act 2003 as an agreement by choice where the person consenting has the freedom and capacity to make that choice. Further, the 2003 Act enacts a number of presumptions in respect of consent in the area of sexual offences. These presumptions will arise only if certain circumstances are proven by the prosecution to have existed at the time of the sexual act in question, provided the defendant has been shown to have been aware of those circumstances. Section 76 creates a conclusive presumption that the complainant did not consent to the sexual act if either of the two following circumstances are proven by the prosecution:

(a) the defendant intentionally deceived the complainant as to the nature or purpose of the act, or
(b) the defendant intentionally impersonated a person known to the complainant in order to induce consent to the act.

The first of these circumstances essentially enacts the decisions in *Flattery* and *Williams*. The second circumstance goes further than the pre-existing law in that the impersonation of any person known to the complainant will conclusively negate consent; prior to 2003, impersonation of a husband or partner only would negate consent. However, the prosecution must show that the defendant carried out the impersonation in order to induce consent to the sexual act; if the defendant can convince the jury that the impersonation was for another purpose, the conclusive presumption in section 76 cannot arise.

Section 75 of the 2003 Act creates an evidential presumption of absence of consent if any of the following circumstances are shown to have existed:

(a) the complainant was subjected to violence or the fear of immediate violence by any person at the time of or immediately before the act was carried out (or the first such act in the event of there being a series of sexual acts – section 75(3)),
(b) any person was causing the complainant to fear that violence was being used or would be used against another person at the time of or immediately before the act was carried out (or the first such act in the event of there being a series of sexual acts – section 75(3)),
(c) the complainant was being unlawfully detained at the time and the defendant was not,

(d) the complainant was asleep or otherwise unconscious at the time of the act,

(e) the complainant would have been unable, due to a physical disability, to communicate whether or not she consented at the time of the act,

(f) any person had administered to or caused to be taken by the complainant without her consent a substance that was capable, having regard to the time at which the substance was taken, of causing the complainant to be stupefied or overpowered at the time of the act.

It must be emphasised that the presumptions that arise under section 75 are evidential only, not conclusive. If a presumption arises under section 76, then as a matter of law the complainant did not consent to the act in question and this conclusion cannot be rebutted by the defendant. If the presumption arises under section 75, however, the defendant may still argue that the complainant consented, but he will be under an evidential obligation to enter specific evidence of the complainant's consent. Invariably, this will mean that the defendant will have to give sworn testimony, thus exposing himself to cross-examination. The defendant will not have to prove that the complainant gave consent; section 75 does not alter the legal burden of proof, which remains at all times on the prosecution. So, if the defendant succeeds in discharging the evidential burden, the prosecution bears the burden of proving that the complainant did not consent to the act in question. If, however, the complainant is unable or unwilling to rebut the evidential presumption, he will effectively have conceded the issue of consent and can no longer rely on it.

20.6 *Mens Rea*

The *mens rea* of rape is set out in section 2(1)(b) of the 1981 Act. At the time of the intercourse, the defendant must either know that the woman is not consenting or be reckless as to her consent. Recklessness for the purposes of rape will be defined subjectively, and accordingly it is not enough for the prosecution to show that the defendant acted unreasonably. The prosecution must show that the defendant adverted to the possibility that the complainant was not consenting and consciously chose to ignore that risk. In *The People (DPP) v. Creighton* (**1994**), the Court of Criminal Appeal used the word 'heedless' to express this requirement, although the court did not elaborate any further. That the *mens rea* of rape is entirely subjective is best demonstrated in cases in which a defendant claims that he genuinely believed that the complainant had consented. The authoritative decision on this situation was given by the House of Lords in *DPP v. Morgan* (1977), a decision that provides the basis for section 2 of the 1981 Act. In that case, a husband invited three of his friends home to have sex with his wife. He told them that she would pretend to struggle and to fight, but that they should pay no attention to this as it was all part of the fun. They went to the husband's home and had sex with their friend's wife, despite the woman's attempts to fight them off. The friends were convicted of rape, while the husband was convicted of aiding and abetting a rape. The friends appealed on the grounds that it was not necessary, as the trial judge had instructed the jury, for an honest mistake to be reasonable in order to excuse liability for rape. They argued that an honest belief, whether or not it was based on reasonable grounds, was inconsistent with the presence of *mens rea* which was a key element of the prosecution's case. If the jury was satisfied that they had acted under such a belief, the jury would have to conclude that the prosecution had failed to prove its case, and return a verdict of acquittal. The Lords upheld the convictions on other grounds, but on this point, a majority of the Lords agreed. Where a man genuinely believes that a woman is consenting, no rape occurs. This is so even where the belief is mistaken and even unreasonable. The reasoning is that rape requires either knowledge that the woman did not consent or recklessness as to consent. If the defendant genuinely believed that she was consenting, then clearly the defendant could not have had the required *mens rea*. The same reasoning applies where the defendant's belief was unreasonable. Where it was unreasonable, the jury is entitled to take this as evidence that the belief was not genuinely held, but the mere absence of reasonable grounds for the belief could not of itself indicate that the defendant's belief was not genuine.

The *Morgan* decision created a public controversy, and led to the creation of the Heilbron Committee, which, under the chair of Mrs. Justice Heilbron, concluded that the Lords had been correct in their decision. The decision was then implemented into statute by the Sexual Offences (Amendment) Act 1976. In Ireland, the decision was also implemented into statute law in section 2 of the 1981 Act. The Law Reform Commission, in its *Report on Rape and Allied Offences*, published in 1988, saw no reason to recommend any alterations to the law.

The principal objection put forward to the *Morgan* decision is that all a defendant has to do to get an acquittal is simply state that he genuinely believed that the woman had been consenting. However, this objection is overly simplistic, for two reasons. In the first place, the jury is not obliged to believe the defendant's claims. In **The People (DPP) v. F (1993)**, the Court of Criminal Appeal noted that in some cases, the circumstances will be such that it was so clearly obvious that the victim was not consenting that the jury simply will not believe the defendant. So, in *Morgan* itself, the majority of the House of Lords upheld the convictions, holding that a properly instructed jury could not have believed that the appellants' claim of honest mistake.

In the second place, section 2(2) of the 1981 Act specifically states that where the defendant pleads honest mistake in a rape trial, the jury must consider the presence or absence of reasonable grounds for such a belief. The absence of such grounds, while not conclusive in itself, increases the likelihood that the jury will disregard the defendant's claims. The judge must explain the meaning and effect of this provision to the jury in cases where the facts are such that the jury might accept the defendant's explanation. In *The People (DPP) v. Gaffey* (1991), the defendant and the victim knew each other. The victim asked the defendant for a lift on his motorcycle. They went to a graveyard, where they had intercourse. The defendant argued consent and relied on various statements allegedly made by the complainant. It was held that section 2(2) was relevant and should have been included in the trial judge's summary. As it had been omitted, a retrial was ordered. This approach was subsequently endorsed by the Supreme Court in *The People (DPP) v. McDonagh* (1996). In that case, the Supreme Court agreed with earlier decisions of the Court of Criminal Appeal that section 2(2) did not have to be explained to juries in every rape case, or even in every rape case in which consent is an issue. It only has to be explained in any case in which there is evidence that the woman did not consent, and the defendant's mistaken belief is an issue.

The *Morgan* decision will not avail a defendant who realised his error after penetration but continued with the intercourse regardless. In *Kaitamaki v. R* (1985), the Privy Council ruled that the *actus reus* of rape begins with penetration and continues until withdrawal. From the moment the defendant realises his mistake, he forms the *mens rea* necessary for rape: knowledge that the complainant is not consenting to sexual intercourse. If he does not withdraw immediately, he commits the *actus reus* of rape with the required *mens rea* and thus satisfies both elements of the offence. Similarly and by extension, if a woman initially consents to intercourse but changes her mind during the intercourse and communicates this to the defendant, he must stop immediately or face a conviction for rape.

20.7 Rape under Section 4

The Criminal Law (Rape) (Amendment) Act 1990 created a new category of rape, called 'rape under section 4'. This offence is a sexual assault that involves either the penetration of the anus or mouth by a penis, or the penetration of the vagina by any hand-held object. In *The People (DPP) v. JD* (1997), the defendant required children aged between five and sixteen to strip while he stripped, to lick his penis, and to allow him to put his tongue into their vaginas. He pleaded guilty to four counts of rape under section 4 (and three counts of sexual assault), and was sentenced to seven years' imprisonment. The court stated that his offences were very serious, and his appeal for a non-custodial sentence had to be dismissed. Only in very extraordinary circumstances could such a sentence be imposed.

This provision was enacted to take account of the fact that if a man, for example, forced a woman to engage in oral intercourse, he could not, under the 1981 legislation, be convicted of rape. The new offence rectifies that shortcoming. Furthermore, the first form of the offence (penetration of the anus or mouth) can be committed by a man against a woman or a man, while the second form of the offence (penetration of the vagina with any hand-held object) can be committed by a woman against a woman. These are novelties in the law of rape, as until 1990, rape could only be committed by a man against a woman, and followed the recommendations of the Law Reform Commission in its *Report on Rape and Allied Offences* (1988). However, the Commission had also recommended that the penetration of the anus by an object be categorised as rape. This recommendation was not enacted, leaving such incidents to be dealt with as sexual assaults.

The issues of consent and *mens rea* are not addressed directly by the section. However, offences under section 4 are in the first instance sexual assaults, so it would seem that the position on consent and *mens rea* adopted in relation to such assaults would also apply under section 4 (see below – sections 20.11 and 20.12, respectively). Therefore, consent to a sexual assault, within the meaning of section 4, that is either minor or that causes harm is a complete defence. If, however, the sexual assault causes serious harm, then consent is not a defence. The *mens rea* of the offence should be defined subjectively. It is not clear whether recklessness will be sufficient in that for most sexual assaults, the required *mens rea* is intention (see section 20.12). However, for the purposes of rape under section 4, it is submitted that if the prosecution can show that the defendant intentionally carried out any of the acts in section 4 upon the complainant without her consent and did so not caring whether he or she consented, the offence has been made out.

SEXUAL ASSAULT

20.8 Introduction

Until 1990, there were common law offences of indecent assault against women and against men. These offences covered virtually any form of sexual activity that did not constitute rape. Indeed, in *R v. Court* (1988), Lord Griffiths pointed out that indecent assault may 'vary greatly in its gravity from an unauthorised teenage groping at one end of the scale to near rape at the other.' The Criminal Law (Rape) (Amendment) Act 1990, however, provided in section 2 that both offences were to be amalgamated into one, to be known as sexual assault. The penalty for sexual assault, now set by section 37 of the Sex Offenders Act 2001, is imprisonment for up to ten years unless the victim was aged under seventeen at the time of the assault, in which case the maximum penalty is fourteen years' imprisonment. Section 2 of the 1990 Act did not alter the essence of the offence; it merely changed its name and placed it on a statutory footing. Thus, in *The People (DPP) v. EF* (1994), the Supreme Court held that sexual assault was still a common law offence, but that the penalty for the offence was provided by statute. There are two elements to the offence: an assault, and circumstances of indecency. Both of these elements must be established in order to prove the *actus reus*.

20.9 Assault

The definition of an assault in this context is the same as given above in section 2 of the Non-Fatal Offences Against the Person Act 1997 (see section 19.3). A sexual assault, therefore, involves an indecent action that either causes unwanted contact or gives rise to a reasonable belief in the victim of being immediately subjected to such contact. Therefore, there are two kinds of sexual assault: where there is no indecent contact, and where there is indecent contact. In cases where there is no such contact, English authority suggests that there must be evidence of hostility of some kind. 'Hostile' in this sense refers to some form of compulsion. In *Fairclough v. Whipp* (1951), for example, the defendant invited a child to touch his penis. The charge of indecent assault was dismissed because a mere invitation by the defendant to touch him could not be construed as an assault. As there was no assault, there could have been no indecent assault. If the defendant had forced the girl to touch him, or advanced towards her, the situation would have been different, as these actions could be taken as an assault. In a similar, though more controversial, vein, the defendant in *R v. Rogers* (1953) was acquitted of indecent assault where he had put his arm around his eleven-year-old daughter, brought her upstairs and asked her to masturbate him. This happened on two occasions, and in both cases the girl complied. On the second occasion, however, the girl, knowing what was going to happen, did not want to go upstairs, but submitted without resistance. It was held that as the defendant had not forced his daughter to comply, there was no assault. Again, had the defendant used some threat or gesture that could be interpreted as compulsion to force the girl to comply, he could have been convicted.

Where there is actual contact, there is no requirement that the prosecution show that the defendant acted in a hostile or forceful manner. For example, in *R v. McCormack* (1969), the defendant shared a bed with a fifteen-year-old girl. While in bed, he inserted his finger into her vagina. His conviction for indecent assault was upheld, even though there was no evidence of force or compulsion. Indeed, the evidence showed that the girl was a willing participant, but her consent was, by law, irrelevant. Similarly, in *R v. Rolfe* (1952), the defendant exposed himself to the victim, moved towards her and asked her to have sex with him. He was convicted on the grounds that the action of moving towards the victim constituted an assault, while the defendant's words and conduct constituted indecency.

20.10 Indecency

What constitutes indecency varies from case to case, and a precise definition is difficult to frame. However, the matter was considered by the House of Lords in *R v. Court* (1988). The defendant, a shop assistant, struck a twelve-year-old girl, who was in the shop, on the buttocks twelve times. He was asked why he had done this, and replied that he did not know, but thought it might be a fetish. Lord Ackner, who delivered the leading judgment, noted three categories of behaviour in an indecent assault case. First, there is behaviour that is inherently not indecent. For example, if X derives a sense of sexual pleasure by removing Y's coat, his secret pleasure does not alter the fact that removing a coat is not an indecent act. This kind of behaviour will not be sufficient for a charge of sexual assault. Second, there is behaviour that is inherently indecent. For example, if X removes all of Y's clothes without her consent, there are no explanations other than indecency that are consistent with his actions. This kind of behaviour will always be sufficient for a conviction. Third, there is behaviour that could be indecent depending on the circumstances. This third category would be judged according to the view of right-minded people, and should take into account the following factors: the relationship between the parties; whether they were relatives, friends or virtually complete strangers; and where, how and why the defendant had started this course of action. Only if the jury was sure that the circumstances led to an irresistible inference that the defendant had intended to commit the assault in an indecent manner should a guilty verdict be returned.

20.11 Consent

Consent may be a defence depending on two conditions: the age of the victim, and the nature of the assault and its consequences. As to the first condition, section 14 of the Criminal Law Amendment Act 1935 specifies that the minimum age at which a person can consent to a sexual assault is fifteen. Thus, if the victim is a fourteen-year-old girl, the fact that she consented to the assault, and indeed fully participated in it, is irrelevant. Such a child is conclusively deemed to be a victim; as Denham J. explained in *The People (DPP) v. WN* (2003), the 'child is never in control; in reality, defenceless. The abuse is never the child's fault.' Even if the victim is over the age of fifteen and consents to the activity, the consent may be deemed inoperative if the child had insufficient maturity to understand what he or she is consenting to. As to the second condition, consent to a sexual assault follows the same general rule as for all assaults (see section 19.10). Where the assault is minor and does not cause any harm, consent is a defence. Where harm is caused, however, the consent of the victim might be a defence depending on the degree of harm caused. As noted in section 19.10, section 3 of the Non-Fatal Offences Against the Person Act 1997 would seem to allow a defence of consent where the assault causes harm, and it seems that this defence is equally applicable to a charge of sexual assault. Section 4 of the same Act, however, does not allow a defence of consent where the defendant intentionally or recklessly inflicted serious harm on the victim. Therefore, providing the harm caused is not serious, as defined in section 1 of the 1997 Act, consent would seem to be a full defence. This alters the position that existed at common law, as illustrated by *R v. Brown* (1993). The defendant engaged in various forms of sadomasochism, and was convicted of assault under the OAPA 1861. He appealed on the basis that his 'victims' had been fully aware of his intentions and had consented to them. The House of Lords upheld the conviction by a majority on the grounds that consensual sexual gratification was no defence to assaults that caused bodily harm. The decision was essentially policy-based; the Lords were concerned that such activities were dangerous, and wanted to prevent young people from being enticed into them. They were also concerned to avoid asking juries to get involved in decisions relating to the degree of harm involved – whether it was actual bodily harm or grievous bodily harm. The defendant then appealed to the European Court of Human Rights on the grounds that their convictions interfered with the right to privacy enshrined in Article 8 of the European Convention on Human Rights. The court held unanimously that a State has a legitimate interest in the regulation of activities whose purpose is the infliction of physical harm. The determination of what is an acceptable level of harm is one primarily for each State. The Court concluded therefore that there had been no violation of the Convention.

20.12 *Mens Rea*

The *mens rea* of sexual assault appears to be in two parts. As far as the assault is concerned, the ordinary *mens rea* for assault is intention or subjective recklessness. However, there is an extra element of *mens rea* concerning the indecency part of the offence. In *R v. Court* (1988), the House of Lords held that the prosecution would have to show that the defendant intended to assault the victim in a way that right-minded persons would think indecent. The second element of *mens rea* is therefore intention. That being the case, it is difficult to see how recklessness could realistically be sufficient for the first element of *mens rea*; it is hard to see how the defendant could recklessly assault a person while intending to do so indecently. Consequently, as Lord Ackner concluded in *Court*, the prosecution must show:

> (1) that the accused intentionally assaulted the victim; (2) that the assault, or the assault and the circumstances accompanying it, are capable of being considered by right-minded persons as indecent; (3) that the accused intended to commit such an assault as is referred to in (2) above.

Sexual assault is therefore unusual among the various species of assaults in that it requires proof of intention.

20.13 Aggravated Sexual Assault

Section 3 of the Criminal Law (Rape) (Amendment) Act 1990 creates the offence of aggravated sexual assault. This offence is composed of a sexual assault together with serious violence or threats of serious violence, grave humiliation, degradation or injury. It is punishable by up to life imprisonment. The offence may be committed by either men or women. Whether or not the circumstances are aggravated as required by section 3 is objective; it is irrelevant that the defendant himself did not consider them to be so. The *mens rea* follows that for sexual assaults: an intentional assault, and an intention to subject the victim to serious violence or threats thereof, grave humiliation, degradation or injury. As far as consent is concerned, the same position applies as with sexual assault.

EXPLOITATIVE SEXUAL OFFENCES

20.14 Introduction

Irish law makes special provision for the protection from sexual exploitation of certain categories of people who are deemed to be especially vulnerable, principally children and people suffering from a mental disability. Thus, sections 1 and 2 of the Criminal Law Amendment Act 1935 make it an offence for a man to have sexual intercourse with a woman aged under seventeen years, sections 3 and 4 of the Criminal Justice (Sexual Offences) Act 1993 make it an offence to engage in buggery with persons under seventeen years and grossly indecent acts with males under seventeen years, respectively, while section 5 of the 1993 Act makes it an offence to engage in sexual intercourse with a mentally ill person. However, it is important to remember that the more general sexual offences, such as rape and sexual assault, can also be invoked to protect such people if appropriate, and the issue of multiple charges is considered below (see section 20.31).

20.15 Unlawful Carnal Knowledge of Young Girls

This offence is colloquially referred to as 'statutory rape'. The Criminal Law Amendment Act 1935 creates two separate offences involving sexual intercourse between a male and a girl under the age of seventeen. Section 1 applies where the girl was aged under fifteen at the time of the intercourse, and is punishable by up to life imprisonment. Section 2 applies where the girl was aged under seventeen at the time of the intercourse, and is punishable by up to five years' imprisonment for a first offence and up to ten years' imprisonment for a subsequent offence. Sexual intercourse has the same meaning here as for the offence of rape. Hence, proof of the slightest penetration of the girl's vagina is sufficient: *The People (Attorney General) v. Dermody* (1956).

The consent of the young girl is irrelevant to a charge under either sections 1 or 2. In *Attorney General (Shaughnessy) v. Ryan* (1960), the defendant argued that the girl had freely consented to his attempt to have intercourse with her. However, it was held that the purpose of the offence of statutory rape was to 'protect young girls, not alone against lustful men, but against themselves'. In other words, the offence of statutory rape exists to punish the exploitation of young girls: due to their tender years, girls under seventeen are perceived to be in danger of being manipulated by older men to their own disadvantage. Thus, the crucial element of this offence, unlike the offence of rape, is the age of the girl at the time of the intercourse, and precise evidence of this age must be tendered by the prosecution: *The People (Attorney General) v. O' Connor* **(1949)**. Once it is shown that the girl was aged under seventeen at the time of the intercourse, the offence is committed. The fact that the defendant genuinely (even reasonably) believed the girl to be over the age of consent is irrelevant as to the defendant's guilt. This was confirmed recently by the Supreme Court in *CC v. Ireland* **(2005)**. Thus, in *The People (Attorney General) v. Kearns* **(1949)**, the admission of a photograph as evidence that the young girl in question appeared to be over the age of seventeen was ruled relevant only as to sentence. The Law Reform Commission, in its 1988 *Report on Rape and Allied Offences*, criticised the application of strict liability to the offence of statutory rape. The Commission recommended that some form of reasonable belief defence should be introduced, especially for the section 2 offence. This recommendation has not been implemented. Thus, the policy of the Oireachtas of protecting young girls by imposing upon men an absolute risk of prosecution if their partner turns out to be under the age of consent remains in place. The extent of this risk was highlighted before the High Court in *Coleman v. Ireland* **(2004)**, in which the applicant pointed out that a conviction under the 1935 Act could follow even if a man had made a 'full and proper enquiry and been given false information by a precocious female.' While expressing some reservations, the High Court ruled that the necessity to protect young girls from exploitation constituted 'an objective justification for a derogation of the necessity to prove *mens rea*.'

The rationale for the offence of statutory rape is to punish the exploitation of young girls, but the language of the 1935 Act makes it clear that the offence is not limited to such exploitative situations. The offence may in fact be invoked where the parties were of a similar age, or even where the complainant instigated the intercourse. Thus, if a sixteen-year-old boy has sexual intercourse with his sixteen-year-old girlfriend at her request, he commits the offence of statutory rape. It may be thought inappropriate for people of this age to be engaging in sexual intercourse, but labeling a boy as a sex offender in these circumstances is surely objectionable. The Law Reform Commission recommended that such a scenario should not generally fall within the ambit of the offence. The Commission recommended that sexual intercourse between a male and a girl aged fifteen years or more should not be an offence unless the male was at least five years older then the girl or he was in a position of authority over her. Such a person was defined by the Commission as a person having responsibility for the education, supervision or welfare of a person under the age of seventeen. This recommendation also has not been implemented.

One final issue should be noted in relation to statutory rape. The offence seeks only to punish the sexual exploitation of young girls by males; the exploitation of young boys by older women is not subject to any special sanction. Thus, if a mature woman has sexual intercourse with a young boy, the most serious charge that can be brought against the woman is sexual assault, and in such a case, the boy's consent is fully operational if he is aged at least fifteen and is capable of understanding what he is consenting to. Young boys, therefore, do not have the same protection against sexual exploitation as do young girls. However, this discrimination in favour of young girls will almost certainly not be actionable on equality grounds. In the American decision of *Michael M. v. Superior Court of Sonoma County* (1981), the appellant challenged the constitutionality of a statutory provision similar to the 1935 Act. The US Supreme Court upheld the provision largely on the basis of the risk to young girls of pregnancy, a risk that clearly does not apply to young boys. Thus, the legislature was found to have a legitimate and objective reason to enact greater statutory protection for young girls from men than for young boys from women. A similar argument found somewhat reluctant favour with the High Court in *Coleman v. Ireland* (**2004**), which rejected a constitutional challenge to section 1 of the 1935 Act. The applicant argued that the absence of *mens rea* as to the complainant's age constituted an interference with a trial in due course of law. The High Court ruled that the 'societal values expressed in the terms of the Act of 1935 fall within the sphere of the Oireachtas', and that the Oireachtas had a legitimate interest in enacting special protection for young girls. While this was not an equality case as such, the High Court also noted that the equality provision of the Constitution, Article 40.1, does not require equal treatment in all circumstances, and it seems certain that an equality challenge to the statutory rape provisions of the 1935 Act would fail.

20.16 Buggery with Persons under Seventeen

Under the Offences Against the Person Act 1861, section 61, buggery was described as an 'abominable crime', punishable by penal servitude for life. It was a generic term that effectively covered sodomy between males and between males and females, and intercourse between people and animals, although it colloquially refers to intercourse between males. The offence could be committed with or without consent, but in any case, consent was not a defence, and the consenting party could be treated as being just as guilty as the other. However, it seems that where the consent was obtained through duress, a full defence would be granted: *R v. Bourne* (1952) – see section 6.6.

The position has changed considerably in recent years. Following the Supreme Court decision in *Norris v. Attorney General* (**1984**), upholding the prohibition on sodomy between consenting couples, an appeal was launched before the European Court of Human Rights (*Norris v. Ireland* (**1991**)) alleging a breach of

Article 8 of the European Convention on Human Rights, which guarantees a right to personal and marital privacy. This challenge was successful, but Irish law was not altered until 1993. Section 2 of the Criminal Law (Sexual Offences) Act 1993 abolished the offence of buggery between persons aged seventeen and over. The Act did not alter the pre-existing law on intercourse between persons and animals.

In addition to decriminalising buggery between adults, the 1993 Act created a new class of buggery offence that mirrors that of statutory rape. Under section 3, it is an offence, punishable by up to life imprisonment, to commit buggery on a person under the age of fifteen. The same provision makes it an offence to commit buggery on a person under the age of seventeen, which is punishable by up to five years' imprisonment for a first offence, and up to ten years for a subsequent offence. Additionally, section 3 makes express provision for attempts to commit these offences. Thus, an attempt to commit buggery on a person under the age of fifteen is punishable by up to five years' imprisonment for a first conviction, and up to ten years' imprisonment for subsequent convictions. The maximum penalties for attempts to commit buggery on a person under the age of seventeen are two years and five years, respectively. These offences are crimes of strict liability, meaning that, as with statutory rape, it does not matter that the defendant genuinely, and reasonably, believed that the person was over seventeen. It is also irrelevant that the person consented to the buggery.

The offences in section 3 are expressed in gender-neutral terms. Consequently, they can be committed between two males or between a male and a female. It is, however, a defence to show that the parties were married at the time, or that the defendant reasonably believed that he was married to the person that he buggered. So, if X is charged with buggering Y, the fact that X and Y are married will provide him with a full defence. The fact that the marriage is subsequently declared void will not affect this defence, as X had reasonable grounds for believing that he was married to Y. If, however, X was aware that the marriage was not valid, the defence would no longer apply, and he could be convicted.

20.17 Gross Indecency with Males under Seventeen

Gross indecency was originally prohibited by section 11 of the Criminal Law Amendment Act 1885 and could be committed consensually or otherwise. The Act prohibited the commission or attempted commission of any act of gross indecency between males, whether in public or in private. While it was not defined by the Act, gross indecency was taken to include any sexual act between males that did not constitute buggery, and was punishable by up to two years' imprisonment. The 1993 Act repealed section 11, and replaced it with a new offence in section 4: gross indecency with males under seventeen years of age. The new offence appears to be similar to the old one, except that it no longer applies to males over the age of consent. Again, no definition is given, but it is clear from pre-existing case law that some form of concerted activity is required. In other words, the indecent action must be *with* the other man rather than merely *towards* him. In *R v. Preece and Howells* (1976), the defendants were masturbating in two public toilet cubicles. There was a hole in the wall between the cubicles. One defendant admitted watching the other, but the second defendant denied watching the first. It was contended that for a charge of gross indecency with another man to be established, there had to be participation and co-operation between the two. This contention was upheld, although the convictions were also upheld on other grounds. Additionally, it seems that inactivity on the part of one man may be sufficient to constitute co-operation and participation. In *R v. Speck* (1977), the defendant was charged with committing an act of gross indecency with a child.[2] An eight-year-old girl had placed her hand on the defendant's groin, outside his trousers. The defendant had allowed her hand to remain there for approximately five minutes, during which time he had an erection. It was held by the Court of Appeal, upholding the conviction, that inactivity that amounted to an invitation to undertake or continue the act in question could constitute gross indecency.

The 1993 Act also prohibits attempts to commit acts of gross indecency with males under the age of seventeen. The attempt can take many forms, but it must be more than merely a description of the intended activity. In other words, the attempt must consist of some form of solid invitation to participate in grossly indecent conduct. In *The People (Attorney General) v. England* (**1947**), the defendant had a conversation with another man, during which he mentioned a house in which certain homosexual acts were practised. He told the other man where the house was, and the best time to visit. The defendant was convicted of an attempt to procure an act of gross indecency contrary to section 11 of the Criminal Law Amendment Act 1885. The conviction was quashed by the Court of Criminal Appeal on the grounds that the conversation did not constitute an attempt in that there was no proximate act (see section 15.3).

20.18 Child Pornography and Prostitution Offences

Specific legislative measures have been enacted in an attempt to deal with the sexual exploitation of children. The EU Joint Action against Trafficking in Human Beings and the Sexual Exploitation of Children, adopted on 24 February 1997, required all Member States of the EU to review their laws to ensure that that the trafficking of people for the purpose of sexual exploitation constituted a criminal offence. To discharge this obligation as regards children, the Oireachtas

---

2 The charge was made under section 1 of the Indecency with Children Act 1960 which made it an offence in England to commit any act of gross indecency with any child under the age of fourteen. Thus, while the Act was not gender-based, as is the law in Ireland, the essence of the offence – gross indecency – was identical.

enacted the Child Trafficking and Pornography Act 1998. The measures in this Act apply with respect to children under the age of seventeen. The most serious offences under the Act are contained in section 3. Section 3(1) is directed against the organisation or facilitation of child trafficking to, through or from the State, or the provision of accommodation for such children, for the purpose of sexual exploitation. Under section 3(2), it is an offence to take, detain, restrict the liberty of any child or use any child for the purpose of sexual exploitation, or to organise or knowingly facilitate any of these activities. Sexual exploitation for the purposes of section 3 is defined in the following terms:

(a) inducing or coercing the child to engage in prostitution or the production of child pornography,
(b) using the child for prostitution or the production of child pornography,
(c) inducing or coercing the child to participate in any sexual activity which is an offence under any enactment, or
(d) the commission of any such offence against the child.

It is noteworthy that for both offences, the prosecution must be able to prove knowledge on the part of the defendant; it is not sufficient to show that the defendant ought to have been aware that he was engaged in trafficking children for sexual exploitation. The maximum penalty for a conviction under section 3(1) is life imprisonment, while under section 3(2) the maximum penalty is fourteen years' imprisonment. Section 3 can clearly be employed against parents or guardians of children, but section 4 is specifically directed against such people. It provides that anyone who has the custody, care or charge of a child and uses that child for the production of child pornography is guilty of a specific offence.

Sections 5 and 6 are directed against the distribution and possession of child pornography. Child pornography is defined broadly in section 2(1) as follows:

(a) visual representations of a person who is or is depicted to be a child engaging in explicit sexual activity or witnessing such activity, or whose dominant characteristic is the depiction for sexual purposes of a child's genital or anal region;
(b) visual representations or descriptions which indicate or imply that a child is available for such purposes;
(c) audio or visual representations that advocate or encourage any sexual activity by children that constitutes an offence;
(d) audio representations of a child or a person depicted to be a child who is engaged in explicit sexual activity.

The precise means of production, transmission or conveyance is irrelevant and the definition specifically includes representations produced by or from computer graphics or any other electronic or mechanical means. Books that have not been banned and films or videos that have been properly certified are not included. Section 5 prohibits the production, distribution, printing, publication, sale, showing, import or export of child pornography. There is no requirement that these activities be done for profit, and section 5(2) specifically includes as a form of distribution the mere parting with possession of the material. Further, knowingly advertising child pornography is prohibited and this prohibition extends to any advertisement that is likely to be understood as indicating that the advertiser is involved in any of the foregoing activities. Thus, it is not necessary that the advertisement in question explicitly refers to child pornography; providing reasonable people would so understand the advertisement, the offence has been established. Finally, section 6 prohibits knowingly possessing child pornography unless such possession arises for stated official purposes. It is also a defence on a charge under section 6 to show that the possession was due to legitimate research. The burden of proving this defence rests with the defendant.

The Children Act 2001 also contains provisions directed at combating the sexual exploitation of children, and these provisions came into force in May 2002. Under section 248, it is an offence for a person having the custody, care or control of a child to allow that child to reside or be in a brothel. Section 249 makes it an offence for a person having the custody, care or control of a child to cause or encourage unlawful sexual intercourse or buggery with the child, or to cause or encourage the child to be sexually assaulted or to be prostituted. Under section 249(3), such causing or encouraging will be deemed to have occurred if the person in question knowingly allowed the child to consort with, or to enter or remain in the employment of, any prostitute or brothel-keeper. For the purposes of this section, a child is defined as a person under the age of seventeen.

20.19 Intercourse with Mentally Ill Persons

Intercourse with a person suffering from a mental illness is an offence under the Criminal Law (Sexual Offences) Act 1993. Section 5 creates three distinct offences:

(a) intercourse or attempted intercourse with a mentally impaired person, punishable by up to ten years' imprisonment for the full offence, or three or five years for first or subsequent convictions, respectively, for attempts;
(b) buggery or attempted buggery of such persons, punishable in the same way as for intercourse; or
(c) acts or attempted acts of gross indecency by a male with another who is mentally impaired, punishable by up to two years' imprisonment.

Mental impairment is defined in the same provision as a disorder of the mind that renders the person incapable of living an independent life or preventing serious exploitation. The Act also allows two defences. First, if the defendant is married to the mentally ill person or has reasonable grounds for believing that he or she is so married, there is no offence. Second, it is a defence to show that the defendant did not know and had no reason to suspect that the person was suffering from a mental impairment. In *R v. Hudson* (1965), considering an identical English provision, it was held that this requires a subjective test, but that the jury was entitled to take account of all the circumstances in order to prevent the acquittal of a defendant who deliberately failed to consider the mentally impaired person's condition. The jury should, however, also take account of any peculiarities in the defendant himself. So, if the defendant was of limited intelligence or suffered from a mental deficiency, these were factors that should also be considered.

INCEST

20.20 Introduction

Incest is an offence in which the defendant has sexual intercourse with a defined blood relative. Up to 1908, it was not a specific offence, but could amount to an offence under some other heading such as rape, the protection of minors or indecent assault. The Punishment of Incest Act 1908, however, made incest a specific offence in its own right for the first time. Under the Act, the male is conclusively seen as being the dominant party with the female being the passive party. Section 1 makes it an offence for a male to have intercourse with a female who is to his knowledge his granddaughter, daughter, sister or mother. Section 2 prohibits any female person aged seventeen or over from consenting to intercourse with her grandfather, father, brother or son while aware of the relationship. The terms 'brother' and 'sister' include half-brother and half-sister, whether through marriage or not. It should also be noted that there is no age requirement; it is irrelevant that both parties are adults. Indeed, in the event of a consensual incestuous relationship between two adults, and only one is charged, the other may be charged as an accomplice. Furthermore, no offence is committed by the woman under section 2 if the woman is under the age of seventeen, such women being conclusively regarded as victims rather than offenders. This applies even where there is evidence that the under-age woman intiated the encounter. So, if a sixteen-year-old girl persuades her sixteen-year-old brother to have intercourse with her, he commits incest, but she does not.

20.21 Consent

By definition, the male in an incestuous relationship is the principal, while the female is an accomplice. The consent of the woman is no defence to a charge of incest; indeed, if she is aware of her relationship to the man, giving consent may make her guilty of an offence under section 2. As the only evidence against the male defendant is likely to come from the female, the jury must be warned of the dangers of convicting only on the evidence of an accomplice, who may have an incentive to lie. Section 7 of the Criminal Law (Rape) (Amendment) Act 1990, which abolished this requirement in relation to sexual offences, does not apply to this situation because section 7 only relates to cases in which a warning had to be given due to the sexual nature of the offence charged. The requirement of a warning in relation to the dangers of the evidence of an accomplice is unaffected by the provision. If there is no consent, the male may be charged with rape. Where the female is the defendant's daughter and is aged under seventeen, the defendant may be charged with statutory rape as well as with incest (see section 20.31).

20.22 *Mens Rea*

The prosecution must prove that the defendant knew that his or her sexual partner was a blood relative as defined by the Act. Therefore, if X is charged with incest with his daughter but can show that he genuinely did not know that she was his daughter, he should be acquitted. Indeed, even where the evidence suggests that X did not care about the possibility of the woman being his daughter, i.e. he was reckless, he must also be acquitted. In either case, the fact that the girl was in fact X's daughter is irrelevant. Thus, this aspect of incest does not revolve around the issue of paternity. In *R v. Carmichael* (1940), the defendant was charged with three counts of incest with his youngest daughter. The defendant and his wife did not live together, but he visited her at weekends. They had a daughter together, E. However, the wife then began to associate with another man about nine months before the birth of a second daughter, S. The marriage ended, and the defendant married again, but this marriage also ended in failure. The defendant then began living with S, with whom he had three children. He argued that he was not the father of S, and wanted to show that his first wife had told him that S had been begotten by another man. He also wanted to show that he had told his second wife that he was not the father of S. The trial judge, however, refused to admit the evidence, and the defendant was convicted. It was held on appeal that this was valid evidence and went to the issue of the defendant's knowledge that his partner was his daughter. It should therefore have been admitted because if the jury accepted it, an acquittal was inevitable. The conviction was accordingly quashed. Similarly, in *R v. Baillie Smith* (1977), the defendant had intercourse with a female who was lying beside him in his bed. He claimed that he had believed her to be his wife, but it was in fact his thirteen-year-old daughter. This evidence was not included in the trial judge's direction to the jury, and indeed, the trial judge indicated, wrongly, to the jury that knowledge had been admitted by the defendant. As a result, the defendant appealed against his conviction on the basis that his defence had not been put to the jury. It was held by the Court of Appeal that the evidence went to the heart of the case and should have been included in the charge. The conviction was accordingly quashed.

20.23 Penalties

As originally enacted, the 1908 Act made incest under either sections 1 or 2 punishable by up to seven years' imprisonment. However, the maximum punishment available for an offence under section 1, i.e. incest by a male, has since been increased to twenty years' imprisonment by the Criminal Law (Sexual Offences) Act 1993, and again to life imprisonment by the Criminal Law (Incest Proceedings) Act 1995. The maximum sentence for an offence under section 2, i.e. incest by a female over the age of seventeen, has not been altered. Until recently, it was unlikely that the maximum sentence would be imposed if the defendant pleaded guilty. In *The People (DPP) v. FB* **(1997)**, the defendant had operated a form of 'customs post' under which his three daughters were prevented from leaving the house unless they engaged in sexual acts with him. He admitted his guilt from the beginning and pleaded guilty to a token number of charges of rape and incest (the actual number was said by the court to be 'so numerous that they cannot be quantified which certainly run into many hundreds'). The trial judge indicated his belief that a life sentence was appropriate, both due to the large number of offences and because the defendant would be released from a life sentence only when he was no longer a danger to society. However, the trial judge felt compelled by precedent to take account of the defendant's early guilty plea and so imposed a sentence of fifteen years' imprisonment on each count. Since that decision, section 29(2) of the Criminal Justice Act 1999 has been enacted to give the courts the power to impose the maximum sentence even where the defendant has pleaded guilty if there are exceptional circumstances which warrant such a sentence. Thus, if *FB* was decided today, the trial judge would probably have been in a position to impose a life sentence notwithstanding the guilty plea due to the huge number of offences and their egregious nature. However, the imposition of such sentences may have the effect of discouraging guilty pleas, so it seems likely that the courts will use this new power sparingly.

INDECENCY OFFENCES

20.24 Introduction

There is a considerable range of indecency offences punishable at common law or under particular statutes. For the most part, charges brought on the grounds of indecent conduct involve some kind of public sexual activity or the public exposure of sexual organs. The principal difficulty with these offences lies in the definition of indecency. The test for indecency is whether the conduct in question so offended recognised social standards of modesty that right-thinking people would deem the conduct indecent (see *R v. Court* (1988)). However, the courts have recognised the danger in such a vague test. In *Knuller v. DPP* (1972), Lord Simon of Glaisdale sounded this warning:

> 'Outraging public decency' goes considerably beyond offending the susceptibilities of, or even shocking, reasonable people. Moreover the offence is, in my view, concerned with recognised minimum standards of decency, which are likely to vary from time to time. Finally, notwithstanding that 'public' in the offence is used in a locative sense, public decency must be viewed as a whole; and I think the jury should be invited, where appropriate, to remember that they live in a plural society, with a tradition of tolerance towards minorities, and that this atmosphere of toleration is itself part of public decency.

Thus, the indecency offences should not be used simply as a mechanism by which a majority view of propriety is forced on minorities.

20.25   Indecent Exposure

Indecent exposure can be prosecuted at common law, under section 4 of the Vagrancy Act 1824 or under section 18 of the Criminal Law Amendment Act 1935. It typically, though not necessarily, involves the exposure by a man of his penis to a woman in a public place, and is commonly referred to as 'flashing'. In *Evans v. Ewels* (1972), the High Court ruled that indecent exposure as defined in the 1824 Act consisted of the exposure of any part of a man's body that might cause insult to a female if willfully, openly, lewdly and obscenely exposed to her. In this case, the defendant had exposed to a woman a portion of his stomach which was close to his genital area, having previously exposed his genitals to her. The High Court held that such conduct could constitute indecent exposure.

The offence must be committed in public. This is reflected in an old Irish case, *R v. Farell* (1862), where it was held that the act must be capable of being seen by more than one person. There is no necessity that the act was in fact seen by more than one person; that the act could have been seen by more than one person is sufficient. Thus, any exposure in a public place is capable of being seen by more than one person, even if there happened to be only one other person present. Further, it seems that the defendant himself need not be in a public place if his actions can be observed from a public place. In *McCabe v. Donnelly* (1982), the defendant exposed himself to a woman and began masturbating while standing naked in his own home at the window. It was held that where either of the parties was in a public place, the offence was committed.

20.26   Outraging Public Decency

Outraging public decency is an offence at common law. In *R v. Mayling* (1963), it was held that the prosecution must prove that the defendant had committed in public an act of such a lewd, obscene or disgusting nature as to constitute an outrage on public decency. Whether or not an action is lewd, obscene or

304

disgusting is a matter for the jury. Such acts are not necessarily sexual in nature. So, in *R v. Gibson; R v. Sylveire* (1990), the defendants had exhibited a model's head with an earring in each ear made from a freeze-dried human foetus. The Court of Appeal accepted that such a display was capable of outraging public decency. Many cases have involved indecent exposure, although as O'Malley notes, it is likely that such prosecutions would normally be taken under the Vagrancy Act 1824 or the Criminal Law Amendment Act 1935 (see below – section 20.27).[3] The act must be one that outrages public decency as well as being lewd, obscene or disgusting. This is also a matter for the jury to decide, and will probably vary from area to area, and from time to time. In *Knuller v. DPP* (1972), it was held that 'outrage' goes beyond merely offending or even shocking reasonable people, and will depend to a large degree on the circumstances of the incident. So, if X enjoys running naked through the fields around his house in a scarcely populated rural area, it may not be considered to be outrageous. If, however, X moves to Dublin city and runs naked through the streets, an entirely different conclusion may be reached. The act must also be done in public, a requirement that is defined in the same way as for indecent exposure. Finally, in *Gibson and Sylveire*, it was held that the prosecution must prove that the act was done deliberately. It is not, however, necessary to prove an intention to outrage public decency.

20.27 Section 18 of the Criminal Law Amendment Act 1935

Section 18 of the 1935 Act provides as follows:

> Every person who shall commit, at or near and in sight of any place along which the public habitually pass as of right or by permission, any act in such a way as to offend modesty or cause scandal or injure the morals of the community shall be guilty of [an offence].

This provision is drafted sufficiently widely so as to incorporate innumerable possible activities that might cause offence. The offensive act does not have to be done in public as such, but it must be visible from a place in which members of the public have a right to be. Unlike the common law offence of outraging public decency, it is sufficient on a charge under section 18 to show that the defendant's conduct merely offended members of the public. Consequently, this provision can be used for acts of a comparatively minor nature. It is likely that if a case involving facts such as those in *McCabe v. Donnelly* (see section 20.25) were to arise in this jurisdiction, it would be prosecuted under this provision.

---

3 O'Malley, *op. cit.*, p. 160.

20.28 Law Reform Commission Proposals

The Law Reform Commission, in its *Report on Vagrancy and Related Offences* (1985), recommended the abolition of all existing indecency offences, and their replacement with a new offence of intentionally committing an indecent act in a public place or where the act is seen by another person without that other person's consent. Under this proposal, even where the act was committed in private the offence could be established unless the other person consented to it. So, if X is watching television in Y's home, and Y deliberately enters the room naked, a prosecution could be brought. Under the present law, this would not be possible as the act was not capable of being seen by more than one person and did not occur in a public place. The *mens rea* of the proposed offence is in two parts. First, the act would have to be done deliberately. Second, the defendant should either know that the person who sees him does not consent to it or is reckless as to his consent. These recommendations have so far not been implemented.

FINAL POINTS

20.29 Position of the Complainant

The nature of sexual offences is such that often the prosecution must rely almost entirely on the complainant's evidence. This is true with all sexual offences, but especially in rape cases. Typically, there will be few witnesses and forensic evidence will often be inconclusive. Therefore, it is essential for the defendant to attack the complainant's testimony and her credibility if he is to successfully contest the charges against him. As a result, the complainant is in a particularly exposed position; it is not uncommon for rape complainants to describe the trial as being almost as bad as the rape itself. This view of the trial process has also been blamed for the apparently low rate of reports of rape to the gardaí. Since 1981, a number of legislative measures have been enacted to mitigate some of the harshness of the rape trial for complainants without compromising the defendant's right to confront his accuser.

Prior Sexual History

One of the principal complaints made by victims' rights groups about rape trials is the introduction by the defence of evidence concerning the complainant's prior sexual history. Such evidence, by its nature, is highly personal and intimate and its introduction in open court can be very embarrassing for complainants. Further, the relevance of this evidence is debatable; typically, the evidence is introduced more to paint an unflattering picture of the complainant in the minds of the jurors rather than to address an issue at trial. Section 3 of the 1981 Act, as amended by section 13 of the Criminal Law (Rape) (Amendment) Act 1990, requires the defence in a case involving a sexual assault offence to apply to the trial judge in the absence of the jury to introduce evidence of prior sexual history. The trial judge should give permission only if he is satisfied that it would be unfair to the defendant to refuse to allow the evidence. Unfair in this context means that the judge must be satisfied that the defendant might be convicted if the evidence is not heard and that the jury might reasonably acquit the defendant if the evidence is introduced. If leave is given to introduce the evidence, the trial judge retains his power to prevent particular questions being asked or answered.

The practical effect of these restrictions is unclear due to an absence of published research. However, the Sex Offenders Act 2001 provided further protection for complainants from the introduction of prior sexual history evidence by inserting section 4A into the 1981 Act. Under section 4A, if the defendant wishes to apply for leave to introduce evidence of the complainant's prior sexual history, his application should be made before the trial starts or as soon as practicable. Further, the complainant has a legal entitlement to be informed by the prosecution of the defendant's application, to be heard before the judge makes his decision on the application and to be legally represented for that purpose. The cost of this representation will be borne by the State under the provisions of the Civil Legal Aid Act 1995.

Anonymity

Section 7 of the 1981 Act, as amended by section 17 of the 1990 Act, provides that once a person has been charged with a sexual assault offence, no matter may be published that might lead the public to identify the complainant unless authorised by law. The purpose of this provision is to provide a measure of reassurance to complainants who will be required to give highly intimate evidence in open court. However, the defendant or anyone else against whom the complainant might give evidence can apply prior to the trial to the trial judge to lift this restriction providing two conditions are satisfied: that the restriction should be lifted to induce potential witnesses to come forward, and that the defendant's defence would be adversely affected if the restriction is not lifted. The defendant may also make his application after the trial has begun, but in addition to satisfying these two conditions, he must also show a good reason for not making his application prior to the trial. The trial judge may also vary the prohibition if he is satisfied that the prohibition is imposing a substantial and unreasonable restriction on the reporting of the proceedings at the trial and that such a variation is in the public interest. However, this power cannot be exercised solely on the basis of the outcome of the trial. Thus, a trial judge cannot lift the restriction on reporting matters that might identify the complainant simply because the defendant has been acquitted.

It must also be noted that section 8 of the 1981 Act imposes a similar restriction on publishing matters likely to lead to the identification of the defendant once charges have been laid. However, this restriction ends if the defendant is convicted. In *Independent Star Ltd. v. O' Connor* (2002), the defendant sought to prevent the release of his name after he had pleaded guilty to several counts of sexual assault. He argued that releasing his name might lead to the identification of the complainant, which might in turn discourage future complainants from coming forward. The High Court ruled that the only rights of anonymity enjoyed by the defendant were dealt with by section 8, which explicitly removes such rights after conviction. That future complainants might be discouraged from coming forward was a policy matter and could not justify continuing the anonymity of the defendant without legislative authority.

The foregoing discussion relates to the trial of sexual offences generally, but special anonymity provisions have been enacted in relation to the trial of incest charges. The Punishment of Incest Act 1908 imposed an absolute anonymity requirement in relation to complainants and defendants in incest cases, a requirement that cannot be lifted by trial judges. Nor does the anonymity of the defendant in incest cases end with his conviction as in rape cases; the rationale here is that as incest can only occur within the immediate family, the identification of the defendant would likely lead to the identification of the complainant. There is no provision for complainants to waive their anonymity even if doing so would be in their best interests. The anonymity requirement in incest cases was so complete that in *The People (DPP) v. WM* (1995), it was held that members of the press could be excluded from the trial and prevented from reporting whether a sentence had been imposed. This situation was clearly at odds with the constitutional requirement that justice be dispensed in public. Thus, the Criminal Law (Incest Proceedings) Act 1995 was enacted to allow for the attendance of the press at incest trials. The 1995 Act did not affect the absolute anonymity requirement.

20.30 Corroboration

In *The People (DPP) v. Slavotic* (2002), Fennelly J. noted that allegations of sexual offences typically derive from an incident alleged to have occurred in private and to which the only evidence available will likely come from the complainant and the defendant. To convict the defendant in these circumstances would mean relying greatly upon the complainant's testimony alone. Traditionally, the common law has been wary of placing such reliance on the testimony of one person, and developed an approach to corroboration that was specific to allegations of sexual offences. Trial judges were required to determine whether there existed any evidence that was legally capable of amounting to corroboration, and juries were then instructed to determine whether such corroboration in fact existed. Corroboration was defined in *R v. Baskerville* (1916) as 'independent testimony which affects the accused by connecting or tending to connect him with the crime. In other words it must be evidence which implicates him, that is, which confirms in some material particular not only the evidence that the crime has been committed, but also that the prisoner committed it.' Similarly, in *The People (DPP) v. Cornally* (**1994**), O'Flaherty J. defined corroborative evidence as evidence 'of a material nature independent of the injured party's version of events that tends to inculpate the Accused in the crime with which he is charged.' Thus, corroborative evidence must do more than merely bolster the complainant's allegations; it must positively link the defendant to the crime charged. So, in *R v. Sutton* (1967), the Court of Appeal ruled that the presence of semen stains on the complainant's clothing did not corroborate the allegation of rape; the stains showed merely that sexual intercourse had occurred. Further, if certain evidence was capable equally of supporting the testimony of both the complainant and the defendant, then the jury should not be instructed that this evidence is capable of corroborating the complainant's testimony. In *Slavotic*, the trial judge told the jury that a portion of the defendant's statement was capable of corroborating the complainant's testimony, but the Court of Criminal Appeal ruled that the statement was equally open to an innocent interpretation and therefore should not have been viewed as potential corroboration.

If no corroboration existed, the jury was still entitled to convict the defendant, but the trial judge had to warn them of the dangers of doing so. This warning was required in all cases involving allegations of sexual offences that were not corroborated by independent testimony, and a failure to provide such a warning constituted a misdirection. Further, in *The People (Attorney General) v. Cradden* (**1955**), the Court of Criminal Appeal indicated that this warning should be given even if there was evidence legally capable of constituting corroboration. It was for the jury to determine whether the complainant's allegations had been corroborated, and the jury was free to reject any potentially corroborating evidence. Thus, in such a situation there would be no corroboration and the jury should be aware of the danger of returning a conviction in such circumstances.

Implicit in the corroboration rule was a belief that complainants in cases of sexual offences were more willing to lie than in other kinds of cases. One of the most explicit judicial examples of this sentiment was provided by Ritchie J. in the Canadian decision of *Hornsburgh v. R* (1967):

> In any event it appears to me to be clear that the damage to be guarded against in cases of sexual offences is that the complainant, through a motive of spite, vengeance, hysteria or perhaps gain by way of blackmail, may make false accusations against which the accused, by reason of the nature of the charges, has no means of defence except his own unsupported denial.

Given such a rationale, it is not surprising that victims' groups and feminist scholars have with some success directed particular anger at the corroboration rule. In England, section 32(1) of the Criminal Justice and Public Order Act 1994 abolished the corroboration rule in its entirety. In *R v. Makanjuola* (1995), the Court of Appeal ruled that the effect of this provision was that a corroboration warning in sexual offences cases was necessary only where there was an evidential reason to believe that the evidence of a particular complainant was unreliable. Where no such evidential basis existed, the complainant in a sexual case should be regarded as no more reliable or unreliable as a complainant in any other kind of case. The court stressed that the mere fact that the complainant had made an allegation of a sexual nature was not a sufficient reason to give a corroboration warning.

In Ireland, changes have also been made to the common law corroboration rule. The Law Reform Commission, in its *Report on Rape and Allied Offences* (LRC 24–1988), recommended only that the warning should be discretionary rather than mandatory, and this recommendation was enacted in section 7 of the 1990 Act. Despite this provision, the courts did not initially alter their practices in relation to corroboration. In *The People (DPP) v. Molloy* (1995), Flood J. ruled that, notwithstanding section 7, it would be 'prudent practice for the trial judge to warn the jury that unless they are very very satisfied with the testimony of the Complainant that they should be careful not to convict in the absence of corroborative evidence.' However, it seems that the courts' practice has now changed. In *The People (DPP) v. JEM* (2001), the Court of Criminal Appeal ruled that the policy and practice behind section 7 was similar to that behind the English legislation. Accordingly, Denham J. specifically endorsed *Makanjuola* as a guide to the interpretation of section 7. Thus, a corroboration warning should be given by an Irish court now only if there is an evidential basis for believing that the complainant's testimony is unreliable. Further, in *Slavotic* Fennelly J. warned that 'a judge should not decide routinely to give [a corroboration] direction in every case', as to do so 'would undermine the basis of the statutory change.'

20.31 Multiple Charges

A particular incident may be classified as a number of offences. For example, intercourse with a girl of fifteen could give rise to a charge of rape or unlawful carnal knowledge of a young girl. If the girl was also the defendant's daughter, a charge of incest could be added. In *O'B v. Pattwell* (1994), the defendant had been charged with multiple offences, all arising from the same incident. The Supreme Court held that this practice was permissible, but that the jury must be carefully instructed as to each offence. In particular, O'Flaherty J. ruled that the offences of rape and statutory rape must be carefully distinguished: 'There must be a great difference between rape attended by circumstances of force and degradation and a case of having unlawful carnal knowledge with a young girl who consents to the act of intercourse. Both are reprehensible offences but one is more reprehensible than the other.' It was further held that a defendant who is charged with multiple offences arising out of the same incident can be convicted of only one offence.

One last point should be made. In *The People (Attorney General) v. Coughlan* (1968), it was stated by the Court of Criminal Appeal that the prosecution should, when deciding on which charges to bring, remember the effect on the victim of having to testify. Therefore, where the facts disclose, for example, either rape, unlawful carnal knowledge or incest, the charge should be the one that will cause the victim the least distress in terms of testifying. In *Pattwell*, the Supreme Court agreed with this statement, with the proviso that the prosecution could and should insist on the greater charge if necessary, irrespective of the effect the charge might have on the victim.

20.32 Sex Offenders Act 2001

The principal purpose of the Sex Offenders Act 2001 was to make better provision for dealing with sex offenders following their release from prison in an effort to reduce repeat offending. To that end, several new post-release procedures were introduced by the Act.

Sex Offenders' Register

Under Part 2 of the 2001 Act, what amounts to a Sex Offenders' Register was established. Conviction for certain specified sexual offences including rape, aggravated sexual assault, sexual assault and, subject to some exceptions, sexual offences involving children, carries an automatic post-release obligation on the offender to provide certain information to the gardaí. This obligation applies to offenders convicted of relevant sexual offences after the commencement of the Act, as well as to those who were serving sentences for such offences at the time the Act came into force. In *Enright v. Ireland* (2003), the High Court ruled that the Act did not retrospectively impose a penalty on offenders who had already been convicted. The court held that the notification requirements of the 2001 Act did not constitute a criminal penalty as such; rather, these requirements were merely a consequence of the conviction that was designed to ensure public safety. However, in *The People (DPP) v. NY* (2002), the Court of Criminal Appeal accepted that a judge could have regard to the notification requirements in deciding on an appropriate sentence, especially in cases in which the offender constituted little danger to the public. The court also pointed out, however, that the 'additional protection for the public laid down by the Oireachtas [in the 2001 Act] cannot be undermined by the courts reducing punishment for sex offenders who constitute a danger.' Thus, if the court is satisfied that the offender could pose a real danger to the public upon his release, the implications of being subject to the notification requirements should carry little weight in imposing sentence. Greater weight can legitimately be given to those implications in cases in which no such danger exists.

The 2001 Act requires notification to the gardaí of the kind of information needed to keep track of the offender, and includes the offender's name and home address and any changes thereto, his intention of leaving the State for more than seven days and the address at which he will be staying while abroad, and his return to the State. This obligation will not generally apply to consensual teenage sexual activity providing the victim is aged at least fifteen and the offender is no more than three years older; thus, if a sixteen-year-old boy has intercourse with his sixteen-year-old girlfriend, he commits the offence of statutory rape but is exempted from the notification requirements. Similarly exempted are cases involving convictions for sexual assault and incest, providing the victim was aged at least seventeen and the offender was not sentenced to a term of imprisonment.

In cases in which the obligation of notification does apply, section 8 sets out a graduated scale of periods during which the obligation will last. The minimum period is five years in cases in which either a non-custodial sentence or a fully suspended custodial sentence was imposed. A custodial sentence of six months or less carries an obligation of notification for seven years, a period that is increased to ten years if the sentence is for imprisonment for up to two years. If an offender receives a custodial sentence of more than two years, his obligation under Part 2 will last potentially for the rest of his life. These periods are halved in cases involving offenders aged under eighteen at the time of sentencing. Where the obligation is indefinite, the offender may apply to the Circuit Court after a period of ten years to discharge his obligation on the grounds that the common good no longer requires that he remains subject to them. A breach of the notification requirements constitutes a summary offence in its own right.

Post-Release Supervision

Part 5 of the 2001 Act requires the court sentencing a sex offender to consider whether post-release supervision should be required. In making its decision, the court is required to consider the need for such supervision, bearing in mind the need to protect the public from serious harm from, or the commission of further sexual offences by, the offender, and the need to rehabilitate or further rehabilitate the offender. The sentencing court is specifically granted the power to hear evidence on these matters from any party. If the court decides that such supervision is required, it may impose a sentence consisting of a custodial period to be followed by a specified period of supervision by the Probation and Welfare Service. However, the total period of the sentence, i.e. the period of imprisonment and supervision, may not exceed the maximum term of imprisonment permitted for the offence in question. The sentencing court is also permitted to attach conditions to the supervision period. In *The People (DPP) v. Muldoon* (**2003**), the defendant had pleaded guilty to charges of being in possession of child pornography and was sentenced to two and a half years' imprisonment as well as eleven years of post-release supervision. However, the trial judge had also included a condition that during the supervision period, the defendant was not to have personal control of a computer or access to the internet. The defendant appealed against the severity of this condition on the grounds that it severely limited his ability to earn a livelihood in his field of information technology. The Court of Criminal Appeal accepted that this condition would have drastic consequences for the defendant, but ruled that the condition was necessary to protect the public and was 'a restriction which he has brought about himself'.

Sex Offenders' Orders

Part 3 of the Act introduced a new civil order known as a Sex Offenders' Order which may be sought from the District Court by a Garda Superintendent. The order may be granted if the subject of the order has been convicted of a relevant sexual offence, and his behaviour in the community has been such that there are reasonable grounds to believe that the order is required to protect the public from serious harm caused by the subject. Section 16(5) provides that the protection of the public from serious harm means 'protecting a member or members of the public from death or serious personal injury, whether physical or psychological, which would be occasioned if the respondent were to commit a sexual offence at a time subsequent to the making of the application under this section.' If the court is satisfied, on a balance of probabilities, that these conditions have been met, an order may be granted that prohibits the sex offender from doing specified things, and the order will last for at least five years or for such longer period as the court may specify. A breach of a Sex Offenders' Order is an offence that carries a maximum penalty of five years' imprisonment and a fine. However, section 16(4) provides that the order cannot restrict the offender any further than is required to protect the public from serious harm. Thus, if a convicted sex offender has been loitering near a national school, a prohibition from approaching schools would be a reasonable restriction. However, an order that prevented the offender from leaving his house for any reason during school hours would go beyond what was necessary to protect the public.

Information to Employers

Part 4 of the Act imposes an obligation on sex offenders to notify prospective employers of their conviction for a sexual offence when seeking or accepting a position, a regular and necessary part of which involves unsupervised access to children or mentally impaired people. Breach of this requirement is an offence that carries a maximum penalty of five years' imprisonment.

20.33 Further Reading

Alldridge, 'Sex, Lies and the Criminal Law', (1993) 44 *NILQ* 250.
Fennell, 'Reform of the Law on Rape', (1988) 10 *DULJ* 109.
Hanly, 'Corroborating Rape Charges', (2001) 11 *ICLJ* (4) 2.
Home Office, *Setting the Boundaries*, HMSO, 2000.
Law Reform Commission, *Consultation Paper on Rape,* 1987.
———, *Report on Rape and Allied Offences,* LRC 24–1988.

————, *Consultation Paper on Child Sexual Abuse,* 1989.

————, *Report on Child Sexual Abuse*, LRC 32–1990.

————, *Report on Sexual Offences against the Mentally Handicapped*, LRC 33–1990.

McGrath, 'Two Steps Forward, One Step Back: The Corroboration Warning in Sexual Cases', (1999) 9 *ICLJ* 22.

O'Malley, *Sexual Offences: Law, Policy and Punishment*, Dublin: Round Hall Sweet & Maxwell, 1996.

Reed, 'An Analysis of Fraud Vitiating Consent in Rape Cases', (1995) 59 *JCL* 310.

Ryan, "Queering' the Criminal Law: Some Thoughts on the Aftermath of Homosexual Decriminalisation', (1997) 7 *ICLJ* 38.

Temkin, *Rape and the Legal Process*, 2nd ed., Oxford: Oxford University Press, 2002.

Temkin and Ashworth, 'Rape, Sexual Assault and the Problems of Consent', [2004] 328 *Crim LR*.

CHAPTER TWENTY-ONE

ABORTION

21.1 Introduction

Until recently, abortion under any circumstances has always been illegal in Ireland, prohibited by the Offences Against the Person Act 1861. However, the position was complicated by the Supreme Court's decision in *Attorney General v. X* **(1992)** by allowing abortions in some situations. While related issues, such as the right to travel to another country to have an abortion and the right to receive information concerning abortion, have been settled by referenda, the central issue of abortion itself (the so-called 'substantive question') has been left unaltered since *X*. This situation is exacerbated by the fact that there is very little case law on the subject, leaving much of the interpretation of the OAPA 1861 to conjecture.

Section 58 of the OAPA 1861 prohibits the unlawful administration or use by a pregnant woman or anyone else of poisons or other noxious things, or any other instrument or means, in order to cause an abortion. In both cases, the person performing the abortion must act with the intent of procuring the abortion. Thus, if a pregnant woman were to take a poison with the intent of committing suicide, there would be no offence under section 58. Interestingly, the section also specifies that a person other than the mother who attempts to procure an abortion commits an offence even where the mother is not actually pregnant. Accordingly, it would appear that, contrary to *Haughton v. Smith* (1973), physical impossibility is no defence to a charge under section 58 of attempting to cause an abortion. The punishment for the offence is up to life imprisonment.

Section 59 of the 1861 Act prohibits the unlawful supply or procurement of any poison, noxious thing, instrument or other thing with knowledge that it is intended to be used for an abortion, again irrespective of whether or not the woman is actually with child. The penalty for an offence under this section is imprisonment for between three and five years.

Abortion in Ireland was dealt with entirely under these two sections until 1983. In the US, the landmark decision of the federal Supreme Court in *Roe v. Wade* (1973), which legalised abortion in that jurisdiction, built on earlier decisions which had extended the right to privacy to include a right to access to contraception. Following the Irish Supreme Court's decision in *McGee v. Attorney General* **(1974)**, which legalised contraception in Ireland on the basis of the right to privacy, there were concerns that future court decisions might follow the US lead. To prevent this, a referendum was held in 1983 on the Eighth Amendment to the Constitution which proposed to amend Article 40.3 to read as follows:

(3) The State acknowledges the right to life of the unborn and, with due regard to the equal right to life of the mother, guarantees in its laws to respect, and, as far as practicable, by its laws to defend and vindicate that right.

The Amendment was accepted by a two-thirds majority, and has formed the basis of Irish law ever since. Much of the consideration that has been given to this provision has arisen under the related issue of the dissemination of abortion-referral information. The central issue of abortion itself has been relatively ignored. Two referenda have been held in relation to the decision of the Supreme Court in *X*. A proposal to remove the threat of suicide as a ground for abortion was rejected in 1992. Ten years later, the electorate again narrowly rejected a proposal to prohibit abortions except where they occurred during or as a result of a procedure needed to prevent the death of the mother except through suicide.

21.2   The Offence of Abortion

An abortion is committed, contrary to section 58, either where a poison or noxious substance is unlawfully administered, or an instrument is unlawfully used, with the intent of inducing a miscarriage. The use of the term 'instrument' is fairly self-explanatory and is also very wide. It is not necessary to show that the instrument was of a medical nature. The statute specifies that any instrument may be sufficient if it is used unlawfully with the intent to induce an abortion. Therefore, the use of ordinary household implements such as kitchen knives is sufficient to commit the offence.

Where a chemical is used, it is essential that the substance taken is either poisonous or noxious. Therefore, if the defendant administered a substance which she believed to be poisonous or noxious, but was in fact neither, no offence is committed. In *R v. Cramp* (1880), poison was defined as 'that which when administered is injurious to health or life'. In that case, the chemical in question was oil of juniper, which was harmless in small quantities. It was held that if the substance was a recognised poison, then even harmless doses would be sufficient to establish the offence. Oil of juniper was a poison, and was therefore enough for the purposes of section 58.

The definition of a 'noxious thing' was considered in *R v. Marcus* (1981). The defendant put eight sedative and sleeping tablets into a bottle of milk, and the question arose as to whether or not the tablets constituted a noxious thing. Expert evidence established that the dosage was too small to cause even sedation let alone sleep. Hence, little harm would be caused unless the person taking the dose tried to do something potentially hazardous such as driving a car. It was argued by the defence that for a thing to be considered noxious, it must be noxious in itself. A substance that is in itself harmless cannot be made noxious by virtue of the quantity in which it is administered. It was further argued that for something to be noxious, it must be harmful in the sense of harmful to the body; harm only to the mental faculties would not be sufficient. It was held, however, by the Court of Appeal that whether or not a substance is noxious depends not only on its intrinsic qualities and nature, but also on the quantity in question. The court went on to state that:

> The jury has to consider the evidence of what was administered ... both in quality and in quantity and to decide as a question of fact and degree in all the circumstances whether that thing was noxious. A substance which may have been harmless in small quantities may yet be noxious in the quantity administered.

As an illustration, the court gave the example of lacing a glass of milk with alcohol. If the glass was then given to an adult, it might not be noxious, but it might well be if it was given instead to a child. As to the second argument, the court held that it is not necessary that the substance be capable of causing bodily injury for it to be noxious. A noxious thing is something different from, and less serious than, a poison. Thus, a noxious thing is something that, in terms of quantity or quality, is injurious, hurtful, harmful or unwholesome.

Finally, the poison or noxious thing must be either administered or caused to be taken. It is not necessary to show that the defendant actually delivered the substance. It is sufficient that some act or omission on the part of the defendant allowed the substance to be taken by the mother.

21.3 Procuring Poisons, Noxious Things or Instruments

The use of the word 'procuring' in section 58 means to bring about an abortion. However, in the context of section 59, it means to obtain the material necessary to bring about an abortion, with the intention of so doing. In *R v. Mills* (1963), the defendant was visited by a pregnant woman who wished to have an abortion. While in the defendant's flat, they discussed the procedure to be followed. At that point, the police raided the flat and found a kettle boiling on the stove that contained various instruments that could be used to bring about an abortion. The defendant was convicted under section 59 of procuring instruments with intent to procure a miscarriage. The point at issue in the appeal was the meaning of the word 'procure'. It was argued that the word in its natural sense means to obtain from someone else, and that this should be the meaning given to the word in the context of section 59. Furthermore, the section uses the phrase 'procure or supply', which indicates even more strongly that it must be shown that the defendant obtained possession of the instruments from someone else. This argument was expressly adopted by the Court of Appeal, which held that as the defendant already had possession of the instruments, he could not be said to have procured them, and his conviction under section 59 was quashed.

21.4 Unlawful Actions

In both sections 58 and 59, the defendant's actions must be unlawful. This requirement was analysed in *R v. Bourne* (1938). A fourteen-year-old girl had been raped, and was pregnant as a result. The defendant was a surgeon who carried out an abortion in order to safeguard the mental health of the girl. It was held that it was lawful to perform an abortion to save the life of the mother; such an action was not capable of being considered unlawful. The defendant must have acted in good faith, and the prosecution bore the burden of proving that he did not have such good faith. There was, however, a considerable discussion as to the distinction between a danger to life and a danger to health. The opinion of the court seems to have been that there is no clear distinction; a danger to health can result in a danger to life, and a jury should place a reasonable interpretation on the words 'danger to life':

> If the doctor is of the opinion, on reasonable grounds and with adequate knowledge, that the probable consequences of the pregnancy will be to make the woman a physical or mental wreck, the jury are entitled to take the view that the doctor who, under those circumstances and in that honest belief, operates, is operating for the purpose of preserving the life of the mother.

Furthermore, a doctor is not obliged to wait until the mother is actually in immediate danger of death. In other words, where the doctor is of the opinion, based on his knowledge and experience, that the child cannot be delivered without risking the mother's life, then he has a right and a duty to perform the abortion sooner rather than later.

Whether the *Bourne* decision represents the law in Ireland depends on the impact of the Eighth Amendment. The Amendment guarantees equal respect for the lives of the unborn and the mother. The precise effect of the Eighth Amendment was considered by the High and Supreme Courts in the highly controversial case of *Attorney General v. X* (1992). A fourteen-year-old girl was made pregnant by a forty-one-year-old neighbour. She wished to travel to England to have an abortion, and had on a number of occasions indicated that she viewed suicide as a solution to her problems. The Attorney General sought an injunction to prevent her from travelling, pursuant to the Eighth Amendment. In the High Court, Costello P. held that the rights of the unborn child had to be balanced with those of the mother. In effect, the court had to balance the possibility of death to the mother with the certainty of death to the unborn child. In those circumstances, the threat to the child was greater, and therefore required a higher level of protection. As a result, the injunction was granted. The decision was appealed by the girl, with the financial assistance of the State. Before the Supreme Court, the Attorney General conceded that the Eighth Amendment permitted abortion in order to save the mother's life, but argued that the danger had to be immediate or inevitable. However, the court rejected the Attorney

General's contention, holding that it was too narrow. An abortion could be performed within the terms of the Eighth Amendment if there was a real and substantial risk to the mother's life, which included a risk that the mother would commit suicide. The court rejected the view that an abortion could be performed in circumstances where there was a risk to the mother's health. Thus the distinction between a danger to life and a danger to health, rejected in *Bourne*, was applied in *X*. Furthermore, the court also specifically rejected the view expressed in *Bourne* that the mother's life was more precious than that of the child. Abortion was permitted to save the mother's life, not because her life is more precious, but because, in balancing the rights of the mother with those of the child, the courts should have regard to the mother's position in the family, the people upon whom she is dependent and those who depend on her.

As a result of the *X* decision, Irish law will allow an abortion to be performed where there is a real and substantial risk to the life of the mother, even where that risk is caused by suicide. A risk to the health of the mother is not sufficient, although it must be said that the view in *Bourne*, that there is no clear distinction between health and life, is likely to be adopted in practice. Thus, where a doctor believes that there is a danger to the mother's health such that her life might be endangered, an abortion is permissible. It is not, however, clear whether the doctor would be duty-bound to perform the abortion. Finally, it would be nonsensical to suggest that the abortion is lawful where the mother's life is endangered, but the procurement of the materials necessary for that abortion is unlawful. Thus, by extension, a charge under section 59 of the 1861 Act must also result in an acquittal where the mother's life was in danger.

21.5 *Mens Rea*

In the case of charges under both sections 58 and 59 of the 1861 Act, the defendant must be shown to have acted with the intention of inducing an abortion. In the case of a person other than the mother acting to cause an abortion, it is irrelevant that the 'mother' is not actually pregnant. In *R v. Hillman* (1863), it was held, in relation to a charge under section 59, that it is the intention of the person who obtains the material that is crucial, not that of the mother. This is an important point, and applies equally to section 58; it is the intention of the person doing the administering or procuring, as the case may be, that is crucial. Therefore, suppose X procures a poison intending to give it to Y who is pregnant, for the purpose of inducing an abortion. However, Y has no intention of having an abortion, and is in fact looking forward to having a baby. The fact that X's actions are in vain is irrelevant; he has procured a poison with the intention that it be used to cause an abortion, and he is therefore guilty under section 59.

In most instances, intention could be shown with relative ease. However, there are situations, such as cancer of the uterus, in which the mother is suffering from some condition that requires medical intervention, but the required intervention will have the effect of incidentally killing the unborn child. Under the definition of oblique intention (see section 4.3), where a defendant knows that his actions are virtually certain to bring about an undesired result, it may be inferred that he intended that consequence. If this rule were to be applied literally to the example given above, where the mother is suffering from cancer of the uterus and requires immediate treatment, by giving the necessary treatment it could be inferred that the doctor intended to cause an abortion as he would know that the child's death would be a virtual certainty. Hence, the doctor could theoretically be convicted under sections 58 or 59, as appropriate. However, it is almost certain that the doctor's actions would be excused under the *X* decision. Where, however, the condition suffered by the mother is not serious, treatment that will almost certainly result in the death of the child would not be so excused.

21.6 Related Issues

Two other issues relating to abortion should be considered in the light of the Supreme Court's decision in *X*. The first is the so-called right to information, and the second is the right to travel. The right to information arose from a series of cases involving the Society for the Protection of Unborn Children (SPUC) and various groups and individuals who wished to disseminate abortion-referral information. Beginning with *Attorney General (SPUC) v. Open Door Counselling* **(1988)** and again in *SPUC v. Coogan* **(1989)** and *SPUC v. Grogan* **(1989)**, the Irish courts consistently held that the activities of the defendants constituted assistance in the destruction of unborn children. As such, their actions were prohibited by the Eighth Amendment, and injunctions were granted against them. Following the *X* decision, a referendum was held on the issue which would allow for the dissemination of abortion-referral information as regulated by law. This referendum was accepted, and was followed by the Regulation of Information (Services Outside the State for Termination of Pregnancies) Act 1995. This Act allows for non-directive referral information to be made available to pregnant women by certain categories of people, providing the pregnant women are counselled as to the full range of options available to them. Failure to provide such counselling is an offence.

The right to travel to another country to avail of abortion services that are legal in that other country was at the heart of the *X* case. The Supreme Court held that while a right to leave this country did exist within the Constitution, it must give way to the unborn child's right to life. While the issue of European law was raised before the Supreme Court, it was not necessary to decide the matter as a solution lay within domestic law. A further referendum was held which would specifically allow a right to travel to avail of services lawful in other countries. This referendum was also accepted.

21.7 Further Reading

Beaumont, 'The Unborn Child and the Limits of Homicide', (1997) 60 *JCL* 86.

Cox, 'Causation, Responsibility and Foetal Personhood', (2000) 51 *NILQ* 579.

Kingston, Whelan and Bacik, *Abortion and the Law*, Dublin: Round Hall Press, 1997.

McAuley, 'Abortion and the Law', (1983) 1 *ILT* 8.

PART V

OFFENCES AGAINST PROPERTY

CHAPTER TWENTY-TWO

THEFT

22.1 Introduction

The law relating to offences against property has recently been reviewed and consolidated in the Criminal Justice (Theft and Fraud Offences) Act 2001. This statute was built mainly on the recommendations of the Law Reform Commission in its *Report on the Law Relating to Dishonesty* (1992) and the Government's Advisory Committee's *Report on Fraud* (1993). The 2001 Act swept away the myriad forms of larceny contained in the Larceny Act 1916 and replaced them with a single composite offence of theft which was drafted widely so as to incorporate several related offences under the 1916 Act, such as embezzlement and fraudulent conversion. The Act also updated the law on other property offences, including robbery, burglary and handling stolen property. These offences will be considered in the following chapters; this chapter focuses on the new law of theft.

Theft is now an offence under section 4(1) of the 2001 Act, which provides as follows:

> [A] person is guilty of theft if he or she dishonestly appropriates property without the consent of its owner and with the intention of depriving its owner of it.

The maximum penalty for theft is ten years' imprisonment and an unlimited fine. Additionally, under section 56 the sentencing court is entitled to order restitution of the stolen property or the payment of a sum of money representing the value of the stolen property taken from any money that was in the defendant's possession when he was arrested.

There are several constituent elements of the offence of theft that require further elaboration. There is no reported Irish case law as yet, but reference can be made to decisions of the English courts, as the 2001 Act follows the general approach of the English Theft Act 1968.

22.2 Dishonesty

Section 2(1) of the 2001 Act defines dishonesty as acting without a claim of right made in good faith. The offence of larceny under the Larceny Act 1916 contained a similar element, so pre-2001 case law on this element of the offence remains good law. In *The People (DPP) v. O'Loughlin* (1979), a quantity of stolen machinery was found on the defendant's land. At trial, the defendant was refused permission to introduce evidence that he had been owed a debt by the machinery's owner and had believed that he was entitled to take the machinery in lieu of that debt. The Court of Criminal Appeal ruled that this evidence should

325

have been admitted. The court stated that a claim of right would be established if the defendant had honestly believed that he was 'entitled to [take the machinery] … even though his claim to be so entitled was not well founded in law or in fact.' The issue was whether the defendant honestly believed his claim, not whether the claim was justified. This was a matter of fact for the jury to decide. Further, in the earlier case of *The People (Attorney General) v. Grey* **(1944)**, it was suggested that the issue of claim of right did not have to be specifically raised by the defendant; if the evidence raised the possibility of such a claim, and it was in the interests of justice to do so, the trial judge must properly instruct the jury on the issue.

The foregoing remains an accurate statement of the law under the 2001 Act. However, section 4(4) provides that when considering whether a claim of right existed, the jury must consider the presence or absence of reasonable grounds for such a belief in conjunction with any other relevant evidence. This provision is identical to the provision contained in section 2(2) of the Criminal Law (Rape) Act 1981, which arises when a defendant in a rape trial claims an honest belief in the consent of the complainant (see section 20.6). The mere fact that a defendant's claim of right was unreasonable is not of itself grounds for holding that the claim was not honestly held. However, the more unreasonable the claim, the more likely it will be that the jury will find that the claim was not genuine.

22.3 Appropriation

Under the Larceny Act 1916, the offence of larceny was committed when a person took and carried away another person's property. A long series of cases demonstrated that taking and carrying away meant taking possession of the property and physically moving it from its original location. So, in *Wallis v. Lane* (1964), the defendant moved boxes from one part of a truck to another in preparation to remove them from the truck entirely. This was found to constitute taking and carrying away. Similarly, in *The People (Attorney General) v. Mills* **(1955)**, it was held that once the defendant had lifted a woman's purse from her handbag, he had taken and carried it away for the purposes of larceny. Thus, the 1916 Act took a wide view of carrying away; moving the property even slightly from its original location was enough. However, the definition of larceny was limited to the physical movement of the property; any other interference with the rights of the property owner could not be charged as larceny. The 2001 Act revolves around the appropriation of property, the most common example of which remains the physical removal of property without the owner's consent. However, the concept of appropriation is much wider than this.

Appropriation is defined in section 4(5) as the usurpation or adverse interference with the proprietary rights of the owner of the property. The proprietary rights of an owner are not defined in the Act, but presumably they refer to the legal and equitable rights normally associated with ownership, such as the right to possess, use, consume, move, lend and sell the property. The precise proprietary rights of an owner in any particular case will depend on the degree of ownership to which a person is entitled. So, if X has been given a company car by his employer, X has the right to possess and use the car, but he does not have the right to sell it. If X tries to sell the car, then he will have interfered with his employer's proprietary rights in the car and may be charged with theft. The Act refers to either a usurpation of or an adverse interference with the owner's proprietary rights. A usurpation occurs when one person unlawfully steps into the shoes of another. So, if X is leaning against Y's car and purports to sell the car to Z, X has usurped Y's proprietary rights. He has in effect claimed to hold all the rights that properly belong to Y. Usurpation therefore involves the complete seizure of another's proprietary rights. However, it is not necessary that a person seize all the rights of another, as the Act makes clear that an appropriation will also occur if a person adversely interferes with the proprietary rights of the owner. Thus, it is only necessary to show that the defendant interfered with any of the owner's rights to the owner's detriment. So, in *R v. Morris* (1983), the defendant had switched the price label on one product with the label on another, cheaper product and had then paid the cheaper price at the checkout. Lord Roskill confirmed that it was unnecessary to prove that the defendant had interfered with all of the owner's rights; proof that he had interfered with any of the owner's rights was sufficient.

A special provision has been made for a trustee who in the course of business holds property in trust for or on behalf of more than one owner, but who uses that property for his own benefit. In such a case, the property has been transferred consensually, but section 4(3) provides that appropriating the property in this manner has occurred without the consent of the owner; there was 'a genuine entrustment in which the fiduciary ownership has been lawfully obtained but which, so to speak, subsequently went wrong' (*The People (Attorney General) v. Singer* (**1960**)). Under the 1916 Act, a charge of larceny in a case where trust funds had been misappropriated would have failed, the correct charge being one of fraudulent conversion under section 20; by virtue of section 4(3) of the 2001 Act, such a case is now properly dealt with as theft. So, in *The People (Attorney General) v. Heald* (**1954**), the defendant was employed by an order of nuns as matron of a nursing home. In that capacity, she received the sum of £2,000 from two elderly women whom she admitted to the home. The defendant paid this money directly into her own bank account and did not inform her employers of the transaction. The defendant was acquitted of larceny but was convicted of fraudulent conversion. By virtue of section 4(3) of the 2001 Act, such a defendant could now be convicted of theft. The prosecution must be able to prove that property was given to the defendant for the benefit of others and that the transaction occurred in the course of a business. This entrustment does not have to be specifically proven; in *The People (Attorney General) v. Cowan* (**1958**), the Supreme Court ruled that such facts could be implied from circumstances such as a solicitor receiving money for a client. In such circumstances, it would be unnecessary to prove that the client had specifically authorised receipt of the money. Further, if the prosecution shows that there is a deficiency in the property held by the defendant in trust and that the defendant has not provided a satisfactory explanation for the deficiency, there will be a presumption under section 4(3)(c) that the deficiency in question has been appropriated without the owner's consent. This provision clearly shifts the legal burden of proof onto the defendant to prove that he appropriated the property with the owner's consent.

In *Morris*, Lord Roskill ruled that the interference must be adverse to the owner's interests, and suggested that a practical joker who switched price labels merely for fun or to cause confusion would not appropriate property for the purposes of the Theft Act 1968. It was when the label-switching was coupled with taking the product from the shelf that an appropriation came into being. However, in *R v. Gomez* (1993), Lord Keith stated for the majority that any interference would suffice, adverse or not. Thus, it was possible for an appropriation to arise even with the consent of the owner. The practical joker referred to by Lord Roskill in *Morris* had, on this view, committed an act of appropriation and whether he was guilty of theft would depend on his *mens rea*. In Ireland, the definition of appropriation in section 4(5) of the 2001 Act makes it clear that the defendant's actions must have adversely affected the owner's rights, and the definition of theft in section 4(1) makes it clear that the appropriation must have been done without the owner's consent. Accordingly, *Morris* seems to be more illustrative of Irish law than *Gomez*. However, it is submitted that Lord Roskill's practical joker has committed an adverse interference with the proprietary rights of the owner in that by switching the price labels, the joker has adversely interfered with the owner's right to determine the conditions upon which he is willing to sell the property, and has done so without the owner's permission. Therefore, the joker's actions must be considered to constitute an appropriation. If he has sufficient *mens rea*, he could be successfully prosecuted for theft. This point illustrates the fact that at its extreme edge, the concept of appropriation is so wide that the offence of theft under the 2001 Act might depart from the popular understanding of the offence: merely switching price labels would not usually be considered theft. Further, one proprietary right enjoyed by owners is undoubtedly the right to private enjoyment of the property; therefore, arguably, the mere touching of another person's property constitutes an adverse interference with his proprietary rights. If this is done with the appropriate *mens rea* (see section 22.6), the person who has touched the property could be convicted of theft. So, if X touches the door handle of Y's car to see if it is open, and does so with the intent of stealing the car, X has committed a theft, i.e. an adverse interference with Y's proprietary rights over his car with the intention of depriving Y of the car, even though X has not actually taken anything in any real sense of the word. X has really done no more than attempt to steal the car, if even that. Thus, the offence of theft is now so wide that it may overlap with situations more properly dealt with as attempts.

22.4 Consent of the Owner

The dishonest appropriation must occur without the consent of the owner. An owner is defined in section 2(4) as a person who has possession or control of the property or any person who has in it any proprietary right or interest other than an equitable interest arising only from an agreement to transfer or grant an interest. This is a wide definition and includes anyone who has a legitimate interest in the property. So, if X lends his property to Y for one night, and the property is stolen by Z, Z has stolen from both X (the person with legal title to the property) and Y (the person who was in possession and control of the property). It would seem, therefore, that as with the Larceny Act 1916, it is possible for a person to be convicted of the theft of his own goods if another person has an interest in them. In *Rose v. Matt* (1951), the defendant gave a clock to a seller as security for the price of goods he had just purchased. It was agreed that if the defendant had not paid the full purchase price within one month, full title to the clock would pass to the seller. The defendant later returned and took the clock without paying the purchase price. The King's Bench ruled that the defendant had given the seller a special interest in the clock which made the seller the owner of the clock for the purposes of the offence of larceny. A similar result would arise if this case was tried today under the 2001 Act.

Further specific instances of ownership are also given in section 2(4). So, if property has been given in trust, the person who is entitled to enforce the trust is considered the owner of the property. A person who gives property to another to be used in a particular way is the owner as against the person who received the property. A person who is entitled to restoration of property from another who has obtained the property by a mistake is considered the owner of the property to the extent of the obligation to make restoration, as against the person under that obligation. Finally, the property of a corporation sole shall belong to that corporation even if the corporation is vacant.

To successfully convict a person of theft under the 2001 Act, the prosecution must be able to show that the appropriation occurred without the consent of the owner of the property. As in all cases involving consent, the consent must have been freely given to be effective. Section 4(2) specifically states that consent obtained by deception or intimidation is not consent for the purposes of the 2001 Act. Deception is defined in section 2(2) as arising in any of the following circumstances:

(a) where the defendant has created or reinforced a false impression held by the owner, including a false impression as to law, value or intention or other state of mind,

329

(b) where the defendant prevents the owner from acquiring information which would affect the owner's judgment of a transaction, or

(c) where the defendant fails to correct a false impression which he previously created or reinforced or which he knows is influencing another person to whom the defendant stands in a fiduciary or confidential relationship.

So, if X convinces Y that Y's painting is worthless and Y gives the painting to X and it turns out to be very valuable, the consent that Y gave to the transfer of the painting will not be operative. Section 2(2) therefore incorporates into the definition of theft activity that would have been dealt with under the Larceny Act 1916 as obtaining by false pretences. However, if Y simply makes an error as to the value of the painting without any input from X, and X benefits from that error, no theft has occurred.

Occasions may arise when an owner becomes aware of plans to steal his property and decides to go along with those plans in order to trap the thieves. Some care should be exercised in such schemes: if the owner does more than merely facilitate the thieves, he may be taken to have consented to the appropriation of his property. In the old case of *R v. Egginton* (1801), the owner of the goods to be stolen merely facilitated the thieves by allowing them access to his property where the goods had been left in a prominent position. The owner was found not to have consented merely because he made the purported theft that much easier. However, in *R v. Turvey* (1946), the owner of the goods instructed his employee to go along with the planned theft by actually handing over the goods. Lord Goddard C.J. ruled that *Egginton* should be distinguished; the fact that in this case the owner had handed over the goods made all the difference and consent had been given. Similarly, in *R v. Miller; R v. Page* (1965), the owner of the goods instructed his employee to take the truck to the place where the thieves were going to steal its contents, and the employee helped the thieves unload the truck. It was held that the taking of the goods was not done against the owner's will. Consequently, the charge of larceny had to fail.

If the owner gives only a limited form of consent to appropriate property, actions in excess of that consent may be prosecuted as theft. A good example is provided by the facts of ***The People (DPP) v. Morrissey* (1982)**. The defendant went to his local supermarket to buy some meat from the meat counter. He was given the quantity of meat that he requested but then left the shop without paying for it. The fact that the meat was handed over to his possession did not mean that he was free to walk out of the supermarket without paying for it. The High Court held, endorsing an earlier English decision, *Martin v. Puttick* (1968), that the assistant at the meat counter had the authority to give only a limited consent to possess the meat rather than actual title to it. Every customer knows that he or she must approach the checkout to pay for the goods. By walking out of the shop without paying for the meat, the defendant had in effect exceeded the limit of the consent given to him by the owner to possess the meat and had therefore stolen it.

Finally, section 4(2) creates what amounts to a defence of honest belief in consent. Under this provision, there is no appropriation without the consent of the owner in the following circumstances:

(a) if the defendant believed that he had the owner's consent to appropriate the property or that the owner would have so consented had the owner known of the appropriation and the circumstances in which it was appropriated, or

(b) if the defendant appropriates the property in the belief that the identity of the owner cannot be discovered by taking reasonable steps, except where the property came to the defendant as a trustee or a personal representative.

So, if a young man takes his mother's car while she is away, believing that she would allow him to do so, no theft is committed even if it subsequently transpires that his belief was erroneous. Similarly, if X finds a sum of money on the side of the road and he keeps it, believing that that the owner of the money could not be identified, then no theft occurs. In either case, the fact that the belief was erroneous, i.e. the mother would not have allowed her son to take her car, or the identity of the owner of the money could have been easily discovered, is irrelevant providing the belief was genuine. However, section 4(4) provides that in considering whether these beliefs were genuine, the jury must consider the presence or absence of reasonable grounds for those beliefs. As with the belief in a claim of right (see section 22.2), the fact that the belief was unreasonable does not of itself invalidate the defence granted by section 4(2), but the more unreasonable the belief, the more likely it is that the jury will conclude that the belief was not genuinely held.

22.5 Property

For the purposes of the 2001 Act, property is defined in section 2(1) as 'money and all other property, real or personal, including things in action and other intangible property.' There is no stated requirement that the property have value as there was under the 1916 Act, but valueless property is rarely the subject of a theft anyway. In any case, the previous requirement of value was only notional: in *R v. Perry* (1845), the defendant took a void cheque, which obviously had no practical value. The defendant's conviction for larceny was upheld because he had stolen a piece of paper.

For the specific purposes of the offence of theft, section 5 sets out a list of property that will not be considered stolen. Most importantly, under section 5(1), if a person acquires property for value in good faith, the fact that the property was stolen will not make that person guilty of theft. So, if X sells a stolen car to Y, and Y is unaware that the car was stolen, Y will not be convicted of theft. However, the protection offered to Y under section 5(1) requires that he act in good faith when purchasing the car; thus, if Y closed his eyes to suspicious circumstances, he cannot be said to have acted in good faith and can therefore be prosecuted for theft.

Section 5(2) provides that land (not including an incorporeal hereditament) or anything forming part of land cannot generally be stolen. However, there are several exceptions to this general exemption:

(a) if a person with a fiduciary duty to another in respect of land, i.e. a trustee, personal representative, one who holds a power of attorney or a liquidator of a company, appropriates the land or anything part of that land in breach of his position of confidence, he can be prosecuted for theft;

(b) if a person who is not in possession of the land appropriates anything forming part of that land by severing it or causing it to be severed from the land, or appropriates anything forming part of that land after it has been severed, he can be prosecuted for theft; or

(c) if a person has possession of land under a tenancy agreement or a licence and appropriates a fixture or structure that was let or licensed to be used with the land, he may be prosecuted for theft. This applies equally to a person whose tenancy or licence has expired.

Further, under section 5(4), the picking of mushrooms, other forms of fungus, flowers, fruit or foliage that is growing wild on any land will not constitute theft even where the person doing the picking is not in possession of the land in question, unless the picking was done for reward, sale or other commercial purpose. So, if X picks some wild berries from Y's land for his own consumption, X cannot be charged with theft. However, if X picks wild berries from Y's land and then offers those berries for sale to Z, the exception offered by section 5(4) will not apply and X can be prosecuted for theft.

Finally, section 5(5) provides that wild animals, tamed or untamed, will be generally regarded as property. However, an untamed creature not ordinarily kept in captivity (including the carcass of such an animal) cannot be stolen unless it has been made the possession of another and this possession has not been lost or abandoned.

22.6 *Mens Rea*

The prosecution must prove that the defendant appropriated the property with the intention of depriving the owner of that property. Section 4(5) provides that such deprivation may be permanent or temporary. This is a major departure from the law as it was under the 1916 Act. Under the previous Act, the prosecution had to prove that the defendant intended to permanently deprive the owner of his property. So, joyriding (the taking of another person's car for a limited time) could not be prosecuted as larceny unless it could be proven that the person taking the car intended either not to return it or to destroy it. No such difficulties exist under the 2001 Act – a temporary appropriation of property is theft even if there is an intention to return the property. It would seem that appropriation of property for any period of time is sufficient. Further, there is no requirement that the owner actually *feel* deprived of the property; indeed, he may be unaware that his property has been appropriated at all. So, if X takes Y's solid-gold watch in order to impress his girlfriend, it will be no defence for X to argue that Y was not using the watch, or that he did not miss it, or that he did not even know it had been taken.

Two specific instances of intention to deprive the owner of his goods are set out in sections 2(4)(b) and (d). The former provision states that if property is being held in trust, the person who has the right to enforce the trust is to be considered the owner of the property held in the trust. An intention to defeat the trust shall be regarded as an intention to deprive the owner of the trust property. Section 2(4)(d) provides that if property has passed to another person by mistake and this other person has an obligation to make restoration to the rightful owner of the property, then an intention not to make restoration shall be regarded as an intention to deprive the rightful owner of the property.

There is no requirement that the thief intends to benefit from the appropriation. Thus, appropriating property with the intention of giving it away or destroying it still constitutes theft. In *R v. Wynn* (1849), the defendant was employed by the post office to sort letters. He tried to flush two letters down a toilet in order to hide a mistake he had made, thereby avoiding penalties attached to such mistakes. He argued that as he had not sought to derive any benefit from his action, he had not committed a larceny. It was held, however, that taking the letters and attempting to destroy them for whatever purpose was a larceny.

If the property came into the defendant's possession lawfully, the position of the defendant is different under the 2001 Act to that under the 1916 Act. Under the 1916 Act, lawful original possession defeated a charge of larceny. In the old case of *R v. Leigh* (1800), the defendant took possession of goods to prevent their destruction by a fire, but then refused to return them. It was held that as the defendant's intention at the time of taking the goods had been innocent, she could not be convicted of larceny. Under section 4 of the 2001 Act, however, the situation is different; the basis of theft is now an appropriation of the property rather than the taking and carrying away of property. Such an appropriation occurs when a person adversely interferes with the proprietary rights of the owner of the property. Hence, a refusal to return property constitutes an appropriation, and if at that time the defendant had an intention to deprive the owner of his property, the defendant will have committed theft. So, if the facts of *Leigh* arose today, the original removal of the property would be lawful – indeed, it is likely that the defendant would have had the implicit consent of the owner to move his property in order to save it – but the subsequent refusal to return the property would constitute an appropriation. If the defendant had at that time the necessary *mens rea*, the charge of theft would be made out.

Finally, a conditional intention to deprive the owner of his property may now be sufficient for a charge of theft, although such an intention was not sufficient for a charge of larceny under the 1916 Act. In *R v. Easom* (1971), the defendant rummaged through the contents of a woman's handbag. Apparently finding nothing of value, he left the contents of the bag intact. The Court of Appeal ruled that the defendant's intention was conditional best, i.e. he intended to take and keep property only if he found something in the handbag that he deemed worth taking. This was found to be insufficient to support a charge of larceny (which at the time required an intention to permanently deprive the owner of her property). Under the 2001 Act, there is no doubt that the defendant committed an appropriation in the sense that he adversely interfered with the woman's proprietary rights to her handbag and its contents by taking possession of them for a short period of time. Therefore, the defendant must have intended to temporarily deprive the woman of her property at least for as long as it took for him to determine whether there was anything in the handbag worth taking. On this basis, it would seem that the defendant in *Easom* could be convicted of theft under the 2001 Act.

22.7 Further Reading

Gardner, 'Appropriation in Theft: The Last Word', [1993] *Crim LR* 195.

Halpin, 'The Test for Dishonesty', [1996] *Crim LR* 283.

Law Reform Commission, *Report on the Law Relating to Dishonesty*, LRC CP43-1992.

Shute, 'Appropriation and the Law of Theft', [2002] *Crim LR* 450.

Williams, 'Temporary Appropriation Should be Theft', [1981] *Crim LR* 129.

CHAPTER TWENTY-THREE

ROBBERY

23.1 Introduction

Until 2001, robbery was an offence under section 23(1) of the Larceny Act 1916, as inserted by section 5 of the Criminal Law (Jurisdiction) Act 1976. Section 14 of the Criminal Justice (Theft and Fraud Offences) Act 2001 re-enacted the offence of robbery in terms virtually identical to those contained in the earlier legislation. The only difference in the 2001 Act is the use of gender-inclusive language. The offence of robbery is defined now in the following terms:

> A person is guilty of robbery if he or she steals, and immediately before or at the time of doing so, and in order to do so, uses force on any person or puts or seeks to put any person in fear of being then and there subjected to force.

Upon conviction on indictment, the maximum sentence for robbery is life imprisonment. The alternative verdict of guilty of assault with intent to rob that was contained in the 1916 Act as amended has not been re-enacted.

In essence, robbery is a theft that was brought about through the use or threat of force. Consequently, the prosecution must prove each of the elements of the offence of theft (see Chapter 22). If X forcibly appropriates property under a claim of right, his appropriation will not be considered dishonest and a charge of robbery must fail. In *R v. Robinson* (1977), the Court of Appeal confirmed that the claim of right defence applied to robbery and that it was satisfied if the defendant honestly believed that he was entitled to take the property. There was no requirement that the defendant honestly believe that he had the right to use force to take the property.

23.2 Force

The definition of robbery traditionally required proof of the use or threat of violence to effect a theft. However, this requirement was replaced in the Criminal Law (Jurisdiction) Act 1976 with the use or threat of force, and the requirement of force rather than violence was re-enacted by the 2001 Act. It seems that the effect of this change from violence to force has been to increase the scope of the offence of robbery, in that a theft using even very minor force may now be prosecuted as robbery instead of theft. In *R v. Dawson and James* (1976), the defendants jostled a person while stealing his wallet. It was held by the Court of Appeal that this could constitute force for the purposes of robbery. Whether or not force was used is a matter of fact for the jury to decide using its 'common sense and knowledge of the world'. It is a concept that is fully understood by juries, and so does not usually require any explanantion. Similarly, in *R v.*

Clouden (1987), the defendant was found to have used force when he wrenched a shopping basket from a lady's hand. His argument that there was insufficient resistance on the part of the woman was dismissed. Consequently, force for the purpose of robbery should be interpreted in the same way as force for the purpose of assault: the slightest degree would seem to be sufficient. In many cases, then, the prosecution is likely to be in a position to charge a defendant with robbery under section 14 rather than theft under section 4. This in turn raises the stakes for potential thieves: the maximum penalty for larceny from the person is ten years' imprisonment, while for robbery it is life imprisonment.

23.3 Threats of Force

It is not necessary that force is actually used. Where a defendant 'puts or seeks to put any person in fear of being then and there subjected to force', a robbery is committed. As with assault, it is not necessary that the defendant actually 'fears' the imminent force in the sense that he is scared; the word 'fear' in this context simply means 'belief'. The threat must be of immediate force. Thus, if X tells Y, 'give me your money or I'll kill you tomorrow', no robbery has been committed. X can, however, be prosecuted for demanding money with menaces under section 17 of the Criminal Justice (Public Order) Act 1994 (more commonly known as blackmail – see sections 26.2–26.5).

The threat may be expressed or implicit in the circumstances. In *The People (DPP) v. Mangan* (1995), two elderly nuns were in a car which had stopped at a set of traffic lights. The defendant smashed the rear passenger window and grabbed a handbag that was on the back seat of the car. The defendant's conviction for robbery was upheld despite the fact that the force had been directed at the car window rather than either of the occupants. The court reasoned that smashing the window allowed the defendant to grab the handbag, but it also 'put in fear the occupants of the car so that they would be affected with fear and be unable to react so as to be in a position to do anything about the attack.' Thus, the court concluded that the use of force against the car window had a dual purpose and the jury was entitled to find that the threat requirement of the offence of robbery had been met.

23.4 Purpose of Force or Threats

It is not sufficient for the prosecution to prove merely that force or threats were used; it must also be shown that the force or threat of force was used to effect the theft. In *R v. Shendley* (1970), it was held that there is no such thing as robbery without violence. If the jury is satisfied that the defendant stole property but is not satisfied that he used force to effect the theft, he is guilty only of theft. Thus, in *R v. Donaghy* (1981), the defendants threatened a taxi-driver in order to make him take them to London. Once he had done so, they stole his money. They were acquitted of robbery apparently on the grounds that the threats were not used in order to steal, but simply to get a ride to London.

23.5 Coincidence

The force or threats must be used either before or at the time of the theft. In effect, the force or threats must form part and parcel of the theft. In general, therefore, if X steals a woman's purse, and then hits her simply for pleasure, he has not committed a robbery, but should be charged with theft and assault. Difficulties can arise, however, in deciding when the theft has actually been accomplished. For example, suppose X steals a woman's purse and then pushes her to the ground in order to escape. Has he used force to effect the theft? In *R v. Hale* (1979), the defendants tied up their victim to facilitate their escape. It was held by the Court of Appeal that robbery could be a continuing action, beginning with the theft and ending with the force. The court went on to hold:

> We also think that [the jury was] entitled to rely upon the act of tying [the victim] up provided they were satisfied (and it is difficult to see how they could not be satisfied) that the force so used was to enable them to steal. If they were still engaged in the act of stealing the force was clearly used to enable them to continue to assume the rights of the owner ...

In the final analysis, whether or not the theft had been completed was a matter of fact for the jury to decide. Under this authority, it would seem that, in the example given above, X could be convicted of robbery. However, this conclusion seems to run contrary to the literal wording of section 14, which states that the force or threats must be used to accomplish the theft and must occur before or at the time of the theft. The theft is accomplished once an appropriation of the property has occurred with the requisite *mens rea*; in the example above, X has appropriated the property *before* the force is used. Common sense dictates that escape is part and parcel of most robbers' plans, but escape is not part of the formal definition of theft. On a literal interpretation of section 14, then, X should be acquitted of robbery, and the better prosecutorial strategy would be to charge him with theft and assault. However, such a result can be criticised for introducing impossibly fine distinctions into the definition of robbery. For example, if X had pushed his victim to the ground first and then taken her purse, there would be no question that he had committed a robbery. There is no moral distinction between these two examples, and any observer would simply conclude that in both cases, X had robbed a woman of her purse. Accordingly, the approach of the Court of Appeal in *Hale* has much to recommend it.

23.6 Target of the Force or Threats

The force or threats can be directed at any person, whether the person whose property is being stolen or another. Therefore, if X threatens Y's child in order to force Y to hand over money, a robbery is committed. Alternatively, suppose X is in the process of taking a woman's purse without using force, but Y comes to her assistance and X uses force against Y to accomplish the theft, X can also be convicted of robbery.

It is not necessary for the target of the force or threats to be present at the scene of the theft. For example, suppose X and Y break into Z's house. X holds Z's wife and children hostage while Y takes Z to the bank to empty his account. Both X and Y are guilty of robbery. The only condition that must be established is that the threat is continuing at the time of the theft. Thus, if X and Y merely threaten to break into Z's house and hold his wife and children hostage, there is at some point no robbery as there is no present threat. X and Y would, however, be guilty of demanding money with menaces – see sections 26.2–26.5.

23.7 *Mens Rea*

The *mens rea* of the offence is in two parts, reflecting the two elements of the offence. In the first place, as the prosecution must prove that the defendant stole property, the defendant must be shown to have intended to deprive the owner of his property (see section 22.6). However, there must also be an element of *mens rea* in relation to the use of force or threats. Whether or not there must be proof of intention is unclear, but this seems likely. The force or threats must be used to effect the theft; it is difficult to see how this could come about except through an intentional desire on the part of the defendant. Consequently, it seems that reckless force will not be sufficient for a charge of robbery. This accords with the decision of a Divisional Court in *Corcoran v. Anderton* (1980), in which two youths agreed to steal a woman's handbag. One of them tugged at the handbag, causing the woman to fall and to release the bag. She screamed, and the youths ran away, leaving the bag behind them. The court held that this constituted robbery as the defendants had stolen the handbag with 'the intention . . . to steal, that is to say to take the handbag, by force if necessary, away from [the woman] and to permanently deprive her of that handbag and its contents.'

23.8 Further Reading

Andrews, 'Robbery', [1966] *Crim LR* 524.
Ashworth, 'Robbery Reassessed', [2002] *Crim LR* 851.

338

CHAPTER TWENTY-FOUR

BURGLARY

24.1 Introduction

The modern offence of burglary is dealt with under section 12(1) of the Criminal Justice (Theft and Fraud Offences) Act 2001, and replaces section 23A of the Larceny Act 1916, as inserted by section 6 of the Criminal Law (Jurisdiction) Act 1976. Section 12 of the 2001 Act states:

A person is guilty of burglary if he or she –
(a) enters any building or part of a building as a trespasser and with intent to commit an arrestable offence, or
(b) having entered any building or part of a building as a trespasser, commits or attempts to commit any such offence therein.

There are thus two forms of burglary as set out in paragraphs (a) and (b). The first form covers a situation in which the defendant enters a building as a trespasser for the purpose of committing an arrestable offence. The second form arises more opportunistically: the defendant has already entered a building as a trespasser and then decides to take advantage of the situation to commit an arrestable offence. The maximum penalty for either form of burglary upon conviction on indictment is fourteen years' imprisonment.

24.2 Entry

The first element of both forms of burglary is entry into a building or part of a building. At common law, a number of highly technical rules had developed as to what constitutes entry. In effect, once the prosecution had shown that the defendant had inserted any part of his body, no matter how small, into a building, he was deemed to have entered that building. Thus, if X inserted a finger through a broken window, he had entered the building. It is not clear to what extent these rules still survive. In *R v. Collins* (1972), the defendant, naked except for his socks, climbed a ladder to a windowsill, intending to commit a rape. The young woman in the room mistook him for her boyfriend and invited him in. To what extent he had entered the room prior to the invitation was unclear, but it was held that the prosecution would have to show that he had made an 'effective and substantial' entry, thus implying a rejection of the common law rules. In *R v. Brown* (1985), the defendant had inserted the top half of his body through a broken shop window. It was held that the defendant's whole body did not need to be inside the building, and that proof that an effective entry had been made was sufficient. In *R v. Ryan* (1996), the defendant had become trapped with only his head and right arm inside the building. It was held that the fact that his entry was insufficient to complete his purpose was irrelevant. As Smith and Hogan note, the effect of *Brown* and *Ryan* is that, contrary to *Collins*, an entry does not have to be effective or substantial. They suggest that the common law rules be maintained.[1] The matter has yet to be decided by the Irish courts, but the decision in *Collins* seems likely to be the cause of considerable difficulty. Therefore, the common law rule that the insertion of any part of the defendant's body into a building should continue to be taken as an entry. Indeed, it would seem that the English courts are moving in this direction anyway in that they are willing to find that it takes less and less of the body to be inside the building to constitute entry.

24.3 Trespass

The entry into the building must be as a trespasser, a concept that has obvious parallels in the law of tort (although it must be emphasised that trespass itself is not a criminal offence). Effectively, a trespass is committed if a defendant enters another person's property without the consent of that person. This is common to both civil and criminal law, although any parallels should not be overstated; in *R v. Collins* (1972), it was noted that the civil concept of trespass is not the same as trespass for the purposes of criminal law. The principal difference is in the area of *mens rea*. In tort, a person can commit trespass negligently. For the purposes of burglary, however, negligence is not sufficient to establish *mens rea*. Thus, on a charge under section 12, it must be shown that the defendant either knew that he had no permission to enter, or at least that he did not care about such permission, i.e. subjective recklessness.

As always, if it is to be operative, the consent of the owner must be real and free from any form of duress. However, it seems that even where real consent has been given, if it is exceeded, the defendant may be regarded as a trespasser. As was stated by Scrutton L.J. in *The Calgarth* (1927), 'when you invite a person into your house to use the staircase you do not invite him to slide down the banisters.' Limits on permission to enter may therefore be set, either expressly or by implication. Clearly, if X invites Y into his house for dinner, he is not consenting to Y entering the house at night in order to steal the silverware. Similarly, in *R v. Jones and Smith* (1976), the defendants entered a house owned by the father of the second defendant with an intention to steal. The second defendant had the permission of his father to enter the house at any time, but not to remove any articles found in the house. The Court of Appeal had no difficulty in upholding their burglary convictions on the grounds that the owner's permission had been exceeded:

> It is our view that a person is a trespasser . . . if he enters premises of another knowing that he is entering in excess of the permission that has been given to him, or being reckless whether he is entering in excess of the permission that has been

---

1 Smith and Hogan, *Criminal Law*, 11th ed., Oxford: Oxford University Press, 2005, p. 813.

given to him to enter, providing the facts are known to the accused that he is acting in excess of the permission given or that he is acting recklessly as to whether he exceeds that permission ...

Similar reasoning was endorsed in Ireland by the Supreme Court in *The People (DPP) v. McMahon* **(1987).** In that case, members of the gardaí entered a licensed premises, believing they had the authority to do so, to investigate alleged offences against the Gaming and Lotteries Act 1956. In fact, the Acts relied on did not give authority to enter the premises for that reason. The court therefore concluded that they had exceeded their authority, and had therefore entered as trespassers.

If a defendant genuinely believes that he has entered a property with permission, he is not a trespasser. Similarly, if he enters a building believing it to be his, he is not a trespasser. However, what happens if he enters innocently but then realises his mistake, thereby making him aware that his entry was trespassory? From that moment, he becomes a trespasser. However, if he then steals something from the building, is he guilty of the second form of burglary? In *R v. Collins* (1972), the Court of Appeal held that to enter as a trespasser, as required for burglary, a defendant must know that he is a trespasser or be reckless as to that fact. Recklessness, as demonstrated by the extract from *Jones and Smith*, given above, is subjective – he must realise that he might be a trespasser. Lack of such knowledge or recklessness would mean that the defendant did not enter as a trespasser. Furthermore, it was also held in *Collins* that the common law doctrine of trespass *ab initio*, under which a person who enters land with permission but then does something to exceed that permission and is thereby deemed to have entered the land as a trespasser *ab initio*, does not form part of the modern law of burglary. Consequently, in the example given, the defendant cannot be deemed to have *entered* as a trespasser. Nevertheless, Smith and Hogan suggest that the defendant is still guilty of the second form of burglary because that form of the offence, unlike the first form which is committed on entry, is committed only when the ulterior offence is committed, and at that time the defendant knew that he was trespassing.[2] However, this view is difficult to reconcile with the clear wording of section 12(1)(b), which requires proof that the defendant entered the building or part of a building as a trespasser: if X enters a house believing it to be his own, then he lacks the necessary *mens rea* to be a trespasser at the time he entered the house. His subsequent realisation of his mistake does not alter the fact that he did not enter the house as a trespasser. If he then steals something and leaves the house, he has committed theft but not burglary. However, the situation might be different if X, having realised his mistake, then goes into another room and steals property. In such a case, X has entered a part of the building, i.e. the other room, with the knowledge that he has no permission to be there and

---

2 Smith and Hogan, *op. cit.*, p. 815.

therefore does so as a trespasser. Consequently, having entered a part of a building as a trespasser, X commits an arrestable offence and is therefore guilty of burglary.

24.4 Building or Part of a Building

The defendant must be shown to have entered a building or part of a building. Ordinarily, this requirement is not difficult to discharge; most burglaries, by their nature, will occur in what is obviously a building. In *Stevens v. Gourley* (1859), it was held that a building is a 'structure of considerable size and intended to be permanent or at least to endure for a considerable time.' On this basis, it was held in *B and S v. Leathley* (1979) that a freezer container resting on sleepers rather than on its chassis, and used to store frozen food, was a building. However, similar structures, which were still on their chassis and used for similar purposes, were found to be vehicles rather than buildings in *Norfolk Constabulary v. Seekings and Gould* (1986). Notwithstanding this decision, it is clear from section 12(2) that some vehicles are to be included as buildings for the purposes of section 12. Section 12(2) states that references to a building will 'apply also to an inhabited vehicle or vessel and to any other inhabited temporary or movable structure, and shall apply to any such vehicle, vessel or structure at times when the person having a habitation in it is not there as well as at times when the person is there.' This provision clearly extends the definition of a building to include mobile homes and caravans and to any other vehicle that is being used for human habitation. Thus, if the containers in *Seekings and Gould* had been inhabited instead of being used for storage, they would have constituted buildings. The reference in section 12(2) to inhabited temporary or movable structures is an advance on the previous law, and suggests that temporary structures such as tents should also be considered as buildings for the purposes of the law of burglary.

Entry may also be into a part of a building, although 'part' is not defined. Certainly, it is possible for a person to enter a building lawfully and become a burglar by entering, with the necessary intention, another part of the same building, to which he should not have access. For example, suppose X and Y lawfully check in to a hotel, and are given rooms 10 and 11, respectively. When X enters room 10, he is not a burglar as he has permission to be there. However, suppose he then enters room 11 with intent to steal Y's possessions. He has now entered another part of the building which he has no permission to enter. X is therefore a trespasser and is guilty of burglary (the first form). Alternatively, suppose X merely enters Y's room to see what kind of a view Y has, and while there decides to help himself to Y's money and camera. In this situation, he is also guilty of burglary (the second form), because he entered room 11 (a 'part of the building') as a trespasser and then stole Y's property. In *R v. Walkington* (1979), the defendant entered a department store, and paid particular attention to the tills. He approached a till at a counter, which was partially open, but found nothing in it and closed it. It was found by the Court of Appeal that the counter area could constitute a different part of the building which the defendant did not have permission to enter. As such, it was open to the jury to find that he entered that part of the building as a trespasser, and did so with the intent to steal. This decision also illustrates the point that it is not necessary for a building to be physically demarcated into different parts; it is sufficient that there is a point beyond which a person has no permission to go. In either case, it is for the jury to determine whether that building has been divided into parts.

24.5 *Mens Rea*

The *mens rea* of burglary is divided into two parts. First, it was held in *R v. Collins* (1972) that a defendant must have *mens rea* in order to enter a building as a trespasser for the purposes of burglary. It must therefore be shown that the defendant was aware that his entry constituted trespass, or that he was reckless as to the fact. In other words, if the defendant entered the building accidentally, negligently or against his will, a charge of burglary will fail, regardless of his subsequent actions (see the discussion on this point above in section 24.3). Second, as burglary requires some ulterior offence on top of trespass, there must be an element of *mens rea* in relation to that ulterior offence as well. Regarding the first form of burglary, the defendant must intend to commit an arrestable offence. Impossibility is not a defence. For example, suppose X enters a building with the intent to rape Y if she happens to be there. However, unknown to X, Y has in fact gone on holidays for a week and is not there. The fact that it is impossible for him to carry out his purpose in entering the building is no defence because section 12(1)(a) simply requires X to enter with the intent of raping; the fact that the target of the rape is not present does not alter the fact that X had the required intent. X will therefore be convicted. In *R v. Walkington* (1979), the defendant entered a department store intending to steal from a cash till, which turned out to be empty. His conviction for burglary was upheld by the Court of Appeal, which observed that the 'fact that there was nothing in the building worth his while to steal seems to us to be immaterial. He nevertheless had the intention to steal.' In relation to the second form of burglary, the defendant must have the *mens rea* necessary for the arrestable offence he committed.

24.6 The Ulterior Offences

The definition of burglary under the Larceny Act 1916 applied only where the defendant intended to commit or actually committed certain specific offences. The first form of burglary required proof of the defendant's intention to inflict grievous bodily harm upon any occupant or to commit larceny, rape or criminal damage. The second form of burglary required proof that the defendant committed or attempted to commit larceny or inflicted or attempted to inflict grievous bodily harm upon an occupant. With such a specific definition, there was always the possibility that a person charged with burglary might resist the charge on the basis that the offence he intended to commit, or the one he actually committed, did not fall within the offences specified in the definition of burglary. Section 12 of the 2001 Act takes account of this possibility by adopting a more general approach. The first form of the offence requires proof that the defendant entered the building with the intention to commit any arrestable offence, while the second form requires proof that the defendant committed an arrestable offence. Arrestable offences are defined in section 12(4) as offences 'for which a person of full age and not previously convicted may be punished by imprisonment for a term of five years or by a more severe penalty.'

24.7 Offences Related to Burglary

There are a variety of offences that relate to the offence of burglary. The broad purpose of these offences is to prohibit what might be described as acts preparatory to burglary.

Possession of Certain Articles

Section 15 of the 2001 Act makes it an offence to be found outside of one's residence in possession of any article with the intention that the article be used either in the course of or in connection with the following offences:

(a) theft or burglary,
(b) offences under sections 6 or 7 of the 2001 Act (making gains by deception or obtaining services by deception, respectively),
(c) offences under section 17 of the Criminal Justice (Public Order) Act 1994 (blackmail), or
(d) offences under section 112 of the Road Traffic Act 1961 (taking a vehicle without lawful authority).

Further, section 15(2) prohibits the possession without lawful authority or excuse of any article made or adapted for use in effecting any of these offences. Unlike subsection 1, there is no requirement that the person in whose possession such articles are found is outside his residence. Therefore, if the gardaí raid X's house and find a selection of homemade housebreaking implements, X can be charged under section 15(2), and X will need to have a reason for being in possession of such implements. No attempt has been made to specify the kind of articles covered by these two provisions, and this is sensible for the variety of articles that could be used to carry out the specified offences is almost endless. If a person is convicted under section 15, the maximum penalty is a fine, imprisonment for up to five years or both, and the trial court has the power to order the disposal of the articles in question as it sees fit. However, any such order will not take effect until the appeal period has elapsed or, if an appeal has been instituted, until such time as the appeal has been determined or abandoned.

Possession of Weapons of Offence

Section 10 of the Firearms and Offensive Weapons Act 1990 makes it an offence to be found on certain premises as a trespasser while in possession of a knife, blade or sharply pointed object, or any weapon of offence. The premises are defined in subsection 2 as any building, part of a building and any land ancillary to a building. Weapons of offence are defined in the same provision as any article made or adapted to cause injury or incapacitation, or intended by the defendant for such a use (see section 24.10 for discussion of this definition).

Public Order Offences

Two new offences with a bearing on burglary were created by the Criminal Justice (Public Order) Act 1994. Section 11 makes it an offence to enter as a trespasser any building or its vicinity in circumstances that would give rise to a reasonable inference that the entry was with the intent to commit an offence, or to unlawfully interfere with any property in the building. This formulation indicates that the test is objective; if a reasonable person would conclude that the defendant's purpose was unlawful, he may be convicted.

Section 13 makes it an offence for a person to trespass on any building in such a manner as causes or is likely to cause fear in another person. The gardaí have the power to order the offender to stop acting in such a manner and to leave the vicinity immediately. A failure to obey the order is a distinct offence. Therefore, suppose X creeps into an elderly person's garden at night without permission, causing that person anxiety. Section 13 enables the gardaí to order X to leave immediately, and if he refuses to do so, he commits an offence. Furthermore, it is not necessary for X to have actually caused fear to the elderly person; where his actions are objectively likely to cause fear, section 13 may be invoked.

AGGRAVATED BURGLARY

24.8 Introduction

Section 13 of the 2001 Act re-enacts the offence of aggravated burglary formerly contained in section 23B of the Larceny Act 1916, as inserted by section 7 of the Criminal Law (Jurisdiction) Act 1976. Section 13(1) provides as follows:

> A person is guilty of aggravated burglary if he or she commits any burglary and at the time has with him or her any firearm or imitation firearm, any weapon of offence or any explosive.

This definition is identical to the formulation under the 1916 Act except that it uses gender-inclusive language. The essence of the offence is an ordinary burglary which is aggravated by the fact that the defendant was armed at the time he committed the offence. The maximum punishment available is life imprisonment.

The crucial point on any charge under section 13 is the possession at the time of the burglary of any of the stated weapons. This requirement is slightly different depending on which form of burglary the defendant is alleged to have committed: *R v. O'Leary* (1986). If it is the first form, the defendant must have the weapons with him at the time of entry. Therefore, if X enters a house, and then arms himself with a kitchen knife, he is not guilty of aggravated burglary. If it is the second form of burglary, it must be shown that the defendant was armed at the time he committed an arrestable offence. In *R v. O'Leary* (1986), the defendant armed himself after entering a house, but before stealing cash and a bracelet from the occupants of the house. It was held that the material time was when the defendant stole the property; at that time, he was armed, and the conviction was upheld. Similarly, in *R v. Kelly* (1993), the defendant broke into a house using a screwdriver, which he kept with him. He then tried to steal the video recorder in the house, using the screwdriver to threaten the occupants. It was held that a screwdriver could be a weapon of offence if it was intended to be used to cause injury or incapacitiation. As the defendant had the weapon with him when he stole the video recorder, he was armed at the time the burglary was committed. On a similar point, in *R v. Klass* (1998), it was held that where two people are involved in a burglary, aggravated burglary is not committed unless the person who actually enters the building or part of a building is armed. If the armed person remains outside the building or part of the building, aggravated burglary is not committed.

It is unlikely that constructive possession would be sufficient. Section 13 states that the defendant must have the article with him at the time of the burglary. Consequently, it would have to be shown that the defendant had physical possession of the article, or that it was at least immediately available to him. Thus, in *R v. Kelt* (1977), the Court of Appeal noted, in relation to similar wording in section 18 of the Firearms Act 1968, that simply having possession is not sufficient. The prosecution must show that the defendant had the weapon with him, either on his person or in a place where it was immediately available to him. Simply having a firearm at home, which is sufficient for possession, is not enough for the purposes of section 18 of the Firearms Act 1968. This reasoning is equally applicable to aggravated burglary.

24.9   Firearms

Section 13(2) defines firearms for the purposes of aggravated burglary as meaning:

(a) lethal firearms or other lethal weapons from which any shot, bullet or other missile can be discharged,
(b) air guns, including both air rifles and air pistols, or any other weapon incorporating a barrel from which metal or other slugs can be discharged,

(c) crossbows, or

(d) any type of stun gun or other weapon for causing shock or other disablement to a person by means of electricity or other energy emission.

This list is exclusive, so any weapon that falls outside this list cannot be considered a firearm for the purposes of aggravated burglary. So, to take an extreme example, if X is armed with a flame-thrower, he is not in possession of a firearm. However, such a weapon constitutes a weapon of offence (see section 24.10).

Imitation firearms are defined in the same provision to mean anything that is not a firearm but which has the appearance of being a firearm. The fact that the imitation is incapable of discharge – because the firing pin has been removed, for example – is irrelevant; indeed, if discharge is possible, then the thing is more properly considered a firearm.

24.10 Weapons of Offence

Weapons of offence are defined broadly in section 13(2) as meaning:

(a) any article which has a blade or sharp point,

(b) any article made or adapted for use for causing injury to or incapacitating a person, or intended by the defendant for such use or for threatening such use, or

(c) any weapon of any description designed for the discharge of any noxious liquid, noxious gas or other noxious thing.

The first category includes articles that have a blade or a sharp point whether by design or adaptation. Thus, a screwdriver that has been sharpened to a point fits into this first category. The third category is reasonably self-explanatory and includes items such as spray cans which contain mace, pepper spray or other such chemicals. The second category is a catch-all for any item made, adapted or intended to cause injury or incapacitation. Articles that fit into the first and third categories also fit into the second category. So, the adapted screwdriver referred to above fits into the first category as it has a point, but it also fits into the second category as it has been adapted to cause injury. Note that such adaptations do not have to be done for the purpose of the burglary; providing the adaptation was done for the purpose of causing injury or incapacitation, either during the burglary or at any other time, the requirements have been met. An article is made for causing injury or incapacitation if that was its original purpose, regardless of the defendant's intended use of the article. So, in *R v. Simpson* (1983), the Court of Appeal ruled that the fact that a flick-knife could be used for innocent purposes such as making electrical repairs to a car does not alter the original purpose of the flick-knife. The court indicated that a bayonet was similarly designed to cause injury even though it could be used to stoke a fire. Finally, the second category of weapons of offence is so wide that it encompasses even articles made for entirely innocent purposes if those articles were used or intended to be used to cause injuries or incapacitation. Thus, a length of rope could be deemed a weapon of offence in that rope can be used to cause incapacitation.

24.11 Explosives

Section 13(2) defines explosives as any article manufactured for the purpose of producing a practical effect by explosion or those intended by the defendant to have that effect. This is narrower than the definition used by the Dangerous Substances Act 1972 which includes, in section 9(1), articles used or manufactured to produce a pyrotechnic effect. As Smith and Hogan point out, such a definition could include a box of matches, but it is unlikely that section 13 would be interpreted to include matches.[3]

24.12 *Mens Rea*

The *mens rea* of the offence is in two parts. First, as the offence is an aggravated one, the *mens rea* of ordinary burglary must be established (see section 24.5). Second, the prosecution must also show that the defendant was aware that he had the article in his possession at the material time. It is not necessary, however, to prove that the defendant intended to use the weapon to effect the burglary. In *R v. Stones* (1989), the defendant had armed himself with a kitchen knife prior to the burglary for use in self-defence against a gang that he said was after him. It was accepted that the knife, being a kitchen knife, had not been made or adapted for causing injury or incapacitation, but the prosecution alleged that it was intended to be used in that way. The Court of Appeal held that it must be proven that the defendant knew that he had the knife with him at the time of the burglary. It was not necessary for the prosecution to prove that the defendant intended to use the weapon in the course of the burglary; it was sufficient that the defendant intended to use the knife to cause injury to any person. The court reasoned that if the defendant intended to use the weapon against someone unconnected to the burglary, he might be tempted to use it during the course of the burglary as well. Thus, it would be somewhat artificial to separate the two intentions.

In some circumstances, there might be a third element of *mens rea*. If X is charged with aggravated burglary because he had a screwdriver in his possession at the time, the prosecution would have to prove that he intended to use the screwdriver to cause injury or incapacitation. Again, however, following the decision in *Stones*, it would seem that it is not necessary to show that he intended to use the screwdriver against the occupant of the building that he was going to burgle.

---

3 Smith and Hogan, *op. cit.*, p. 827.

24.13 Further Reading

Pace, 'Burglarious Trespass', [1985] *Crim LR* 716.
Reville, 'Mischief of Aggravated Burglary', (1989) 139 *NLJ* 835.

CHAPTER TWENTY-FIVE

HANDLING STOLEN PROPERTY

25.1 Introduction

If property has been stolen, Irish law punishes not only the thief, but also anyone who subsequently handles that property. Handling stolen property is an offence under section 17 of the Criminal Justice (Theft and Fraud Offences) Act 2001. Further, two related offences are created by sections 18 and 19: being in possession of stolen property and failing to account for stolen property, respectively. These related offences will be considered later in this chapter. Section 17(1) of the 2001 Act provides as follows:

> A person is guilty of handling stolen property if (otherwise than in the course of the stealing) he or she, knowing that the property was stolen or being reckless as to whether it was stolen, dishonestly –
> (a)   receives or arranges to receive it, or
> (b)   undertakes, or assists in, its retention, removal, disposal or realization by or for the benefit of another person, or arranges to do so.

There are thus eighteen possible forms of handling stolen property, but the most common form of the offence is receiving; indeed, until 1990, the offence was formally known as receiving stolen property. The Law Reform Commission concluded in its 1987 *Report on Receiving Stolen Property* that the offence of receiving stolen property was too narrow. This conclusion was adopted in section 3 of the Larceny Act 1990, which abolished the old offence and replaced it with the new offence of handling stolen property. Section 17 of the 2001 Act essentially re-enacts this offence. In *R v. Deakin* (1972), it was said in respect of a similar English provision:

> [The provision] sets out to do two things: first, to preserve the old offence of receiving stolen goods which involved proof of control or possession, and secondly, to enable the conviction of somebody who had dishonestly dealt with stolen goods albeit without necessarily taking them into his control or possession.

A similar policy underlies section 17. The maximum penalty available for handling stolen property is a fine or imprisonment for up to ten years or both, but the maximum penalty cannot exceed the maximum penalty for the principal offence, i.e. the offence by which the property became stolen.

25.2 Dishonesty

Dishonesty for the purposes of handling stolen property has the same meaning as for the purposes of theft (see section 22.2). Thus, if the defendant handles stolen property under a claim of right, a charge of handling must fail.

25.3 Handling

As noted above, there are eighteen different forms of this offence, but the most common is receiving stolen property. Indeed, in *R v. Bloxham* (1982), Lord Bridge suggested that the identical English offence broadly created two offences: receiving stolen property, and all other forms of dealing with stolen property. It is important to note that the other forms of dealing with the property must be done for the benefit of a person other than the person charged with handling. In *Bloxham*, the defendant had purchased a car in good faith but later realised that it was in fact stolen. He then sold the car to an innocent third party. The prosecution alleged that the defendant had disposed of the car for the benefit of the innocent third party, but this contention was rightly rejected. The court accepted the view that a person sells property largely for his own benefit and doing so clearly did not fit the definition of handling by disposal of property. So, the beneficiary of the forms of handling other than receiving must be someone other than the person charged with handling. If the allegation is that the defendant merely received the property, there is no requirement to show that he was acting on someone else's behalf.

Receiving

The central element of receiving is possession; it must be shown that the defendant took possession himself or constructively, even if the possession is only temporary. In *The People (Attorney General) v. Kelly and Robinson* (**1953**), it was held that it was not necessary to show that the defendant himself took possession; it is possible for property to be received by one person on behalf of another. For example, if X takes possession of property on behalf of his father Y, Y can be convicted of receiving. In *The People (Attorney General) v. Lawless* (**1968**), the defendant asked another man if he would allow stolen spirits to be stored in his yard. It was held that the defendant had possession if the goods were in the custody of another person over whom the defendant had control. In other words, the defendant was effectively acting as the other man's principal, while the other man was the defendant's agent.

It is also essential that the prosecution be able to show that the defendant knew of the existence of the property. In *The People (Attorney General) v. Nugent and Byrne* (**1964**), a sum of stolen money was found in a car belonging to the first defendant and in which the second defendant was travelling as a passenger. There was no evidence that either defendant knew that the money was there. In relation to the second defendant, the Court of Criminal Appeal held that a passenger could not be presumed to have knowledge of the contents of someone else's car. In relation to the first defendant, as it was his car, he would normally be considered to have knowledge as to its contents. This, however, was a constituent element of the offence which had to be proven by the prosecution. As a result, both convictions for receiving stolen property were quashed.

Retention

Retaining means keeping or continuing to have possession. In *R v. Bloxham* (1982), it was held that a retaining offence could be committed in one of two ways:

(a) where the defendant undertakes to retain stolen property for the benefit of another person, which implies a degree of agency; or

(b) where another person undertakes to retain the property and the defendant assists him.

A good example of the first form is *R v. Pitchley* (1972), in which the defendant lodged £150 to his own bank account, having been asked by his son to look after the money. At that time, he was unaware that the money was stolen. He realised that it was stolen some time later, but did nothing about it until he was interviewed by the police. It was held by the Court of Appeal that his conduct amounted to retaining stolen property on behalf of another, i.e. his son. In other words, he had allowed the money to remain in his control, despite having discovered that it was stolen. Indeed, the court endorsed the use of the dictionary definition of the word – to keep possession, to not lose, to continue to have.

For this first form of the offence, there must be evidence that the defendant committed some action; a mere failure to act is generally not enough. The required action, however, may be very slight. In *R v. Kanwar* (1982), the defendant, when asked by the police about various items of property in her house, replied that she had bought them. As it turned out, her answers were lies. It was held by the Court of Appeal that simply lying to the police as to the origin of the goods was sufficient to establish assisting in the retention of stolen property. Note that such a scenario now satisfies the offence of failing to account for property created by section 19 (see section 25.8).

R v. Brown (1969) is a good example of the second form of retaining. In that case, a man broke into a café and stole some cigarettes and food, which he hid in the defendant's flat without the defendant's knowledge. Some time later, he told the defendant about them. The police raided the flat and, while the defendant denied any knowledge of the stolen goods, he did not impede the police search. It was held by the Court of Appeal that the defendant's failure to reveal the existence of the goods did not amount to assisting in their retention. However, his knowledge that the goods were in his flat, and that they were stolen, did constitute the offence in that the defendant had effectively assisted the thief in retaining possession of the goods.

Removal

Removing property simply refers to the action of moving the property from one place to another. It is not necessary to show that the defendant took possession –

if he did so, his actions constitute receiving instead. It is also sufficient to show that the defendant helped to move the goods.

Disposal and Realisation

Realisation involves the exchange of the goods for money and must be done for the benefit of another. In *R v. Deakin* (1972), twenty-five cartons of spirits had been stolen from British Rail and were bought by the defendant, who was aware that they had been stolen. It was held that this constituted a realisation that was done for the benefit of the seller. The fact that it was also for the benefit of the defendant was irrelevant.

Disposal in its ordinary sense means getting rid of the property. This could refer to either destroying the goods or selling them, or both. It is likely that it refers only to their destruction; if it meant or included selling them, the word 'realisation' would become redundant. As *Deakin* shows, realisation has a distinct meaning.

Arranging

Arranging arises where the defendant has agreed to receive goods or undertakes or assists in their retention, removal, disposal or realisation. The crucial point is making an agreement; in this respect, arranging is similar to conspiracy: once the agreement has been made, the offence is committed. Therefore, as with conspiracy, it is immaterial that the defendant later abandoned the arrangement. However, as far as arranging to receive stolen property is concerned, it was established in *R v. Park* (1988) that the goods must have been stolen prior to the arrangement being made. Where this is not the case, it would be appropriate to bring conspiracy charges instead.

25.4 Stolen Property

It is essential for the prosecution to prove that the property in question was in fact stolen. Section 2(1) of the 2001 Act provides that the phrase 'stolen property' includes 'property which has been unlawfully obtained otherwise than by stealing.' Thus, the prosecution must establish that the property has been unlawfully obtained through a principal offence which includes any of the offences contained in the 2001 Act. A failure to offer such proof must result in the acquittal of the defendant: *Attorney General v. Conway* (**1925**). It must also be shown that the defendant did not come into possession of the stolen property while in the course of stealing it; this requirement is explicit in the definition of the offence. Further, the Court of Criminal Appeal ruled in *The People (DPP) v. Fowler* (**1995**) that a failure to so inform the jury would amount to a misdirection that would result in a conviction for handling being quashed.

Section 20 of the 2001 Act extends the application of section 17 to property stolen before the commencement of the 2001 Act, and to property stolen outside the State providing the stealing constituted an offence where and at the time the property was stolen. So, if X steals a television set in Belfast and passes it to Y in Dublin, Y has handled stolen goods within the meaning of the 2001 Act. Further, section 20(2) includes in the definition of stolen property the direct or indirect proceeds of the disposal or realisation of the whole or part of the stolen property. However, section 20(3) provides that property will no longer be stolen if it has been restored to the rightful owner of the property or other lawful possession or custody, or the original owner's rights to the property have terminated. In *Attorney General's Reference No.1 of 1974* (1974), the Court of Appeal ruled that once stolen property came under police control, it ceased to be stolen, having been returned to lawful custody. Similarly, in *Haughton v. Smith* (1973), the police had intercepted a quantity of stolen corned beef, but allowed the goods to proceed in an effort to trap the persons waiting to receive the goods. It was held that the goods were under the control of the police from the moment of interception and were therefore no longer stolen. Further, if X finds stolen property and takes possession of it in order to bring it to the police, he is not guilty of handling as he would have the implicit authority of the owner to take possession in those circumstances.

It is not generally necessary to prove the identity of the rightful owner of the property. However, in *R v. Gregory* (1972), it was suggested that such proof might sometimes be required, such as when there was evidence that the goods alleged to have been stolen might not have been manufactured at the time they were alleged to have been stolen. This is likely to be a rare situation, and in *R v. Deakin* (1972) it was suggested that *Gregory* should be confined to its own facts.

Finally, there is authority to the effect that goods taken by someone who lacks capacity to steal cannot be considered to be stolen. In *Walters v. Lunt* (1951), a child took home a tricycle that did not belong to him and his parents took possession of it. The child was *doli incapax* at the time, and it was held that as he was incapable of stealing, the tricycle could not have been stolen, and therefore his parents could not have received stolen property. However, as indicated in Chapter 12, this decision should be treated as suspect. The principle of *doli incapax* excuses young children from criminal responsibility; the principle does not deny that an offence was committed by the child. In this case, the child took property that belonged to someone else but was excused from any responsibility for so doing on account of his age. However, the tricycle was still stolen and his parents, by taking possession of the tricycle, had received stolen property.

25.5 Relationship with Other Offences

The offence of handling is ancillary to the principal offence by which the property is obtained unlawfully. Section 2(1) of the 2001 Act explicitly includes in the definition of stolen property any property that is unlawfully obtained by means other than theft. However, handling is distinct from these principal offences. In *The People (Attorney General) v. Carney and Mulcahy* (1953), it was held that where it is shown that the time of the defendant's possession is so close to the time of the theft as to reasonably exclude the possibility of another person being involved, the defendant should be charged with larceny. This point has been consistently upheld by the Irish courts, most recently by the High Court on a case stated in *O'Kelly v. DPP* (1997). The defendant had been charged with stealing a wallet under section 14 of the Larceny Act 1916, and with handling stolen property. The section 14 charge was dismissed, but the defendant was convicted of handling. The High Court held that such a conviction could not be maintained in the absence of evidence that the wallet had been stolen by someone else, and that the defendant had received the wallet from someone else.

Despite the decision in *Carney and Mulcahy*, it is permissible to charge a defendant with larceny and handling in respect of the same incident. This situation was considered by the Court of Criminal Appeal in *The People (DPP) v. Fowler* (1995). It was held that the jury should look at the larceny charge first. Only where there is a reasonable doubt as to the defendant's guilt on that charge should the jury consider the handling charge. A conviction on that charge could only be sustained where there is evidence that the property was stolen by someone else.

Finally, it is worth noting also that section 17(3) specifically allows a person to be convicted of handling even though the perpetrator of the principal offence has not been convicted or is no longer amenable to justice. Thus, it is no answer to a charge of handling for X to argue that the property was stolen by Y and as Y has not been charged, the charges against X should fail.

25.6 *Mens Rea*

There are two elements of *mens rea* required for the offence of handling. First, as noted above (section 25.2), the defendant must have acted dishonestly. In other words, if he believed that he had a right to take possession of the property, the charge of handling must fail. Second, section 17 explicitly requires proof that the defendant either knew that the property was stolen or that he was reckless as to whether or not it was stolen. Recklessness for the purpose of handling is defined in section 16(2) as follows:

> A person is reckless if he or she disregards a substantial risk that the property handled is stolen, and for those purposes 'substantial risk' means a risk of such a nature and degree that, having regard to the circumstances in which the person acquired the property and the extent of the information then available to him or her, its disregard involves culpability of a high degree.

Thus, the *mens rea* of the offence of handling is entirely subjective; a person cannot disregard a substantial risk without first being aware that the risk exists. The prosecution must prove at the least that the possibility of the property being stolen must have crossed the defendant's mind and that he disregarded that possibility in highly culpable circumstances. Further, section 17(2) provides that the defendant should be taken to have known that the property was stolen or was reckless as to that fact if it is shown that he handled stolen property in circumstances in which it is reasonable to conclude that he so knew or was so reckless unless all the evidence in the case creates a reasonable doubt as to the defendant's state of mind. Thus, an ostensibly subjective *mens rea* may be established on an objective view of the circumstances. This provision exists to prevent wholesale acquittals of people who could easily claim that they had no idea that the property they were handling was stolen, and whose claims would be difficult for the prosecution to resist. Relevant factors to be considered in assessing the circumstances might include the nature of the property, and the price being quoted for that property, the location of any transaction, the identity and reputation of the person from whom the defendant obtained the property and the extent to which the defendant was aware of that identity and reputation. So, if X buys a solid-gold watch for €10 from Y, who X knows to be a 'fence', in a place known by X to be frequented by disreputable characters, there is plenty of evidence from which a jury can conclude that X consciously disregarded a substantial risk that he was buying stolen property. On the other hand, if X is a tourist and is approached by Y who offers him a solid-gold watch for €10, and perhaps has a plausible explanation for such a low price, the jury should conclude that X acquired the property innocently. It must be stressed, however, that merely because a reasonable person would have realised that the property might be stolen is not sufficient in itself. Section 17(2) makes it clear that all the evidence in the case must be considered, and if evidence other than the circumstances in which the property was handled creates a reasonable doubt as to the defendant's state of mind, he must be acquitted. The defendant's own testimony as to his knowledge and belief will be especially important in this respect; if he has a plausible explanation as to why he did not appreciate facts or risks that would have been obvious to a reasonable person, the court would have to accord great weight to such testimony.

25.7 Possession of Stolen Property

Section 18(1) creates a distinct offence of possession of stolen property:

> A person who, without lawful authority or excuse, possesses stolen property (otherwise than in the course of the stealing), knowing that the property was stolen or being reckless as to whether it was stolen, is guilty of an offence.

As with handling, section 18(2) allows the defendant's state of mind to be determined according to a reasonable view of the circumstances in which he came into possession of the stolen property, subject to reference being had to all the evidence in the case. This provision makes specific reference to the purchase of the property at a price below the property's market value as a circumstance by which the defendant's knowledge or recklessness may be determined. In effect, the section 18 offence is a particular form of handling that is punishable by up to five years' imprisonment. The construction of the offence is almost identical to that of receiving stolen property, the essence of which is possession, and a person guilty of this offence is also guilty of handling stolen property under section 17. However, the presence of the section 18 offence allows the DPP to charge a lesser alternative in appropriate cases. Most likely, section 18 will be used to charge the ultimate receiver of the stolen goods, while section 17 will be retained for use against those involved in the organised and large-scale disposal of stolen property.

25.8 Failure to Account for Property

Section 19 makes it an offence to fail to properly account for property that is found in a person's possession. The obligation to account arises if certain circumstances exist:

(a) a member of the gardaí has reasonable grounds for believing that an offence of theft or handling has occurred,
(b) the member finds a person in possession of any property,
(c) the member has reasonable grounds for believing that this property includes or may include, in whole or in part, the property stolen or handled or represents the proceeds of such property, and
(d) the member must inform the person found in possession of his or her belief.

Thus, the gardaí do not have the power under section 19 to quiz members of the public in general about their property; rather, they must have grounds to believe that the property was stolen. Further, the gardaí must be able to relate the property they suspect to be stolen to a specific instance of theft or handling. In other words, if a member of the gardaí knows that a particular silver clock was stolen, he is not justified in holding to account any member of the public who happens to own a silver clock. However, if the garda reasonably believes that the silver clock that is in X's possession might be the particular silver clock that was stolen, the garda would then be justified in asking X to account for his possession of that clock. If X fails to do so without reasonable excuse, or if he gives misleading information, he is guilty of an offence, providing he has been informed in ordinary language by the garda of the consequences of his failure. In other words, X must be placed on notice that failure to account for his property constitutes an offence. Finally, if X complies with the garda's request, any information that he gives cannot then be used against him or his spouse in criminal proceedings other than proceedings for an infringement of section 19.

25.9 Further Reading

Law Reform Commission, *Report on Receiving Stolen Property*, LRC 23–1987.

McCutcheon, 'Revision of the Larceny Code: Two New Offences', (1991) 1 *ICLJ* 23.

Spencer, 'Handling and Taking Risks – A Reply to Professor Williams', [1985] *Crim LR* 440.

———, 'Handling, Theft and the *Mala Fide* Purchaser', [1985] *Crim LR* 92.

Williams, 'Handling, Theft and the Purchaser Who Takes a Chance', [1985] *Crim LR* 432.

CHAPTER TWENTY-SIX

THEFT-RELATED OFFENCES

26.1 Introduction

The main property offences are theft, robbery, burglary and handling, all of which have already been covered. In addition, there are a number of theft-related offences concerning property contained in the Criminal Justice (Public Order) Act 1994 and the Criminal Justice (Theft and Fraud Offences) Act 2001. The essence of these offences is the obtaining of other people's property by unlawful means in circumstances that do not amount to outright theft.

BLACKMAIL

26.2 Introduction

Strictly speaking, Irish law does not recognise any offence called 'blackmail'. The term is colloquial, and is derived from the old term used by English landowners to denote the tribute they paid to Scottish chieftains to prevent Scottish raids on their property. Modern law, while not officially recognising the term, prohibits the kind of behaviour that gave rise to the term. Until 1994, blackmail was prohibited by sections 29, 30 and 31 of the Larceny Act 1916, which collectively contained six different forms of the offence. There was a considerable amount of duplication, and there was a need for consolidation and updating. This was done by section 17 of the Criminal Justice (Public Order) Act 1994, which provides:

> (1) It shall be an offence for any person who, with a view to gain for himself or another or with intent to cause loss to another, makes any unwarranted demand with menaces.

26.3 Unwarranted Demands

A demand may be made either expressly or by implication from the circumstances. However, a mere request will not be a demand; there must be some element of a threat accompanying the request. So, if X asks Y for £10, there is no demand for the purposes of this offence. If, however, X asks Y for £10 while casually noting how flammable Y's house appears to be, a demand has been made. A good example of an express demand is *R v. Clear* (1968), in which a case was being taken against the defendant's employer, and the defendant was called as a witness. He approached the employer and demanded £300 in exchange for changing his testimony. The court had no trouble in seeing this as a demand. Alternatively, a demand can be implied from the defendant's words or actions which, in themselves, seem innocent. In *R v. Robinson* (1796), the defendant stated to the victim: 'Remember, sir, I am now only making an appeal to your benevolence.' This was held to be capable of being construed as a demand. Similarly, in *R v. Collister; R v. Warhurst* (1955), the defendants were police officers who tried to extort money from a member of the public in exchange for not prosecuting him for importuning. At no time was any request for money made, but it was held that a demand could be inferred from the circumstances of the case.

Furthermore, section 17(2)(b) provides that it makes no difference to the charge what the defendant demands from the victim. Therefore, blackmail is committed under section 17 whether the defendant demands money, property, books or anything else.

The prosecution must show not only that a demand was made, but also that it was unwarranted or unjustified. This is similar to the provision in the old section 29 of the 1916 Act, which also allowed demands to be made if there was a reasonable cause. Unlike the old provision, however, section 17 provides a definition of 'unwarranted'. Section 17(2)(a) provides that a demand will be unwarranted unless:

(i) the defendant believed that he had reasonable grounds for making the demand, and
(ii) the defendant also believed that the demand was a proper method of enforcement.

In *R v. Harvey* (1981), the defendant agreed to pay S a sum of £20,000 to obtain a quantity of cannabis. S failed to obtain the cannabis, so the defendant kidnapped S's wife and young child to force him to repay the money. The Court of Appeal noted that where the defendant thought his actions were a proper means of enforcement, he would have a defence. The word 'proper' is wider than the word 'lawful', but the latter was incorporated into the definition of the former. Therefore, no act could be believed to be proper unless it was also believed to be lawful. So, where X is owed money by Y and he threatens to sue Y unless the debt is paid, X's demand will not be unwarranted. Furthermore, even where the debt is not legally enforceable, X will still have a good defence, providing he genuinely believed that he was owed money. In effect, therefore, section 17(2)(a) provides a claim of right defence to a person charged with blackmail.

26.4 Menaces

The demand must be accompanied by menaces of some kind, and under section 17(2)(b), it is immaterial that the defendant threatens to do something himself or through someone else. What will constitute a menace will vary according to each case, but in *Thorne v. Motor Trade Assoc.* (1937), it was held that 'menace' has a very wide meaning, and refers to anything unpleasant or detrimental. In *R v. Lawrence and Pomroy* (1971), it was held that 'menaces' was an ordinary English word that did not generally require any special direction from the judge as to its meaning. However, the jury must be satisfied that a menace or threat has been made. In *R v. Clear* (1968), the Court of Appeal discussed the effect that a menace must have:

> Words or conduct which would not intimidate or influence anyone to respond to the demand would not be menaces . . . but threats and conduct of such a nature and extent that the mind of an ordinary person of normal stability and courage might be influenced or made apprehensive so as to accede unwillingly to the demand would be sufficient for a jury's consideration.

This is clearly an objective test, so it is immaterial that the particular recipient of the threat did not himself feel threatened. Providing the prosecution can show that a normal person with normal courage would have felt threatened, this element of the offence is made out.

26.5 *Mens Rea*

The *mens rea* requirement is an intention on the part of the defendant to either make some gain for himself or for another person, or alternatively to cause a loss to another person. It is therefore not necessary for the prosecution to show that the defendant wanted to make some profit for himself. Thus, if X wishes to stop the manufacture of a product made by his rival Y, and he threatens to cause Y financial ruin unless production ceases immediately, X can be convicted of blackmail.

GAINING BY DECEPTION

26.6 Introduction

The use of deception to deprive another person of his money or property has a long history, as has the efforts by the law to punish such actions. If such actions constitute a dishonest appropriation without the owner's consent, they can be prosecuted under section 4 of the Criminal Justice (Theft and Fraud Offences) Act 2001. Indeed, section 4(2) specifically states that consent gained by deception is no consent for the purposes of a charge of theft. However, there will be occasions not covered by section 4 when a person is induced by deceit to part with his property or services. In those instances, charges might be possible under section 6 (making a gain or causing a loss by deception) or section 7 (obtaining services by deception). In both cases, the definition of deception is the same as for section 4(2): the creation or reinforcement of a false impression as to law, value or intention, preventing the other party from acquiring information that would affect his judgement of a transaction, or the failure to correct a false impression previously created by the deceiver or which the deceiver knows is influencing the mind of another person to whom the deceiver owes a fiduciary duty (see section 22.4).

26.7 Making Gains or Causing Losses by Deception

Section 6(1) of the 2001 Act makes it an offence for a person to dishonestly induce by deception another person to do or to refrain from doing an act, with the intention of making a gain for himself or causing a loss to another person. Gains and losses are defined in section 2(3) as extending only to gains or losses in money or other property, whether such gain or loss is permanent or temporary. The maximum penalty available for this offence is a fine or imprisonment for five years or both. The definition of dishonesty is the same here as for the offence of theft (see section 22.2), so an honest belief in the correctness of the impression created will preclude a conviction under this provision. There is no requirement that the person deceived and the person who suffers the loss caused by the deception be the same person, although invariably that will be the case. The *mens rea* of the offence is an intention to induce another person to do or to refrain from doing something, so recklessness as to the impression being created will not be sufficient for a conviction.

26.8 Obtaining Services by Deception

Section 7 makes it an offence to dishonestly induce another person by deception to provide services, with the intention of either making a gain for himself or causing a loss to another person. This is a parallel offence to that created by section 6 and the maximum penalties available for both offences are identical. Section 7(2) defines obtaining a service as the conferral of a benefit on some person by doing an act, or causing or permitting an act to be done, on the understanding that the benefit has been or will be paid for. Section 7(3) provides that the conferring of a loan with the understanding that a payment has been or will be made is a specific example of such a benefit.

OTHER OFFENCES

26.9 Introduction

The 2001 Act creates several other theft-related offences, all of which have as a common thread the dishonest making of a gain for one's self or the causing of a loss to another person. As with the deception offences, gains and losses are defined in section 2(3) to extend only to money or other property, whether temporary or permanent. Thus, gains or losses to intangible factors such as reputation are not included in these offences.

26.10 Making Off Without Payment

Section 8(1) makes it an offence for a person to dishonestly leave without paying for goods obtained or services rendered when he knew that payment on the spot was required or expected and with the intention of avoiding making payment. A typical example of such an offence is leaving a restaurant without paying for the meal. This offence does not arise, however, where the goods obtained or the services rendered are illegal or the contract is legally unenforceable. Hence, refusing to pay a prostitute for sexual services will not constitute an offence under section 8. The *mens rea* of the offence is knowledge that immediate payment is required or expected and an intentional desire to avoid making payment. Thus, if X honestly forgets to make payment, he has a complete answer to a section 8 charge. Similarly, as the offence must be committed dishonestly, a genuine belief that payment is not required for the goods obtained or services rendered will also provide the defendant with a complete answer.

Section 8(3) allows anyone to arrest a person who has made off without payment. In the usual course of events, the arrest will be made, if not by members of the gardaí, then by the person to whom payment is owed. However, an arrest by someone who has no interest in the matter is equally valid. But if the arrest is made by someone other than a member of the gardaí, such arrest will only be valid under section 8(5) if the person making the arrest reasonably believes that the person so arrested would otherwise attempt to avoid or is avoiding arrest by the gardaí. So, if X is challenged by a shopkeeper to pay for his newspaper and X tries to flee, he can be arrested by the shopkeeper or any bystander. However, if X is returning to the shop to make payment and Y purports to arrest him, Y has committed an assault and a false imprisonment. If a valid arrest is made by a citizen, then the person arrested must be turned over to the gardaí as soon as practicable. Members of the gardaí may arrest without warrant anyone they reasonably suspect to have made off without payment.

26.11 Unlawful Use of a Computer

Under section 9, it is an offence to dishonestly use a computer with the intention of making a gain for himself or another person, or causing a loss to another person. The provision makes it clear that the offence can be committed from within the State or outside the State providing the computer being so used is within the State. This offence is directed at the actions colloquially referred to as 'hacking' and is relatively serious in that it attracts a maximum penalty of ten years' imprisonment and an unlimited fine. No doubt the severity of the penalties is a reflection of the gains that can be made or losses caused relatively quickly by computer hackers. As with all of these theft-related offences, the offence under section 9 must be committed dishonestly; consequently, an honest belief by the defendant that he was entitled to act as he did will offer a complete defence.

26.12   False Accounting

Dishonest false accounting is an offence under section 10(1) if it is done with the intention of making a gain for oneself or another person or to cause a loss to another person. The section sets out what constitutes a false accounting:

(a) destroying, defacing, concealing or falsifying any account or any document made or required for accounting purposes,
(b) failing to make or complete any account or any such document, or
(c) in furnishing information for any purpose, the production or use of any account or any such document which to the person's knowledge is or may be misleading, false or deceptive in a material manner.

Under section 10(2), a person will be taken to have falsified an account if he makes or concurs in the making in the account any entry that is or may be misleading, false or deceptive in a material particular, or if he omits or concurs in the omission from the account of a material particular. Thus, someone charged with an accounting responsibility is under a duty to properly include in the account all material particulars. What constitutes a material particular is not specified in the Act, but presumably this duty will be construed similarly to the duty of an insured person to disclose all material facts to an insurance company. Such material facts are those that would influence an insurer in his decision whether to offer insurance and the premium to be charged. Applied to a situation within the contemplation of section 10, a material particular would be any entry that would influence a person relying on the account. Whether or not a particular entry is material ultimately is a matter of fact to be decided by the jury.

Once again, the false accounting must be done dishonestly and with the requisite intention. Accordingly, an honest belief in the correctness of the entry or omission will provide a complete answer to a charge under section 10. The maximum penalty available for this offence is ten years' imprisonment or an unlimited fine or both. The relative severity of these maximum sanctions reflects the reliance that is customarily placed on accounts, and the damage that can be done when such accounts are falsified.

26.13   Suppression of Documents

Under section 11(1), it is an offence to dishonestly interfere with certain official documents with the intention of making a gain or causing a loss to another person. The interference must consist of destroying, defacing or concealing the document. The documents in question are valuable securities, wills or other testamentary documents or any original documents of, belonging to, filed in or deposited in any court or government department or office. By virtue of section 2(1), documents include maps, plans, graphs, drawings, photographs or records, or reproductions in permanent legible form of information in non-legible form, whether by a computer or any other means. Under section 11(2), dishonestly procuring by deception the execution of a valuable security is a separate offence. The maximum penalties available for the offences in either subsection are ten years' imprisonment or an unlimited fine or both.

26.14 Further Reading

Aldridge, 'Attempted Murder of the Soul: Blackmail, Privacy and Secrets', (1993) *Ox JLS* 368.

Halpin, 'The Test for Dishonesty', [1996] *Crim LR* 283.

Law Reform Commission, *Report on the Law Relating to Dishonesty*, LRC CP43-1992.

CHAPTER TWENTY-SEVEN

CRIMINAL DAMAGE

27.1 Introduction

Until 1991, the law relating to criminal damage was governed by a series of common law rules and Malicious Damage Acts, especially the Malicious Damage Act 1861. However, in 1988, the Law Reform Commission, in its *Report on Malicious Damage*, recommended sweeping changes to this area of law. These recommendations resulted in the Criminal Damage Act 1991. The Act had two principal objectives. First, it reformed the law on criminal damage. Second, it applied these changes to interfering with data stored in computers. Therefore, any of the criminal damage offences can be invoked where computer data have been destroyed or damaged. In achieving these objectives, the legislators used two pieces of English legislation as their models, the Criminal Damage Act 1971 and the Computer Misuse Act 1990. English case law in this area will therefore be very helpful in the interpretation of the Irish Act.

As far as damaging property is concerned, the 1991 Act creates three basic offences: damaging property (section 2), threats to damage property (section 3) and possessing anything with intent to damage property (section 4). The Act further provides that where any of these offences are committed by fire, the defendant should be charged with arson. Damaging property is dealt with in section 2, which creates three distinct forms of the offence: damaging property, damaging property with intent to endanger life and damaging property with intent to defraud. As far as interfering with computers is concerned, due to the wide definition of property, damaging data can be prosecuted under any of these provisions. The Act also, however, creates a specific offence of unauthorised accessing of data (section 5). It should be noted that in addition to the infliction of punishment for causing criminal damage, the 1991 Act as originally enacted also authorised the courts to make compensation orders (section 9). Such orders were limited to the value of the damage caused only and could not include any consequential loss. However, section 9 was repealed by section 13 of the Criminal Justice Act 1993, which gives the courts a general power in criminal cases to order a convicted defendant to pay compensation to his victim (see section 1.16).

DAMAGING PROPERTY

27.2 Introduction

Section 2(1) establishes the basic form of the offence:

> A person who without lawful excuse damages any property belonging to another intending to damage any such property or being reckless as to whether any such property would be damaged shall be guilty of an offence.

This provision is different to the comparable English provision in that the latter refers to destroying or damaging property. However, as destruction is merely an extreme form of damage, it is difficult to see the advantage of incorporating the extra term, and the Irish provision has adopted this rationale. The maximum penalty for this offence is up to ten years' imprisonment, a fine or both.

27.3 Without Lawful Excuse

Under the 1861 Act, it was essential that the prosecution prove that the damage was carried out unlawfully. The 1991 Act preserves this element by requiring that the damage be done without lawful excuse. Section 6 elaborates on this requirement, and includes what amounts to two statutory defences that revolve around the defendant's belief in the owner's consent or circumstances of necessity. Furthermore, section 6(3) provides that, in relation to the defendant's belief, there will still be a lawful excuse even where the belief is not justified. In other words, the belief required is entirely subjective. Under section 6(5), these defences operate in addition to any of the general defences recognised by the law.

The first defence is under section 6(2)(a), which provides that the defendant has a lawful excuse if he has an honest belief that the owner of the property had consented to the damage, or would have so consented had he known of the damage. For example, suppose X tells Y that he would love a new doorway in the side of his house, and Y proceeds to knock a hole in the side of the house as a surprise, in preparation for the insertion of a new door. Y can plead that he honestly believed that X would have consented to the damage, even if X had subsequently changed his mind. In *R v. Denton* (1982), the defendant set fire to his employer's mill, believing that his employer had encouraged him to do so. His conviction for arson was accordingly quashed. Furthermore, in *Jaggard v. Dickinson* (1980), the defendant broke a window in a house that she honestly thought belonged to a friend with whom she was staying. At the time, the defendant was intoxicated, and the mistake occurred as a result of the intoxication. It was held that the defence applies to any situation in which the defendant has an honest belief, irrespective of the source of that belief. Indeed, the court stated that what is material to this defence is the existence of the honest belief, 'not its intellectual soundness; and a belief can be just as much honestly held if it is induced by intoxication, as if it stems from stupidity, forgetfulness or inattention.'

The second defence applies in situations of necessity and arises under section 6(2)(c), as amended by section 21 of the Non-Fatal Offences Against the Person Act 1997. As originally enacted, section 6(2)(c) provided an answer to a charge of criminal damage if the defendant had acted to protect himself, others or property from immediate harm if he believed that his actions were reasonable in the circumstances. The potential breadth of this defence was such that a person could conceivably justify any act of criminal damage in order to prevent even minor harm to his property. The 1997 amendment now restricts the availability of the defence to situations in which the defendant damages property in order to prevent harm occurring to actions that were reasonable in the circumstances as he believed them to be. Thus, under the former formulation, X could have been acquitted of the destruction of a chemical plant if he reasonably believed that the plant was responsible for harming his vegetable garden.[1] Under the present formulation, any such defence would necessarily fail, as the destruction of a chemical plant is scarcely a reasonable way in which to protect one's vegetables. The fact that the defendant's view of the circumstances turns out to have been mistaken is not fatal to the defence, providing that view was honestly held. So, if X believes, mistakenly, that the house in which he is staying is on fire and he breaks a window to get out, his actions will be judged on the basis that the house really was on fire. In those circumstances, was it reasonable for him to break a window in order to get out of the house? Finally, the courts will be reluctant to allow this defence to be used in order to justify acts of criminal damage that are committed due to one's political beliefs. In *The People (DPP) v. Kelly* (**2004**), the defendant was charged with causing criminal damage to a warplane belonging to the US Navy. She claimed that her actions were lawful in that they were necessary to protect life in Iraq. The Circuit Court judge restricted the defendant's defence on the basis that he did not want the case to become a political debate on the legitimacy of the US invasion of Iraq.

27.4 Damage

There are different definitions of damage in section 1, according to whether the property is tangible or in data form. Damaging tangible property may be done by destroying, defacing or dismantling it, or rendering it inoperable or unfit for use or by preventing or impairing its operation, whether temporarily or not. Damaging data means adding to, altering, corrupting, erasing or moving them to a different storage medium or a different location within the same storage medium, or doing any act that contributes towards the addition, alteration,

---

1 Derived from Smith and Hogan, *Criminal Law*, 8th ed., London: Butterworths, 1996, p. 705.

corruption, erasure or movement of the data. In relation to either form of property, doing any act within the State to damage property outside the State, or vice versa, or making any omission that causes damage to property, will be included in the definition.

Generally, the damage will be brought about by a positive action on the part of the defendant, but section 1 specifically includes omissions in the definition of damage, providing those omissions cause the damage in question. In *R v. Miller* (1983), the defendant was a squatter who fell asleep on a mattress while smoking a cigarette. He awoke to find the mattress on fire, but made no attempt to put the fire out, going instead into another room. It was held by the House of Lords that having created the danger, he was under a duty to take all reasonable steps to put it out. His failure to do so allowed the fire to spread, thereby causing further damage. Providing the defendant had at that point the necessary *mens rea*, he could be convicted of arson.

27.5 Property of Another

Property is defined in section 1 as meaning property of a tangible nature, whether real or personal, and includes money and animals capable of being stolen, or data held in a form that is accessible by a computer. Despite the fact that section 2(1) refers to damaging property belonging to another, section 7(2) provides that in any prosecution for any offence under section 2, it is not necessary to identify the actual owner of the property. Furthermore, section 7(2) creates two rebuttable presumptions: first, that the property damaged belongs to another person, and second, that the owner did not consent to the damage. Therefore, if X smashes a car, it will be presumed that the car belonged to someone else, whose identity it is not necessary to prove, and that the owner did not consent to the damage being done. In both respects, the onus of proof shifts to X to show either that the car belonged to him, or that the real owner did in fact consent to the damage being done. This onus may be discharged on a balance of probabilities instead of beyond reasonable doubt.

27.6 *Mens Rea*

The *mens rea* of the offence is intentionally or recklessly damaging property. In England, recklessness was judged objectively by virtue of *MPC v. Caldwell* (1981) until 2003. In that year, the House of Lords ruled in *R v. G* (2003) that recklessness arose only where the defendant had adverted to a risk and consciously decided to run it (see section 4.5). In Ireland, section 2(6) also requires proof of subjective recklessness by providing that 'a person is reckless if he has foreseen that the particular kind of damage that in fact was done might be done and yet has gone on to take the risk of it.' Not only is recklessness subjective, therefore, it is restricted to foresight of the kind of damage that was actually done. Thus, if X foresees that by kicking over a television set he will damage it, he will be liable for all the damage done to the television. If, however, the television falls and splits open, causing sparks that ignite the carpet, he is not liable for the resulting fire damage. Therefore, if a case arose before the Irish courts with facts similar to those in *Miller*, the prosecution would have to prove that the defendant either intended the fire to spread, or foresaw the danger of the fire spreading, and decided to do nothing to prevent it.

DAMAGING PROPERTY WITH INTENT TO ENDANGER LIFE

27.7 Introduction

Section 2(2) sets out the first and most serious of the aggravated forms of damaging property:

> A person who without lawful excuse damages any property, whether belonging to himself or another –
> (a) intending to damage any property or being reckless as to whether any property would be damaged, and
> (b) intending by the damage to endanger the life of another or being reckless as to whether the life of another would be thereby endangered, shall be guilty of an offence.

The maximum penalty for this offence is life imprisonment, a fine or both. The precise sentence obviously will vary from case to case, but the more aggravated the circumstances, the heavier the sentence will be. In *Attorney General's Reference No.35 of 1996* (1997), the defendant lived in an apartment, which was part of an apartment complex. He got into arrears in his rent and set fire to the apartment by placing a mattress over an electric fire, while knowing that there was at least one other person in the complex. It was held that there were a number of aggravating factors in the offence: it was deliberate; it was done as a form of revenge against the landlord; it was done while the defendant knew there were other people in the complex; and it was done late at night. The court therefore raised the sentence of two years' probation and 100 hours of community service to a sentence of eighteen months' imprisonment.

27.8 Damage without Lawful Excuse

The offence under section 2(2) is the most serious of the property offences created under this Act. It has a number of elements, some of which, such as 'damage' and 'property', are the same as under section 2(1). It is important to note that it must be shown that it was the damage to the property that endangered the other person's life, rather than the action of the defendant. In *R v. Steer* (1987), the defendant had fired a number of rifle bullets through a window of a house owned by another person. His conviction for endangering life by damaging property was unanimously quashed by the House of Lords because the victim was endangered by the bullets, not by the broken window. There must be proof that the endangerment comes from the damage to the property. In the circumstances of this case, therefore, the prosecution would have to have shown that the defendant had either intended or foreseen a danger to the occupant's life from flying glass rather than from the bullets.

The requirement that the damage take place unlawfully is an element of this offence as in the offence in section 2(1), but has a somewhat broader meaning. In particular, the two statutory defences under section 6 (see section 27.3) do not apply to an offence under section 2(2). Therefore, a defendant is restricted to using the general defences recognised by the criminal law.

27.9   Ownership

Under section 2(1), no offence is committed if the property damaged belongs to the defendant. Under section 2(2), the ownership of the property is irrelevant as the intention of the provision is to penalise a defendant who places another person in danger through criminal damage, rather than for creating the damage itself. Therefore, if X lives in a terraced house, and he sets it on fire, the fire is likely to spread to the adjoining houses, thereby placing the occupants of those houses in danger. The fact that it was his own house that was damaged by his action is irrelevant. In the context of computer data, if X were to alter information relating to patients held in hospital computers, thereby knowingly or recklessly placing them at risk, he is also guilty under this section.[2]

27.10   *Mens Rea*

The *mens rea* of the offence is in two parts. First, the defendant must act with the same *mens rea* as under section 2(1), namely an intention to damage the property or recklessness as to whether or not the property is damaged. Second, the defendant must intend to endanger life by causing the damage or be reckless as to such endangerment. Recklessness in this context is, again, by virtue of section 2(6), of the subjective variety. Therefore, the prosecution must prove that the defendant actually foresaw the risk of endangering another person's life. The fact that any reasonable person would have foreseen the risk is irrelevant. It is, however, necessary to show that the endangerment arose as a result of the damage intended or foreseen by the defendant. Actual damage that was not intended or foreseen by the defendant, but which nevertheless caused an endangerment to life, will not be sufficient: *R v. Dudley* (1989). So, if X fires a bullet through a window, he intended to damage the window, or was reckless as

---

2 As noted by Jackson in her annotations to the Act, *Irish Current Law Statutes Annotated,* Dublin: Round Hall Sweet & Maxwell, 1991.

to the window being broken. If it could be shown that he had intended to endanger the lives of the occupants by flying glass, or had been reckless as to that possibility, he can be convicted. Otherwise he must be acquitted. Suppose, however, that the bullet had hit a chandelier, causing it to fall and narrowly miss Y. Can the prosecution use the damage to the chandelier to establish intent or recklessness to endanger life? It would seem that unless X at least foresaw the possibility of the bullet hitting some fixture and causing it to fall and thereby endanger life, he must be acquitted – intent or recklessness must be inferred from the damage X intended to do or was reckless about doing, which in this case was breaking a window. Finally, it is not necessary to prove that anyone's life had in fact been endangered by the damage; providing it is shown that the defendant intended to endanger life or was reckless about doing so, the offence is established. Consequently, impossibility is no defence to a charge under this section.

DAMAGING PROPERTY WITH INTENT TO DEFRAUD

27.11 Introduction

This form of the offence has no equivalent under the (English) Criminal Damage Act 1971. Section 2(3) provides:

> A person who damages any property, whether belonging to himself or another, with intent to defraud is guilty of an offence.

Penalties for the offence are the same as for damaging property under section 2(1). The most obvious example of this offence occurs where a defendant destroys his own property in order to collect compensation from an insurance company. There is no provision made for lawful excuse; even if there was, it is hard to conceive of any excuse that would justify trying to defraud others. As a result, if the defendant destroyed someone else's property with their consent, as happened in *R v. Denton* (1982) (see section 27.3), he will have no defence to a charge under this section, as the consent of the owner is irrelevant. However, the defendant is still able to rely on the general criminal defences, such as duress. Therefore, if X can show that Y had threatened to kill him unless he handed over €50,000, and he had no other way to collect that money, he would probably have a good defence.

27.12 *Mens Rea*

Strictly speaking, there are two elements of *mens rea*. First, there is the *mens rea* as to the action of damaging property. This element is not made clear, but it seems that the defendant must act intentionally: it is hard to see how a defendant could act recklessly with an intent to defraud. Second, it must be shown that the defendant damaged the property with the intent of defrauding others. It is not necessary to show that someone had actually been defrauded; the defendant's intent is sufficient. Furthermore, as with an offence under section 2(2), the prosecution must show that the defendant intended to defraud another person through the damage to the property.

ARSON

27.13 Introduction

At common law, it was a felony to wilfully and maliciously burn another person's house, and a misdemeanour to burn one's own house. The Malicious Damage Act 1861 then penalised a considerable number of specific forms of arson, such as the burning of churches, warehouses, offices and shops. Some highly technical rules developed as to the meaning of 'burning'; for example, evidence that the property was charred was sufficient, but mere scorching was not. The key requirement in any arson case was proof that the defendant had acted maliciously. Therefore, where a fire resulted accidentally from a defendant's actions, a charge of arson could not be sustained. A good example of this is the old Irish case of *R v. Faulkner* (1877). The defendant was a sailor on board a ship carrying a cargo of rum, sugar and cotton. He went into the cargo hold and attempted to steal some of the rum. To see what he was doing, he lit a match, which then accidentally came into contact with some of the rum. The rum ignited, causing a fire that destroyed the ship. It was held that the defendant had not intended to harm the ship in any way, and therefore he did not have the *mens rea* for arson. His conviction was quashed.

27.14 The 1991 Act

Section 14(1) of the 1991 Act abolished the common law offence of arson, and section 15 repealed all of the arson provisions in the 1861 Act. In their place, section 2(4) provides:

> An offence committed under [section 2] by damaging property by fire shall be charged as arson.

The penalty on conviction on indictment is up to life imprisonment. Arson is now, therefore, a specific form of damaging property, rather than a totally distinct offence. Consequently, there are three forms of arson: arson, arson with the intent to endanger life and arson with the intent to defraud. The construction of each of these offences is exactly the same as in sections 2(1), (2) and (3), respectively, with the exception that in each case the prosecution must prove that the damage was caused by fire. The comments made above in relation to each of the offences therefore hold good for each different type of arson. Whether or not a modern court would follow the common law rules on fire damage is unclear. For example, suppose X tries to burn down his mother-in-law's house, but succeeds only in scorching it. At common law, this would not be sufficient for an arson charge. Would a modern court agree? The Act is silent on this point, but it is likely that the modern court would disagree: the Act simply requires that the property be damaged, as defined in section 1. Scorching clearly constitutes defacing the property, and would therefore be considered to be damage.

RELATED OFFENCES

27.15 Threats to Damage Property

Under section 3, it is an offence to threaten, without lawful excuse, to damage property with or without an intent to endanger life, providing it is intended that the person so threatened will believe the threat will be carried out. This provision[3] could be used, for example, where X owes Y money, and Y threatens to burn X's house unless he pays the debt off. It is irrelevant whether the property belongs to the person threatened, or whether the life endangered is that of the person threatened. The provisions under section 6, i.e. the statutory defences, apply with respect to lawful excuses unless the defendant knew that his threat would endanger life. It is not necessary that the threat be carried out, and indeed if it is carried out, the charge should be made under section 2 instead. The *mens rea* of the offence is intention: it is difficult to see how a defendant could recklessly threaten to damage property with the intention that the threat be believed.

27.16 Custody or Control of Implements

Section 4 makes it an offence for a person to be found having in his custody or under his control without lawful excuse anything that he intends to use, or that could be used by others, to cause an offence under section 2. The penalties are the same as under section 3. The phrase 'lawful excuse' has generally the same meaning as under section 2(1). It will not, however, apply to an offence under section 4 if the defendant intended to use or allow the use of the article in a way in which he knows is likely to endanger life. The precise scope of the *actus reus* of the offence is unclear. Despite the name of the offence used in the Act (possessing anything with intent to damage property), it could be argued that its scope is wider than just possession. Custody and control are two distinct concepts. Control, either actual or constructive, refers to possession, while custody simply refers to having the article physically near: *Minister for Posts and Telegraphs v. Campbell* (**1966**) (see section 3.2). Section 4, however, includes both concepts. If the provision is interpreted in this way, it will be no defence for a defendant

---

3 This provision should be read in conjunction with section 11 of the Non-Fatal Offences Against the Person Act 1997, which deals with unreasonable demands for the payment of a debt (see section 19.22).

found to have custody of such implements to argue that the articles in question were actually under the control, and therefore the possession, of someone else. Be that as it may, it is clear that knowledge of the existence of the articles is required for either concept; one can hardly intend to use an article to damage property if one is unaware of its existence.

27.17 Unauthorised Accessing of Data

Each of the offences under sections 2 and 3 can be committed against data stored in computers. Section 5 provides further protection to such data by making it an offence to access the data without proper authorisation. The main target of this provision is obviously the computer hacker. It provides that a person who operates a computer, without lawful excuse, to access data with intent to do so commits an offence. Where the computer is within the State, it is irrelevant whether the data are held within or outside the State. If the computer is outside the State, however, the data must be within the State if an offence is to be committed. In either case, the offence is committed even where the defendant was unsuccessful in accessing the data. The offence is also committed whether or not the defendant had any particular target or data in mind. The *mens rea* of the offence is therefore very wide; it is no defence for X to argue that he had intended to access Y's data instead of Z's. In this respect, the provision operates in a manner similar to that of the doctrine of transferred intent (see section 4.3). It is also unnecessary to show that the defendant intended to destroy or damage the data; an intention to look at them is sufficient. The penalty for the offence is a fine of up to €625, imprisonment for up to three months or both.

The provisions relating to lawful excuse in section 6 apply to offences under section 5. Therefore, it is a defence if the defendant honestly believed that the owner of the data had consented, or would have consented had he known of the access. It is also a defence to show that the accessing was done by the defendant in order to protect himself, another person or property, providing his actions were reasonable in the circumstances as he believed them to be. Further, section 6(2)(b) provides an additional defence specific to section 5 offences, namely that the defendant is himself the person who would have the power to consent to the accessing. Quite why the legislature inserted this provision is unclear as a defendant who was accessing his own data, or data to which he had lawful access, would not be liable to prosecution, having lawful authority to do so. However, if the defendant accessed his own data, but intended to access someone else's instead, the offence is committed.

27.18 Further Reading

Elliot, 'Endangering Life by Destroying or Damaging Property', [1997] *Crim LR* 382.

Law Reform Commission, *Report on Malicious Damage*, LRC 26–1988.

PART VI

PUBLIC ORDER OFFENCES

CHAPTER TWENTY-EIGHT

PUBLIC ORDER OFFENCES

28.1 Introduction

Public order offences mainly relate to conduct that causes annoyance, distress or alarm to general members of the public. The main such offences are riot, violent disorder, affray, public intoxication and abusive conduct in a public place. Until recently, public order offences were governed by common law rules. Further minor offences were prohibited by the Vagrancy Acts, especially the Act of 1824. Much of the force of the Vagrancy Acts was removed, however, by the Supreme Court in *King v. Attorney General* **(1981)**, which declared that much of section 4 of the 1824 Act, dealing with loitering with intent, was unconstitutional due to its inherent arbitrariness and ambiguity. The common law rules relating to the more serious public order offences were abolished and replaced by the Criminal Justice (Public Order) Act 1994, which also introduced a new offence of the display of offensive material. Irish law is now modelled on English law contained in the Public Order Act 1986.

28.2 Intoxication in a Public Place

Under section 4(1), it is an offence for any person to be intoxicated in a public place to the extent that there is a reasonable apprehension that he might endanger himself or others in his vicinity. 'Public place' in this context includes any highway, cemetery or churchyard, or any train, vessel or vehicle used to carry people for reward, or any outdoor area used for public recreational purposes to which the public has access at the material time in whatever capacity, or any premises or other place to which the public has access at the material time whether as of right or by permission or on payment of a fee. 'Material time' in this context means the time at which the defendant is found to be intoxicated. 'Intoxicated' means being under the influence of alcohol, drugs, solvents or any other substance. It is not sufficient that the prosecution demonstrate that the defendant was merely drunk while in a public place. It must also be shown that the defendant was so drunk that there was a reasonable fear that he could be a danger to himself or to others. The fear should be one that a reasonable person would perceive, and is therefore objective.

The gardaí also have powers of confiscation under section 4(3). Under this provision, where a person is in a place other than a place used as a dwelling, and a member of the gardaí has reasonable cause to believe that an offence under section 4(1) or under sections 5 (disorderly conduct in a public place) or 6 (threatening, abusive or insulting behaviour in public) is being committed by that person, the garda may confiscate without warrant any bottle or container in that person's possession that the garda reasonably believes to contain an intoxicating substance. When used in connection with an offence under sections 5 or 6, however, the garda must reasonably suspect that the bottle or container is relevant to the offence that he believes the person to have committed.

28.3 Disorderly or Threatening Conduct in a Public Place

Under section 5(1), it is an offence for any person to engage in offensive conduct in a public place either (a) between twelve o'clock midnight and seven in the morning, or (b) at any other time having been asked to stop by the gardaí. It is not necessary to give the defendant any warning where the conduct occurs between the hours specified. 'Offensive conduct' means any unreasonable behaviour which in the circumstances is likely to cause serious offence or annoyance to anyone who is, or might reasonably be expected to be, aware of that behaviour. Suppose, for example, that a group of teenagers is listening to loud music near a residential area at four o'clock in the morning, to the extent that the people in the houses cannot get to sleep. The gardaí are entitled to arrest the teenagers under section 5 without giving any warning or chance to lower the music. Even where the music is being listened to at a more reasonable time, the occupiers of the houses may call the gardaí, who may ask that the music be turned down. If this request is refused, and the music level is such that it is likely to cause serious annoyance or offence, a prosecution may be brought.

A more aggravated form of this offence is provided for in section 6. Under this section, it is an offence for any person in a public place to use or engage in any threatening, abusive or insulting behaviour, or words, either with the intent to breach the peace or while being reckless as to whether or not such a breach occurs. The kind of behaviour contemplated by this provision is of a different order to that covered by section 5. Conduct under that section must cause serious annoyance or offence, so the conduct proscribed in section 6 should be considerably worse. The behaviour or words should either be calculated to cause a breach of the peace, or the defendant should be reckless as to their effect. In *R v. Howell* (1982), it was held that a breach of the peace occurs whenever harm is or is likely to be done to a person or to his property, or creates a fear in that person of being harmed through an assault, an affray, a riot or other disturbance. Thus, the language or actions used should be sufficient to create such a fear. However, in view of the constitutional right to free speech, the conduct should probably be more than merely hostile language.[1]

---

1 Hogan suggests that this provision, and indeed sections 5 and 7, may be unconstitutional due to the fact that they are all intended to curtail some form of constitutionally protected conduct (section 5 – assembly; sections 6 and 7 – speech); see Hogan's commentary on the 1994 Act, *Irish Current Law Statutes Annotated,* Dublin: Round Hall Press, 1994.

28.4 Display of Obscene Material

Section 7 prohibits the distribution or display in a public place of any writing, sign or visible representation which is either threatening, abusive, insulting or obscene with the intention of causing a breach of the peace, or while being reckless as to whether or not such a breach is caused. What exactly constitutes such material is unclear. As far as obscenity is concerned, in *R v. Hicklin* (1868) it was held that obscene material is material that is such as would tend to deprave and corrupt those whose minds are open to immoral influences, and into whose hands a publication of this sort may fall. Smith and Hogan comment that in practice, where it was shown that material fit the ordinary definition of obscenity, i.e. filthy, lewd or disgusting, this was sufficient, and proof of a tendency to deprave and corrupt was unnecessary, being presumed.[2] While this definition probably still stands, it must be construed according to prevailing social standards. Thus, what constitutes obscenity in the twenty-first century is likely to be considerably different from what constituted obscenity in the mid-nineteenth century. As for threatening, it could be defined in much the same way as 'menaces' for the purposes of blackmail. If that turns out to be the case, the courts could use the definition in *R v. Clear* (1968) that the threats must be such that it would unsettle a person of ordinary firmness and courage (see section 26.4). Insulting or abusive behaviour may be given their ordinary meanings. In *Lewis v. DPP* (1995), the High Court considered whether the display of graphic photographs of an aborted foetus outside an abortion clinic could be considered abusive or insulting. The appellant argued that the photographs were an accurate representation of the results of an abortion, and that 'what is truthful cannot be abusive or insulting'. The High Court ruled that the truth of the photograph notwithstanding, such a display was capable of being abusive or insulting to people attending for lawful procedures being conducted in the clinic. However, while the photograph in question was clearly shocking and distressing, the court did not explain how shock and distress can or should be equated with abuse and insult. It is debatable whether this decision could be maintained in Ireland in light of the constitutional guarantee of free speech and the similar guarantee of free speech contained in the European Convention on Human Rights.

28.5 Wilful Obstruction

It is an offence under section 9 for any person, without lawful authority or reasonable excuse, to wilfully prevent or interrupt the free passage of any person or vehicle in any public place. Therefore, protesters or strikers who block the roads or pathways as part of their protest or strike may be prosecuted under this section.

---

2 Smith and Hogan, *Criminal Law*, 11th ed., Oxford: Oxford University Press, 2005, p. 945.

28.6 Further Penalties

Section 8 gives the gardaí extra powers in addition to those specified in sections 4, 5, 6, 7 or 9. Where the gardaí suspect a person to be acting contrary to any of these provisions, or to be loitering in a public place without lawful authority or reasonable excuse in a manner that raises a reasonable fear for the safety of people or property or the maintenance of public peace, they may order the person to do one or both of two things:

(a) to stop acting in such a manner, or
(b) to leave the vicinity immediately.

A failure by that person to comply with the order is an offence unless the person has lawful authority or a reasonable excuse for not complying with the order.

28.7 Riot

The common law offence of riot was defined in ***O'Faolain v. Lord Mayor of Dublin*** (**1996**) as occurring where three or more people assemble together to execute a common purpose with the intent of using force if necessary to help each other against anyone who might try to stop them, and actually use force or violence in such a manner as would alarm at least one person of reasonable firmness and courage. The common law offence of riot was abolished by section 14(4) of the 1994 Act, and section 15(5) provides that references to the common law offence in any statute passed prior to the 1994 Act are to be considered as references to the new statutory offence of violent disorder in section 15 (see section 28.8). The 1994 Act created a new statutory offence of riot in section 14, which is defined in section 14(1) as requiring the following elements:

> Where –
> (a)   12 or more persons who are present together at any place (whether that place is a public place or private place or both) use or threaten to use unlawful violence for a common purpose, and
> (b)   the conduct of those persons, taken together, is such as would cause a person of reasonable firmness present at that place to fear for his or another's safety,
> then, each of the persons using unlawful violence for the common purpose shall be guilty of the offence of riot.

Where these elements are present, any of the people who use unlawful violence commit the new offence of riot. It does not have to be shown that the people used or threatened to use violence simultaneously. Therefore, where a group of twelve or more threatens to use or actually uses violence to effect a common purpose, riot is committed as soon as any member of that group uses violence.

What actually constitutes violence for the purposes of a riot is not clear. In particular, it is not clear if it differs from the concept of force under the common law offence. In ***O'Faolain v. Lord Mayor of Dublin*** (**1996**), one of the men involved in a riot stared at a woman in such a way that she left the scene. It was held that it was reasonable to assume that if the stare had not forced the woman to leave, the man would have resorted to violence. Therefore, this stare constituted force under the common law definition of the offence. Whether such a stare could constitute violence for the new offence is unclear. In practice, it is likely to be a matter of degree. Where the defendant uses any degree of force, and it is decided that it would cause a reasonable person to fear for his own safety, then regardless of how violent the action actually was, it will constitute violence. Finally, the requirement that a person of reasonable firmness would fear for his own safety or that of others creates an objective test. The prosecution does not have to prove that a person at that place actually feared for his own safety, or was even present at that place.

28.8 Violent Disorder

The common law offences of rout and unlawful assembly were abolished by section 15(6), and replaced by the offence of violent disorder created by section 15. Section 15(1) defines this new offence as arising in the following circumstances:

Where –
(a) three or more persons who are present together at any place (whether that place is a public place or a private place or both) use or threaten to use unlawful violence, and
(b) the conduct of those persons, taken together, is such as would cause a person of reasonable firmness present at that place to fear for his or another person's safety,
then, each of the persons using or threatening to use unlawful violence shall be guilty of the offence of violent disorder.

This offence is similar to the definition of riot except in three respects. First, the number of people required to be present is only three as opposed to the twelve required for riot. Second, there is no requirement that the individuals be pursuing a common purpose; indeed, they may be using or threatening violence to each other. Third, section 15(3) provides that before a person can be convicted of violent disorder, it must be shown that he either intended to use or threaten to use violence or was aware that his conduct may be violent or threaten violence. There is no similar provision relating to the offence of riot. Subsection 3's reference to an awareness on the part of the defendant that his conduct might threaten violence indicates that the threats do not have to be verbal but may be inferred from gestures and acts. As with riot, the test for violent disorder is objective and is based on whether a reasonable person present at that place would have thought his own safety or that of another was in peril. However, section 15(2)(b) provides that such a reasonable person need not be shown to have been present at the disorder.

Finally, section 15(5) provides that any reference in any statute passed prior to the 1994 Act that contains a reference to the common law offences of riot or riot and tumult should be construed as a reference to violent disorder. For example, the Malicious Injuries Act 1981 refers to damage caused by three or more people tumultuously and riotously assembled. By virtue of section 15(5), this Act now refers to damage caused by three or more people engaged in a violent disorder.

28.9 Affray

At common law, an affray occurred where two or more people engaged in a fight in a public place to the terror of the general public. Common law affray, however, was abolished by section 16(5) and replaced by a new offence of affray created by section 16. This offence requires the following elements:

> Where –
> (a) two or more persons at any place (whether that place is a public place or a private place or both) use or threaten to use violence towards each other, and
> (b) the violence so used or threatened by one of those persons is unlawful, and
> (c) the conduct of those persons taken together is such as would cause a person of reasonable firmness present at that place to fear for his or another person's safety,
> then, each such person who uses or threatens to use unlawful violence shall be guilty of the offence of affray.

In *Reid v. DPP; Kirwan v. DPP* (2004), the Court of Criminal Appeal ruled that proof that the defendant was using or threatening to use violence against another person involved in the affray was essential. In that case, there was evidence that the first defendant had used force against the arresting garda only. Consequently, there was no *prima facie* case against the first defendant and the issue of affray should not have gone to the jury.

Where these elements are established, any person who actually uses or threatens to use violence commits affray. As with riot and violent disorder, it is not necessary to show that a person of reasonable firmness was actually present. The threats cannot be made merely by words. Consequently, there must be evidence of some hostile action as well as words, such as the swinging of clubs or the shaking of fists. Finally, there is also a *mens rea* provision similar to that for violent disorder: the defendant must either intend to use or threaten to use violence, or be aware that his conduct may be violent or threaten violence.

28.10 Assault Offences

The Act creates two assault offences. Section 18 makes it an offence to assault any person with intent either to cause bodily harm or to commit an indictable offence. As common law assault has now been abolished, assault, for the purposes of this Act, must be read in the light of the new statutory definition of assault contained in the Non-Fatal Offences Against the Person Act 1997 (see section 19.3). Section 18 effectively creates two offences: assault with the intent to cause bodily harm, and assault with the intent to commit any indictable offence. In both cases, the defendant must be shown to have acted intentionally; it is not sufficient to show that he acted recklessly.

Section 19 concerns assaults on members of the gardaí, and replaces section 38 of the Offences Against the Person Act 1861. Section 19 covers four separate offences, three of which are in section 19(1):

(a) assault on a garda acting in the course of his duty, knowing that the person is a garda or being reckless as to whether he is a garda;
(b) assault on any other person assisting a garda;
(c) assault on any other person with the intention of resisting or preventing his own arrest or that of any other person for any offence.

These offences may be tried either summarily or on indictment, at the election of the defendant. If he chooses trial on indictment, the matter will ordinarily be heard before a jury. However, anyone who commits an offence under section 19(1) also commits the offence of assault under section 2 of the Non-Fatal Offences Against the Person Act 1997, which is triable summarily. In *DPP (Travers) v. Brennan* **(1998)**, the Supreme Court ruled that the DPP has discretion to decide to bring a charge under section 19 of the 1994 Act or section 2 of the 1997 Act. By selecting summary trial under section 2 of the 1997 Act, the DPP can therefore effectively remove a defendant's right to be tried before a jury.

Section 19(3) provides a fourth form of the offence: resisting or wilfully obstructing a member of the gardaí acting in the course of his duty or any person assisting a garda in the execution of his duty, while knowing that he is a garda or being reckless as to whether or not he is a garda.

The first and fourth of these offences have similarities in construction to capital murder, and should be read in the light of the Supreme Court decision in *The People (DPP) v. Murray* **(1977)** (see section 18.10). Consequently, it must be shown that the defendant either knew that the person being assaulted or obstructed was a garda, or was reckless as to whether he was a garda. Recklessness in this respect is subjective. The second offence also requires some knowledge on the part of the defendant that the person being assaulted is assisting a member of the gardaí. The third offence requires an intention on the part of the defendant to resist the arrest of some person, whether himself or anyone else. Therefore, the prosecution must show that the defendant was aware that an arrest was being made, although it is not necessary that he knows for what offence the arrest was being made. It is also apparently irrelevant whether the person trying to make the arrest is a member of the gardaí or a member of the public, providing the arrest is lawful. For a member of the public to make a lawful arrest, it is necessary, under section 4 of the Criminal Law Act 1997, that the member of the public believe with reasonable cause that an arrestable offence has been or is being committed, and that the person being arrested would attempt to avoid arrest by the gardaí. Where these conditions have been complied with, any assault committed with the intention of preventing the arrest of a person constitutes the third offence under section 19.

28.11 Further Penalties

The Criminal Justice (Public Order) Act 2003 was enacted to provide further measures to control public disturbances. Under section 3, anyone convicted under sections 4, 5, 6, 7, 8 or 9 of the 1994 Act may be made the subject of an Exclusion Order issued by the District Court. An Exclusion Order prohibits the subject from entering or being in the vicinity of a specified catering premises between specified times and for as long as the court may specify, subject to a maximum of twelve months. Catering premises are defined in section 2(1) as licensed premises or food premises, and clearly includes public houses, restaurants and fast food establishments. A breach of such an order is a summary offence.

Under section 4, a member of the gardaí of at least the rank of inspector may apply to the District Court for a Closure Order in respect of a catering premises on one of two grounds. First, that there has been a disorder on the premises or in its vicinity involving people in the premises. Alternatively, a Closure Order may be sought because of noise from the premises, or from its vicinity caused by people who were on the premises, and the noise has been 'so loud, so continuous, so repeated, of such duration or pitch or occurring at such times as to give reasonable cause for annoyance to persons in that vicinity.' In either case, the applicant must also be of the view that the disorder or noise is likely to recur. Before any such application may be made, however, the gardaí must give written notice to the operator of the premises in question of their view that a disorder or noise has occurred, and a request that preventative measures be put in place within a reasonable period but not more than seven days from service of the notice. Once these requirements have been met, the order should be granted if the District Court is satisfied that the disorder or noise has occurred, and that closure is necessary to prevent any recurrence. The order will direct the closure of the premises between specified times on specified days during a specified period, but the duration of the order cannot exceed seven days for a first order or thirty days for any subsequent order. However, the gardaí may apply under section 7 to the District Court for the extension of a Closure Order before its expiration, and that extension may be granted if the court is satisfied that the continued closure of the premises is required to prevent a recurrence of disorders or noises. Once issued, a copy of the order must be affixed in a conspicuous place on the premises during the currency of the order. Employees of a premises closed by any such order are not to be disadvantaged because of the order; in other words, employees are entitled to still be paid while the premises are closed. When making any such order, the District Court may also direct the operators of the premises to take specified future measures, including the installation of a closed-circuit television system, the restriction of the number of people to be admitted to the premises or restrictions on the type of substances to be sold in the premises.

28.12 Further Reading

Carey, 'The Rule of Law, Public Order Targeting, and the Construction of Crime', (1998) 8 *ICLJ* 26.

———, '*Mens Rea* and the Irish Riot', (2000) 10 *ICLJ* 4.

CHAPTER TWENTY-NINE

PROSTITUTION

29.1 Introduction

Prostitution is not in itself an offence. Therefore no offence is committed where a person offers to have intercourse with another in return for payment, providing the intercourse is not otherwise illegal, such as due to age. However, the law does not approve of such actions, and tries to control the public activities of prostitutes by controlling their public actions. The Criminal Law (Sexual Offences) Act 1993 therefore contains a number of offences which, taken together, have the object of controlling the public manifestation of prostitution. Hence, despite the obvious connection between prostitution and sexual activity, prostitution is not a sexual offence as such. Rather, prostitution is treated as a public order issue.

29.2 Definition of Prostitution

A number of cases have put forward definitions of what is meant by the word 'prostitute'. In *R v. De Munck* (1918), the Court of Criminal Appeal considered the meaning of a common prostitute. The defendant was charged with the attempted procuring of the prostitution of her sixteen-year-old daughter, controlling the activities of a prostitute and with causing and encouraging the prostitution of her daughter. There was evidence that while the girl had engaged in lewd actions, she had never engaged in sexual intercourse, and the question arose as to whether the girl could be considered a prostitute. The defence argued that prostitution could not arise unless there was evidence of actual intercourse. This argument was rejected, the court holding that a common prostitute was a woman who offers her body commonly for acts of lewdness in return for payment, although there is no act or offer of an act of ordinary sexual intercourse. A woman who does so on a one-off basis is therefore not a common prostitute, but would apparently still be classified as a prostitute. In a more recent case, *R v. McFarlane* (1994), the defendant was charged with living on the earnings of prostitution. The alleged prostitute in question was his partner, with whom he lived. She gave evidence that she was not a prostitute, but was what was called a 'clipper' – a woman who took money in return for sexual favours without any intention of performing those favours. It was argued by the defendant that sexual services must be performed before a person could be viewed as a prostitute. The Court of Appeal held that the essence of prostitution is the making of an offer of sexual services for reward. An intention to perform those services is irrelevant, as is the fact of failing to provide them. Given the archaic use of language in *De Munck*, it is likely that an Irish court would prefer the decision in *McFarlane*.

This is subject, however, to one express proviso contained in section 1(4), that any reference to a prostitute includes a male person who acts as a prostitute. Thus, a prostitute is any person who offers sexual services of any kind in return for payment, whether or not those services are actually performed.

29.3 Soliciting or Importuning

The Act contains two provisions dealing with solicitation or importuning. Section 6, as inserted by section 250 of the Children Act 2001, prohibits soliciting or importuning a person, whether for the purposes of prostitution or otherwise, for the commission of an offence under sections 3 (buggery with a person under the age of seventeen), 4 (gross indecency with a male under the age of seventeen) or 5 (sexual intercourse or buggery with a mentally impaired person) of the 1993 Act, or sections 1 or 2 of the Criminal Law Amendment Act 1935 (unlawful carnal knowledge of a young female). This offence is not confined to soliciting or importuning in public places; as the purpose of the provision is the protection of children, the Act applies equally to solicitation or importuning of young people in private places as well. Section 7 makes it an offence to solicit or importune another person in a street or public place for the purpose of prostitution. A public place is defined in section 1(1) as any place to which the public has access either as of right or by permission, irrespective of charges. A street is defined in the same provision as including any road, bridge, lane, footway, subway, square, court, alley or passage which is open to the public, and further includes any doorway, entrance, garden or car park facing onto such a street. By virtue of section 1(1), soliciting or importuning from a car may be considered soliciting or importuning for the purposes of the Act, thereby including 'kerb-crawling' in the definition. Furthermore, section 1(2) provides that any of the following actions will be considered soliciting or importuning:

(a) offering services as a prostitute to another person;
(b) soliciting or importuning another person to obtain that person's services as a prostitute; or
(c) soliciting or importuning another person on behalf of another for the purposes of prostitution.

The soliciting or importuning may, therefore, be done either by the prostitute, the client or anyone acting on behalf of the prostitute or client.

It is clear that neither the prostitute nor the client have to make any clear request or offer in order to be soliciting or importuning. In *Dale v. Smith* (1967), it was held that when the defendant said 'Hello' to another person in a public toilet, he could be considered to have importuned that other person for immoral purposes. However, that case revolved around an English statutory offence of persistently soliciting or importuning for immoral purposes. The court took the view that as the defendant had used the same word to another person on a previous occasion, and followed it with an invitation to look at some obscene photographs, the defendant was persistently importuning. As the Irish offences are somewhat different, it is likely that an Irish court would require evidence of something in excess of merely greeting another person before considering a conviction for importuning, although the circumstances of the case may themselves provide that extra evidence.

It is clear that an express invitation is not required. In *Behrendt v. Burridge* (1976), the defendant was sitting on a high stool in a bay window of a house, lit by a red light and wearing provocative clothing. All sides agreed that she did so in order to advertise her services. However, the defendant made no movements or attempts at communication of any kind to possible clients. It was held that she was tempting prospective customers to enter the house for the purpose of prostitution, and might just as well have hung a sign to that effect outside the front door. She was therefore soliciting. Similarly, in *Smith v. Hughes* (1960), the High Court ruled that 'it can matter little whether the prostitute is soliciting while in the street or is standing in a doorway or on a balcony, or at a window, or whether the window is shut or open or half open; in each case her solicitation is projected to and addressed to somebody walking in the street.' Furthermore, in *Horton v. Mead* (1913), the defendant was a male prostitute who was observed loitering around a public toilet. He smiled at male passers-by, pursed his lips and made gestures, but never spoke to anyone. It was suggested that because there was no evidence that the defendant had succeeded in attracting the attention of male passers-by, he could not be considered to have engaged in solicitation. It was held that it is immaterial that the person to whom the invitation was addressed did not perceive it to be an invitation. The fact that the defendant had tried to do so was sufficient.

29.4 Loitering for the Purposes of Prostitution

Section 8 allows the gardaí to order any person whom they reasonably suspect to be loitering in a street or public place in order to solicit or importune others for the purposes of prostitution to leave the area immediately. Under section 8(2), it is an offence for the person so ordered to refuse to obey that order without reasonable cause. 'Street' and 'public place' have the same meanings as under section 7. Thus, it is not an offence *per se* to loiter for the purposes of prostitution; it is only when an order to leave the area has been refused without good cause that an offence is committed.

This section was considered by the High Court by way of a case-stated from the District Court in **The People (DPP) v. Keogh (1998)**. A garda sergeant had ordered the defendant to move on under section 8, but found her still in the same place an hour and a half later, and accordingly arrested her. The sergeant gave evidence that the area was well known as a 'red light' district, and that he had known the defendant for two and a half years, and had seen her in that area approaching cars on previous occasions. The defence objected to this evidence, and the District Court stated a case to the High Court. During the High Court hearing, the objection to the evidence about the nature and type of the area was withdrawn. However, the court held that the prosecution could not rely on evidence of the defendant's previous activities or character because it was unduly prejudicial, unless the defendant put her character in issue. The fact that it was the defendant's failure to obey a garda order that formed the basis of the charge rather than her activities or character was irrelevant; the sergeant had no right to give the order unless he had reasonable grounds to do so, and he was not entitled to base his suspicion on his prior knowledge of the defendant. However, Kelly J. also expressed the opinion that finding four women standing in a known red light area at 1.20 in the morning would be sufficient to found a reasonable suspicion.

29.5 Organisation of Prostitution

Section 9 makes it an offence to either control or direct the activities of prostitutes in relation to prostitution, or to organise prostitution by controlling or directing the activities of prostitutes, or to coerce a person to be a prostitute. This is a relatively serious offence and can be punished with imprisonment for up to five years, and reflects the fact that persons charged under this section are exploiting the prostitutes whom they control. The targets of the section are those people popularly known as 'pimps'. It is probably not necessary that the prosecution prove that the defendant had a formal structure or premises for running his prostitution activities. It should be sufficient that the defendant had the power to give directions to prostitutes regarding how and when they were to offer their services. It is also not necessary that the prosecution proves that the defendant received any money from the prostitutes; if this is the case, the defendant may be charged under section 10 as well.

29.6 Living on the Earnings of Prostitution

It is an offence under section 10 for any person to knowingly live in whole or in part on the earnings of the prostitution of another person, and to aid and abet that prostitution. Section 10 thus differs from the similar offence under the Vagrancy Act 1898 (now repealed) which was restricted to males living on the earnings of a prostitute. There are three elements in the new offence. First, the defendant must be living on the earnings of the prostitution of another person, in whole or in part. It is irrelevant whether the other person is male or female. In *R v. Stewart* (1986), the defendant had let a number of flats at high rents to persons whom he knew to be prostitutes. The Court of Appeal held that 'living on the earnings' implies a parasitic relationship, and could therefore include a situation in which a person lets out rooms for use in prostitution, or someone who supplies goods and services to the prostitute. The court suggested that a good working test is for the jury to decide whether or not the prostitute and the supplier were in the business of prostitution together. Therefore, a person who merely supplies groceries to the prostitute would not be guilty under section 10. For such a person to be convicted, there must be evidence of a closer relationship between the receipt of money for the groceries and the trade of prostitution.

Second, the defendant must know that he is living on the proceeds of prostitution. It is not sufficient that the defendant was reckless as to the source of his money. Therefore, where a husband suspects that his wife is engaging in prostitution, but deliberately does not seek clarification, and uses her money for his own purposes, he is not living on the earnings of prostitution for the purposes of section 10, unless his suspicions were so strong as to be considered knowledge.

Third, the defendant must be aiding and abetting the prostitution of the other person. It is therefore necessary to show that all the elements of the offence relate to the same prostitute or prostitutes. Irish law accepts a wide definition of the phrase 'aiding and abetting', but requires knowledge on the part of the defendant of the nature of the offence: *The People (DPP) v. Egan* (**1989**) (see Chapter 6). While this requirement is a complicating factor, and is absent from the corresponding English offence (section 30, Sexual Offences Act 1956), if it were not there, then strictly speaking the child of a prostitute could be prosecuted for living on the earnings of prostitution. Preventing such prosecutions appears to be the purpose of the requirement. However, where the child assists in his or her mother's prostitution, by helping to advertise her services, for example, a prosecution may proceed, subject to the principle of *doli incapax* (see Chapter 12).

29.7 Brothel Keeping

Section 11 penalises the use of premises as a brothel. The section applies to three categories of people:

(a) persons who manage, act or assist in the management of a brothel;
(b) tenants, lessees, occupiers or persons in charge of premises who knowingly permit those premises to be used as a brothel or for habitual prostitution; or
(c) landlords or lessors who let their premises knowing that the premises or part of the premises will be used as a brothel, or who wilfully act as a party to the continued use of the premises as a brothel.

The last category explicitly includes agents of landlords or lessors. In *Durose v. Wilson* (1907), the defendant was a porter employed to look after a block of eighteen flats in which he lived. Twelve of the tenants were women who used the premises for the purposes of prostitution. The main door to the complex was locked at twelve midnight, but the defendant had on a number of occasions admitted the women accompanied by men after that time. When the men left, he would sometimes call cabs for them, and receive tips from them. It was held that, on the evidence, he could be convicted of wilfully being a party to the continued use of the premises as a brothel. As far as *mens rea* is concerned, people in the last two categories must act knowingly, while people in the first category may apparently act knowingly or recklessly, although in practice it is unlikely that a person could manage a brothel without knowing the nature of the premises.

There is no definition of a brothel in the Act. In *Singleton v. Ellison* (1895), it was held that where a prostitute exclusively operated from her own rooms, she was not guilty of keeping a brothel. In other words, it must be shown that the premises are used for the purposes of prostitution by persons other than the occupant of the premises. In *Gorman v. Standen; Palace-Clarke v. Standen* (1963), the first defendant was a tenant of a premises in which she lived with the second defendant, her stepdaughter. They were observed on a number of occasions bringing men to the premises. It was argued by the defence that the fact that the first defendant was the tenant meant, on the authority of *Singleton v. Ellison*, that she could use the premises for prostitution without it being considered a brothel. Therefore, effectively, the second defendant was the only prostitute who was using the premises for the purposes of prostitution. It was held that a brothel is a premises to which people of opposite sexes may go in order to have illicit sexual intercourse. It was essential that there was proof that the premises was used by more than one prostitute, although they need not use the premises at the same time. The fact that one of the prostitutes was also the tenant was irrelevant. Further, it was held in *Kelly v. Purvis* (1983) that proof that acts of sexual intercourse occurred in a premises is unnecessary; if acts of indecency such as masturbation are performed, then those premises constitute a brothel.

29.8 Advertising of Brothels and Prostitution

Section 23 of the Criminal Justice (Public Order) Act 1994 prohibits any person from publishing, distributing or causing to be published or distributed any advertisement for brothels or prostitutes in the State. The advertisement should be such that it gives rise, from its terms, circumstances or manner, to a reasonable inference that the premises being described is a brothel, or the services being advertised are those of a prostitute. The provision is thus wide enough to include advertisements that do not use the words 'brothel' or 'prostitute', but instead use words such as 'massage parlours'.

Advertisements include, under section 23(5), every form of advertising or promotion, including posters or notices whether by publication or display, or circulars, leaflets, pamphlets or cards, or any other form of advertising such as by way of radio, television, computer monitors, telephones, faxes, photographs or films. Thus, advertisements posted on the Internet that may be accessed by a computer are prohibited. However, the advertisement must be for a brothel or prostitute located within the State. Advertisements for brothels in other countries are not covered by the Act.

Section 23(3) provides a defence for those whose business it is to publish, distribute, or to arrange for the publication or distribution of, advertisements. For such persons, it is a defence to show that the advertisement was received by them in the ordinary course of their business, and that they did not know and had no reason to suspect that the advertisement related to a brothel or a prostitute. The phrase 'had no reason to suspect' indicates that wilful blindness will not be a defence. Where a reasonable person would have suspected the true nature of the advertisement, the defendant may be convicted. It is not, however, clear what steps the defendant should take to ascertain the nature of the advertisement. Much will depend on the nature of the premises or person advertised. For example, if X, a newspaper publisher, receives an advertisement from Y for a massage parlour which turns out to be a brothel, a jury might conclude that X must have suspected the true nature of the premises because of the common connotation that 'massage parlours' have. If the advertisement, however, is for a health club, such a conclusion might not be warranted.

29.9 Ancillary Prostitution Offences

A number of other statutes contain offences related to prostitution. Section 2 of the Criminal Law Amendment Act 1885 penalises the procuring or attempted procuring of a woman or girl to become a common prostitute in Ireland or elsewhere, or to have her live in or frequent a brothel in Ireland or elsewhere, or, where the woman or girl has a known immoral character, to have her engage in unlawful sexual intercourse in Ireland or elsewhere.

Section 3 of the same Act makes it an offence to procure or attempt to procure by threats, intimidation or false pretences a woman to have unlawful sexual intercourse. In *R v. Broadfoot* (1976), it was held that procuring means to bring about a course of conduct. Therefore, what is penalised under sections 2 and 3 of the 1885 Act is conduct designed to persuade or force a woman to engage in unlawful sexual intercourse, rather than simply employing a woman as a prostitute.

Finally, section 8 of the 1885 Act makes it an offence to detain a woman or girl against her will either in a brothel or so that she can be subjected to unlawful sexual intercourse by any man. In this context, denying the woman or girl her clothes or other property, or threatening to sue her if she leaves with clothes that the defendant has lent her, will be considered a form of detention.

29.10 Further Reading

Law Reform Commission, *Report on Vagrancy and Related Offences*, LRC 11–1985.

O'Malley, *Sexual Offences: Law, Policy and Punishment*, Dublin: Round Hall Sweet & Maxwell, 1996, Chapter 9.

Index